ATLAS OF BRITISH OVERSEAS EXPANSION

Spanning the entire period from the late fifteenth-century beginnings of Britain's growth as a maritime commercial power to her withdrawal from most colonial possessions and her alignment with continental Europe in the 1970s and 1980s, this atlas traces the history of Britain's changing presence overseas. Each map is accompanied by an explanatory text.

The shifting territorial pattern of empire over more than four centuries, from the colonization of Virginia to the dismemberment of African empire is naturally prominent. British exploration is also covered, showing the routes taken and discoveries made from Frobisher and Ralegh to Cook and Livingstone. War, conquest and non-European military resistance are touched on, especially in the American War of Independence, the Indian Mutiny, the South African War of 1899–1902 and recent world wars.

In addition, the atlas illustrates the considerable influence and power, albeit of less formal kinds and at different times, brought by Britain's trade and investments, the patterns of imperial defence and communications, the spread of white settlement and the presence of her consuls, shipping and missionaries.

A. N. Porter is Professor of History and Head of the History Department at King's College, University of London.

ATLAS OF BRITISH OVERSEAS EXPANSION

EDITED BY A.N. PORTER

London

First published in 1991 by Routledge

First published in paperback 1994
by Routledge
11 New Fetter Lane, London EC4P 4EE

Typeset by Colset Private Ltd, Singapore

Printed in England by Clays Ltd, St Ives plc

British Library Cataloguing in Publication Data

Atlas of British overseas expansion.
    1. Great Britain, Foreign relations, history
    I. Porter, A. N. (Andrew Neil)
    327.41

ISBN 0–415–06347–7 pbk

CONTENTS

CONTRIBUTORS

Dr P. J. Beck, Kingston Polytechnic.
  Maps and text pp. 209–14.
Professor Peter Burroughs, Dalhousie University.
  Maps and text pp. 74–6, 84–6, 118–24, 221.
Dr Edward Countryman, University of Warwick.
  Maps and text pp. 41–4, 51–3, 219–20.
Professor B. W. Higman, University of the West Indies, Mona.
  Maps and text pp. 62–3, 86–9, 220–1.
Dr R. F. Holland, Institute of Commonwealth Studies, London.
  Maps and text pp. 158–63, 170–2, 177–9, 187–205, 207–9.
Dr David Killingray, Goldsmiths' College, London.
  Maps and text pp. 152–8.
Dr Martin Lynn, The Queen's University, Belfast.
  Maps and text pp. 76–80, 103–9, 234–7.
Dr David McLean, King's College, London.
  Maps and text pp. 93–6, 101–3, 233–4.

Professor P. J. Marshall, King's College, London.
  Maps and text pp. 36–8, 44–50, 53–7, 64–5, 89–93, 230–3.
Dr Gwenda Morgan, Sunderland Polytechnic.
  Maps and text pp. 26–36, 218.
Professor A. N. Porter, King's College, London.
  Maps and text pp. 80–4, 109–18, 124–37, 144–52, 163–7, 205–7, 222–5.
A. N. Ryan Esq., University of Liverpool.
  Maps and text pp. 1–26.
Dr A. J. Stockwell, Royal Holloway and Bedford New College, London.
  Maps and text pp. 97–101, 142–4, 168–70, 172–7, 180–7, 214–7.
Dr J. L. Sturgis, Birkbeck College, London.
  Maps and text pp. 60–1, 66–74, 137–41, 226–9.
Professor Glyn Williams, Queen Mary and Westfield College, London.
  Maps and text pp. 38–40, 57–60.

PREFACE

The history of Britain's connections and interests overseas has long been a major subject of study in both universities and schools. It continues to be so, both for reasons of genuine intellectual curiosity about vital aspects of Britain's own history, and because of a consciousness that the world as a whole continues to live with the legacies of a British past. Today that study takes many forms, for it has always reflected both the changing interests and the new insights of successive generations of scholars.

To a long-standing concern with the growth of formal territorial empire, first in the Americas and West Indies, later in India and Africa, has been added more recently an interest in the changing patterns of twentieth-century imperial rule, in the activities of the Commonwealth and in the process of decolonization. Moreover, it is now widely accepted that empires may exist not only as formal structures: Britain's presence and expansion overseas do not relate only to areas where her officials actually ruled and administered. Her trade and investments, the emigration of her population and the presence of her consuls, shipping and missionaries have also brought considerable influence and power of less formal kinds at different times.

Not only has the study of 'informal' been added to that of 'formal' empire. The history of expansion has also been affected by the proliferation in recent decades of many more specialized historical studies. Alongside the traditional fields of the military historians and the students of maritime or overland explo-

ration, there are now to be found the new estates of urban history, the detailed study of emigration, disease and ecology, of colonial administration, education and technology.

A sense of geography, place and distance, as well as of period and the passage of time, is essential for historians and for none more, perhaps, than students of British expansion. Certainly the judicious use of maps offers one way in which the sometimes bewildering variety of the subject can be contained. Yet there is no modern collection of maps or an atlas which provides a broad selection of the basic cartographical supports for this field of study. The present volume is designed to supply this need.

Using nearly 140 maps, it spans the entire period from the late-fifteenth-century beginnings of Britain's growth as a maritime commercial power to her withdrawal from most colonial possessions and alignment with continental Europe in the 1970s and 1980s. The changing pattern of territorial empire over more than four centuries, from the colonization of Virginia to the dismemberment of African empire, is naturally given particular prominence. British exploration is followed through from Frobisher and Ralegh to Cook and Livingstone. The themes of war, conquest and non-European military resistance are touched on, especially, for example, in the American War of Independence, the Indian Mutiny, the South African War of 1899–1902 and the First World War. The development of colonial resources and aspects of British trade, the shifting patterns of imperial defence and

communications and the spread of white settlement are also represented as of great importance. Small-scale area maps and many town
plans are included, from colonial America
and the St Lawrence valley to Hong Kong,
Canberra and the Suez base. The maps are
accompanied by short explanatory texts, and
suggestions are provided for further reading.

Limited space and the constraints of
black-and-white cartography have unfortunately made it necessary to exclude much of
potential interest. Users of the volume will
undoubtedly regret particular omissions, just
as contributors would have welcomed the
chance to chart such things as the paths of
labour migration, the progress of Admiralty
or geological surveys, the extension of consular appointments or patterns of Aboriginal
and Maori settlement. The final selection has
been influenced particularly by the demands of
undergraduate teaching familiar to the editor
and contributors.

To the contributors I am extremely grate-
ful, not only for all their work but for the
good humour with which they have borne an
editor's badgering and eccentricities as well
as unavoidable delays. To the cartographer,
Jayne Lewin, special thanks are due from all
of us, for her expert advice, her skill in inter-
preting our early designs and in reconcil-
ing conflicting purposes and her patience in
coping with belated changes. The assistance of
colleagues and librarians, unfortunately too
numerous to mention, has also been indispens-
able. Richard Stoneman's initiative in launching the project and the work of his successive
assistants – Alan Jarvis, Anita Roy, Jackie
Dias and Kate Morrall – in keeping it afloat
have been much appreciated.

Andrew Porter
King's College, London

Bristol and the Atlantic, 1480–1509

Evidence of English contributions to fifteenth-century European Atlantic discovery is sparse, and mostly formal. No journals, narratives or charts have survived. The first recorded information is of a voyage from Bristol in 1480 for the 'island of Brasylle in the west part of Ireland'. In 1481 two more ships sailed from Bristol 'to serch and fynde a certaine Isle called the Isle of Brasile'. 'Brasil' is located on fifteenth-century maps at varying distances to the west and south-west of Ireland. Knowledge of its alleged existence had probably been acquired in Bristol through commercial links with the Iberian peninsula and Madeira, probably supplemented by reports from Ireland. The incentive to search for it had nothing to do with imperial ambition. The people involved were interested in finding fishing grounds less heavily exploited than those in Icelandic waters. The exact outcome of their endeavours is unknown. Almost certainly the Newfoundland banks were reached and adjacent coasts sighted between 1481 and 1494–5, the likely date of the arrival in Bristol of the Venetian navigator John Cabot.

Cabot placed Bristol discovery in a new context. He shared Christopher Columbus's view that the western Atlantic was bordered, within realistic sailing distance from Europe, by Asia. According to reports of Italians resident in London he claimed in 1497 on return from his one successful transatlantic voyage (he was lost at sea in 1498) to have made an Asiatic landfall. Whether his Bristol allies shared this conviction is doubtful. They seem to have been more impressed by the wealth of the fishery. And John Day, an informed English correspondent of Columbus, says nothing in his one surviving letter to support Cabot's claim. He identified the 1497 discovery with that 'found and discovered in the past by the men from Bristol', thus asserting an earlier English discovery of what would soon come to be known as North America. The coast traversed by Cabot cannot be accurately identified. A reasonable estimate, based with qualifications on the reckonings of Day, is that its southern and northern limits are 42°N and 54°N.

After 1498 any lingering idea that Cabot had reached Asia was abandoned. By 1502 the English were talking of 'the newe founde launde' and were already trying to exploit it. A series of voyages for purposes of trade were made from Bristol between 1501 and 1505 under letters patent granted by Henry VII to syndicates made up of Bristol merchants with Azorean associates. Little is known of them except that items brought to England included 'haukes', 'wylde cattes & popyngays'. Two American Indians dressed as Englishmen were seen at court in 1504. Efforts to establish a profitable trade failed, however. Interest in the new land flagged. The last references to any syndicate occur in 1505–6.

Sebastian Cabot, son of John, was meanwhile performing shadowy service 'in and aboute the fyndynge of the newe founde

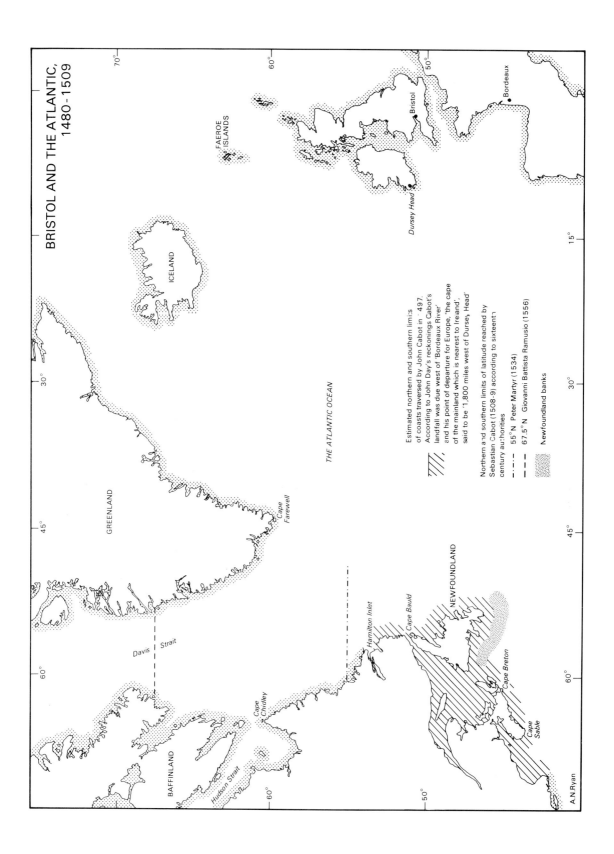

BRISTOL AND THE ATLANTIC, 1480-1509

ICELAND

FAEROE ISLANDS

Bristol

Dursey Head

Bordeaux

70°

60°

50°

15°

GREENLAND

30°

45°

THE ATLANTIC OCEAN

Cape Farewell

Estimated northern and southern limits
of coasts traversed by John Cabot in 1497.
According to John Day's reckonings Cabot's
landfall was due west of 'Bordeaux River'
and his point of departure for Europe, 'the cape
of the mainland which is nearest to Ireland',
said to be '1,800 miles west of Dursey Head'

Northern and southern limits of latitude reached by
Sebastian Cabot (1508-9) according to sixteenth
century authorities

— · — · — 55°N Peter Martyr (1534)

— — — — 67.5°N Giovanni Battista Ramusio (1556)

Newfoundland banks

30°

BAFFINLAND

Davis Strait

Hudson Strait

Cape Chidley

Hamilton Inlet

Cape Bauld

NEWFOUNDLAND

Cape Breton

Cape Sable

60°

60°

50°

45°

A.N.Ryan

2

landes'. After 1505 he revived his father's ambition of reaching Asia by sailing beyond the transatlantic discovery. What Sebastian achieved is unclear largely because he himself, the chief witness speaking to us through sixteenth-century historians, is unclear. All that we can be sure of is that he later convinced many people in England and abroad that he had during 1508–9 discovered the entry to a navigable passage around the new land to Asia. He thus created the concept of the North-West Passage, the most enduring aspect of the Cabot family's legacy to the English.

Sixteenth-century English oceanic enterprise: the northern hemisphere

Between 1509 and 1550 English interest in oceanic endeavour, the Newfoundland fishery excepted, was spasmodic. The writings of Robert Thorne (1527) and Roger Barlow (1540–1) in favour of establishing trade with Asia by a passage through the Arctic seas elicited little public or private response. Economic difficulties in mid-century, including those associated with the export of English cloth, prompted reappraisal. By 1553 Englishmen were ready to venture capital in searching for trans-Arctic routes to Asia, said to be shorter than the routes of the Iberian powers around southern America and Africa, and in finding new cloth markets in lands bordering the way. This led in the first instance to voyages beyond the North Cape of Norway to open a North-East Passage.

The first voyage (1553) commanded by Hugh Willoughby and Richard Chancellor reached Archangel, through which port a regular trade with Russia was established. It was monopolized by the Muscovy Company, chartered in 1555. The company continued to promote exploration east of the White Sea. Stephen and William Borough attempted a reconnaissance (1556) as far as the River Ob, but failed to get beyond Vaygach Island near Novaya Zemlya. Arthur Pett and George Jackman struggled into the Kara Sea (1580) only to find themselves, like the Boroughs, blocked by a barrier of ice. Henry Hudson was turned back (1608) without entering the Kara Sea.

These defeats in the icefields encouraged advocates of Sebastian Cabot's North-West Passage to press their case. Delayed by legal wrangles arising out of the Muscovy merchants' monopolistic claims over navigation in the northern seas, a sustained English search, frequently hampered by muddled geographical concepts, began in 1576 with the first of Martin Frobisher's three voyages to the northwest (1576–8). Sponsored by the Cathay Company, Frobisher revealed parts of the coasts of Greenland, Baffin Island, Labrador and Frobisher Bay, but ruined the company by propagating the fantasy that he had found gold. John Davis, with more modest financial support, explored the coast of Greenland to 72°N as well as coasts on the opposite side of Davis Strait in three voyages (1585–7). The search was renewed by George Waymouth (1602) under the auspices of the East India Company. He found the promising Hudson Strait, through which Henry Hudson sailed (1610) to enter Hudson Bay. Murdered by a mutinous crew, Hudson did not fully explore the bay, but his discovery enkindled hopes that a North-West Passage had been found. A North-West Passage Company was established which sent out Thomas Button (1612–13) and William Baffin and Robert Bylot (1615–16), whose findings discouraged hopes that a North-West Passage was open either by way of the bay or to the north of Davis Strait. The last voyages in the series were by Luke Foxe and Thomas James in 1631, both of whom through

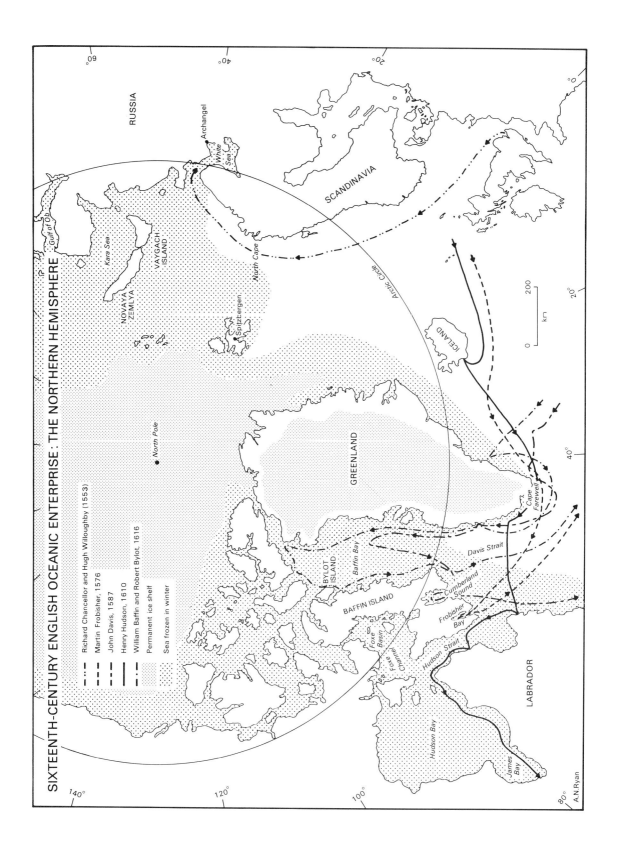

SIXTEENTH-CENTURY ENGLISH OCEANIC ENTERPRISE: THE NORTHERN HEMISPHERE

Richard Chancellor and Hugh Willoughby (1553)
Martin Frobisher, 1576
John Davis, 1587
Henry Hudson, 1610
William Baffin and Robert Bylot, 1616
Permanent ice shelf
Sea frozen in winter

RUSSIA

Archangel

White Sea

Gulf of Ob

Kara Sea

NOVAYA ZEMLYA

VAYGACH ISLAND

North Cape

Spitzbergen

SCANDINAVIA

North Pole

Arctic Circle

ICELAND

GREENLAND

Cape Farewell

Davis Strait

BYLOT ISLAND

Baffin Bay

BAFFIN ISLAND

Cumberland Sound

Frobisher Bay

Foxe Basin

Foxe Channel

Hudson Strait

Hudson Bay

LABRADOR

James Bay

0   200
km

60°

40°

20°

0°

20°

40°

80°

100°

120°

140°

A.N.Ryan

4

their discoveries are named in modern charts of Hudson Bay and Foxe Basin just north of the Arctic Circle.

The Arctic seas were impassable in fragile wooden sailing ships. The wonder is not that the pioneers failed to break through but that they got as far as they did and in many cases lived to write their historically price-less reports. They significantly enlarged geographical knowledge; they helped to reveal rich fishing grounds, that off Spitzbergen being a case in point. Though practical seamen rather than scholars, they made their distinct contribution to the application of science in man's discovery of the sea.

Sixteenth-century English oceanic enterprise: the southern hemisphere

Until the 1570s contacts between Englishmen and South America had been limited to voyages to Brazil in the 1530s made by William Hawkins the elder of Plymouth. In March 1574 Richard Grenville and his associates, among them William Hawkins the younger, petitioned the queen for permission to make a voyage for the 'discovery, traffic and enjoying for the Queen's Majesty and her subjects of all or any lands, islands and countries southwards beyond the equinoctial'. Despite an emphatic statement that they sought no possession in places 'already subdued and inhabited by the Spaniard or Portingal', the queen refused permission. Her refusal points to South America, then thought to be effectively occupied by Spain and Portugal to about 30°S of the equator, as the object of the enterprise. Had it been, as has been argued, *Terra Australis*, the unknown southern continent, she would have had no cause for anxiety that her subjects might become embroiled in conflicts with Iberian settlers.

Plans for the armed reconnaissance of South America were resumed in 1577 following a deterioration in Anglo-Spanish relations. Backed by the anti-Spanish group at court, and approved by the queen, Francis Drake sailed from Plymouth in November with orders to prospect unoccupied lands southwards of the Rio de la Plata, pass through the Strait of Magellan, reconnoitre the Pacific coast of America as far as 30°S and return by the same route. It was understood by all concerned that pillage was part of the programme. There are no grounds for believing that Thomas Doughty, executed at Port St Julian in June 1578 on a charge of treachery, was the agent of a 'peace party' determined to curb Drake's piratical ambitions. It is also important not to miss the point that Drake and his backers took the reconnaissance seriously as a step towards the establishment of an English colony and base for expansion in South America.

The looting began at Valparaiso in December 1578 and culminated in March 1579 in the capture of the so-called *Cacafuego*, bound from Callao to Panama with a cargo of silver, near Cape San Francisco. The voyage of reconnaissance now became a voyage of circumnavigation because Drake could not return by the same route. Running northwards in search of signs of the North-West Passage, he reached California (which he named New Albion) and then struck out across the Pacific. He crossed the equator shortly after a visit to Ternate in the Moluccas and returned to Plymouth in September 1580 by way of the Cape of Good Hope.

After Drake's return, English interest in both colonization and trade in South America gradually petered out. People were deterred in part by Spanish demonstrations of force and in part by the unpromising outcome of ventures to Brazil. Drake's principal legacy was

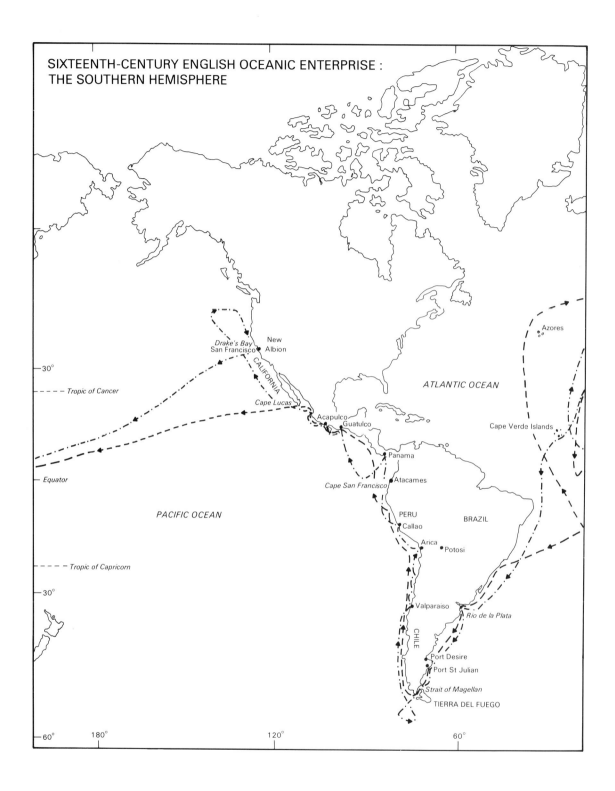

SIXTEENTH-CENTURY ENGLISH OCEANIC ENTERPRISE :
THE SOUTHERN HEMISPHERE

Azores

Drake's Bay
San Francisco
New
Albion

CALIFORNIA

30°

- - - Tropic of Cancer

Cape Lucas

ATLANTIC OCEAN

Acapulco
Guatulco

Cape Verde Islands

Panama

Equator

Cape San Francisco
Atacames

PACIFIC OCEAN

PERU
Callao

BRAZIL

Arica
Potosi

Tropic of Capricorn

30°

Valparaiso

Rio de la Plata

CHILE

Port Desire
Port St Julian

Strait of Magellan

TIERRA DEL FUEGO

60°

180°

120°

60°

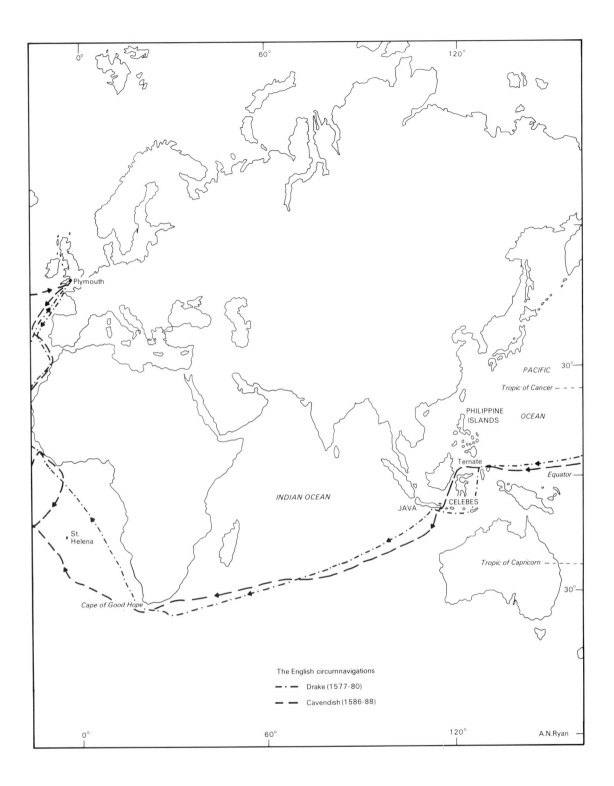

Plymouth

PACIFIC

30°

Tropic of Cancer ---

PHILIPPINE
ISLANDS

OCEAN

Ternate

Equator ---

CELEBES

JAVA

INDIAN OCEAN

St.
Helena

Tropic of Capricorn ---

30°

Cape of Good Hope

The English circumnavigations

—·—·— Drake (1577-80)

— — — Cavendish (1586-88)

A.N.Ryan

7

to privateering. He was followed by Thomas Cavendish who circumnavigated (1586–8) and 'made' the voyage financially by taking that year's Manila galleon off Cape Lucas. John Chidley failed to get through the Strait of Magellan (1589), and Cavendish died at sea on a second venture in 1591. Richard Hawkins, on a marauding mission to the Peruvian coast, was made prisoner of war in the Bay of Atacames in 1594. This ended English efforts to enter the Pacific by the strait and wage war there. In this region at least Spain won the victory.

Early attempts at settlement in North America

English interest in the settlement of North America dates from the 1560s when news was received of an attempted French settlement of Florida. It was not, however, until the 1570s that efforts, which coincided with North-West Passage voyages, were made to translate the interest into action. People who supported active measures included the elder Richard Hakluyt, a lawyer associated with overseas speculators, the younger Richard Hakluyt, propagandist for, and chronicler of, English maritime enterprise, and Elizabeth I's principal secretary Francis Walsingham. The prime mover was Humphrey Gilbert of Devonshire gentry stock. His qualification was experience of colonization in Ireland. In 1578 he received a patent from the queen to colonize unoccupied lands. Gilbert envisaged a settlement, without having any exact idea of its whereabouts, on the American coast north of Spanish Florida. A badly organized reconnaissance (1578) failed. Gilbert was not thereby deterred from disposing of territory to would-be transatlantic landowners. In 1583 he was lost at sea on a second reconnaissance.

The new patentee, Gilbert's half-brother Walter Ralegh, organized a reconnaissance by Philip Amadas and Arthur Barlowe (1584). They presented an idyllic report on the Carolina Outer Banks and drew attention to Roanoke Island, which was selected by Ralegh as the first settlement. As a leading object of the promoters was the establishment of a base for profitable operations against Spanish shipping, this was an unsuitable choice. While dilating on the charms of the land and its people, Amadas and Barlowe glossed over the inadequacy of the harbour at Roanoke. The first colonial pioneers, an all-male party of 108 under Ralph Lane, were put ashore by Sir Richard Grenville in 1585 on an exploratory mission. They were to survey the land and its natural resources, look for gold, examine the prospects of relations with American Indians and carry out agricultural experiments. They were also to search for a better harbour, for which purpose Lane proposed a reconnaissance, which was never made, of the Chesapeake Bay region. Neither Lane nor his men had the appropriate skills and experience to complete their mission successfully. As supplies ran low they made harsh demands of the Indians for provisions, and as relations between the two races deteriorated they became increasingly dependent for survival upon the promised arrival of help from England in the early summer of 1586. When their sponsors failed to meet the deadline, the pioneers returned home.

The first effort to establish an English community, as opposed to a military garrison, in America was made in 1587, again at Roanoke, under the leadership of John White. The party, which included women and children, was landed in July 1587. The weakness of the second settlement, as of the first, was dependence for subsistence upon Indian goodwill and regular supplies from England, both uncertain factors. The uneasiness of the settlers is reflected in their insistence that White

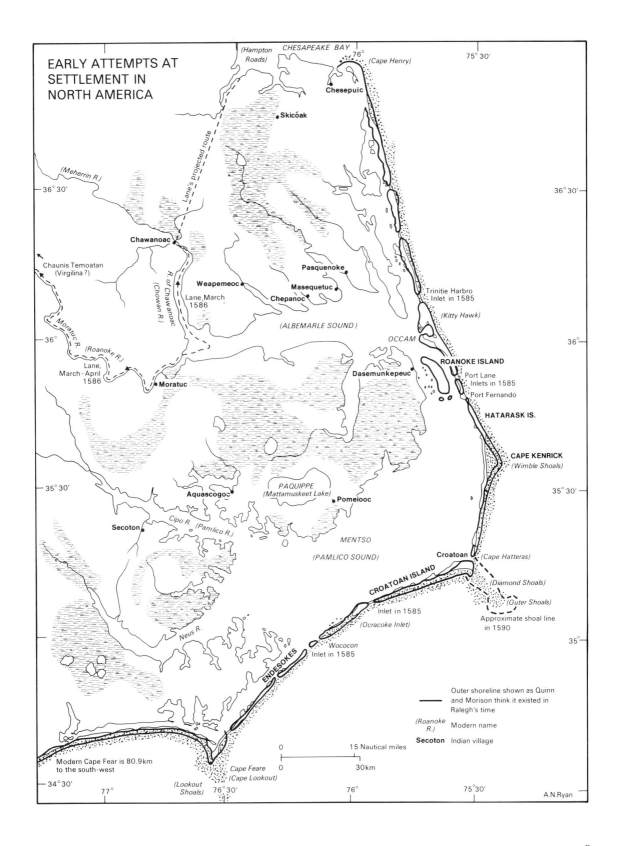

EARLY ATTEMPTS AT
SETTLEMENT IN
NORTH AMERICA

CHESAPEAKE BAY
(Hampton Roads)
(Cape Henry)
76°
75° 30'

● **Chesepuic**

● **Skicóak**

(Meherrin R.)

36° 30'   36° 30'

Lane's projected route

● **Chawanoac**

Chaunis Temoatan
(Virgilina?)

● **Pasquenoke**

● **Weapemeoc**   ● **Masequetuc**
● **Chepanoc**

Lane, March
1586

R. of Chawanoac
(Chowan R.)

(ALBEMARLE SOUND)

Trinitie Harbro
Inlet in 1585

(Kitty Hawk)

OCCAM

36°   36°

● **Dasemunkepeuc**   **ROANOKE ISLAND**

Moratuc R.

(Roanoke R.)

Lane,
March-April
1586

● **Moratuc**

Port Lane
Inlets in 1585
Port Fernando

HATARASK IS.

CAPE KENRICK
(Wimble Shoals)

PAQUIPPE
(Mattamuskeet Lake)

● **Aquascogoc**   ● **Pomeiooc**

35° 30'   35° 30'

● **Secoton**   *Cipo R.* *(Pamlico R.)*

MENTSO

(PAMLICO SOUND)   ● **Croatoan**   *(Cape Hatteras)*

(Diamond Shoals)

CROATOAN ISLAND

(Outer Shoals)

Approximate shoal line
in 1590

Neus R.

Inlet in 1585
(Ocracoke Inlet)

35°   35°

Wococon
Inlet in 1585

ENDESOKES

Outer shoreline shown as Quinn
and Morison think it existed in
Ralegh's time

(Roanoke
R.) Modern name

Secoton Indian village

0   15 Nautical miles

0   30km

Modern Cape Fear is 80.9km
to the south-west

Cape Feare
(Cape Lookout)

34° 30'

77°   76° 30'   76°   75° 30'

(Lookout
Shoals)

A.N.Ryan

9

return to England with the ships to organize supplies, leaving behind as sureties his family. He was never to see them again. Detained by wartime conditions, he next sighted Roanoke only in 1590, to find that the colonists had disappeared.

Victims of insufficient support, inadequate knowledge and national absorption in the Spanish war, the 'lost colonists' did not disappear without trace. There are indications that some went south to Croatoan and others north to the Chesapeake Bay region where they may have survived until the early seventeenth century. Elizabethan England had neither the resources nor the interest to fund on a proper scale colonial ventures which were to the majority peripheral activities.

Virginia: early settlement

Through the deliberately ambiguous wording of the clauses appertaining to the rights of the two powers in the transatlantic world the Anglo-Spanish peace treaty of London (1604) did not contain any formal acknowledgement by the English of Spanish monopolistic rights in North America. Reconnaissances, combined with privateering, had been a feature of the war years, and anti-Spanish groups in English society were determined to resume the colonial enterprises of the 1580s. As in the days of Queen Elizabeth I (d. 1603), the initiative lay with private citizens, many of whom had long associations with warlike maritime activities. Interest was strongest in Plymouth, Bristol and Exeter and among 'Adventurers of and for our Cittie of London'.

The Virginia Company, chartered in April 1606, was responsible for England's first systematic effort to colonize North America. Privately organized and financed, it received royal approval through the creation by James I of the royal council for Virginia which was to oversee the affairs of the colony without taking responsibility for them. The company consisted of two branches: that based on Plymouth being allocated 'North Virginia' (later called New England) between 38°N and 45°N; that based on London, 'South Virginia' between 34°N and 41°N. The overlap was of no consequence since neither branch had an interest in that region. In any case the Plymouth branch failed as a result of disappointing returns from the fur trade, of which much had been expected,

the unsuitability of the land for agricultural development and the harshness of the 1607–8 winter. The settlement started around Fort St George on the Kennebec River was evacuated in 1608 (see p. 13).

The London branch was interested in the Chesapeake region. Its fleet, led by the *Susan Constant* under Christopher Newport, entered Chesapeake Bay in April 1607 and founded a site well up the James river in an unhealthy location at Jamestown, well placed to resist attack and with a good anchorage. The pioneers attempted to investigate the fate of the 'lost colonists', but their energies were largely consumed in a struggle for survival. Organizational defects, highlighted by bitter quarrels, were partly to blame. They were probably less to blame than the fact that the pioneers were more interested in the discovery of precious metals and the cultivation of Mediterranean produce, calculated to attract investment, than in the achievement of self-sufficiency. Following the issue of a new and more satisfactory charter in 1609 and the imposition of military discipline the colony survived precariously, with a dangerously high death rate. It was still confined to the limits of Jamestown, and settlers found it difficult to come to terms with the environment or to create a healthy economy.

Economically the colony was to be saved by tobacco. Experiments (in which John Rolfe, son-in-law of the great Indian chief Powhatan, was prominent) in the cultivation of tobacco acceptable to English taste, began in 1612. By

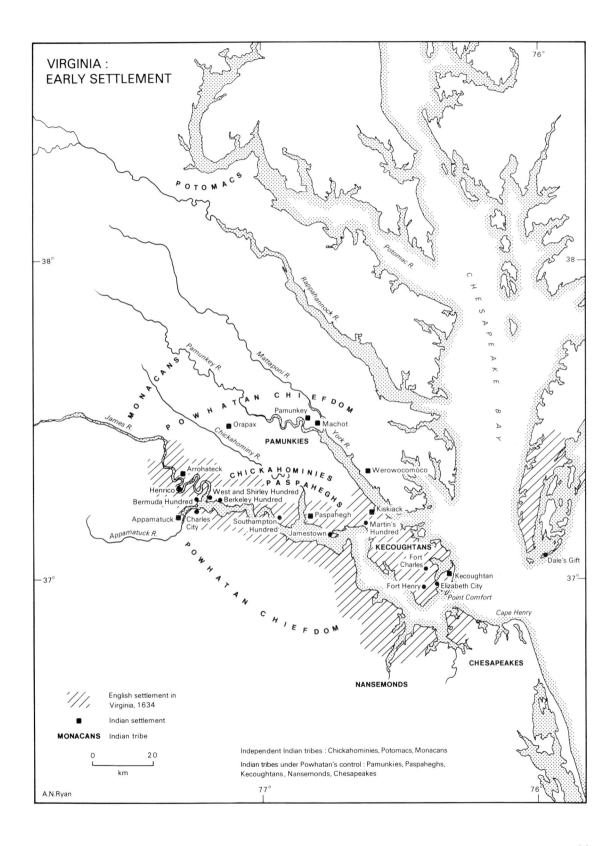

VIRGINIA :
EARLY SETTLEMENT

POTOMACS

CHESAPEAKE BAY

Potomac R.

Rappahannock R.

MONACANS

Pamunkey R.

Mattaponi R.

POWHATAN CHIEFDOM

James R.

Pamunkey
■ Orapax   ■ Machot
Chickahominy R.   York R.
PAMUNKIES

CHICKAHOMINIES
PASPAHEGHS
■ Werowocomoco

Arrohateck
Henrico ■
West and Shirley Hundred
Bermuda Hundred ●   ● Berkeley Hundred
Appamatuck ■   ● Charles   Southampton   ● Paspahegh   Kiskiack
City   Hundred   ■ Martin's
Appamatuck R.   ● Jamestown   Hundred

POWHATAN CHIEFDOM

KECOUGHTANS
Fort
Charles ●
■ Kecoughtan
Fort Henry ●   ● Elizabeth City   ● Dale's Gift
Point Comfort

Cape Henry

CHESAPEAKES

NANSEMONDS

///// English settlement in
Virginia, 1634

■ Indian settlement

MONACANS Indian tribe

0   20
km

Independent Indian tribes : Chickahominies, Potomacs, Monacans

Indian tribes under Powhatan's control : Pamunkies, Paspaheghs,
Kecoughtans , Nansemonds, Chesapeakes

A.N.Ryan

11

1617 the commercial advantages of a staple crop not only produced a new confidence in survival but attracted fresh waves of settlers and nurtured ideas of territorial expansion, first seen in the establishment of new plantations higher up the James River. Expansion disturbed the pattern of Anglo-Indian relations, hitherto marked by an odd mixture of mutual tolerance and suspicion. The Indian uprising of 1622 caused the deaths of some 350 colonists and was followed by a bitter war. It was a setback to the credibility of the company at home, which was in any case rent by dissension and increasingly seen as incapable of discharging colonial responsibilities. James I dissolved the company and replaced it by royal commissions, thus creating a royal colony. As such Virginia entered upon an era of prosperity associated with its prolific tobacco plantations.

New England colonies: early settlement

The Plymouth and New England colonies in North America were populated primarily by 'vexed and troubled' Englishmen, dissatisfied with religious and constitutional developments in England under James I and Charles I and concerned about the persecution of people who dissented from the practices and doctrines of the established Anglican Church. The area acquired a poor reputation, following the experiences there of the Plymouth branch of the Virginia Company, as a harsh and barren land. Apart from tiny coastal settlements under the auspices of the Council for New England in what are now New Hampshire and Maine, it was neglected by the English.

The first tentative steps towards the colonization of New England took place in 1620 when a party of some one hundred people on board the *Mayflower* made a landfall at Cape Cod and settled in Plymouth. Many of the group, known as the Pilgrim Fathers, had originally belonged to a separatist congregation at Scrooby near Gainsborough, which had emigrated to Leiden in the Netherlands. Its leader and first governor, William Bradford, became inspired by the idea of the New World as a secure haven for English separatists. Although the Pilgrims were by no means destitute, they emigrated on borrowed capital and had to toil in a difficult environment at agriculture, fishing and the fur trade to achieve economic independence. For many years the settlement remained small and weak. It none the less survived with modest growth and was eventually absorbed into Massachusetts in 1691. Plymouth was the first permanent northern outpost of England in America.

Its early difficulties were a warning to English Puritans of the need for adequate financial backing within a corporate company as the basis of colonial settlement. In 1629, when the prospects facing Puritanism in England seemed bleaker than ever, a wealthy group, mainly Puritanical in sympathy, obtained a royal charter as the Massachusetts Bay Company with authority to establish a self-governing settlement in America. In 1630 over 1,000 persons with provisions, livestock and equipment established at Boston a community which escaped the initial horrors of Virginia and Plymouth, partly through stern ecclesiastical and theological discipline and partly through applied knowledge of the experiences of earlier ventures. Though hardly opulent, Massachusetts rapidly became prosperous enough through fur trading, agriculture and fishing to attract more settlers. By 1640, 20,000 people had emigrated to New England. The population of the Chesapeake settlements stood in comparison at about 6,000. Massachusetts was the great success story of early English colonization, its urban element emphasized by the growth of Boston, Charles Town,

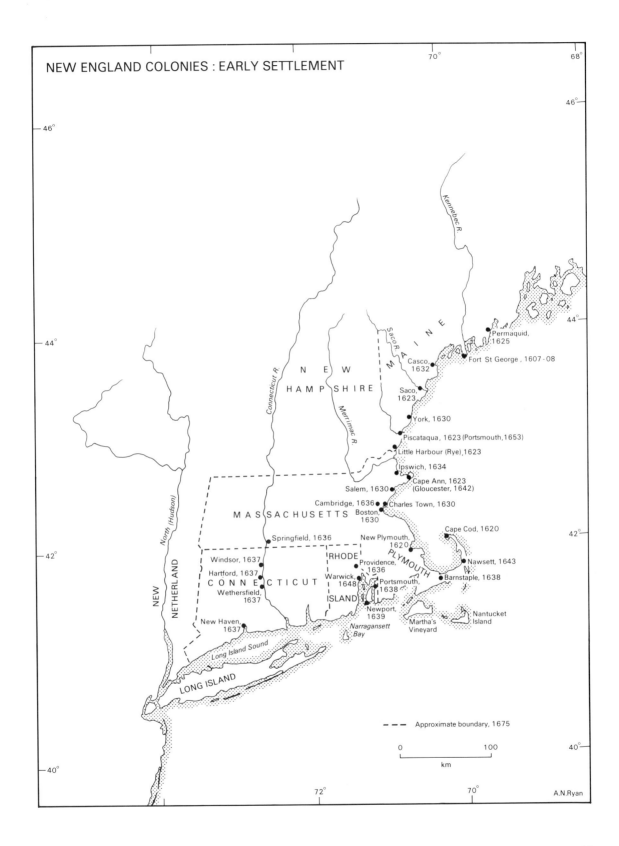

NEW ENGLAND COLONIES : EARLY SETTLEMENT

Permaquid, 1625

Casco 1632

Fort St George , 1607-08

Saco, 1623

York, 1630

Piscataqua, 1623 (Portsmouth,1653)

Little Harbour (Rye),1623

Ipswich, 1634

Cape Ann, 1623 (Gloucester, 1642)

Salem, 1630

Cambridge, 1636

Charles Town, 1630

Boston, 1630

Springfield, 1636

New Plymouth, 1620

Cape Cod, 1620

Windsor, 1637

RHODE

Providence, 1636

Nawsett, 1643

Hartford, 1637

Warwick, 1648

Portsmouth, 1638

Barnstaple, 1638

Wethersfield, 1637

ISLAND

Newport, 1639

New Haven, 1637

Narragansett Bay

Martha's Vineyard

Nantucket Island

MAINE

NEW HAMPSHIRE

MASSACHUSETTS

CONNECTICUT

PLYMOUTH

NEW NETHERLAND

LONG ISLAND SOUND

LONG ISLAND

Kennebec R.

Saco R.

Connecticut R.

Merrimac R.

North (Hudson)

- - - Approximate boundary, 1675

0   100
km

A.N.Ryan

13

Cambridge (the site of Harvard College, 1636) and Salem.

During the 1630s the New England settlement, originally confined to a narrow strip of the eastern shore, expanded southwards and northwards along the Atlantic coast. This was caused both by religious dissent, not necessarily of a liberal tendency, and secular expansionist ambitions. Emigrant congregations from Massachusetts brought new colonies into existence. They founded Newport, Portsmouth, Providence and Warwick (Rhode Island), and Hartford, New Haven, Wethersfield and Windsor (Connecticut), and also attached themselves to the small settlements in Maine and New Hampshire. They were creating beyond the Atlantic a new England, already significantly different from old England. The freedoms or opportunities these colonies had to offer do something to explain the remarkable willingness of seventeenth-century Englishmen to begin life anew in the New World and to lay the firm foundations of Anglo-Saxon North America.

Chartered companies: the eastern seas

In 1580 Philip II of Spain absorbed the kingdom of Portugal, and by the same act the Portuguese overseas empire, into his dominions. With English entrepreneurs and seamen already showing scant regard for Spanish claims to imperial monopoly in the overseas world, the Portuguese empire in the east became for them an equally legitimate target. In the same year Francis Drake returned from his voyage of circumnavigation to report that the ruler of Ternate in the Spice Islands was discontented with the Portuguese and ready to trade with the English. Taken together the two events seemed to point the way to an English entry into the eastern seas by way of the Portuguese route around the Cape of Good Hope.

Twenty years were to pass before the foundation of the East India Company in 1600. The reasons for the delay are clear enough. English seamanship and shipping had not yet quite come of age in the struggle for oceanic dominion.

The results of voyages in the 1580s and 1590s, beginning with Edward Fenton's 'troublesome voyage' of 1582, were discouraging to investors, who were also conscious that Drake's fleeting visit shed little light on either conditions of trade or the likely strength of Portuguese opposition. Investment in the prosperous Levant Company and speculation in Atlantic privateering were strong counter-attractions. Ironically members of the Levant Company played a major part in launching the East India Company. In 1595 the Dutch, much better furnished with commercial and navigational intelligence, entered the eastern seas. The prospect of such formidable rivals impeding the transit of spices to the Levant through a monopolization of the Indian Ocean confronted the Levant Company with a challenge it could not ignore.

Chartered on 31 December 1600, the East India Company sent its first ships from the Thames in February 1601 under James Lancaster, who had led an unprofitable venture ten years earlier. Its aim was to obtain a footing in the Indonesian trade in pepper and spices. Lancaster did some business in pepper at Bantam, as did Henry Middleton, who led the second expedition of 1604. It soon became clear, however, that the Dutch were not intent upon ousting the Portuguese from Indonesia and the Moluccas in order to let the English in. Their object was monopoly. Less well organized, less reliably funded and less certain of state support, the English company fought an uphill battle to maintain a footing in the pepper and spice trades. It was never in fact totally excluded from them, even after expulsion from Amboina (1623), but it did come

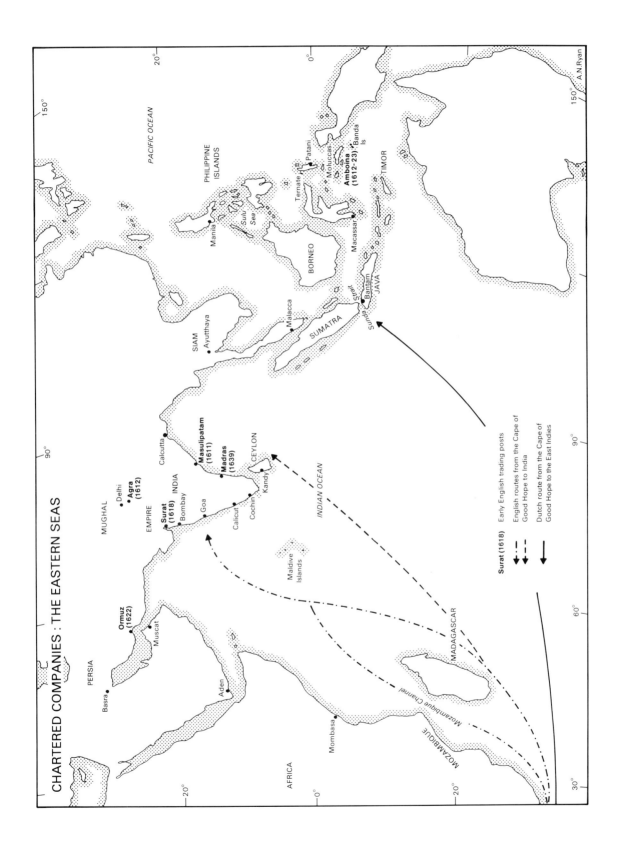

CHARTERED COMPANIES : THE EASTERN SEAS

PERSIA

Basra

Ormuz (1622)

Muscat

Aden

MUGHAL

Delhi

Agra
(1612)

Surat (1618) INDIA

EMPIRE

Bombay

Goa

Calicut

Cochin

Kandy

CEYLON

Madras
(1639)

Masulipatam
(1611)

Calcutta

SIAM

Ayutthaya

Malacca

SUMATRA

Sunda Strait

Bantam

JAVA

Macassar

TIMOR

Amboina
(1612-23)

Banda
Is

Moluccas

Ternate

Patani

BORNEO

Sulu
Sea

Manila

PHILIPPINE
ISLANDS

PACIFIC OCEAN

INDIAN OCEAN

Maldive
Islands

MADAGASCAR

Mozambique Channel

Mombasa

AFRICA

MOZAMBIQUE

Surat (1618)   Early English trading posts

English routes from the Cape of
Good Hope to India

Dutch route from the Cape of
Good Hope to the East Indies

20°   0°   90°   150°

20°   0°   20°

30°   60°   90°   150°

A.N.Ryan

to rely increasingly upon its activities in the Indian subcontinent.

India, however, was not selected as an alternative to Java, Sumatra and the Spice Islands. The third voyage of 1607 was sent under William Hawkins to Surat to obtain Indian textiles, a marketable commodity in the Spice Islands, as well as pepper and indigo. As a result of negotiations with the Mughal Empire the company was able to establish trading posts in India, the two most important being Surat and Masulipatam, and to make its commercial influence felt in the Persian Gulf and Red Sea. It consolidated its position by victories in 1612 and 1614 over the Portuguese, with whom by the 1630s it was collaborating. The company's great days were in the future. Despite successes, its monopoly was not consistently supported by the early Stuart monarchy, and the English civil wars were detrimental to its progress. It entered upon an era of prosperity following the restoration of its monopoly under a new charter granted by Oliver Cromwell in 1657.

Chartered companies: the Mediterranean

In the early sixteenth century trade between England and the Mediterranean, including the Levant, flourished. Imports included alum, spices and wine; the principal export was English cloth. The troubled state of the Mediterranean and the growth of Turkish power, especially in its eastern parts, between the late 1530s and early 1570s resulted in the disappearance of English ships. The Venetian Republic held most-favoured-nation status with the Ottoman Empire and was the principal carrier of the trade, English cloth brought overland from Antwerp to the head of the Adriatic being one of its components.

Owing to the increasing insecurity of the transcontinental route and the rise of problems for Venice, English ships returned to the Mediterranean in the early 1570s, appearing first at the Italian ports of Livorno and Civita Vecchia with cargoes of cloth, herring, lead and tin. Penetration of the eastern Mediterranean soon followed. There are documentary references both to English ships making for Zante and Cephalonia as early as 1575 and to leading Mediterranean merchants establishing contacts with the Levant, terminal of traditional sea routes from Asia. Such activities were the prelude to the mission to Turkey in 1578 of William Harborne to negotiate the regulation of commerce. Aided by the Ottoman Empire's need for gun metals, Harborne succeeded, not without occasional alarms, in establishing conditions which led in 1581 to the foundation of the Levant Company, one of the most powerful and successful of the chartered companies created in the sixteenth century to promote English overseas trade. In 1592 it was enlarged to include members of the Venice Company, which had enjoyed since 1583 a monopoly over the import of currants, oils and wines from the Venetian settlements. The company's activity can be measured by the establishment of warehouses at Constantinople, Smyrna and Aleppo and by the appointment at its own expense of diplomatic representatives, ambassadorial and consular, within the Ottoman Empire.

In the late sixteenth and early seventeenth centuries the Mediterranean was a dangerous place because of the Anglo-Spanish war and the activities of North African pirates. The company's well-armed ships of 400–500 tons sailing in their own convoys were easily able to survive such hazards and, because of the security they afforded, to attract freights in the Mediterranean carrying trade from foreign merchants, despite vigorous Dutch competition. The importance of the Levant trade in the history of English expansion lay not in the acquisition of territory but in the acquisition of

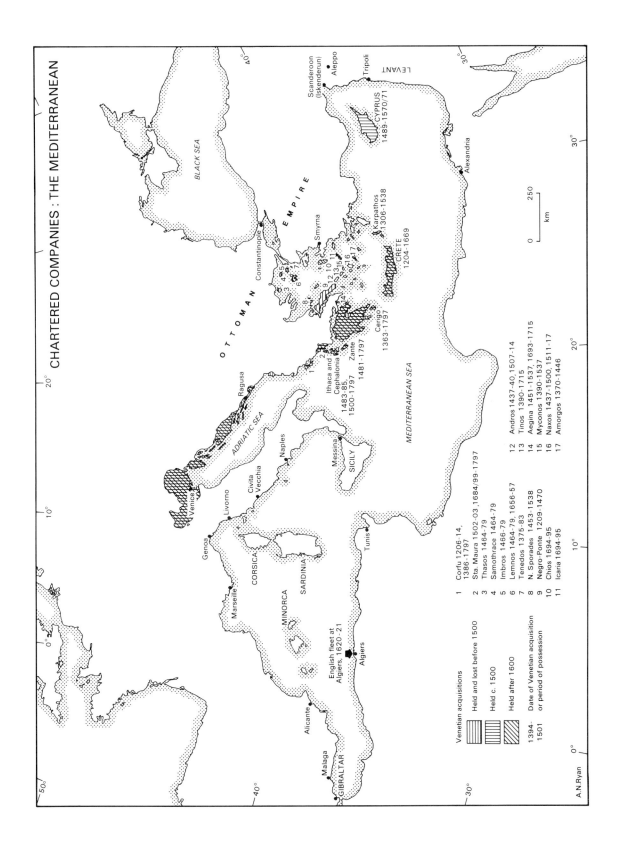

CHARTERED COMPANIES : THE MEDITERRANEAN

BLACK SEA

OTTOMAN EMPIRE

LEVANT

Scanderoon (Iskenderun)
Aleppo
Tripoli

CYPRUS
1489-1570/71

Smyrna

Alexandria

Karpathos
1306-1538

CRETE
1204-1669

Cerigo
1363-1797

Constantinople

MEDITERRANEAN SEA

Ragusa

ADRIATIC SEA

Ithaca and
Cephalonia
1483-85,
1500-1797

Zante
1481-1797

Venice

Genoa

Livorno

Naples

Civita
Vecchia

Messina

SICILY

CORSICA

SARDINIA

MINORCA

Marseille

Tunis

Alicante

Malaga

GIBRALTAR

Algiers

English fleet at
Algiers, 1620-21

0   250
|————————|
km

Venetian acquisitions

Held and lost before 1500

Held c. 1500

Held after 1600

1394-   Date of Venetian acquisition
1501   or period of possession

1   Corfu 1206-14,
     1386-1797
2   Sta. Maura 1502-03, 1684/99-1797
3   Thasos 1464-79
4   Samothrace 1464-79
5   Imbros 1466-79
6   Lemnos 1464-79, 1656-57
7   Tenedos 1375-83
8   N. Sporades 1453-1538
9   Negro-Ponte 1209-1470
10   Chios 1694-95
11   Icaria 1694-95

12   Andros 1437-40, 1507-14
13   Tinos 1390-1715
14   Aegina 1451-1537, 1693-1715
15   Myconos 1390-1537
16   Naxos 1437-1500, 1511-17
17   Amorgos 1370-1446

A.N.Ryan

17

nautical skills and capital for investment in other maritime endeavours, notably the East India Company.

In dealing with English commerce and shipping in the Mediterranean it would be wrong to overlook that in the western basin outside the monopoly of the company. Much of it was conducted in traditional English exports and imports through the port of Livorno in Tuscany. Like the Levant company, these Englishmen also participated successfully in the competition for freights in the carrying trade. English activity in the Medi-terranean was privately financed and organized, but the state could not ignore the growing English presence there. Ultimately the flag followed trade. In 1620 the government participated in an ineffective international expedition against the North African pirates. The force led by Sir Robert Mansell was the first English squadron to pass beyond the Straits of Gibraltar and hence the first demonstration of English naval power in the inland sea. The occupations of Gibraltar and Minorca, however, did not take place until the first decade of the eighteenth century.

Chartered companies: Africa

The first Englishmen to trade with Africa were merchants established in Anglo-Iberian commerce who extended their activities southwards to Morocco and possibly to Guinea in the late fifteenth century. Apart from certain knowledge of seemingly profitable activities by William Hawkins the elder of Plymouth at Guinea in the 1530s, evidence of early Anglo-African connections is slight. The first recorded account of a venture to Morocco (often referred to as Barbary) is a voyage in 1551 of the *Lion* of London commanded by Thomas Wyndham, who made his way to Agadir. By this time Morocco had largely cast off Portuguese control and its Atlantic ports were open. Wyndham, backed by London magnates, went again in 1552, calling at Safi and Agadir. These voyages were the beginning of a steady trade, with Morocco importing cloth, timber and other goods and exporting to England sugar and saltpetre. A Barbary Company was incorporated in 1585. It ceased to exist after 1597, but trade continued much as it had done on a modestly profitable basis during the Spanish war and after.

The business magnates behind the voyages of 1551–2 had another ambition, nothing less than a thrust further south in search of Guinea gold, Malagueta pepper and ivory. This was an intrusion into an area over which Portugal claimed monopolistic rights, with the result that the trade was conducted against a background of diplomatic protest and increasingly stiff opposition on the spot. Undeterred by either the Portuguese or the death rate, which was disastrously high on Wyndham's first and last voyage to Guinea and Benin in 1553, the English sent armed commercial missions to Guinea for the rest of the 1550s and into the 1560s. The earlier ones were profitable, but want of a base, more effective Portuguese opposition and the doubtful attitudes of Negro merchants made trade increasingly hard to come by despite crown support under Elizabeth I. In 1562 John Hawkins of Plymouth, already familiar with the Canary Islands, made his first attempt to enter the transatlantic slave trade by shipments to the Caribbean from the region extending from the Senegal to Sierra Leone. He made two further voyages, but declining profitability and, to a lesser degree, Spanish resistance persuaded him to abandon the trade in 1568. Falls in profits also caused the English effectively to abandon the Guinea trade after 1571.

There was a revival of interest in trade and privateering in African waters during the Anglo-Spanish war up to 1591, after which there is no continuous history of trade until 1607. The renewed trade was

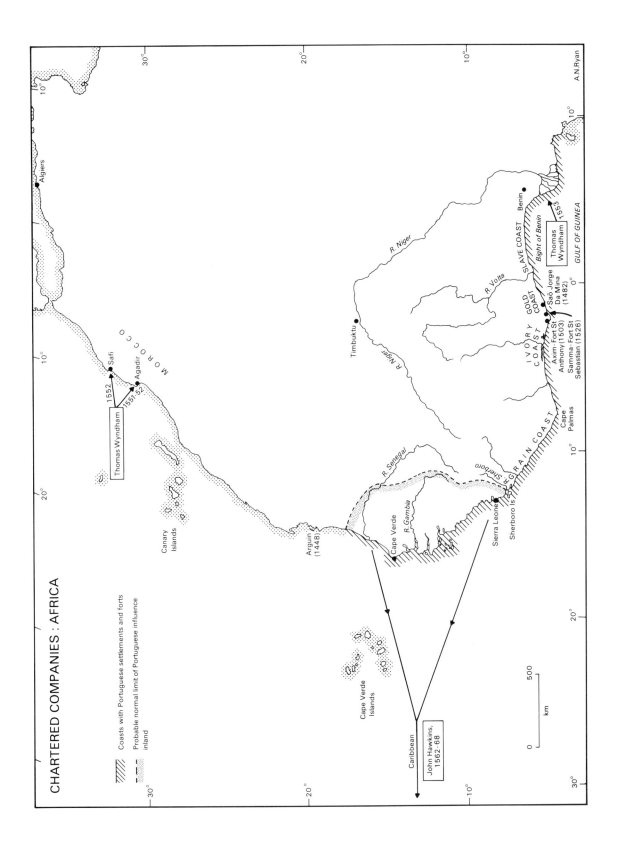

CHARTERED COMPANIES : AFRICA

Coasts with Portuguese settlements and forts

Probable normal limit of Portuguese influence inland

Algiers

MOROCCO

Safi
1552
Agadir
1551-52

Thomas Wyndham

Canary Islands

Arguin (1448)

R. Senegal

Cape Verde
R. Gambia

Sierra Leone
Sherboro Is.
Sherboro

GRAIN COAST

Cape Palmas

IVORY COAST

GOLD COAST

Axim–Fort St Anthony (1503)
Samma–Fort St Sebastian (1526)

Saõ Jorge Da Mina (1482)

SLAVE COAST

Bight of Benin

Benin

Thomas Wyndham 1553

GULF OF GUINEA

R. Volta

R. Niger

R. Niger

Timbuktu

Cape Verde Islands

Caribbean

John Hawkins, 1562-68

km
0   500

A.N.Ryan

10°
20°
30°
10°
20°
30°

30°
20°
10°
0°
10°
10°

19

largely a matter of individual enterprise directed towards Sierra Leone and the Sherboro, Gambia and Senegal rivers in Malagueta pepper, gold, ivory and redwood. John Davies of London, one of the trade's principal participants, was largely responsible in 1618 for its being chartered as the Company of Adventurers of London trading to Gynney and Bynney. The company, despite being reinforced in the 1620s by Humphrey Slany, who dealt in redwood, had a difficult existence largely because of shortage of capital and competition from the Dutch and Portuguese. It was regrouped in 1631 with a particular, though largely unrewarding, interest in the search for sources of gold. It seems to have been insufficiently well organized to preserve its monopoly against English interlopers, some of whom were forerunners of the greatest English trade with Africa from the mid-century onwards, that in slaves.

Chartered companies: Russia and the Eastland

The Eastland of the sixteenth and seventeenth centuries defies exact political or geographical definition. In its most precise form it denoted the south-east coast of the Baltic Sea, particularly the ports of Danzig, Elbing, Königsberg and Riga, perhaps even Narva. The great rivers of the Eastland, the Vistula, the Niemen and the Dvina, were gateways to the markets of central and eastern Europe; they were also outlets to the Baltic Sea for timber, hemp, flax and corn from the forests and plains of the hinterland. There was a great demand for this produce from the building and shipping industries, as well as for subsistence, in western and southern Europe from Norway to the Mediterranean.

The charter of privileges granted to the Eastland Company in 1579 extended beyond the traditional Eastland by covering Norway and Sweden as well as the Baltic, though the port of Narva was excluded on the grounds that it lay within the monopoly of the Muscovy Company, chartered in 1555 after the opening of trade with Russia through the port of Archangel. The timber trade with Norway was conducted mainly through the port of Tønsberg, the pitch, tar and iron trades with Sweden through Stockholm.

The Eastland Company was chartered not in order to create trade but to give the many private traders, not only from London but also from the east coast ports, a corporate identity in matters such as negotiations with the kings of Denmark over the tolls levied on shipping in the Sound or the pursuit of commercial privileges at places like Elbing and Danzig. The prosperity of the Eastland through the corn trade in the sixteenth century created a demand there for fine English cloth, including the expensive dyed cloth of Suffolk and Essex. Favoured by this, the export trade of the company increased steadily between 1579 and the late 1590s. Thereafter it encountered increasingly competitive Dutch rivalry, Dutch finished broadcloth emerging as a rival and gaining at the expense of the English product, the price of which continued to rise because of domestic economic problems.

The English also faced a challenge from the Dutch mercantile marine in the Baltic trade. As a carrier of bulk cargoes the Dutch *fluitschip* was technically superior to English ships and therefore more cost effective. This gave the Dutch an advantage in the struggle for freights and created a crisis not only for the English company but also for the English government; with the growth in mid-century of the state navy the role of Dutch shipping in the carriage of timber, hemp and other naval stores was seen as detrimental to the national interest. In 1651 the government intervened with the Navigation Act to achieve through state

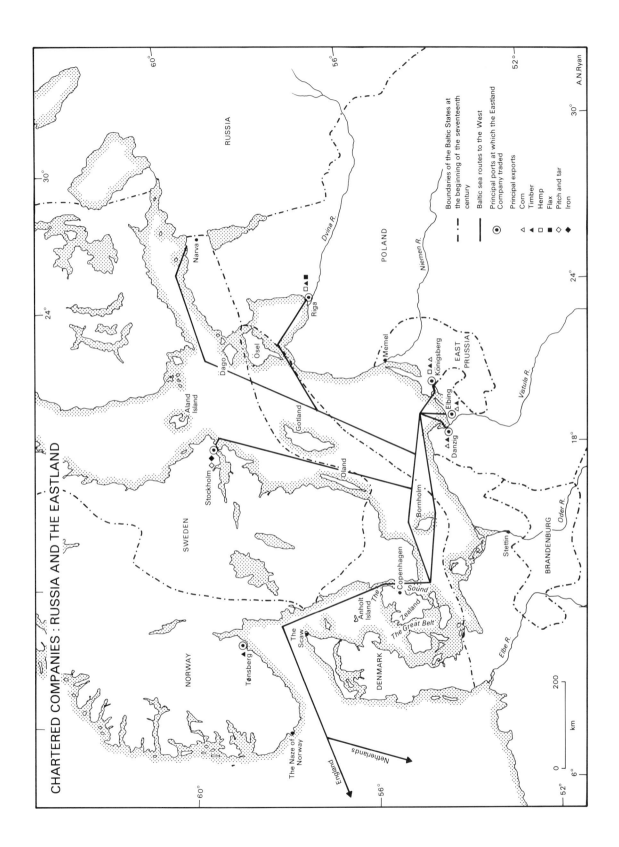

CHARTERED COMPANIES : RUSSIA AND THE EASTLAND

A.N.Ryan

Boundaries of the Baltic States at
the beginning of the seventeenth
century

Baltic sea routes to the West

Principal ports at which the Eastland
Company traded

Principal exports
△ Corn
◀ Timber
□ Hemp
■ Flax
◇ Pitch and tar
◆ Iron

RUSSIA

POLAND

Narva

Riga □■

Memel

EAST PRUSSIA

Königsberg □▲△

Elbing △▲

Danzig ▲◆

Dvina R.

Niemen R.

Vistula R.

Oder R.

Elbe R.

Dago

Osel

Åland
Island

Gotland

Oland

Bornholm

SWEDEN

Stockholm ◉◇

NORWAY

Tønsberg ◉◀

The Scaw

The Naze of Norway

DENMARK

Copenhagen

The Sound

Anholt
Island

Zealand

The Great Belt

Stettin

BRANDENBURG

England

Netherlands

km
0   200

21

regulation and control the protection of English shipping which the company had increasingly failed to provide. The Eastland Company thus became largely redundant, and its monopoly lapsed in 1673.

Ireland: mid-sixteenth to late seventeenth centuries

In the early sixteenth century English government in Ireland was largely ineffective beyond the Pale, an area limited in 1537 to Dublin and parcels of land in Counties Louth, Meath and Kildare within the province of Leinster. In the midlands and south of Ireland the English presence was represented by the magnates known as the Old English, who were descendants of the Anglo-Norman settlers and were effectively autonomous; in the north and west the Gaelic chieftains conducted affairs with little reference to English administration and according to their own customs and laws. From the point of view of the Tudor monarchy Ireland was a political vacuum which might be filled by internal or external opponents of the crown.

After crushing the rebellion of Thomas Fitzgerald, son of the viceroy the ninth Earl of Kildare, and thereby breaking the power of the house of Kildare, Henry VIII assumed the title of King of Ireland (1541) and set about making himself *de facto* ruler by persuading Old English and Gaelic lords to accept his rule in return for holding land under more secure (English) conditions of legal tenure. He thus introduced the principle, which was to dominate Irish history for four centuries, of making landowning synonymous with loyalty. In 1556 Mary I extended the principle by introducing a practice, the effects of which still influence Irish affairs: that of plantation. She allocated estates, confiscated following insurrection, in Counties Offaly and Laois to settlers from England and the Pale, as did Elizabeth I on a larger scale in Munster in the 1580s, after the defeat of the Desmond rebellion which had been provoked by her policy of Anglicization, ecclesiastical and secular.

Elizabeth encountered her greatest difficulties in Ulster, where the Gaelic lords led by Hugh O'Neill, Earl of Tyrone, resisted stubbornly. They defeated the English at Yellow Ford (1598) and opened the gates of Ireland to Spain. But the Spanish force sent to Kinsale in 1601 (like that sent to Smerwick, County Kerry, in 1580) was too small to make a decisive contribution, and Tyrone's effort to join it resulted in defeat there. Victory over the northern lords and their voluntary departure to the Continent in 1607 were followed by the most thoroughgoing plantation of all, that of English and Scots into Ulster. It is estimated that by 1618 the Scots in Armagh, Derry, Donegal, Tyrone, Fermanagh and Cavan numbered 40,000. The plantation of these counties was accompanied by the plantation of Antrim and Down and followed by smaller, though significant, plantations in other parts of Ireland. The process of the transfer of land from Irish into English and Scottish hands was carried further by Oliver Cromwell, who decreed that Catholic landowners should be transplanted to the province of Connacht and to County Clare and their lands elsewhere confiscated.

At the beginning of the seventeenth century most of the land in Ireland was still, despite the Tudor plantations, owned by Catholics both Gaelic and Old English. By 1660, with Catholic landowning confined to areas west of the Shannon, Ireland was in the hands of new landowners, English and Scots who had settled in Ulster in the early decades of the century and new settlers in Leinster and Munster in the wake of Cromwell's armies in the 1650s. The seventeenth-century plantations altered permanently the character of Ulster and

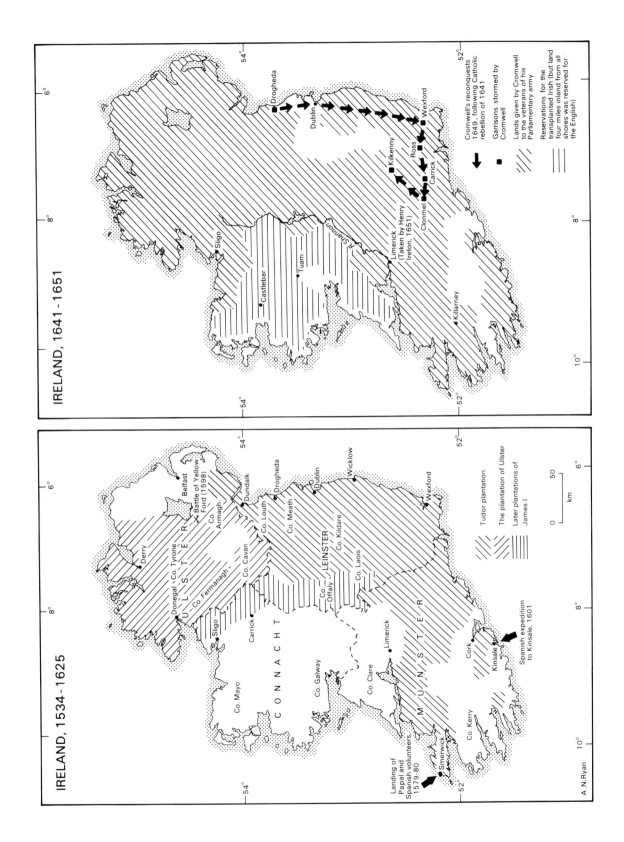

IRELAND, 1641-1651

Cromwell's reconquests
1649, following Catholic
rebellion of 1641

Garrisons stormed by
Cromwell

Lands given by Cromwell
to the veterans of his
Parliamentary army

Reservations for the
transplanted Irish (but land
four miles inland from all
shores was reserved for
the English)

Drogheda
Dublin
Kilkenny
Ross
Carrick
Wexford
Clonmel
Limerick
(Taken by Henry
Ireton, 1651)
R. Shannon
Sligo
Tuam
Castlebar
Killarney

IRELAND, 1534-1625

Derry
Donegal Co. Tyrone
U L S T E R
Co. Fermanagh
Co. Cavan
Co. Armagh
Belfast
Battle of Yellow
Ford (1598)
Co. Louth
Dundalk
Drogheda
Co. Meath
Dublin
Co. Kildare
Wicklow
Co. Offaly
Co. Laois
L E I N S T E R
Wexford
Sligo
Carrick
C O N N A C H T
Co. Mayo
Co. Galway
Co. Clare
Limerick
M U N S T E R
Co. Kerry
Cork
Kinsale
Spanish expedition
to Kinsale, 1601
Smerwick
Landing of
Papal and
Spanish volunteers,
1579-80

Tudor plantation

The plantation of Ulster

Later plantations of
James I

0   50
km

A.N.Ryan

23

transformed landowning throughout Ireland. Like the American Indians the Irish experienced the consequences of large-scale emigration from Great Britain by people in search of land and fresh opportunities.

The West Indies: plunder and acquisitions in the sixteenth and seventeenth centuries

Opportunities for personal aggrandizement and profit arising out of Spanish exploitation of the Americas were first seized by the French during the Habsburg–Valois wars through an extension into the Atlantic and Caribbean of the traditional privateering war against enemy shipping. The first English foray into the Caribbean was of a different order. In 1562 John Hawkins and his partners made the first of three attempts to participate in the transatlantic slave trade, over which Spain claimed a monopoly, by shipping African slaves to the markets of the Caribbean. Although customers were to be found, the Spanish government was determined to enforce its ban on foreign interlopers. In 1568 the third voyage ended in defeat for Hawkins in the Mexican harbour of San Juan de Ulúa.

If the slave trade first brought Englishmen to the Caribbean, it was silver which brought them back again. The flow of silver from the mines of the empire to Spain was by now a standing temptation to anti-Spanish Europeans both to enrich themselves and, as they saw it, to undermine the power of Spain by severing her financial sinews. Francis Drake, who had been at San Juan de Ulúa, formed a following in the West Country to commit profitable acts of revenge. Voyages of reconnaissance in 1570–1 were followed by a successful raid on the silver train on its way across the isthmus from Panama to Nombre de Dios in 1573. It made Drake's fame and his first fortune and, as Anglo-Spanish relations deteriorated, provided an incentive to patriotic plunderers as well as encouraging unrealistic expectations that the Spanish war-machine could be crippled cheaply and profitably in the Caribbean. It was no coincidence that one of the government's first acts of war in 1585 was to back a large expedition led by Drake across the Atlantic. It returned with modest profits and many unheeded warnings of the vulnerability to disease in the West Indies of large-scale expeditions. Ten years later Drake and Hawkins were to die of sickness on the ill-fated raid of 1595–6 against San Juan de Puerto Rico and coastal towns on the mainland. Caribbean offensives were conducted mainly by flocks of privateers, of which 235 are calculated to have visited the area between 1586 and 1603. This continuous, though uncoordinated, harassment cost Spain no colonies and little treasure, but it created a state of chronic insecurity in the Caribbean, helped to open its ports to illicit trade and forced up defence expenditure.

Privateering also stimulated the English shipping industry and fostered the skills and aptitudes which made possible England's oceanic advances and the foundation of permanent overseas plantations in the seventeenth century. The plantations included those in the Caribbean. Post-war enterprise first centred upon the coast between the Orinoco and Amazon rivers. There was also growing recognition of both the attractiveness of the Caribbean islands, encouraged perhaps by the success of the Atlantic island colony of Bermuda (1609), and the limitations of the Spanish hold over remoter islands, many of which were uninhabited or inhabited by Caribs. These factors led in the 1620s, especially after the outbreak of Charles I's Spanish war in 1625, to the occupation of islands: St Kitts (1624), Barbados (1625), Nevis (1628), Antigua and

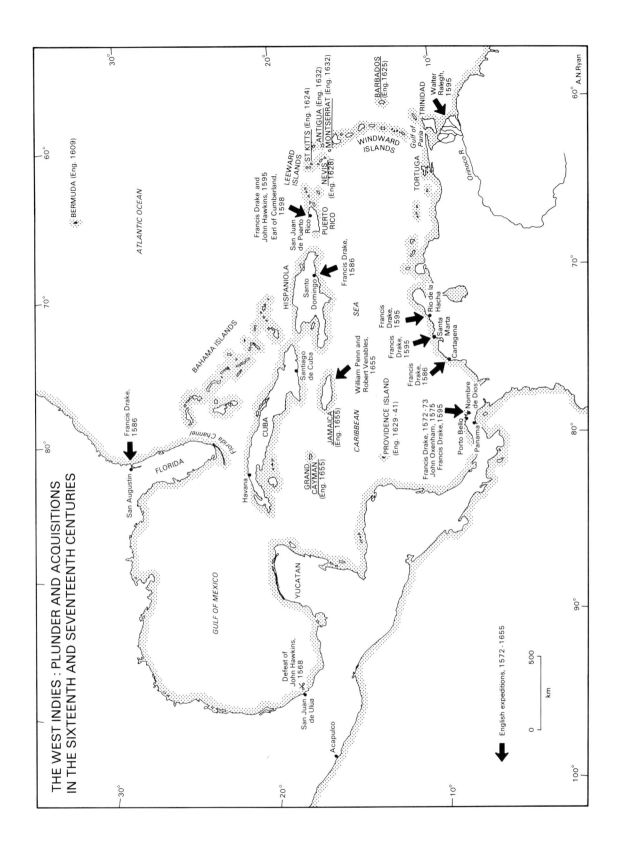

THE WEST INDIES : PLUNDER AND ACQUISITIONS
IN THE SIXTEENTH AND SEVENTEENTH CENTURIES

BERMUDA (Eng. 1609)

ATLANTIC OCEAN

Francis Drake and
John Hawkins, 1595
Earl of Cumberland,
1598

San Juan
de Puerto Rico

PUERTO
RICO

LEEWARD
ISLANDS

ST KITTS (Eng. 1624)
ANTIGUA (Eng. 1632)
MONTSERRAT (Eng. 1632)
NEVIS
(Eng. 1628)

BARBADOS
(Eng.1625)

WINDWARD
ISLANDS

Francis Drake,
1586

Santo
Domingo

HISPANIOLA

TORTUGA

Walter
Ralegh,
1595

TRINIDAD

Gulf of
Paria

Orinoco R.

Santiago
de Cuba

William Penn and
Robert Venables,
1655

CARIBBEAN

SEA

Francis
Drake,
1595

Rio de la
Hacha

Santa
Marta

Cartagena

BAHAMA ISLANDS

CUBA

Havana

JAMAICA
(Eng. 1655)

PROVIDENCE ISLAND
(Eng. 1629–41)

Francis
Drake,
1595

Francis
Drake,
1586

Florida Channel

GRAND
CAYMAN
(Eng. 1655)

Francis Drake, 1572–73
John Oxenham, 1575
Francis Drake, 1595

Porto Bello
Nombre
de Dios

Panama

Francis Drake,
1586

San Augustin

FLORIDA

GULF OF MEXICO

YUCATAN

Defeat of
John Hawkins,
1568

San Juan
de Ulúa

Acapulco

English expeditions, 1572 - 1655

km

0   500

A.N.Ryan

Montserrat (1632), as well as smaller islands. Not until 1655, however, when they occupied Jamaica, did the English wrench a colony from the grip of Spain, though Santa Catalina, renamed Providence Island, was held by them during 1629–41. Tobacco cultivation and subsistence farming were the main activities of the early settlements, which attracted a flow of adventurers and indentured servants from England. The first switch to sugar as the staple crop occurred in Barbados after 1640. The age of the 'sugar islands' and the slave societies was about to dawn.

South Carolina, North Carolina and Georgia

Charles II granted full title to all the land lying between 31°N and 36°N to eight of his friends and supporters in 1663. Two years later the grant was extended two degrees south to include the Spanish settlement at St Augustine and to 36°30″ to absorb Virginia settlers in the north. Their title enabled the Lords Proprietors, as they were known, to create a private or proprietary colony similar to Maryland, distinct from a royal colony such as Virginia or a corporate colony such as Rhode Island, whose primary purpose would be to enrich its owners.

Immigrants from Barbados who settled on Goose Creek, a tributary of the Cooper River, quickly established their political and economic ascendancy in South Carolina. Anglicans and slave holders, they thwarted proprietary policies of religious toleration, land distribution and taxation at every turn. In 1674 Dutch immigrants arrived from New York, settling on land south of the Ashley near the Stono River, and in 1680 the first French Huguenots arrived. A vigorous promotional campaign in the mother country between 1682 and 1685 attracted over 500 Presbyterians and Baptists, who settled below Charles Town on the Edisto River. In 1695 Congregationalists from Massachusetts founded Dorchester on the Ashley River. By 1700 settlers were established at Port Royal, and in 1711 the town of Beaufort was created on Port Royal Sound. The first grant of land at Winyah Bay was made in 1705, but there was only a handful of families living north of the Santee River in 1712.

A profitable trade in deer skins, furs and Indian slaves secured the colony's immediate future. Proprietary attempts to regulate the Indian trade led to conflict with the Goose Creek men and a war of extermination against the Westo Indians. The colony exported naval stores to England and cattle and lumber to the West Indies. Rice cultivation, possibly introduced by West African slaves, developed in the 1690s, becoming as significant to the economy of colonial South Carolina as sugar was to that of the West Indies and tobacco to the Chesapeake. In 1708, 4,100 African slaves, 4,080 whites and 1,400 Indian slaves were reported in the province.

Political stability continued to elude the province until the permanent establishment of royal government in 1729. A period of rapid economic expansion followed, bringing great wealth to Low Country planters and thus perpetuating their domination of the colony.

North Carolina, though not formally separated from South Carolina until 1701, had its own administration from the beginning of English settlement. Poor communications retarded North Carolina's economic development. A haven for pirates, the coast was hazardous to shipping, and access to markets was difficult. Settlement did not spread outwards from a single centre as in South Carolina but from a number of points.

In the 1660s colonists from Virginia traversed the swamps south of the James River, establishing plantations on fertile necks of land between the rivers flowing into Albemarle

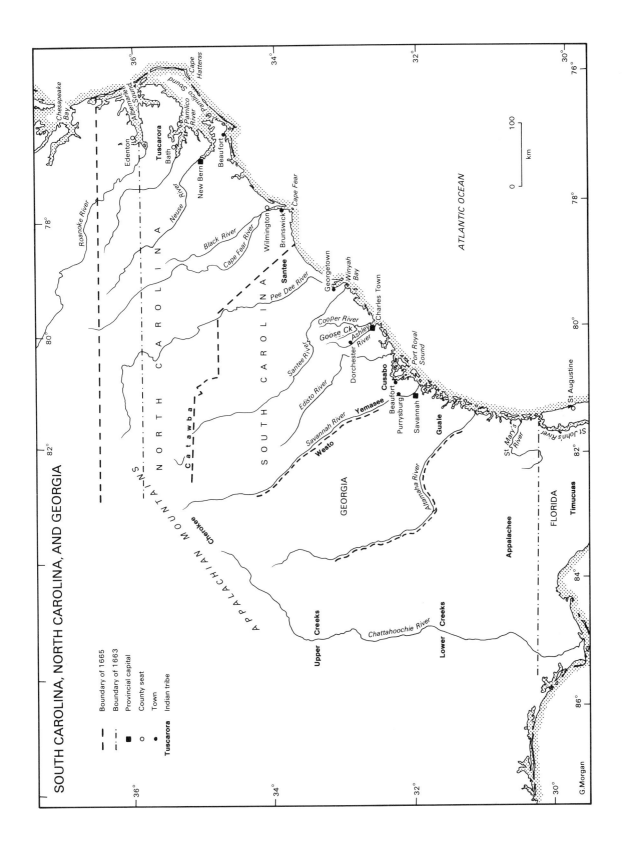

SOUTH CAROLINA, NORTH CAROLINA, AND GEORGIA

Boundary of 1665

Boundary of 1663

■ Provincial capital

○ County seat

● Town

Tuscarora Indian tribe

ATLANTIC OCEAN

100

km

0

Chesapeake Bay

Roanoke River

Edenton

Tuscarora

Bath

Albemarle Sound

Pamlico River

Pamlico Sound

Cape Hatteras

New Bern

Neuse River

Beaufort

Cape Fear

NORTH CAROLINA

Black River

Cape Fear River

Cape Fear

Wilmington

Brunswick

Pee Dee River

Santee

Georgetown

Winyah Bay

SOUTH CAROLINA

Santee River

Cooper River

Goose Ck

Ashley River

Charles Town

catawba

Dorchester

Cusabo

Port Royal Sound

Beaufort

Purrysburg

Savannah

Edisto River

Yemasee

Guale

St Augustine

St John's River

APPALACHIAN MOUNTAINS

Cherokee

Westo

Savannah River

GEORGIA

Altamaha River

St Mary's River

FLORIDA

Timucuas

Appalachee

Upper Creeks

Chattahoochie River

Lower Creeks

G.Morgan

27

Sound. In 1696 the county of Bath was created, including most of the land between Albemarle Sound and the Pamlico River. French Huguenots from Manakin Town, Virginia, entered this area in 1704–5. Swiss colonists led by Christopher von Graffenried founded the town of New Bern in 1710. Provoked by abuses in the Indian trade, Tuscarora Indians attacked settlers along the Neuse River in 1711. Aid from South Carolina led to their defeat but triggered off a war against the Yemasee.

In the 1720s South Carolinians moved north into the Cape Fear region, the site of a number of earlier abortive attempts at settlement, where they established large-scale plantations based on slave labour. Welsh, Scots and Scots-Irish colonists settled beyond them in the Cape Fear River valley and on the Black River. Less structured and hierarchical than either of its neighbours, North Carolina was, for the most part, a society of small planters and farmers. Its population did not grow rapidly until the late colonial period when immigrants came overland from the north.

Conceived as a philanthropic enterprise and military buffer, Georgia was the last of the mainland colonies to be established. In 1733, 120 colonists founded Savannah. Protestant refugees arrived the following year. By the time it became a royal colony in 1753, Georgia was exhibiting traits similar to South Carolina.

Maryland, Pennsylvania, Delaware and New Jersey

Founded in 1634, Maryland provided the model for later proprietary grants; but, with the exception of James, Duke of York, none enjoyed such extensive powers as the second Lord Baltimore. In other respects Maryland resembled neighbouring Virginia. Most immigrants entered the colony as indentured servants, their passage paid for by others in return for head-rights to land. As in other tobacco-growing areas, dispersed settlement patterns quickly developed.

Maryland's early society, made up of a few Catholic gentlemen and large numbers of Protestant servants, lasted barely a decade. It gave way to one of small planters which survived until depression hit the tobacco economy in the 1680s. As large planters turned increasingly to African slave labour, many small planters quit the colony, and Maryland became a society of masters and slaves. Marylanders took the opportunity afforded by the Glorious Revolution to curtail proprietary policies of religious toleration, by barring Catholics from public office and requiring all taxpayers to support the Anglican Church.

When the New Netherlands fell to the English in 1664, the area between the Delaware and the Hudson containing a few Dutch, Swedes and Finns was granted by the Duke of York to two of the Carolina proprietors. Towns were established at Elizabethtown, Woodbridge, Piscataway, Middletown and Shrewsbury. Disaffected New Haven Puritans founded Newark and Scots Presbyterians Perth Amboy. A large influx of Yorkshire and London Quakers into West New Jersey in 1676 led to the foundation of Burlington. Settlers flowed southward and eastward, reaching Cape May by 1700. New England Congregationalists settled at Fairfield, Baptists on the Cohansey River and Lutheran Swedes at Penn's Neck and Swedesboro. New Jersey changed hands many times, was split in two and passed into multiple ownership. Contentious East New Jersey was incorporated into the Dominion of New England in 1686 but returned to private ownership six years later. In 1702 when the population of farmers and fisherman numbered around 15,000, East and West New Jersey were reunited as a royal province.

William Penn sought permission from the

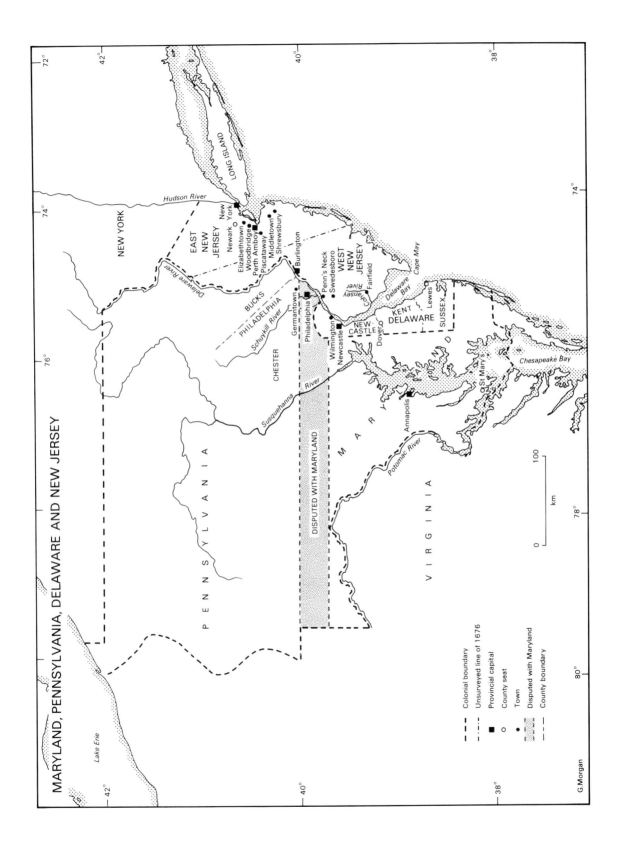

MARYLAND, PENNSYLVANIA, DELAWARE AND NEW JERSEY

Lake Erie

NEW YORK

LONG ISLAND

Hudson River

New York
Newark
Elizabethtown
Woodbridge
Perth Amboy
Piscataway
Middletown
Shrewsbury

EAST NEW JERSEY

WEST NEW JERSEY

Burlington
Penn's Neck
Swedesboro
Fairfield
Conansey River
Cape May

Delaware Bay

PENNSYLVANIA

BUCKS
PHILADELPHIA
Germantown
Philadelphia
Schuylkill River
CHESTER
Wilmington
Newcastle
NEW-CASTLE
Dover
KENT
DELAWARE
Lewes
SUSSEX

Delaware River

Susquehanna River

DISPUTED WITH MARYLAND

MARYLAND

St Mary's
Annapolis
Chesapeake Bay

Potomac River

VIRGINIA

Colonial boundary
Unsurveyed line of 1676
Provincial capital
County seat
Town
Disputed with Maryland
County boundary

0   100

km

G.Morgan

42°
74°
76°
40°
78°
38°
80°

72°
42°
40°
74°
38°

29

Indians to settle the tract of land granted him by Charles II in 1681, and Indian–settler relations in Pennsylvania were in marked contrast to those experienced in other English colonies, but his boundaries overlapped those of his neighbours. The Proprietor of Maryland disputed his southern boundary, obliging him to return to England to defend his interests, while New York governor Thomas Dongan contested his northern boundary. The latter was resolved when the Duke of York recognized Penn's title, but the former had to wait until Mason and Dixon surveyed their famous line in 1767. In 1682 Penn also obtained the three lower counties which comprised Delaware: Newcastle, Kent and Sussex, an area taken over by the Dutch from the Swedes in 1655. The Swedes had founded Fort Christina in 1638 (later Wilmington) and established small settlements along the Delaware River. After 1701 Delaware had its own assembly but not its own governor.

Early settlers were mainly English and Welsh and mostly Quaker, but Penn's promotional tracts, translated into French, German and Dutch, brought German pietists and French dissenters to the colony. His policies

of cheap land, religious toleration and liberal politics were attractive to other settlers, and 8,000 arrived by the end of 1685. By 1700 the population numbered 18,000, a quarter of whom lived in Philadelphia. The city flourished by providing goods and services for the many immigrants who passed through it and by exporting foodstuffs to the West Indies. Settlers moved south from Philadelphia along the Delaware into the lower counties and north into Bucks County. After 1700 settlers moved westward into areas north and south of the Schuykill. By 1710 a few families had settled beyond the Susquehanna River. The pattern of settlement was dispersed rather than nuclear, and few compact villages or townships of the sort Penn envisaged came into existence.

Despite Pennsylvania's economic success, the colony failed to achieve political harmony. Penn was no more successful in resolving the conflict between his authority and the perceived interests of his colonists than proprietors elsewhere. Although there was no overt rebellion in 1688 or 1689, Penn's charter was suspended in 1692 when he was accused of Jacobite sympathies. It was restored in 1696.

New York and New Hampshire

In 1664 the Duke of York dispatched a deputy governor, Richard Nicholls, three other officials, four frigates and 450 regular troops to take possession of the Dutch colony of the New Netherlands, granted to him by charter in 1663 by his brother Charles II. The Dutch surrendered without a struggle. Thus, the English acquired a colony which assumed unparalleled importance in imperial policy because of its strategic location with regard to French Canada and its centrality to other mainland English colonies. Settled for forty years before the English assumed control, the colony remained Dutch in character for another generation.

Although English colonists found New York

less attractive than other areas of settlement, settlers from New England constituted one of the three centres of population in the former Dutch colony. Founded by Walloon families in 1624, 150 miles up the Hudson River, Albany was the centre of the fur trade and long remained a stronghold of Dutch influence. In 1625 a few families settled New Amsterdam at the other end of the Hudson. Settlers at Albany moved north and west, some establishing themselves at Schenectady on the Mohawk while those at New Amsterdam, renamed New York by the English, expanded into adjacent parts of King's County and Staten Island. As Dutch settlers spread out along the Hudson River valley in the 1640s, English settlers

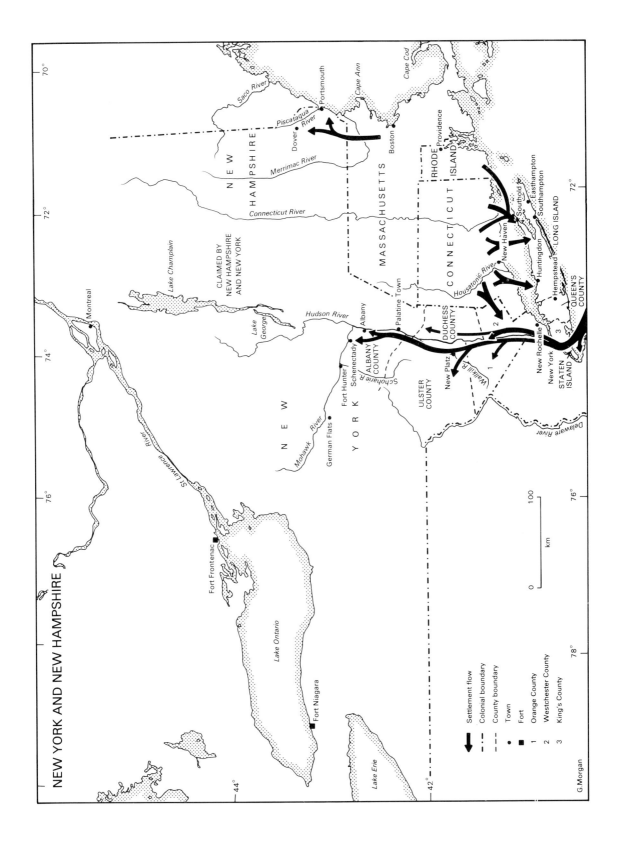

NEW YORK AND NEW HAMPSHIRE

Settlement flow
Colonial boundary
County boundary
● Town
■ Fort
1 Orange County
2 Westchester County
3 King's County

G.Morgan

entered the eastern end of Long Island from Connecticut. They established towns on the New England model at Southold, Easthampton, Southampton and Hempstead. Others moved overland into Westchester County.

The economy grew slowly. Large land grants stimulated neither significant population growth nor economic development. Like other Restoration colonies, New York was unstable, disorderly and faction-ridden. Resentment over taxation, economic monopolies, special privileges, Catholic influence, the French, arbitrary government and finally absorption into the Dominion of New England all contributed to the discontent which culminated in Leisler's Rebellion in 1689. Not until 1691 did New York acquire a legislative assembly, sixty-seven years after its foundation and twenty-seven years after the conquest.

Religious diversity and a multi-ethnic population distinguished colonial New York and especially New York City. French Huguenots began arriving after 1685, the wealthiest among them settling in New York, others at New Rochelle and a few at New Platz. Two and a half thousand Germans from the Palatinate came in 1710, the majority of whom established themselves in the Mohawk and Schoharie valleys at Palatine Bridge, German Flats and other centres. Small groups of Scots, Irish, Swedes, Portuguese Jews and African slaves further augmented New York's population.

New Hampshire, lying between the Merrimac and the Piscataqua, originated as part of a proprietary grant. Massachusetts assumed control of its few straggling settlements for three decades until it became a royal colony in 1679. In 1686 this exposed frontier area was made part of the Dominion of New England. A royal colony again in 1691, the towns of Dover and Portsmouth grew steadily as centres of the lumber trade supplying masts to the Royal Navy and staves to the West Indies. As a consequence of New York's policy of extensive land grants, eighteenth-century New Hampshire became involved in a bitter boundary dispute with its neighbour which was not resolved until after the Revolution.

European rivalries in the New World, 1650–1713

European powers confronted each other in three major areas: the Caribbean, the south-east and Canada. Spain had colonized the larger islands of Cuba, Hispaniola, Puerto Rico and Jamaica in the sixteenth century, leaving the smaller islands to be seized by other European countries. The English established themselves in the Leeward Islands in the 1620s (see p. 25). The Caribbean was the richest and most vulnerable part of Europe's overseas empires. Difficult to defend and exposed to privateers who flourished there in the seventeenth century, islands changed hands frequently. International rivalries intensified as Spanish power crumbled. In 1655 the English seized Jamaica.

Spanish resistance to English settlement on the American mainland was one of the hazards faced by early English colonists. Although Spain recognized English possessions in the New World in the Treaty of Madrid in 1670, English expansion in the south-east was thwarted by the Spanish presence in Florida, which continued to threaten the Carolina coastline.

In 1660 the European population of English North America was approximately 70,000, of the Dutch New Netherlands 5,000, of French Canada 3,000, and there were fewer still in Spanish Florida. While the second wave of English colonial expansion originated as a means of rewarding those who remained loyal to the crown during the Civil War or were instrumental in securing the Restoration, it

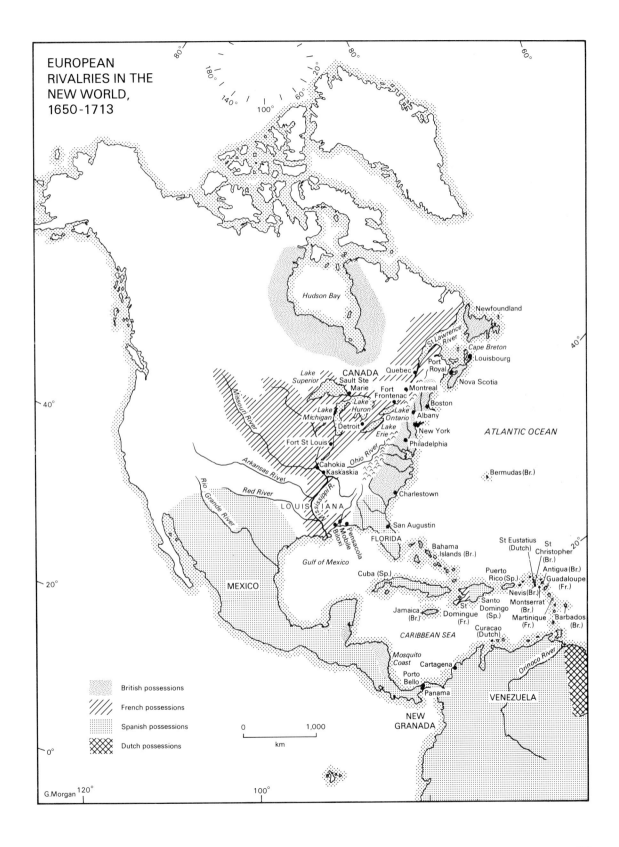

EUROPEAN
RIVALRIES IN THE
NEW WORLD,
1650-1713

Hudson Bay

Newfoundland

St Lawrence River

Cape Breton
Louisbourg

CANADA   Quebec   Port Royal

Lake Superior   Sault Ste Marie   Nova Scotia

Fort Frontenac   Montreal

Lake Huron   Boston

Lake Michigan   Lake Ontario   Albany

Detroit   Lake Erie   New York   ATLANTIC OCEAN

Fort St Louis   Philadelphia

Missouri River

Cahokia   Ohio River
Kaskaskia   Bermudas (Br.)

Arkansas River

Rio Grande River   Red River   Charlestown

LOUISIANA

Pensacola   San Augustin
Mobile
Biloxi   FLORIDA

Gulf of Mexico   Bahama Islands (Br.)

St Eustatius (Dutch)   St Christopher (Br.)

Cuba (Sp.)   Puerto Rico (Sp.)   Antigua (Br.)

MEXICO   Guadaloupe (Fr.)

Nevis (Br.)   Montserrat (Br.)

Jamaica (Br.)   St Domingue (Fr.)   Santo Domingo (Sp.)   Martinique (Fr.)   Barbados (Br.)

CARIBBEAN SEA   Curacao (Dutch)

Mosquito Coast   Cartagena   Orinoco River

Porto Bello
Panama   VENEZUELA

British possessions
French possessions
Spanish possessions   0   1,000
Dutch possessions
km   NEW GRANADA

G.Morgan

33

was also a continuation of the aggressive commercial and expansionist policies of the Cromwellian years. The Dutch were eliminated as serious contenders for power, but the French proved a more formidable foe. Louis XIV and his chief minister Colbert assumed control of New France in 1663. They aimed to create a vast inland empire encircling the English. By the early 1680s the French had established a string of forts and trading posts north and west of the English colonies, and by 1700 had outposts in the south at Mobile and Biloxi where they encountered South Carolina traders. Opposition to French ambitions in Europe and America led to war on both continents between 1689 and 1697 and between 1701 and 1713.

The English struck at Port Royal and Quebec but captured only the former. French and Indian forces raided frontier areas of New York, Maine and Massachusetts, but the English failed to mobilize their Iroquois allies, who chose neutrality. In 1702 South Carolinans and their Indian allies made a precmptive strikc against Spanish Florida but failed to capture the fort at San Augustin (St Augustine). Two years later the English attacked again, destroying all but one of the fourteen Spanish missions in Apalachee. In 1706 French, Spanish and Indian forces retaliated with raids on the South Carolina coast. In 1711 France's chief allies in the south-east, the Choctaw, were attacked by the English, but the Creeks prevented them from taking control of the area. In the Caribbean, French and Spanish privateers attacked English commerce and settlements, wiping out the Bahama colony in 1703.

The Anglo-Americans lacked the military expertise to dislodge the French, and the mother country declined to supply it, despite an interest indicated by the reorganization of colonial administration under the Board of Trade in 1696 and earlier attempts to foster colonial unity through the creation of the ill-fated Dominion of New England in 1686. In 1713 the French ceded Nova Scotia, Newfoundland, Hudson Bay and St Kitts to the English in the Treaty of Utrecht, while the Spanish granted the English the monopoly of supplying slaves to Spanish America. The boundaries between Carolina, Florida and Louisiana remained unsettled.

The disparity in European resources, population and patterns of settlement pointed to the ultimate domination of North America by the English, but that victory was not to be assured until 1763.

Emigration from Britain in the seventeenth century

As many as 400,000 people may have crossed the Atlantic from the British Isles during the seventeenth century, half of them between 1630 and 1660. In these decades of religious and political upheaval, harvests were poor and wages low; there was much unemployment and underemployment. Some 200,000 people went to the Caribbean, the main thrust of English colonizing activity in the 1620s. Mortality rates were high, and many perished. Conversion of the island economies to sugar production signalled their end as colonies of settlement and their development as colonies of exploitation. Unable to compete with the large capital-intensive plantations dependent on African slave labourers – of whom more than 250,000 were brought to the English Caribbean in the seventeenth century – there was an outmigration of small planters, many of them to South Carolina.

Between 75 and 80 per cent of the 100,000 estimated to have gone to the Chesapeake in the seventeenth century were servants. For most of the seventeenth century, the population was young, male, single and immigrant. Unable to sustain themselves until the last

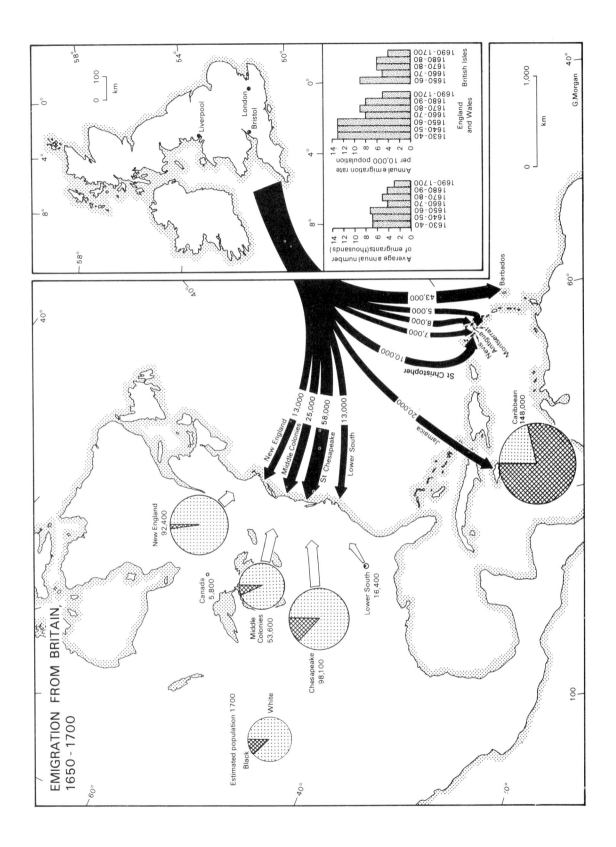

EMIGRATION FROM BRITAIN, 1650 - 1700

Estimated population 1700

White

Black

New England 92,400

Canada 5,800

Middle Colonies 53,600

Chesapeake 98,100

Lower South 16,400

Caribbean 148,000

New England 13,000
Middle Colonies 25,000
Chesapeake 58,000
Lower South 13,000

Jamaica 20,000

St Christopher 10,000

Nevis 7,000
Antigua 8,000
Montserrat 5,000

Barbados 43,000

Liverpool

London
Bristol

km
0   100

Annual emigration rate per 10,000 population

14 12 10 8 6 4 2 0

1630-40
1640-50
1650-60
1660-70
1670-80
1680-90
1690-1700

England and Wales

1650-60
1660-70
1670-80
1680-90
1690-1700

British Isles

Average annual number of emigrants (thousands)

14 12 10 8 6 4 2 0

1630-40
1640-50
1650-60
1660-70
1670-80
1680-90
1690-90

km
0   1,000

G.Morgan

35

quarter of the century, without a continuous flow of immigrants the Chesapeake colonies would have failed. Half were unskilled agricultural workers and minors, and the remainder were from agricultural occupations and various trades and crafts. While servants came from towns and villages across England and Wales, London dominated the trade, although Liverpool and Bristol increased their share of the market in the latter part of the century. Sixty per cent of servants emigrating from Bristol came from within a forty-mile radius of the city, as did 70 per cent of those emigrating from Liverpool. Servants going to the Chesapeake were part of a much larger migration of people moving from town to town in search of greater opportunities. Tobacco prices regulated the flow of immigration to the Chesapeake. When they were high, large numbers of small merchants, traders and mariners invested in servants; when low, the rate of immigration declined. Between 1680 and 1700 the labour system of the Chesapeake was transformed as the supply of servants shrank while that of slaves was enhanced. Of the 20,000 Africans imported into the mainland colonies before the end of the century, most went to the Chesapeake.

The majority of settlers who paid their own way went to New England. 'The Great Migration' between 1629 and 1642 averaged 1,600 a year. The outbreak of the Civil War terminated the flow of immigrants, causing a slump in the local economy. The earliest settlers had strong East Anglian links, but all regions were represented in the migration. Unlike the Chesapeake, this was a migration of families. Moreover, groups from the same parish or village might migrate together. They created discrete communities with well-defined boundaries and strong institutions. New England's population growth was striking. Again unlike that of the Chesapeake, it grew by natural increase. In contrast with Europe, women married younger, households were larger, and mortality was lower.

A further 38,000, not only from England and Wales but also from Scotland and Ireland, migrated to the Restoration colonies in the last four decades of the seventeenth century. They comprised family groups and servants; some were dissenters. They were the vanguard of a much larger movement of population from the outregions which flooded the back-country from Pennsylvania to Georgia between the 1720s and 1770s.

Beginnings of empire in India, to 1765

In the middle of the eighteenth century British interests in India were still managed by the East India Company. The Company's main trading settlements, Calcutta, Bombay and Madras, had grown into important towns under British rule. The Company shipped goods from Asia worth up to £1,000,000 a year. In Bengal, in particular, its trading networks spread far into the hinterland, and Englishmen and Indians living under its protection also traded very extensively on their own behalf. The India in which these great commercial operations took place was no longer effectively subject to the Mughal imperial system, but the relationship between Mughal failure and the transformation of the Company into a ruling power over large parts of India, as illustrated by this map, is by no means clear cut. Older assumptions that the British were forced to defend themselves from anarchy and chaos have been discarded. Post-Mughal India was not necessarily an unstable world. In Bengal the British traded under the aegis of an apparently well-established regional state ruled by its own dynasty of nawabs. Bombay was effectively hemmed in by the power of the Marathas. In south-eastern India regional states were also emerging, but

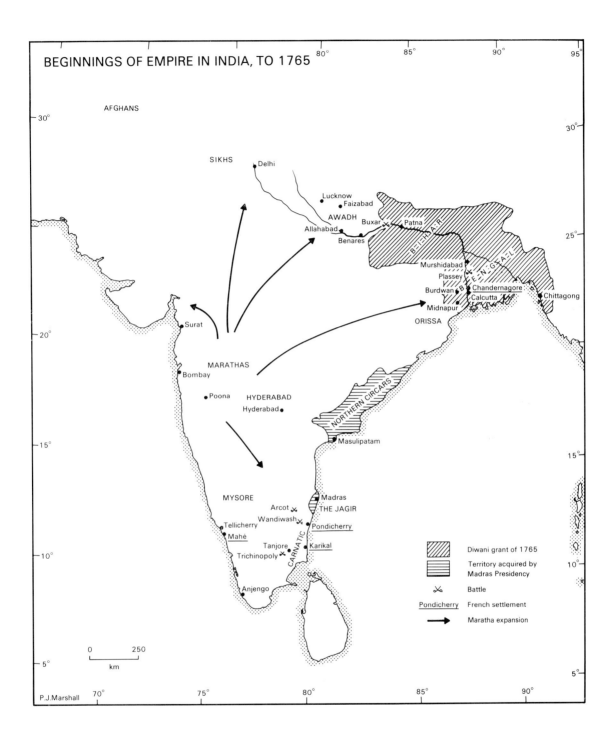

BEGINNINGS OF EMPIRE IN INDIA, TO 1765

AFGHANS

SIKHS
• Delhi

• Lucknow
• Faizabad
AWADH
Allahabad •
Benares •
Buxar
Patna
B-I-H-A-R

Murshidabad •
Plassey
Burdwan •
Midnapur •
B-E-N-G-A-L
Chandernagore
Calcutta
Chittagong

ORISSA

• Surat

MARATHAS
Bombay •

• Poona   HYDERABAD
Hyderabad •

NORTHERN CIRCARS

Masulipatam •

MYSORE

Arcot
Wandiwash
Tellicherry •
Mahé •
Tanjore •
Trichinopoly •
CARNATIC
Madras
THE JAGIR
Pondicherry
Karikal

Anjengo •

	Diwani grant of 1765
	Territory acquired by Madras Presidency
✗	Battle
Pondicherry	French settlement
→	Maratha expansion

0   250
km

P.J.Marshall

37

in the coastal strip called the Carnatic, in which Europeans traded, local rivalries were leading to open conflict.

It is through becoming participants in such conflicts that Europeans became significantly involved in Indian politics for the first time. From 1744 the British and the French East India Companies at Madras and Pondicherry respectively tried to exploit local rivalries for their own ends. By using troops sent from Europe and forces of Indian soldiers, the British and the French tried to establish the dominance of Indian allies, first in the Carnatic and then in Hyderabad, in return for concessions that would ensure their own commercial supremacy. A long period of confused fighting, made more intense by the outbreak of formal war in Europe, ended in 1761 with total British success. Thereafter, the rulers of the Carnatic owed their throne to the British and were effectively their puppets. Some territory was even ceded outright to the East India Company.

In Bengal the British had acquired a vast territorial dominion by 1765. There were crucial differences as well as close similarities with what happened in the south. French rivalry was less important than conflict with the Indian rulers, the nawabs of Bengal. The extent of the Company's commercial penetration of Bengal posed serious problems for its rulers. Repeated attempts to curb the Company in Bengal failed because of the military strength of the British and their ability to exploit divisions within the Bengal state. In 1756 the Nawab actually succeeded in taking Calcutta. His troops were driven out the following year, and he was deposed in favour of one of his rivals, after his army had been dispersed at the battle of Plassey by British troops under Robert Clive. In 1760 and 1763 other nawabs were forcibly removed when they proved to be insufficiently pliant to British demands. Conflict in 1763 spread as the defeated Nawab called in allies from northern India. By the time the British had recovered complete control of Bengal, it had become clear that no autonomous Indian authority could coexist with the East India Company. Moreover, the Company's demands on the resources of this rich region, in order to pay for its troops and to subsidize its trade, were so great that some degree of direct British involvement in the government of Bengal had become inevitable. Involvement to a limited degree was formally sanctioned by the titular Mughal emperor, who ceded to the Company what was called the *diwani*, or financial administration, of Bengal and Bihar by the treaty of Allahabad, extracted from him by Clive in 1765. The *diwani* of 1765 was, however, only a stage in the transformation of Bengal into a British province.

Canada at the British conquest, 1763

Rivalry between the English and French in North America had existed since their first settlements, and by the eighteenth century the sporadic frontier skirmishes of early days had turned into something altogether more purposeful and threatening. By 1750 the two North American empires faced each other across frontiers which the expansion of trade and settlement had brought close to contact point. In the north the fur traders of the English Hudson's Bay Company were engaged in a strenuous if often unseen rivalry with their French counterparts operating out of Montreal and Quebec. While the English remained in their posts along the shores of Hudson Bay the more enterprising French had established a string of posts reaching as far west as the Forks of the Saskatchewan, and the difference of approach was reflected in the trade figures. Quebec's trade greatly exceeded that of

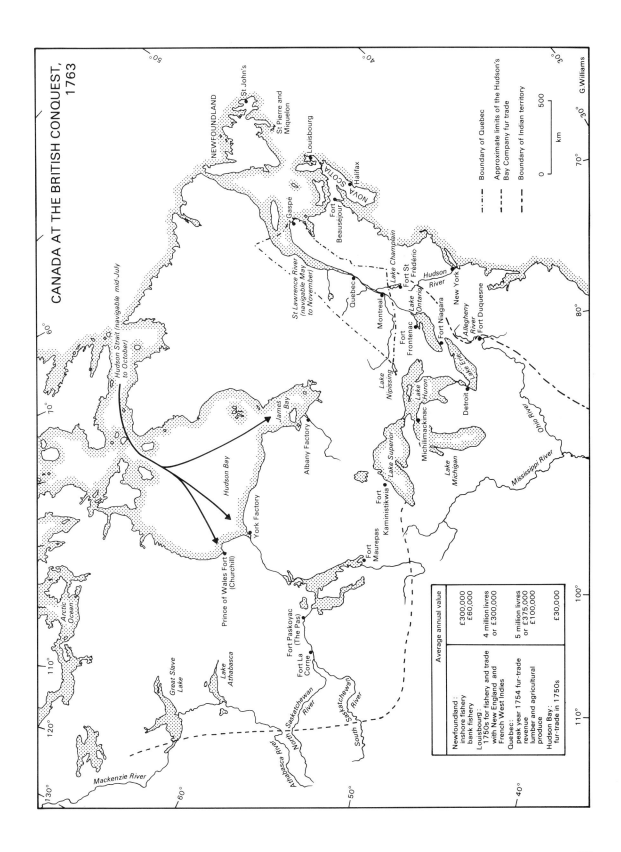

CANADA AT THE BRITISH CONQUEST, 1763

NEWFOUNDLAND

St John's

St Pierre and Miquelon

Louisbourg

NOVA SCOTIA

Halifax

Fort Beauséjour

Gaspé

St Lawrence River (navigable May to November)

Quebec

Montreal

Lake Champlain

Fort St Frédéric

Hudson River

New York

Lake Ontario

Fort Frontenac

Fort Niagara

Allegheny River

Fort Duquesne

Lake Erie

Detroit

Lake Nipissing

Lake Huron

Michilimackinac

Lake Michigan

Ohio River

Mississippi River

Lake Superior

Fort Kaministikwia

Albany Factory

James Bay

Hudson Bay

York Factory

Hudson Strait (navigable mid-July to October)

Prince of Wales Fort (Churchill)

Fort Maurepas

Fort Paskoyac (The Pas)

Fort La Corne

North Saskatchewan River

South Saskatchewan River

Great Slave Lake

Lake Athabasca

Athabasca River

Mackenzie River

Arctic Ocean

Boundary of Quebec

Approximate limits of the Hudson's Bay Company fur trade

Boundary of Indian territory

0   500
km

G.Williams

Average annual value	
Newfoundland : inshore fishery bank fishery	£300,000 £60,000
Louisbourg: 1750s for fishery and trade with New England and French West Indies	4 million livres or £300,000
Quebec: peak year 1754 fur-trade revenue lumber and agricultural produce	5 million livres or £375,000 £100,000
Hudson Bay: fur-trade in 1750s	£30,000

39

Hudson Bay, and in commercial terms Quebec itself was being overtaken by Louisbourg. This new port and citadel, built in the 1720s, not only commanded the Cape Breton fishing banks but, less obstructed by ice than the St Lawrence, had become a focal point in the expanding Canadian trade with New England and the French West Indies. On the Atlantic seaboard the British annexation of Acadia in 1713 had led by the 1750s to the expulsion from the region (now Nova Scotia) of most of its French inhabitants, and to the establishment of a naval base at Halifax to match Louisbourg. Along the inland frontiers the most sensitive among several areas of possible confrontation was the Ohio valley, and there fighting broke out around Fort Duquesne in 1754 – two years before any formal declaration of war. During the Seven Years War the deployment by the Pitt government of massive land and sea forces led to the overwhelming of New France. The network of French forts, so impressive on the map, marked rather than commanded the strategic points. Few had a garrison of more than a hundred men, and some were simply wooden stockades sheltering a few huts and a score of soldiers and traders. Only Louisbourg with its garrison of 3,000 approached European standards, and without a permanent naval squadron on station the great stone fortress was little more than a trap. In 1758 it fell to a powerful amphibious force, and in the same summer another British army began its advance in the Ohio valley. In 1759 thrusts by British forces took the key post of Fort Niagara in one direction, and Quebec, capital of New France, in another; and in 1760 the surrender of Montreal marked the collapse of the French empire in North America.

Peace negotiations were difficult and complex, but the Treaty of Paris in February 1763 confirmed the British determination to retain Canada, even at the cost of restoring valuable French sugar islands. All French territory in North America east of the Mississippi was conceded to Britain, and although France kept some fishing rights in the Gulf of St Lawrence, and the tiny islands of St Pierre and Miquelon as fishing stations, its loss of Louisbourg strengthened British dominance of the North American fisheries. The importance of this trade lay not only in its nominal value but in the number of men and vessels it engaged.

The Proclamation of 1763 gave a more detailed definition to the vast territories which now lay under British control. A much reduced colony of Quebec, in shape an irregular parallelogram, took in a broad strip of territory along the St Lawrence from Gaspé to a point just above Montreal; but it was cut off from the fur-trade country to the west, Quebec's natural hinterland, which was viewed by the British government as a giant Indian reserve. In the vacuum to the west which had been created by the military operations of the war, the subsequent boundary changes and the major Indian rising of Pontiac in 1763–4, the Hudson's Bay Company now held sway; but its domination was short lived. By 1765 traders from Quebec, English, Scottish and American as well as French, were being issued with licences at the western forts – Niagara, Detroit and Michilimackinac – and were heading for the fur-trade country. While affairs within the new British colony of Quebec were cramped within tight and unfamiliar boundaries until the Quebec Act of 1774 brought both territorial expansion and a fresh form of government, far to the west the old commercial rivalry of the St Lawrence and Hudson Bay was renewed in a setting which by the 1770s was to take Canadians to Athabasca and on towards the Arctic and Pacific oceans.

The British North American empire in 1776

Geographically the Thirteen Colonies that declared independence comprised only a small sector of the area of British dominion. Five other organized colonies – East and West Florida, Nova Scotia, Newfoundland and Quebec – did not join in the Revolution, and a vast territory to the far north was under the nominal jurisdiction of the Hudson's Bay Company. To British policy-makers, moreover, none of the mainland provinces was as important as the sugar colonies of the Caribbean. After France entered the War of American Independence in 1777, the protection of the islands became the central concern of British western hemisphere policy.

To most colonials the interior was far more important than the Caribbean. The claims of some of the provinces were enormous. The most liberal construction of Virginia's original grant would have given it a large fraction of the continent, and several other colonies had pretensions to 'sea-to-sea' control within their northern and southern boundaries. Speculators made the most of such claims, and of the uncertainties caused by ill-defined provincial lines. The Wyoming valley of Pennsylvania, which was claimed by Connecticut; the region around modern Pittsburgh, which was disputed between Pennsylvania and Virginia; and the present state of Vermont, claimed by both New York and New Hampshire: all were the scenes of particularly intense conflict.

But colonial claims meant nothing while Native Americans still controlled their own land and their own affairs. Some of them, especially the Iroquois confederacy, had become adept diplomats, playing off different European groups against each other. After the French withdrawal from Canada in 1763 most Indians recognized that the distant British government was their best ally. In that year the government established a western limit to settlement, in the hope of preventing further frontier warfare. This 'Proclamation Line' ran from Chaleur Bay, on the Gulf of St Lawrence, down the crest of the Appalachian chain of mountains to the Georgia–Florida border. Even then white settlement was pushing close to the areas of Indian control, especially in New York's Mohawk valley and in western Virginia and the Carolinas. By the mid-1770s the line had been breached in what are now central Kentucky and north-eastern Tennessee. In 1774 the British transferred jurisdiction over the Indian lands that lay south of Lakes Ontario and Erie east of the Mississippi and north of the Ohio River to the provincial government of Quebec. This 'Quebec Act' was statesmanlike in its recognition both of the Native Americans' interests and of the Catholic religion and French culture of the *habitants* of the St Lawrence valley. But to the land-hungry Protestant whites of the Thirteen Colonies, the Act was just one more grievance.

One of the greatest triumphs of the independence movement came not on the battlefield but in Paris, during the peace negotiations. A skilful American team persuaded Britain to recognize American control over all the land south of the Great Lakes, east of the Mississippi and north of Florida, which itself was ceded to Spain. One result was to leave the eastern Indians wholly defenceless before American policy; and, though some resisted, their subjugation and removal were swift. The other great result, aided by the surrender of most state claims, was the creation of a national domain, the first step in the expansion of the United States to the dimensions of a continental empire.

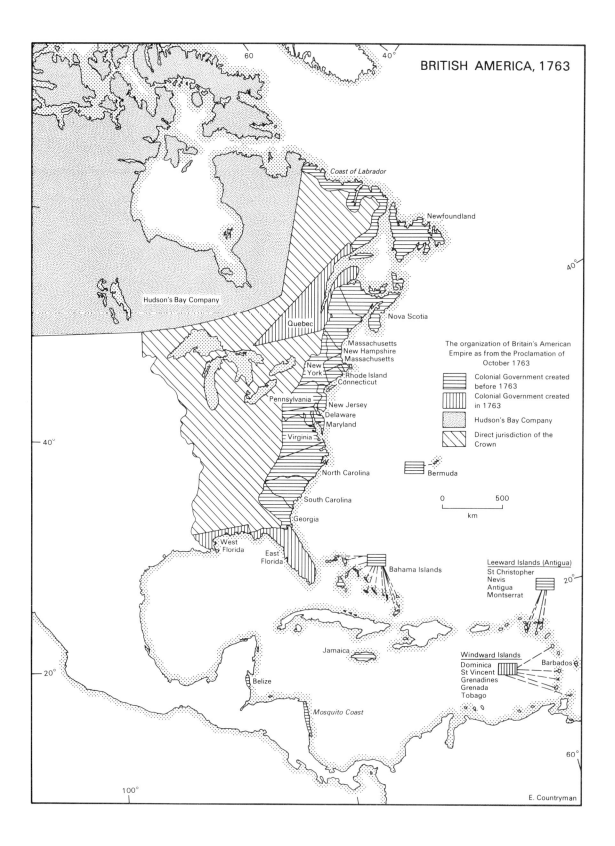

BRITISH AMERICA, 1763

Coast of Labrador

Newfoundland

Hudson's Bay Company

Nova Scotia

Quebec

Massachusetts
New Hampshire
Massachusetts
New York
Rhode Island
Connecticut
Pennsylvania
New Jersey
Delaware
Maryland
Virginia

North Carolina

South Carolina

Georgia

West
Florida
East
Florida

Bahama Islands

The organization of Britain's American
Empire as from the Proclamation of
October 1763

Colonial Government created
before 1763

Colonial Government created
in 1763

Hudson's Bay Company

Direct jurisdiction of the
Crown

Bermuda

0   500
km

Leeward Islands (Antigua)
St Christopher
Nevis
Antigua
Montserrat

Windward Islands
Dominica
St Vincent
Grenadines
Grenada
Tobago

Barbados

Jamaica

Belize

Mosquito Coast

E. Countryman

42

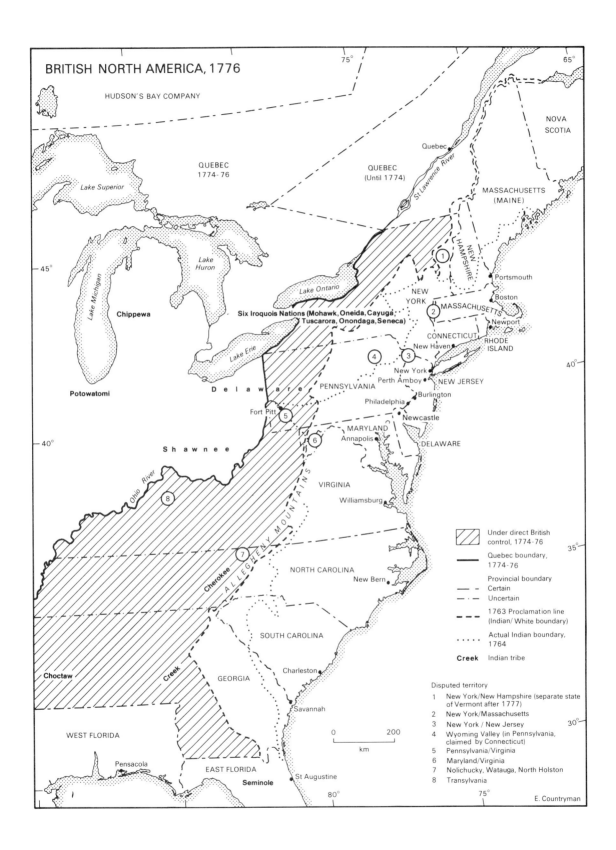

BRITISH NORTH AMERICA, 1776

HUDSON'S BAY COMPANY

NOVA SCOTIA

QUEBEC 1774-76

QUEBEC (Until 1774)

St Lawrence River

Quebec

MASSACHUSETTS (MAINE)

Lake Superior

Lake Huron

Lake Michigan

Chippewa

Lake Ontario

Six Iroquois Nations (Mohawk, Oneida, Cayuga, Tuscarora, Onondaga, Seneca)

NEW HAMPSHIRE

Portsmouth

Boston

NEW YORK

MASSACHUSETTS

Lake Erie

CONNECTICUT

New Haven

RHODE ISLAND

Newport

Potowatomi

D e l a w a r e

PENNSYLVANIA

New York

Perth Amboy

NEW JERSEY

Burlington

Philadelphia

Newcastle

Fort Pitt

MARYLAND

Annapolis

DELAWARE

S h a w n e e

Ohio River

VIRGINIA

Williamsburg

A L L E G H E N Y   M O U N T A I N S

Cherokee

NORTH CAROLINA

New Bern

SOUTH CAROLINA

Choctaw

Creek

GEORGIA

Charleston

Savannah

WEST FLORIDA

Pensacola

EAST FLORIDA

Seminole

St Augustine

Under direct British control, 1774-76

Quebec boundary, 1774-76

Provincial boundary
Certain
Uncertain

1763 Proclamation line (Indian/White boundary)

Actual Indian boundary, 1764

Creek   Indian tribe

0   200
km

Disputed territory
1   New York/New Hampshire (separate state of Vermont after 1777)
2   New York/Massachusetts
3   New York / New Jersey
4   Wyoming Valley (in Pennsylvania, claimed by Connecticut)
5   Pennsylvania/Virginia
6   Maryland/Virginia
7   Nolichucky, Watauga, North Holston
8   Transylvania

E. Countryman

43

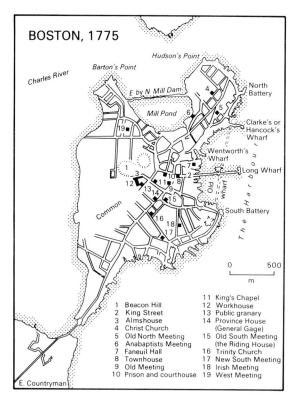

BOSTON, 1775

Charles River
Hudson's Point
Barton's Point
E by N Mill Dam
Mill Pond
North Battery
Clarke's or Hancock's Wharf
Wentworth's Wharf
Long Wharf
Old Wharf
The Harbour
Common
South Battery

0   500
        m

1 Beacon Hill
2 King Street
3 Almshouse
4 Christ Church
5 Old North Meeting
6 Anabaptists Meeting
7 Faneuil Hall
8 Townhouse
9 Old Meeting
10 Prison and courthouse
11 King's Chapel
12 Workhouse
13 Public granary
14 Province House (General Gage)
15 Old South Meeting (the Riding House)
16 Trinity Church
17 New South Meeting
18 Irish Meeting
19 West Meeting

E. Countryman

Boston

Legally, Boston, Massachusetts, was only a town until early in the nineteenth century, governing itself by the same system of town meeting and selectmen used in the smallest farming communities of the New England interior. In fact, it was always much more.

Founded in 1630, it was the most important English population centre in North America until the mid-eighteenth century, when New York and Philadelphia both overtook it. Its prosperity came from fishing, shipbuilding and the carrying trade, not from a rich hinterland of its own. Boston's colonial population peaked at about 15,000 people around 1750; thereafter economic stagnation and a simple lack of space limited its growth.

Colonial Boston occupied a small peninsula, connected to the mainland by the narrow spit called Boston Neck. It was a 'walking city', where most people knew one another by face, if not name. From August 1765, when lower-class Bostonians staged the first American rising against the Stamp Act, to December 1773, when they dumped the East India Company's tea into their harbour, the town was in the forefront of American resistance to British authority. The 'Boston Massacre' of 5 March 1770, in which British troops opened fire on a crowd and killed five of its members, was the Revolution's first bloodshed. The town's Puritan heritage, its economic plight, the determination of such 'Sons of Liberty' as the Harvard-educated cousins Samuel and John Adams and the silversmith Paul Revere, and intense hostility between Bostonians and the representatives of British authority all contributed to its assertive, defiant stance. In 1774 the British government closed its port as a punishment for the Tea Party, and from then until the withdrawal of British troops in March 1776 it was under military rule.

The British North Atlantic trading system of the later eighteenth century

North America, the Caribbean, West Africa and even the Spanish and Portuguese colonies in South America were closely linked in what can be regarded as a single Atlantic trading area. During the eighteenth century Britain's Atlantic trade grew more rapidly than her

trade with any comparable part of the world. British exports and imports around the Atlantic amounted to 12 per cent of the British total in each case at the beginning of the century; in the years 1772–4 the proportion of imports from the Atlantic region had risen to 37 per cent, while 42 per cent of British exports went

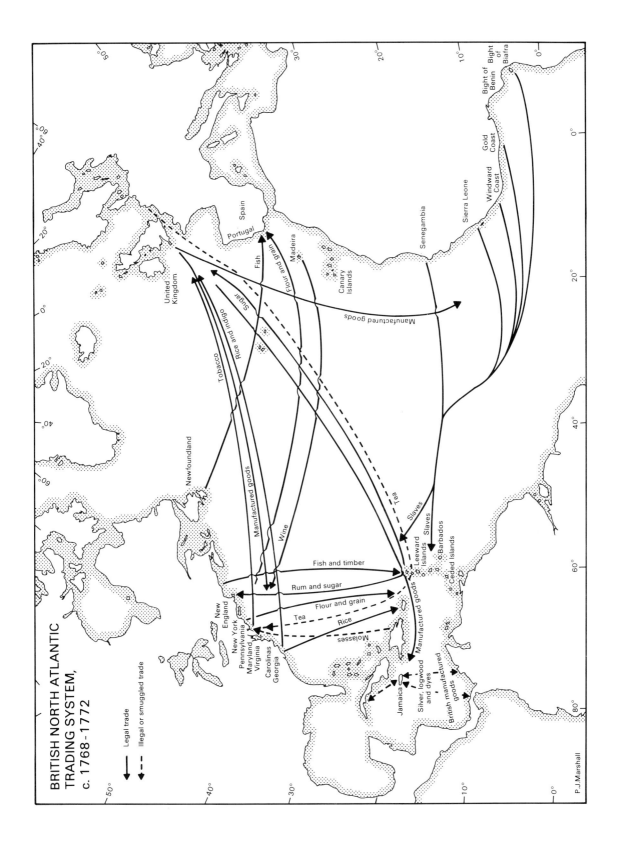

BRITISH NORTH ATLANTIC
TRADING SYSTEM,
c. 1768–1772

Legal trade
Illegal or smuggled trade

United Kingdom

Spain
Portugal
Madeira
Canary Islands
Senegambia
Sierra Leone
Windward Coast
Gold Coast
Bight of Benin
Bight of Biafra

Fish
Flour and grain
Sugar
Rice and indigo
Tobacco
Manufactured goods
Tea
Slaves
Slaves
Leeward Islands
Barbados
Ceded Islands

Newfoundland
Manufactured goods
Wine

New England
New York
Pennsylvania
Maryland
Virginia
Carolinas
Georgia

Fish and timber
Rum and sugar
Flour and grain
Tea
Rice
Molasses
Manufactured goods

Jamaica
Silver, logwood and dyes
British manufactured goods

P.J.Marshall

45

there. The central axis of the British Atlantic trading area consisted of exports of British manufactured goods to the West Indies and North America in return for tropical or semi-tropical products, either for consumption in Britain or for re-export to European markets; by 1772–4 the value of British re-exports (a large proportion of which originated in the Americas) was almost equal to the value of exports of goods actually produced in Britain.

The growth of the North American market for British goods was particularly spectacular. On the eve of the Revolution the white population of the colonies had increased by about nine times during the course of the century. Furthermore, by eighteenth-century standards, this population enjoyed a high standard of living, some 20 per cent higher, it is supposed, than that of Britain itself. A very high proportion of the clothes the colonists wore, the tools and equipment they used and the crockery off which they ate came from Britain. Outnumbered by blacks by ten to one, the white population of the West Indies was minuscule by comparison with that of North America, but the West Indies were still a major export market for Britain, many consignments of goods finding their way illegally into Spanish America, having been imported initially into Jamaica. The principal items in the reverse trade of tropical and semi-tropical commodities for Britain originated either in the southern continental colonies – tobacco from Maryland and Virginia, rice and indigo from South Carolina – or from the West Indies, sugar above all, with some cotton and coffee.

The main east–west axis of the trans-atlantic trade was supplemented by other axes running north and south as well as across the Atlantic. Britain exported manufactured goods to West Africa and shipped slaves to the American plantations. The West Indies and the northern colonies traded with one another on a very large scale. Fish, timber and foodstuffs were shipped from the continental colonies in return for rum and sugar from the British West Indian islands and molasses and silver from the French and Spanish ones. The northern colonies also sent fish and farm products to 'southern Europe', that is, to Spain, Portugal and the Mediterranean, and to the 'wine islands' of the Atlantic, Madeira and the Canaries.

The famous Navigation Acts of the seventeenth century with their later amendments constituted the rules by which the British Atlantic trading system was supposed to operate. By these rules it was illegal for colonies to import manufactured goods that had not been shipped from Britain, or for them to export listed, or 'enumerated', commodities to any destination other than Britain, with some exceptions. When these rules were first imposed, it is likely that they involved considerable disruption of existing trade patterns. By the middle of the eighteenth century, however, the growth of Britain's manufacturing capacity and of her demand for tropical produce probably ensured that the pattern of trading laid down by law had in fact become a 'natural' one for most of the participants. It was certainly one within which striking growth had been achieved, both for those sections of the British economy engaged in Atlantic trade and also for the colonial economies as a whole, for which exports appear to have been the main engine of expansion during the eighteenth century (see p. 48).

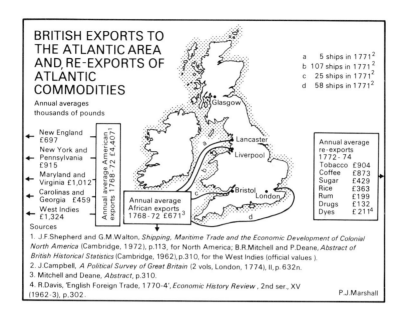

BRITISH EXPORTS TO
THE ATLANTIC AREA
AND, RE-EXPORTS OF
ATLANTIC
COMMODITIES

Annual averages
thousands of pounds

a   5 ships in 1771[2]
b 107 ships in 1771[2]
c   25 ships in 1771[2]
d   58 ships in 1771[2]

← New England £697
← New York and Pennsylvania £915
← Maryland and Virginia £1,012
← Carolinas and Georgia £459
← West Indies £1,324

Annual average American exports 1768-72 £4,407[1]

Glasgow
Lancaster
Liverpool
Bristol
London

Annual average African exports 1768-72 £671[3]

Annual average re-exports 1772-74
Tobacco £904
Coffee £873
Sugar   £429
Rice   £363
Rum   £199
Drugs   £132
Dyes   £211[4]

Sources
1. J.F.Shepherd and G.M.Walton, *Shipping, Maritime Trade and the Economic Development of Colonial North America* (Cambridge, 1972), p.113, for North America; B.R.Mitchell and P.Deane, *Abstract of British Historical Statistics* (Cambridge, 1962), p.310, for the West Indies (official values).
2. J.Campbell, *A Political Survey of Great Britain* (2 vols, London, 1774), II, p.632n.
3. Mitchell and Deane, *Abstract*, p.310.
4. R.Davis, 'English Foreign Trade, 1770-4', *Economic History Review* , 2nd ser., XV (1962-3), p.302.

P.J.Marshall

British exports to the Atlantic area

The great commercial metropolis of London inevitably had a huge stake in the growth of Atlantic trade. A large volume of shipping based on the Thames traded with Africa, the West Indies and North America. By the 1760s and 1770s over twice as much sugar was being sold in London as in all other British ports. A large part of the Atlantic commerce of other ports was ultimately financed by London. But the growth of Atlantic trade also injected a new vitality into some of the British 'outports'. Early in the eighteenth century Bristol overhauled London in the African trade, and Bristol merchants became heavily engaged in American trade. By the middle of the eighteenth century, however, the chief challenge to London's predominance in the Atlantic was coming from Liverpool and Glasgow. On the eve of the American Revolution some 67 per cent of British African trade was passing through Liverpool, while Glasgow had become the major centre for the North American tobacco trade; up to half the total of British imports were handled by its port.

Assessments of the role of Atlantic trade in Britain's overall economic performance raise complex issues. It is especially difficult to relate commercial expansion to that now rather elusive concept 'the industrial revolution'. Two obvious potential links do, however, suggest themselves: the generation through commercial profits of capital for other kinds of investment in the British economy, and the stimulus provided by largely new Atlantic markets to the growth of British manufacturing. Theories about capital accumulation through commercial profits encounter difficulties in demonstrating either that Britain was short of savings from many sources in the eighteenth century or that profits made overseas were directly invested in other sectors of the economy. The overall role of exports in stimulating industrial output is a very controversial topic. Nevertheless, contemporaries were in no doubt of the importance of the American market for British manufactures, and it is hard to disagree with them.

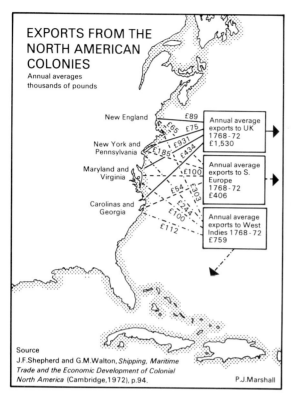

EXPORTS FROM THE
NORTH AMERICAN
COLONIES
Annual averages
thousands of pounds

New England   £89

New York and
Pennsylvania

Maryland and
Virginia

Carolinas and
Georgia

£75
£931
£185   £434
£100
£54
£303
£244
£100
£112

Annual average
exports to UK
1768-72
£1,530

Annual average
exports to S.
Europe
1768-72
£406

Annual average
exports to West
Indies 1768-72
£759

Source
J.F.Shepherd and G.M.Walton, *Shipping, Maritime
Trade and the Economic Development of Colonial
North America* (Cambridge,1972), p.94.

P.J.Marshall

Exports from the North American colonies

Comparison of this map with the maps on pp. 47 and 49 suggests certain conclusions about the overseas trade of the North American colonies on the eve of the Revolution. Manufactured goods from Britain made up a very large proportion of their imports. This is certainly what British law and British colonial policy intended to be the case, but it is likely to have been a situation that would have developed regardless of law and policy. Although the colonies were obliged to export most of their so-called enumerated commodities to Britain, the extent of their exports, especially those of the more northern colonies, did not balance the amount that they imported from Britain. To some extent unfavourable balances with Britain could be mitigated by earnings through exporting commodities which were not enumerated, above all agricultural produce and fish, to the West Indies or to southern Europe. The major elements in enabling the northern colonies to balance their trade with Britain seem, however, to have been invisible earnings, especially profits made on colonial shipping, together with the expenditures incurred by Britain through the troops and warships which she maintained in America.

The economy of eighteenth-century colonial America grew rapidly, largely, it would seem, through overseas trade within the framework laid down for it by the Navigation Acts. Any case for suggesting that growth would have been even more rapid without the Acts probably has to rest on assumptions that the pattern of colonial exports could have been diversified with advantages to the colonies. The most that can be said is that in view of the very large quantities of tobacco and rice that were re-exported from Britain (see p. 47), southern planters perhaps had some grounds for speculating on what might have been the consequences for them had they been enabled to ship their produce directly to its ultimate destination.

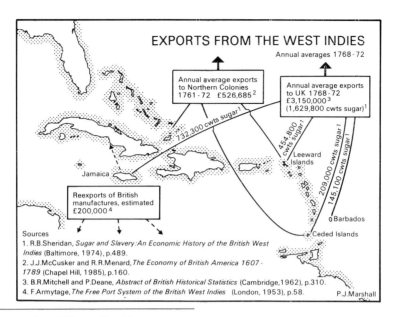

EXPORTS FROM THE WEST INDIES
Annual averages 1768-72

Annual average exports
to Northern Colonies
1761-72 £526,685[2]

Annual average exports
to UK 1768-72
£3,150,000[3]
(1,629,800 cwts sugar)[1]

732,300 cwts sugar[1]

454,800 cwts sugar[1]

209,000 cwts sugar[1]

145,100 cwts sugar[1]

Jamaica

Leeward
Islands

Barbados

Ceded Islands

Reexports of British
manufactures, estimated
£200,000[4]

Sources
1. R.B.Sheridan, *Sugar and Slavery:An Economic History of the British West Indies* (Baltimore, 1974), p.489.
2. J.J.McCusker and R.R.Menard, *The Economy of British America 1607-1789* (Chapel Hill, 1985), p.160.
3. B.R.Mitchell and P.Deane, *Abstract of British Historical Statistics* (Cambridge,1962), p.310.
4. F.Armytage, *The Free Port System of the British West Indies* (London, 1953), p.58.

P.J.Marshall

Exports from the West Indies

Led by Barbados and later by some of the Leeward Islands, the British West Indies became major sugar producers in the later seventeenth century, when they enjoyed a commanding position in the world market. By the 1760s the competition of the French islands, especially of St Domingue, had eroded this position to some extent. As the map on p. 47 suggests, relatively little British sugar was now being re-exported to European markets. The British home market, to which the Navigation Acts ensured protected access for British colonies, was, however, extremely buoyant. It was capable of absorbing the increasing output of the British islands at a generally remunerative price. By the mid-eighteenth century the great land mass of Jamaica, with much potential sugar land still to be cultivated, dominated British output. Older, smaller producers – Barbados and the Leeward Islands, St Kitts, Antigua and Nevis – were still producing large quantities of sugar and rum efficiently. British sugar cultivation was in fact being extended to the islands ceded by France in 1763: Dominica, St Vincent and, especially, Grenada. Arguments that the British Caribbean was entering into irremediable

decline after the Seven Years War or that it was to do so after the ending of the War of American Independence now seem to have little substance. At least a part of the huge favourable balance of trade between the West Indies and Great Britain consisted of the profits which planters were accumulating for their return to Britain.

The British West Indies also traded with other parts of the Atlantic. They imported ever increasing numbers of African slaves, both to maintain the labour force on established plantations, where births rarely matched the very high death rate, and to extend cultivation in Jamaica and the Ceded Islands. The British Caribbean, especially the smaller islands, was not self-sufficient in food or timber, relying largely on imports from British North America. Sugar and rum were exported in return. Finally, some British islands, notably Jamaica and Dominica, which were given the status of 'free ports' after 1766, did a vigorous trade with French and Spanish islands. British manufactured goods were channelled through Jamaica in return for silver, hides, logwood and dyes illegally shipped from Spanish ports.

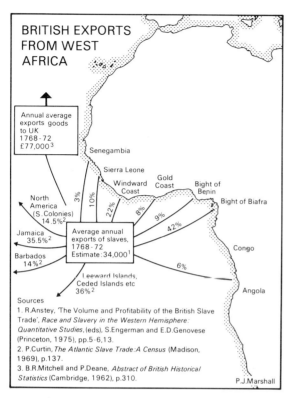

BRITISH EXPORTS FROM WEST AFRICA

Annual average exports goods to UK 1768-72 £77,000[3]

Senegambia

Sierra Leone

Windward Coast

Gold Coast

Bight of Benin

Bight of Biafra

North America (S.Colonies) 14.5%[2]

Jamaica 35.5%[2]

Barbados 14%[2]

3%

10%

22%

8%

9%

42%

6%

Congo

Angola

Average annual exports of slaves, 1768-72 Estimate:34,000[1]

Leeward Islands, Ceded Islands etc 36%[2]

Sources
1. R.Anstey, 'The Volume and Profitability of the British Slave Trade', *Race and Slavery in the Western Hemisphere: Quantitative Studies*, (eds), S.Engerman and E.D.Genovese (Princeton, 1975), pp.5-6,13.
2. P.Curtin, *The Atlantic Slave Trade:A Census* (Madison, 1969), p.137.
3. B.R.Mitchell and P.Deane, *Abstract of British Historical Statistics* (Cambridge, 1962), p.310.

P.J.Marshall

British exports from West Africa

Early in the eighteenth century the British had become the largest carriers of slaves from West Africa, ahead of the Portuguese and the French. With the failure of the Royal African Company, the trade was taken over by a large number of individual merchants or small partnerships based on Bristol, London and, increasingly in the second half of the century, Liverpool. In an average year in the 1760s or 1770s these merchants dispatched some three-quarters of a million pounds' worth of goods to Africa in about 150 ships. Textiles, metals and manufactured metal goods, such as guns, were the main items of export. Some of the ships came back to Britain with gold, gum or hides purchased in Africa, but the majority bought slaves and took them to America.

Slaves were obtained at many different points along the West African coasts from Senegal in the north to Angola to the South. As the map shows, in 1768–72 the largest purchases were being made in the Bight of Biafra (now Nigeria and Cameroon). Calculations about the price and availability of slaves, the extent of competition from other slavers and the preferences of American customers all seem to have influenced the destination of the slaving ships. In the Gambia and Senegal rivers and along the Gold Coast, traders could operate from permanent British posts. Elsewhere they traded from their ships or from temporary quarters on shore. Depending on where they landed, Europeans had to sell their goods and obtain their slaves either through African merchants or through the agents of African rulers. Their loading completed, the ships crossed over to the Caribbean or North America, estimates of the average slave deaths on British ships in this period during the 'middle passage' varying from under 10 per cent to up to 13 per cent. Jamaica was the largest single destination of British slave ships. Having disposed of their cargo, slavers usually tried to obtain some American produce for their return voyage to their home ports. For most slaving ships, however, the trade was not strictly a triangular one, since they were not major carriers to Britain of West Indian staples.

The War of the American Revolution

The War of American Independence began with a skirmish between colonial irregulars and British troops at Concord, Massachusetts, in April 1775. It ended as a world war, involving Britain, France, Spain and the Netherlands as belligerents, several German states as suppliers of troops to Britain, and much of the rest of Europe in a League of Armed Neutrality. There was military action in places as distant as Nicaragua, Cape Town and Padang.

On such a global scale the North American campaigns seem small, but this was the longest war the United States fought until Vietnam. The sea-borne force that drove the American army from New York City in August 1776 was the mightiest the world had seen to that date. The Americans won, despite Britain's enormous strength, for four main reasons. The first was George Washington's ability to keep the American army together, despite intense privation. The British captured every major city, but this was a political war in which the prize was the ability to govern, not control of territory or capitals. The second reason was American fighting ability, demonstrated at 'Bunker' (actually Breed's) Hill, near Boston, just after fighting began, in Washington's victories at such places as Trenton and Princeton, and in the battle of Saratoga in 1777, which persuaded France to enter the war. French aid was the third; without Admiral de Grasse and his fleet, Washington could never have trapped Lord Cornwallis at Yorktown, Virginia, in 1781, bringing the American campaigns to an effective end. The last was repeated British blunders. Among the most notable were Sir William Howe's failure to pursue Washington after he drove him from New York and Sir Henry Clinton's failure to link up with General John Burgoyne's army when it marched south from Montreal in 1777.

The war divides both chronologically and geographically at the early summer of 1779. Prior to that, most of the fighting was in the north, centred in turn on Boston, New York City and Philadelphia. Thereafter the south was the main theatre, with the British trying to extend their control northwards from a secure base at Charleston. The very first fighting was a disaster for Britain. General Thomas Gage sent an expedition from Boston, which he controlled as military governor and commander-in-chief, to Concord to capture arms known to be stored there. It found little, but the shots it exchanged with the local militia provoked sniping, with heavy British losses, throughout its retreat to Boston. A self-created American army immediately placed the capital under siege. After Washington took command and placed cannon on Dorchester Heights, overlooking the town, the British withdrew and regrouped at Halifax. Then their fortunes turned. After taking New York City, they established control along a line from Newport, Rhode Island, almost to Philadelphia, the seat of the American Congress. But brilliant generalship by Washington during the winter of 1776–7 regained American control of most of New Jersey.

The year 1777 saw the formulation and the frustration of a great British plan to cut the rebellion in half, using New York and Montreal as bases. Burgoyne was to march south through the Champlain and Hudson valleys, and either Howe, the commander-in-chief, or Clinton was to march north to meet him. Burgoyne carried out his orders, but at the price of overextending his supply lines and in the face of strong resistance from Vermont militiamen and from an American army under Horatio Gates. But a smaller British expedition coming along the Mohawk valley from the west was turned back at Fort Stanwix; Howe chose to move on Philadelphia instead; and Clinton never carried out his orders. Howe did defeat Washington at Brandywine Creek,

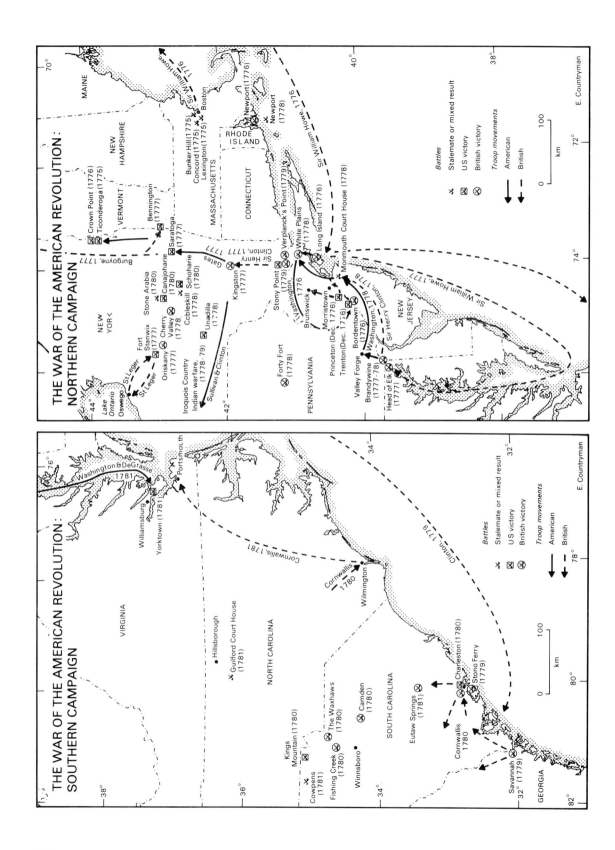

THE WAR OF THE AMERICAN REVOLUTION:
NORTHERN CAMPAIGN

THE WAR OF THE AMERICAN REVOLUTION:
SOUTHERN CAMPAIGN

E. Countryman

Battles
⨂ Stalemate or mixed result
⊠ US victory
⊗ British victory

Troop movements
→ American
⇢ British

0   100
km

52

taking the rebel capital, but Burgoyne was forced to surrender his whole army.

The next year, 1778, saw serious fighting along the axis from Philadelphia to Newport and in the lower Hudson valley, but the net result was to return Philadelphia to American hands and end major fighting in the north. In 1779 the British switched to a southern strategy, taking Savannah and moving on Charleston. In the spring of 1780 they took Charleston and captured a sizeable American army under Benjamin Lincoln. But General Gates, the victor of Saratoga, and General Nathanael Greene drew Cornwallis ever deeper into the back-country, until he finally transferred his base of operations to Virginia. There, in October 1781, Washington and de Grasse trapped him at Yorktown, on the peninsula between the James and York rivers. With his defeat, Britain lost the will to fight.

Washington's great goal was always to command 'a respectable army'. Throughout his tenure as American commander he insisted on the punctilio of eighteenth-century warfare, once refusing a British communication because it was improperly addressed. The British, in their turn, held back from full use of their might, recognizing that in a war like this mere conquest was not enough. The worst fighting of the war was thus among Americans, the revolutionaries on one side and the loyalists and many Indians on the other. The western frontier of New York and the interior of the Carolinas, in particular, were decimated. One of the war's major consequences was the destruction of the ability of the Iroquois in the north and the 'civilized' tribes in the south to resist white penetration of their territory.

British expansion in India, 1765–1805

The Indian empire created by 1765 (see p. 37) was generally assumed in Britain to have been an exceptional response to exceptional circumstances. Further territorial aggrandizement was indeed specifically forbidden. As the map on p. 54 shows, a huge gap existed between official intentions and what actually happened; over the next forty years the British frontier rolled forward, incorporating much new territory.

Contemporary Englishmen in India usually explained the extension of empire as the inevitable response to the instability of Indian politics. Only by imposing their will on their neighbours could the British quell aggression and create a peaceful order in India. Most historians have not found it easy to accept this at face value. Even when the East India Company appeared to be solely concerned with defending itself against what it regarded as an implacable foe, the ruler of Mysore in southern India, it is still not difficult to see how the Mysore ruler in his turn could regard the

Company's interpretation of what was needed for its security as extremely threatening to him. After three wars against Mysore, the British under a new governor-general, Lord Wellesley, made little pretence of standing on the defensive. Mysore was attacked in 1799, and its power was broken for ever. For good measure territory was annexed from it to the British dominions, as it had been in 1792, after a previous war. Enlargement of the Company's territory in southern India was carried much further in 1801 by the formal annexation of the lands of the company's old clients, the nawabs of the Carnatic.

The Ganges valley was the other main axis of territorial advance. The Company's initial concern was to provide a secure frontier for the *diwani* lands of Bengal and Bihar. Turning the neighbouring kingdom of Awadh into a client state under British influence seemed to be the most effective device for protecting Bengal. As he had done in the south, Wellesley decided to

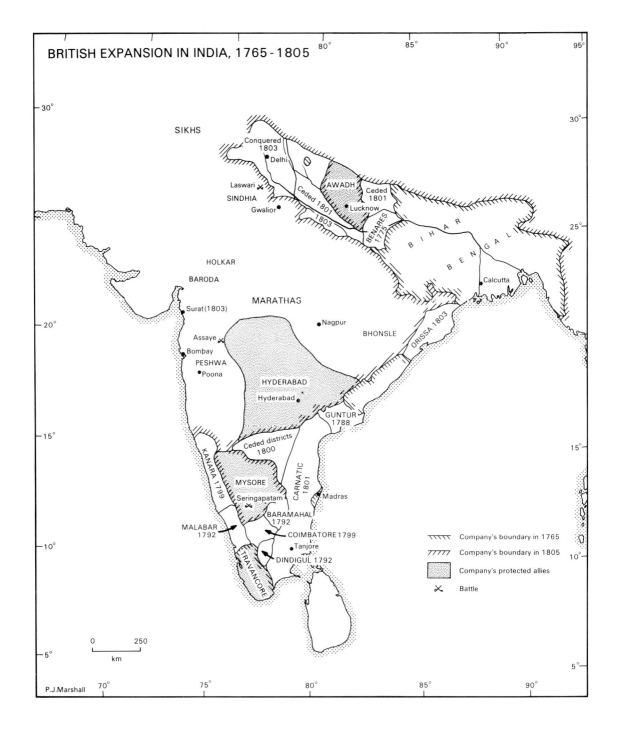

BRITISH EXPANSION IN INDIA, 1765-1805

SIKHS

Conquered 1803

Delhi

Laswari

SINDHIA

Gwalior

Ceded 1801 1803

AWADH

Ceded 1801

Lucknow

BENARES 1775

B I H A R

B E N G A L

Calcutta

HOLKAR

BARODA

MARATHAS

Surat (1803)

Nagpur

BHONSLE

ORISSA 1803

Assaye

Bombay

PESHWA

Poona

HYDERABAD

Hyderabad

GUNTUR 1788

Ceded districts 1800

KANARA 1799

MYSORE

Seringapatam

CARNATIC 1801

Madras

BARAMAHAL 1792

MALABAR 1792

COIMBATORE 1799

Tanjore

DINDIGUL 1792

TRAVANCORE

⟋⟋⟋	Company's boundary in 1765
⟋⟋⟋	Company's boundary in 1805
▦	Company's protected allies
✂	Battle

0 250

km

P.J.Marshall

bring a long period of indirect influence to
an end by outright annexation. In 1801 he
took large slices of territory from Awadh,
which became the Company's Ceded Provinces. These annexations carried the Company's territory far into northern India and
brought it into close contact with the Maratha
powers. Wellesley's attempts to impose his

54

ideas of a British order on the Marathas provoked them to war in 1803, out of which more annexations followed, the Company's stake in northern India being rounded out by new 'Conquered' districts.

Thus Wellesley's period as governor-general spectacularly accelerated what was still likely to have been a process of slow creeping expansion. There is abundant evidence that Wellesley was impelled by high ambitions to create a new imperial system in India. Important as his ambitions certainly are, they cannot be a complete explanation of why the British territorial empire grew so relentlessly in this period. Commercial motives, which might have driven the British to conquer new markets or new sources of commodities, appear to have only a limited application. There is, however, a rather stronger case for arguing that new territory was taken for the revenue that could be extracted from its inhabitants in the form of taxation, above all to pay for the company's enormous army. Indeed, the role of the army seems crucial, both because it was the instrument of expansion and because its needs seem often to have been the motive for expansion in the first place.

India, south-east Asia and China, 1784–1826

By the end of the eighteenth century the export of tea had become the most dynamic sector of the East India Company's trade. After a major reduction of the duties imposed on tea in Britain in 1784, the company's sales quickly grew to the point where some twenty ships a year from England called to collect tea at Canton, the only place at which under tight restriction European trade with China was permitted. A buoyant tea trade stimulated trade between India and China, since a large part of the funds needed to purchase tea came from the sale of Indian commodities in Canton. For most of the period western Indian cotton, shipped out of Bombay, was the largest Indian export to China. In the 1820s, however, raw cotton was being overtaken by opium. The largest part of the opium was produced under the East India Company's monopoly in its Bengal Presidency and dispatched from Calcutta. The import of opium into China was illegal, but a large smuggling operation ensured that Indian opium reached its destination. The huge growth of this smuggling in the 1820s eventually produced the crisis that led to the Opium Wars.

Increased trade with China also stimulated British interest in what was to become Malaya and Indonesia. Throughout the eighteenth century locally based British traders at Calcutta, Bombay and Madras had taken their 'country' ships into the archipelago with Indian commodities, such as opium and cotton cloth, and later with British goods. They linked up with trading networks operated by Chinese junks and Indonesian praus, selling their Indian cargoes and buying commodities, such as tin and pepper, for China. The tin-producing island of Banka off Sumatra, for instance, became an important trading point. Other English ships went to the Spanish port of Manila to obtain silver for China from Spanish America. A British base in the region was frequently sought as a trading entrepôt. The first permanent lodgement was established in 1786 at Penang, a position somewhat off the main trading routes. In 1819 a much more promising site was obtained by Raffles on the island of Singapore.

British activity in the archipelago was inevitably a challenge to the Dutch. The Dutch East India Company claimed the right to restrict the access of other Europeans to parts of the region and to control the trade in certain commodities. Outside Java and the Moluccas, Dutch claims were, however, very difficult to

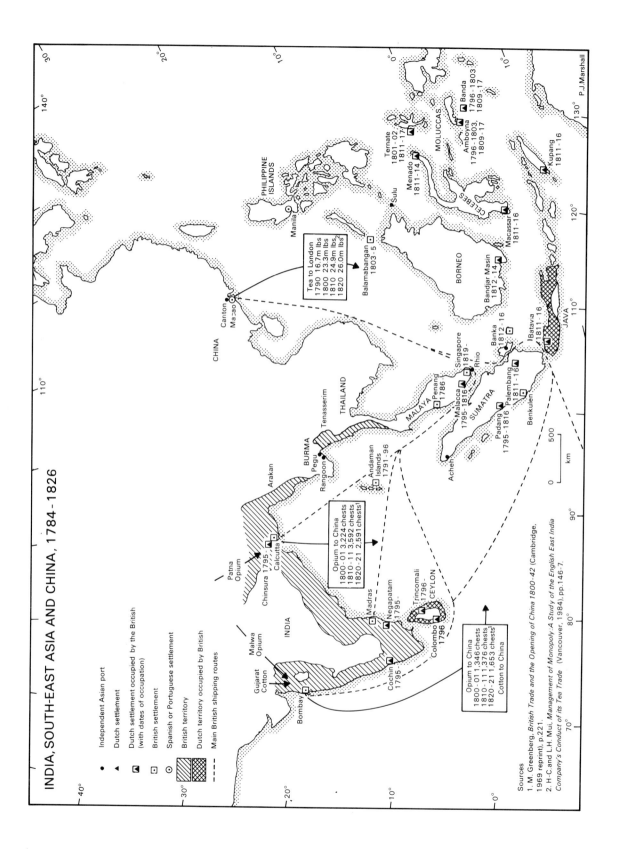

INDIA, SOUTH-EAST ASIA AND CHINA, 1784-1826

Independent Asian port
Dutch settlement
Dutch settlement occupied by the British
(with dates of occupation)
British settlement
Spanish or Portuguese settlement
British territory
Dutch territory occupied by British
Main British shipping routes

Tea to London
1790 16.7m lbs
1800 23.3m lbs
1810 24.9m lbs
1820 26.0m lbs

Opium to China
1800-01 3,224 chests
1810-11 3,592 chests
1820-21 2,591 chests

Opium to China
1800-01 1,346 chests
1810-11 1,376 chests
1820-21 1,653 chests
Cotton to China

Sources
1. M. Greenberg, *British Trade and the Opening of China 1800-42* (Cambridge, 1969 reprint), p.221.
2. H-C. and L.H. Mui, *Management of Monopoly: A Study of the English East India Company's Conduct of its Tea Trade* (Vancouver, 1984), pp.146-7.

P.J. Marshall

Patna Opium
Chinsura 1795-
Calcutta
Arakan
BURMA
Pegu
Rangoon
Tenasserim
THAILAND
Andaman Islands 1791-96
Malwa Opium
Gujarat Cotton
Bombay
Cochin 1795-
Madras
Negapatam 1795-
Trincomali 1796-
Colombo 1796
CEYLON
INDIA
Acheh
Penang 1786
Malacca 1795-1816
MALAYA
Singapore 1819-
Rhio
SUMATRA
Padang 1795-1816
Benkulen
Palembang 1811-16
Banka 1812-16
Batavia 1811-16
JAVA
Banjar Masin 1812-14
BORNEO
Macassar 1811-16
CELEBES
Kupang 1811-16
MOLUCCAS
Menado 1811-14
Ternate 1801-02 1811-17
Amboyna 1796-1803, 1809-17
Banda 1796-1803, 1809-17
Sulu
Manila
PHILIPPINE ISLANDS
CHINA
Canton
Macao
Balamabangan 1803-5

0   500
km

enforce, and the whole Dutch position in Asia was at the mercy of the military and naval power of the British. Englishmen in Asia often argued that the Dutch should be swept away, but the strategy of the British government was generally to try to preserve the Dutch as potential British allies in Europe. After 1795, when the Netherlands were effectively under French domination, the Dutch Empire was systematically attacked to exclude the French and keep open the trade routes between India and China. Such attacks culminated in the invasion of Java and the establishment of British rule there from 1811 to 1816. At the end of the Napoleonic Wars the policy of a Dutch alliance again prevailed. By now the extent of British trading contacts within the region was so great that some kind of demarcation limiting Dutch control was regarded as imperative. Following Raffles's initiative in settling Singapore, an agreement was signed in 1824 by which the Dutch gave up all claims to the Malay peninsula, including their old base at Malacca, in return for Britain abandoning her old established pepper settlements round Benkulen on the west coast of Sumatra. Along this line of demarcation the colonial empires that were to lead to modern Malaya and Indonesia slowly developed.

British interest in mainland south-east Asia was limited for most of the period. In 1824 the East India Company turned on its Burmese neighbours for what seemed to be persistent encroachment on the Company's territory. A major war resulted, leading to a sea-borne invasion of Burma and cession of territory along the Burmese coast – Arakan, bordering on Bengal, and Tenasserim, far to the east. With the occupation of Tenasserim in 1826, Britain was brought into contact with Thailand, a power also entering into British calculations due to her claims on territory in the Malay peninsula in the hinterland of Penang.

Exploration and exploitation of the Pacific in the late eighteenth century

As late as the middle of the eighteenth century the Pacific presented a series of baffling problems to geographers. Although Magellan had crossed the great ocean as early as 1520, attempts at systematic exploration had been hindered by the difficulty in finding longitude at sea, by the ravages of scurvy on oceanic voyages and by the strait-jacket of wind and current which cramped the movements of sailing ships into predictable tracks. Two hundred and fifty years after Magellan, the two main problems of the Pacific remained unresolved; no European knew whether a huge fertile continent, *Terra Australis Incognita*, stretched across its southern latitudes, or whether in the north an open sea route, the North-West Passage, offered a short cut between Atlantic and Pacific oceans.

After the end of the Seven Years War in 1763 a number of expeditions left England and France to explore the Pacific. Byron, Bougainville, Wallis and Carteret made scattered discoveries of some significance; but the navigator who opened the Pacific to the modern world was James Cook, an explorer who added to his superb technical ability a determination 'not only to go farther than any man had ever been before, but as far as it was possible for man to go'. On his first voyage of 1768–71 Cook explored more than 5,000 miles of coastline and charted the outlines of the twin islands of New Zealand, the hitherto unknown east coast of Australia and the Torres Strait separating Australia and New Guinea. This he accomplished without any losses from scurvy. On his second voyage (1772–5), carrying for the first time the newly developed chronometer to establish longitude, Cook discovered

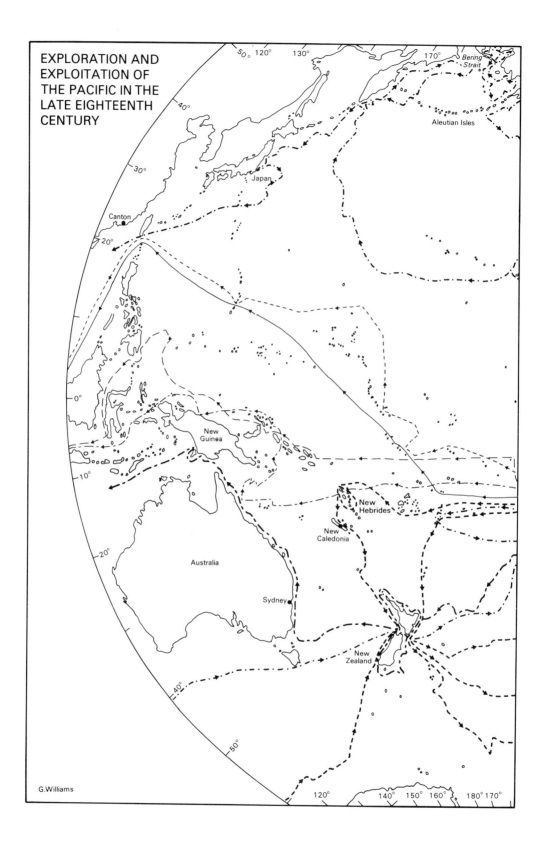

EXPLORATION AND
EXPLOITATION OF
THE PACIFIC IN THE
LATE EIGHTEENTH
CENTURY

Bering Strait

Aleutian Isles

Japan

Canton

New Guinea

New Hebrides

New Caledonia

Australia

Sydney

New Zealand

G.Williams

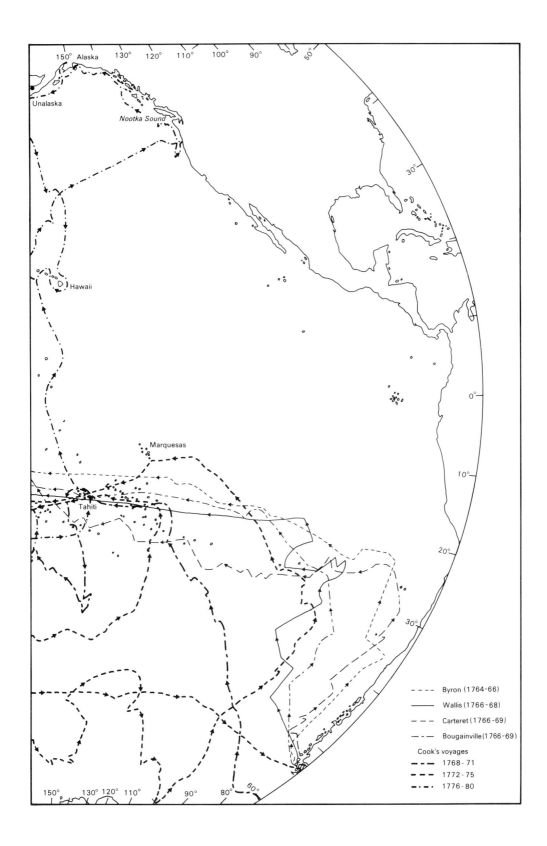

150° Alaska 130° 120° 110° 100° 90° 50°

Unalaska

Nootka Sound

30°

Hawaii

Marquesas

10°

Tahiti

20°

30°

- - - - Byron (1764-66)
——— Wallis (1766-68)
– – – Carteret (1766-69)
–·–·– Bougainville(1766-69)

Cook's voyages
–··–··– 1768-71
– – – 1772-75
–···–···– 1776-80

150° 130° 120° 110° 90° 80° 60°

a myriad of Pacific islands and in a series of sweeps far to the south reached nearer the Pole than any man before him. He discovered the only southern continent that exists, not the fertile land mass of the theorists, but the frozen Antarctic. On his third and final voyage of 1776–80 (Cook was killed in 1779 at Hawaii) he turned to the North Pacific in search of the western entrance of the North-West Passage. There was none to find; but in a single remarkable season of exploration (1778) along the north-west coast of America, Cook closed the gap between the Spanish and Russian explorations, determined the shape of the Alaskan peninsula and sailed through Bering Strait.

There were further voyages of exploration to the Pacific before the end of the century– by La Pérouse from France, Vancouver from England and Malaspina from Spain – but although they did useful work of a detailed nature, after Cook the main features of the Pacific were known. The aftermath of his voyages showed the connection between exploration and exploitation. In the South Pacific, Cook had described the east coast of Australia as suitable for European colonization, and in 1788 the first British settlement was established at Port Jackson (Sydney). Cook's reports of whales in far southerly latitudes soon attracted British and American whalers to

Antarctic waters, and to the Pacific islands to victual and refit. Also arriving at the islands by the end of the century were traders, searching for sandalwood and for exotic foodstuffs for the China market. The activities of the whalers and traders did incalculable harm to the Pacific islanders, and the only protective influence came from the missionaries. The London Missionary Society sent missionaries to Tahiti in 1797, and American and French societies soon followed suit. In the North Pacific a clash in 1789 between British traders and Spanish officials at Nootka Sound (Cook's old watering place on the west coast of Vancouver Island) precipitated an international crisis which was settled in favour of Britain. In effect, Spain conceded the right to other nations to trade and establish posts along the north-west coast of America. This determination to ignore the vast spheres of influence established in an earlier age by the Spaniards and Dutch in both the Pacific and the eastern seas was a cardinal feature of British policy and activity in the late eighteenth century. John Douglas, the editor of Cook's final journal, summed up the matter well when he wrote: 'Every nation that sends a ship to sea will partake of the benefit [of the accounts of exploration]; but Great Britain herself, whose commerce is boundless, must take the lead in reaping the full advantage of her own discoveries.'

The Hudson's Bay Company

Driven on by the European demand for beaver pelts, traders from New France established an ascendancy by 1660 over the ever westward-moving fur trade. In a blatant attempt to outflank the French and foreshorten the distances involved, the Hudson's Bay Company, under the direction of Prince Rupert, was granted a charter in 1670. Although the grant theoretically laid a claim to all lands draining into the Hudson and James bays, the Company for the next century was strangely content to wait upon Indian middlemen to arrive

at its posts along the bays. French-Canadian traders therefore retained the upper hand. They reduced travelling times and expenses somewhat by the establishment of Grand Portage by the 1740s as a point of trans-shipment to Montreal. Meanwhile, they continued to explore and to set up new posts further north and west.

The viability of the Company was in even greater jeopardy after the British conquest of New France in 1759–60. The emergence of mainly Scottish entrepreneurs in Montreal led

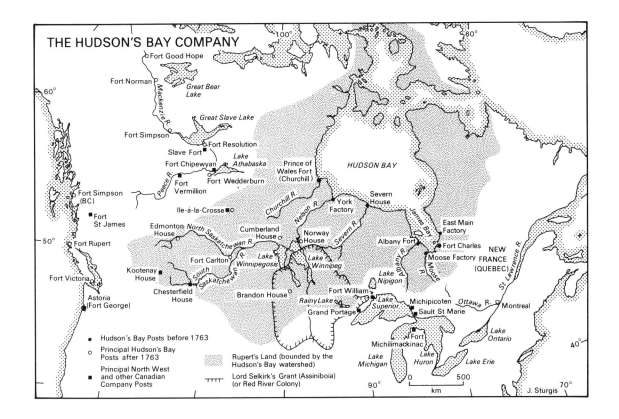

THE HUDSON'S BAY COMPANY

Fort Good Hope

Fort Norman

Great Bear Lake

Mackenzie R.

60°

Great Slave Lake

Fort Simpson

Fort Resolution

Slave Fort

Fort Chipewyan

Lake Athabaska

Prince of Wales Fort (Churchill)

HUDSON BAY

Peace R.

Fort Vermillion

Fort Wedderburn

Fort Simpson (BC)

Ile-à-la-Crosse

Churchill R.

Nelson R.

York Factory

Severn House

Severn R.

East Main Factory

Fort St James

Edmonton House

North Saskatchewan R.

Cumberland House

Norway House

James Bay

Albany Fort

Fort Charles

NEW FRANCE (QUEBEC)

St Lawrence R.

Fort Rupert

Fort Carlton

Lake Winnipegosis

Lake Winnipeg

Moose Factory

Albany R.

Moose R.

Kootenay House

South Saskatchewan R.

Lake Nipigon

Fort Victoria

Chesterfield House

Brandon House

Fort William

Rainy Lake

Lake Superior

Michipicoten

Ottawa R.

Montreal

Astoria (Fort George)

Grand Portage

Sault St Marie

Lake Ontario

40°

Fort Michilimackinac

Lake Michigan

Lake Huron

Lake Erie

70°

• Hudson's Bay Posts before 1763

○ Principal Hudson's Bay Posts after 1763

■ Principal North West and other Canadian Company Posts

Rupert's Land (bounded by the Hudson's Bay watershed)

Lord Selkirk's Grant (Assiniboia) (or Red River Colony)

0   500   km

90°

J. Sturgis

---

eventually to the creation of the North West Company in 1779–80. Already Hudson's Bay Company officials could see the necessity of emulating their rivals' strategy of moving inland, a policy begun in 1774 with the founding of Cumberland House. Likewise, the HBC adopted the policy of profit sharing for its employees, and even more forceful direction came about when Lord Selkirk gained control of it in 1810. Indeed, by this time the rivalry was so intense that the Colonial Office leaned very heavily on both companies to effect a merger in 1821. What had most upset the balance of things was Selkirk's determination to set up a colony at Red River. From 1812 onwards this colony came to resemble a time bomb; the explosion occurred when the infant Dominion of Canada began negotiations to purchase Rupert's Land from the Hudson's Bay Company. It was the threat posed to the traditional way of life of the *métis* people, of French and Indian parentage, by the prospect of the arrival of Canadian settlers which led to the championing of their cause by Louis Riel. The ensuing conflicts in 1869–70 and 1885 were to inflame ethnic and religious tensions within the Dominion (see p. 139).

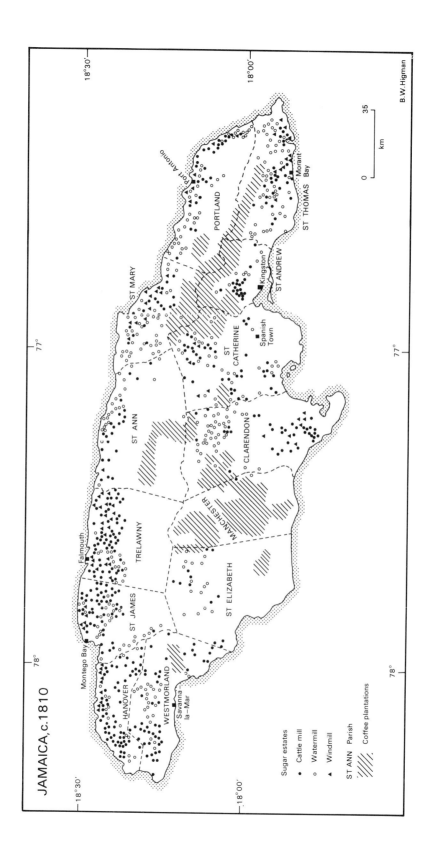

JAMAICA, c.1810

Sugar estates
• Cattle mill
○ Watermill
▲ Windmill

ST ANN Parish

//// Coffee plantations

B.W.Higman

Jamaica, c. 1810

Jamaica's importance as a producer of tropical export staples was at its peak around 1810. In 1805 the island shipped almost 100,000 tons of sugar, making it the world's leading exporter. Coffee had its maximum in 1814 when 15,200 tons, accounting for 30 per cent of the world total, were exported. These two crops were not the colony's only products. Pimento and dyewoods were also exported, and grazing-pens produced livestock for the internal market. The port towns supported a vibrant commercial sector. Nevertheless, sugar and coffee dominated the landscape.

Sugar emerged as the most profitable crop at the end of the seventeenth century, and by 1730 the colony was firmly established as the major exporter in the Empire. Settlement was concentrated at first in the southern and eastern parts of the island, plantations being most common in the parishes of Clarendon, St Catherine, St Andrew and St Thomas. Between 1730 and 1790 plantations spread along the north coast and penetrated the plains of Westmorland and St Elizabeth. In 1670 there were 57 sugar plantations in Jamaica, but the number increased to 419 in 1739 and 1,061 in 1786.

Whereas the eighteenth century was characterized by expansion, the nineteenth saw contraction and decline in Jamaica's sugar industry. Exports fell from the peak of 100,000 tons in 1805 to a mere 5,000 tons by 1913. The climacteric of 1807 saw the abolition of the British Atlantic slave trade, to be followed by emancipation in 1833, equalization of the British sugar duties between 1847 and 1854 and the removal of all duties on sugar imports in 1874. In consequence, the number of sugar plantations in Jamaica dropped to 670 in 1834, 330 in 1854 and 125 in 1900. Even before emancipation, decline occurred along the wet coastal fringe of Portland. Contraction spread steadily westward. By 1900 few estates remained in the eastern half of the island; sugar production was then centred on the parishes of Clarendon and Westmorland, and the specialized rum-producing estates of Trelawny and St James.

Jamaica's sugar mills were powered initially by cattle and mules. During the eighteenth century these were gradually replaced or augmented by water-mills, and wind was employed on a small number of favourably located plantations. Steam came to predominate only after 1850. Regional differences in the types of power employed were clearly evident around 1810. The typical sugar plantation then covered 1,000 acres, with 250 acres planted in cane, and was worked by 230 slaves. The Jamaican estate was a truly large-scale enterprise.

In Jamaica, sugar was a lowland crop. Few estates were situated above 1,000 feet. Coffee, however, was confined to the highlands, almost all of the plantations being located above 1,000 feet and nearly one-third of them above 3,000 feet. Around 1810 coffee production was concentrated in two distinct regions. The eastern, Blue Mountain region was characterized by steep slopes and produced high-quality coffee on large plantations. The western region, centred on Manchester, had gentler slopes but produced coffee of a lower grade and was abandoned to small farmers by the end of the nineteenth century.

Coffee came to Jamaica relatively late, but experienced a spectacular boom between 1783 and 1838. This boom resulted from the reduction of the British import duty in 1783. It was brought to an end by devastating soil erosion and, less importantly, abolition and emancipation. Abandonment of plantations continued throughout the period from 1815 to 1900, with exports falling to a low of 1,520 tons in 1849. At the time of emancipation coffee plantations accounted for 14.4 per cent of Jamaica's slaves, while 49.5 per cent lived on sugar estates.

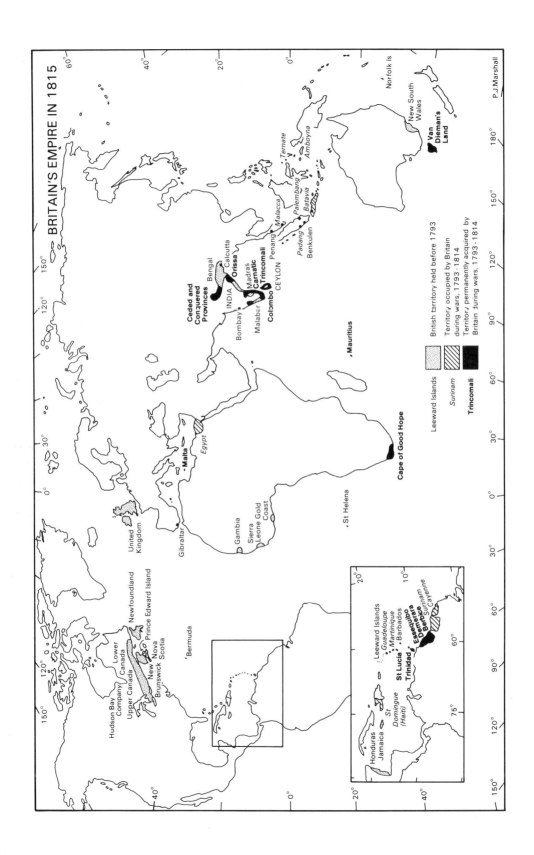

BRITAIN'S EMPIRE IN 1815

P.J.Marshall

Ceded and Conquered Provinces
Bengal
INDIA
Calcutta
Orissa
Madras
Carnatic
Bombay
Malabar
Colombo
Trincomali
CEYLON

Penang
Malacca
Padang
Palembang
Batavia
Benkulen
Ternate
Amboyna

Norfolk Is
New South Wales
Van Dieman's Land

Mauritius

Cape of Good Hope

Egypt
Malta

St Helena

Gambia
Sierra Leone Gold Coast

Gibraltar

United Kingdom

Newfoundland
Prince Edward Island
Lower Canada
Hudson Bay Company
Upper Canada
New Brunswick
Nova Scotia

Bermuda

Honduras
Jamaica
St Domingue (Haiti)
Leeward Islands
Guadeloupe
Martinique
St Lucia
Barbados
Trinidad
Essequibo
Demerara
Berbice
Surinam
Cayenne

British territory held before 1793
Territory occupied by Britain during wars, 1793-1814
Territory permanently acquired by Britain during wars, 1793-1814

Leeward Islands
Surinam
Trincomali

Britain's empire in 1815

The titanic European struggles against Revolutionary and Napoleonic France, lasting from 1793 to 1815 with only a brief interval of peace in 1802–3, tend to mask the extent to which Britain was also engaged in a world-wide war. British troops and warships were deployed round the coasts of the United States of America, on the River Plate, in Egypt, at the Cape of Good Hope and throughout Indonesia, as well as in the traditional cockpits of European rivalry, the Caribbean and India. The scale of the conflict in the West Indies and India leaves little doubt that, whatever else the great wars may have been, they were also 'wars for empire' in the conventional eighteenth-century sense. Britain not only attacked the empires of her old enemies, France and Spain, but she also dismembered that of the Netherlands. The map shows that Britain had made sizeable territorial gains by the end of the wars.

If Britain appears to have emerged as a successful predator, her motives for making war overseas were in fact more complex than simple imperial aggrandizement. In the Caribbean, the overseas theatre where Britain made by far her largest commitment of force, over 70,000 troops in the 1790s, objectives were defensive as well as offensive. Not only were the British islands threatened by periodic French expeditionary forces, but there was intense fear of the spread of 'Jacobin' subversion among the British slaves producing an uprising comparable to that which had devastated St Domingue after 1791. Occupation of territory thus seemed to be the best method both of protecting the flow of British Caribbean produce and of making valuable additions to it. By the late 1790s the seizure of foreign colonies had gone far beyond the needs of defence alone. An extremely costly attempt to subjugate St Domingue had been abandoned, but the other French islands were to be taken, together with Spanish Trinidad and the rich sugar lands of the Dutch mainland colonies, Essequibo, Demerara, Berbice and Surinam, the first three and Trinidad being retained after the wars. In the later stages of the wars British interests even turned to projects of conquest or liberation in Spanish America. Apart from an opportunist and unsuccessful attempt to establish a British presence on the River Plate in 1806–7, these schemes came to very little.

India dominated Britain's interests in the eastern hemisphere. From 1798 to 1805, in the governor-generalship of the Marquess Wellesley, territorial expansion in India moved rapidly forward on a dynamic of its own (see p. 53), whose relationship to the European wars was not necessarily very close. But European war was certainly responsible for extensions of British power round the Indian Ocean in efforts to frustrate French threats. British troops expelled the French from Egypt in 1801, the Dutch from the coasts of Ceylon in 1796 and from the Cape in the same year and again in 1806, and the French from Mauritius in 1810. Deemed to be essential bases for the defence of India, Ceylon, the Cape and Mauritius remained in British hands after the war. In Indonesia, as in the Caribbean, British motives were mixed. The strategy of the metropolitan government was generally to limit British intervention to what was needed to prevent the French from getting control of Dutch settlements. A major expedition was sent to Java in 1811 to achieve this end. There was, however, a vigorous 'sub-imperialism' among Englishmen in the east, most notably in Stamford Raffles. His designs for a permanent British colonial presence in Indonesia were rejected when the Dutch were restored after the war (see p. 57).

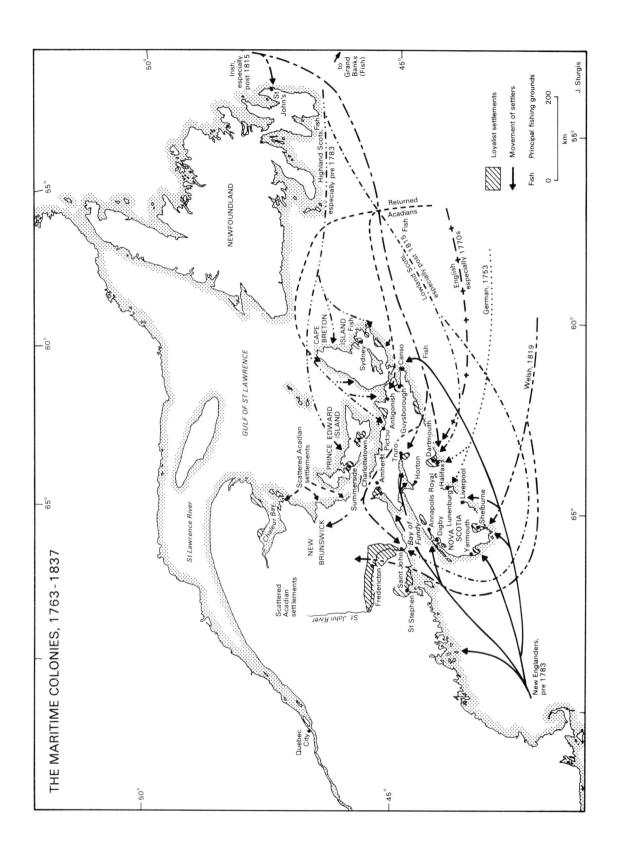

THE MARITIME COLONIES, 1763–1837

NEWFOUNDLAND

Irish, especially post 1815

St John's

Highland Scots, especially pre 1783

to Grand Banks (Fish)

Returned Acadians

Lowland Scots, post 1815 Fish

English, especially 1770s

German, 1753

GULF OF ST LAWRENCE

CAPE BRETON ISLAND

Fish

Sydney

Canso

Fish

Welsh, 1819

St Lawrence River

Chaleur Bay

Scattered Acadian settlements

PRINCE EDWARD ISLAND

Summerside

Charlottetown

Antigonish

Guysborough

Pictou

Truro

Dartmouth

Halifax

Horton

Amherst

NEW BRUNSWICK

Scattered Acadian settlements

Fredericton

Saint John

St Stephen

St John River

Bay of Fundy

Annapolis Royal

Digby

Lunenburg

NOVA SCOTIA

Yarmouth

Liverpool

Shelburne

New Englanders, pre 1783

Quebec City

Loyalist settlements
Movement of settlers
Principal fishing grounds
Fish

0   200
km

J. Sturgis

50° 55° 60° 65°

45° 50° 55° 60° 65°

66

The Maritime Colonies, 1763-1837

Four of Canada's future provinces – New-foundland, Prince Edward Island, New Brunswick and Nova Scotia – had been, because of their location, the cockpit of the Anglo-French struggle for the mastery of North America. On the one hand, the decline in French power was confirmed in the region by France's loss of most of her territories by the Treaty of Utrecht in 1713; and, on the other, the determination to defend Canada was evident in France's retention of Cape Breton and the subsequent building there of the imposing fortress of Louisbourg. Its walls, however, could not safeguard the French presence in North America, which ended with the Treaty of Paris in 1763. Humanity suffered in the transition. During the renewed warfare in the 1750s the British authorities took the decision to deport over 10,000 Acadians, the self-sufficient peasantry remaining since the original French emigration of the seventeenth century, to other widely scattered sites, such as Louisiana. The Seven Years War was barely over before the Acadians, enduring great hardships, began to drift back to Nova Scotia, where they were once more given the right to own land. The result was that by the turn of the eighteenth century the number of Acadians was restored to that prior to their exile. Although some were inevitably assimilated into the dominant British culture, enough were not to ensure the survival of a distinctive presence, especially in New Brunswick. The original Indian population, the Micmacs, fared less well and suffered declining numbers and economic marginalization as the fur trade lost its importance.

The seriousness with which the British took the Maritimes can be gauged by their decision to set up Halifax as a new town and naval base in 1749. Although the 3,000 original inhabitants were recruited in England, prevailing policy after 1763 was to encourage the movement of population from within North America. As a result 6,000 or so New Englanders did make the trek north-wards, most settling around the Bay of Fundy. Unsettled conditions in Highland Scotland led to an extensive migration to Cape Breton, the north shore of Prince Edward Island and mainland sites such as Pictou.

Undoubtedly a turning-point for the Maritimes was the onset of the American Revolution. Economically tied to Britain much more directly than were the Thirteen Colonies, the region became the preferred refuge for Loyalists. Over 30,000, including nearly 4,000 free blacks, streamed into the Maritimes. One result was the clamour for the creation of a uniquely Loyalist province; hence the establishment of the colony of New Brunswick in 1784. Although the nature of the land discouraged any large-scale immigration in succeeding years, the area continued to attract significant numbers of British settlers. The economy was never more vibrant than in the days of sail when the timber trade and the recurrent, though not wholly successful, attempts to entrench Maritime traders in the West Indian trade ensured a degree of optimism about the future. Prince Edward Island also attracted its fair share of emigrants due to its naturally fertile soil. However, progress was not what it might have been, due to the failure to wrest control of the land from an absentee landed class dating from 1767 when a few of the king's friends were granted extensive holdings. The issue was still smouldering in the 1860s, at the time of Confederation. Cape Breton, separated from Nova Scotia in 1784, had little agricultural potential, and industry could not be allowed to flourish in the face of prevailing mercantilist tenets. As a result it was returned to the jurisdiction of Nova Scotia in 1820, despite having attracted some Loyalist and Scottish emigrants. Newfoundland remained an anomaly. Britain stubbornly clung to the fiction that it was not a colony, despite the all too evident fact that

West Countrymen and Irish were establishing permanent sites. In 1824 Parliament finally acknowledged the logic of events by passing an Act which paved the way for the setting up of a regularized system of civil government.

The expansion of settlement in Upper and Lower Canada, 1783 to the 1830s

In 1759 the 60,000 inhabitants of New France underwent the trauma of conquest. The British victors were now faced with the problem of how to govern a people of alien culture. Partly because of an increasingly threatening situation in the Thirteen Colonies, they tended to deal liberally with the new subjects by allowing, for example, the retention of French civil law. By the terms of the Quebec Act of 1774 the outlines of the former French empire were retraced when Canada's jurisdiction was extended north of the Ohio and east of the Mississippi rivers. This attempt to seal off the west from colonization was one of the sparks igniting the revolution which was to leave British North America with its northern complexion. The arrival of 10,000 Loyalists, the majority of them settling west of the Ottawa River, led to the division into Upper and Lower Canada by the Constitutional Act of 1791.

Issues concerning land and settlement were to become contentious in succeeding decades. Britain had chosen not to interfere with the seigneurial system of land-holding where it already existed, but was loath to extend it into new areas of settlement such as the triangle of land on the south side of the St Lawrence River known as the Eastern Townships. Since the rugged Canadian Shield discouraged expansion northwards, there soon developed a land crisis for the rapidly growing French population whose birth rate meant a doubling of numbers every twenty-five years. The seigneurial system, which had worked benevolently during the French regime by allowing land use (in the form of the characteristically long strips fronting on the major rivers) in return for the fulfilment of certain dues and tasks, now began to operate on more clearly capitalistic principles. Seigneurs, perhaps a quarter of them now British, preferred to retain unparcelled land in its virgin state awaiting its timber profits and future rise in value. By the 1820s a landless class was developing; one result was the beginnings of a drift of population into the New England states which greatly alarmed the indigenous religious and political leadership. When the Eastern Townships were opened up by the government in the early 1800s the obvious, if unstated, intention was to encourage sales to large land companies and to incoming British or American settlers. Thus nationalist leaders, such as L. J. Papineau, were to find a receptive audience in their agitation against the ethnic exclusivity of British rule which culminated in the rebellions of 1837–8.

In 1837 there was a rebellion in Upper Canada as well, but one much less popularly backed and not so directly linked with the issue of land and settlement. Although the Canadian Shield did invade the peninsula in its eastern half, the agricultural potentialities were greater and soon exploited. In the production of wheat, Upper Canada began to dominate the market. At first, the colony benefited from the continental movement of population westwards, resulting in the arrival of many American settlers. However, the tensions arising from the Anglo-American war of 1812 led to official discouragement of this source; instead, military settlements along the recently constructed Rideau Canal were

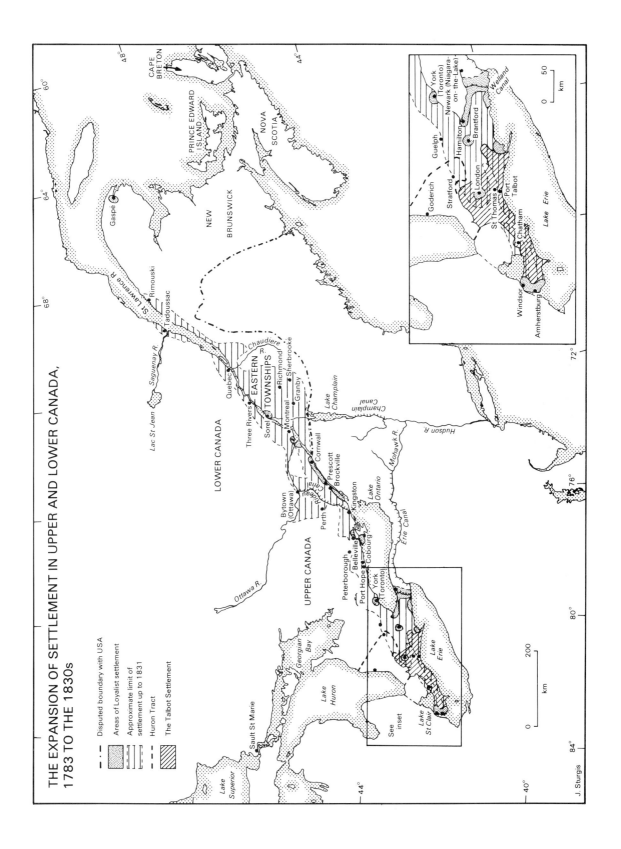

THE EXPANSION OF SETTLEMENT IN UPPER AND LOWER CANADA, 1783 TO THE 1830s

Disputed boundary with USA
Areas of Loyalist settlement
Approximate limit of settlement up to 1831
Huron Tract
The Talbot Settlement

J. Sturgis

69

promoted. In addition, several state-sponsored schemes were launched, most notably in the settlement of Scots and Irish in the Rideau district and Peterborough area respectively. In time these projects, combined with push factors in Britain, were to act as a syphon for a voluntary flow of British settlers. In the 1830s they were to be a stabilizing force in counteracting the increasingly rebellious Reform movement led by William Lyon Mackenzie. As in Lower Canada, the government also made use of private companies and individuals for the disposal of land. The eccentric, but effective, Colonel Thomas Talbot developed the north-west shore of Lake Erie as far inland as London, while the Canada Company purchased the Huron Tract for future development. The expansion of immigration continued apace after the Act of Union of 1841, so that by 1850 the largely English-speaking population of Canada West outnumbered that of Canada East.

The expansion of settlement in eastern Australia to 1835

From the inception of European settlement in Australia until nearly the mid-nineteenth century, the underlying dilemma for British policy-makers was to what extent to treat the continent as a vast gaol and to what extent as a potentially useful colony. Alongside the convicts transported there from Britain there were free men, of course, from the beginning; the first free settlers arrived as early as 1793, although even by 1810 they numbered only about 1,000. Until that same date another source of free men was the officers and men of the New South Wales Corps who remained in Australia and were often the favoured recipients of extensive grants of land and convict labour. One such was John Macarthur, who more than anyone else developed the wool trade which became the staple of trade with Britain. He epitomized the pretensions of a small elite know as 'the exclusives' to form a class of gentry in the colony of New South Wales. Because the expense of emigrating to the Antipodes was four times that of going to North America, only fairly prosperous families, such as the Hentys of Sussex, could contemplate such a voyage. Indeed, early land policy based the size of grant on an individual's capital.

It could be argued that the Bigge Reports of 1822–3 represented a transitional stage in the evolution of the British view of Australia. True, it was still to be a stern place of punishment, but Bigge also believed that future prosperity depended on the encouragement of free settlers. Punishment could be reconciled with profit if the most useful convicts were assigned to agriculturalists rather than to government service. The prevailing image of Australia in Britain, however, was still not one to encourage very much migration. Edward Gibbon Wakefield's *A Letter from Sydney* (1829) only added to the portrayal of Australia as a den of iniquity. Nevertheless, slowly accommodation was being made to a new state of things. Criticisms of the despotic nature of the governor's rule led to the first rudimentary civil institutions such as a legislative council in 1823. The dangers of population dispersal were dealt with in the setting up of the Nineteen Counties in 1829. The influence of E.G. Wakefield's ideas concerning land distribution was evident in the Ripon Regulations of 1831 whereby the costs of emigration would be met by the proceeds from the auction of crown lands at a minimum price of five shillings per acre. The concern of the authorities to improve the social tone of the colony was immediately evident in the decision to give free passage to suitable single women, of whom 3,000 arrived between 1832 and 1836.

As for the transportation system, it came under increasing attack in both Britain

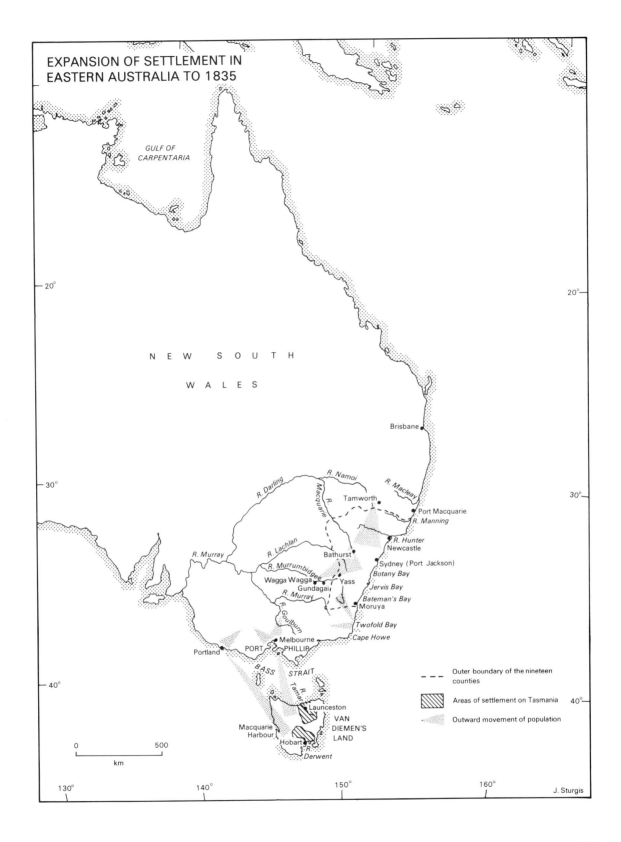

EXPANSION OF SETTLEMENT IN
EASTERN AUSTRALIA TO 1835

GULF OF
CARPENTARIA

N E W   S O U T H

W A L E S

Brisbane

R. Darling

R. Namoi

Macquarie

R. Macleay

Tamworth

Port Macquarie

R. Manning

R. Murray

R. Lachlan

Bathurst

R. Hunter
Newcastle

R. Murrumbidgee

Wagga Wagga
Gundagai

Yass

Sydney (Port Jackson)
Botany Bay

R. Murray

Jervis Bay

Bateman's Bay
Moruya

R. Goulburn

Twofold Bay

Cape Howe

Melbourne

PORT   PHILLIP

Portland

B A S S   S T R A I T

R. Tamar

Launceston

VAN
DIEMEN'S
LAND

Macquarie
Harbour

Hobart
R.
Derwent

0   500

km

Outer boundary of the nineteen
counties

Areas of settlement on Tasmania

Outward movement of population

130°   140°   150°   160°   J. Sturgis

20°   20°

30°   30°

40°   40°

71

and Australia. In particular, the Benthamites defined the terms of debate by demanding a more scientific approach to punishment and reformation. Colonists without capital objected to its devaluing of labour, whereas those who yearned for free institutions realized what a barrier convictism represented. In total 162,000 convicts reached Australian shores, the vast majority of them prior to 1840 when transportation to New South Wales was suspended. In that year convicts or ex-convicts (emancipists) represented more than half the population within the Nineteen Counties. In fact, the chief political and social division within the colonies was that between the exclusives and the emancipists.

The British authorities took a stubbornly Lockeian view of the Aboriginal population. Since they did not cultivate the land, they had no rights to it. Thus European settlement proceeded with disastrous consequences for the Aborigines, of whom recent estimates suggest there were perhaps 750,000 in 1788. Disease and callous treatment took their toll. Attempts were made to safeguard their welfare, but often the private opinions of officials and the public actions of settlers conspired together to result in the ineffectuality of all policies which might have reversed their marginalization and decline.

The Australian colonies and their expansion to the 1850s

By 1835 the boundary of the Nineteen Counties in New South Wales had already been breached by pastoralists in search of new pastures for their flocks. Those who took to the interior were called squatters – a title at first of disapprobation but which in time became purely vocational. From Van Diemen's Land (Tasmania) came the intrepid settlers who began the same process of squatting at Melbourne and in the Port Phillip district. It was all too evident that the government could do little to restrain this movement of a few prosperous men and a great many sheep. In time, the authorities bowed to the inevitable by making provisions whereby such an influential class could protect their holdings. Nevertheless, after the Australian colonies had gained the right of responsible government in 1856, the fact that so few individuals had engrossed so many acres led the eastern legislatures to pass Acts with the aim of unlocking the land. Such a movement of population also necessitated the redrawing of colonial boundaries. By 1850 the settlers in Melbourne and its environs were successful in establishing the colony of Victoria. The last great surge from New South Wales moved northwards in the 1840s and 1850s with the result that Queensland broke away from the same parent in 1859.

The 1830s were the last decade in which significant numbers of convicts were sent to Australia. By the early 1840s the numbers of free settlers arriving each year began to dwarf convict numbers. Not surprisingly, some individuals in Britain began to look to Australia for purposes of satisfying pecuniary or utopian ambitions. One such venture resulted in the founding of the Swan River colony in Western Australia in 1829. Founded by private settlers, it did not fare well due to a misreading of its climate and the high proportion of absentee landlords. Its difficulties were all grist to the mill of Edward Gibbon Wakefield, who blamed its shortcomings on the low price of land. Wakefield then took a leading part in forming a pressure group to establish a colony based upon his principles. When sufficient capital had been amassed, Parliament passed an Act establishing the colony of South Australia in 1834. Even though the price of land was set higher than elsewhere, it did not satisfy Wakefield, who dissociated himself from the venture.

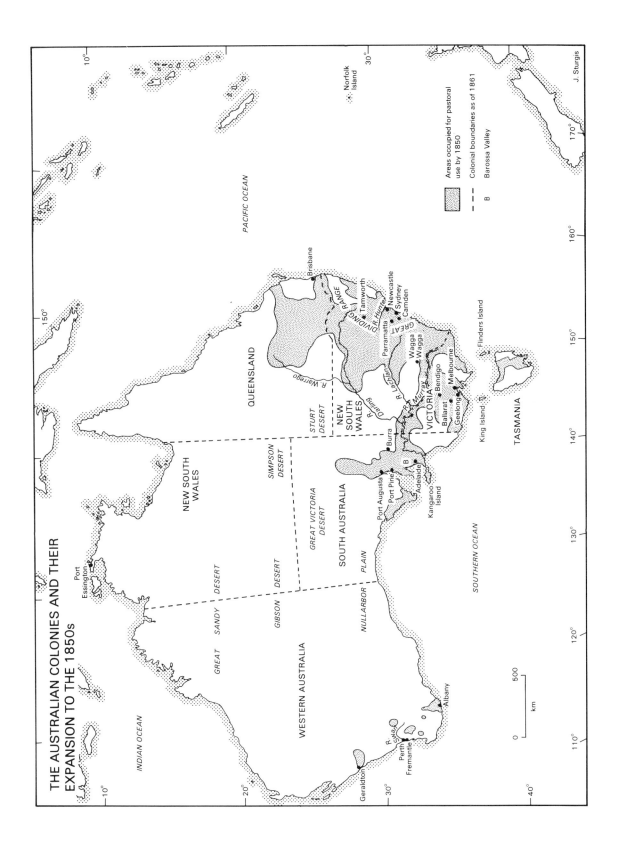

THE AUSTRALIAN COLONIES AND THEIR
EXPANSION TO THE 1850s

J. Sturgis

Areas occupied for pastoral
use by 1850

Colonial boundaries as of 1861

B   Barossa Valley

INDIAN OCEAN

PACIFIC OCEAN

SOUTHERN OCEAN

WESTERN AUSTRALIA

SOUTH AUSTRALIA

NEW SOUTH WALES

QUEENSLAND

NEW SOUTH
WALES

VICTORIA

TASMANIA

GREAT SANDY DESERT

GIBSON DESERT

GREAT VICTORIA DESERT

SIMPSON DESERT

STURT DESERT

NULLARBOR PLAIN

GREAT DIVIDING RANGE

Port Essington

Geraldton

Perth
Fremantle
R. Swan

Albany

Port Augusta
Port Pirie

Adelaide
Burra
B

Kangaroo
Island

King Island

Flinders Island

Brisbane

R. Warrego

R. Darling

R. Lachlan

Wagga
Wagga

R. Murray

Bendigo
Ballarat
Geelong
Melbourne

Tamworth
Newcastle
R. Hunter
Parramatta
Sydney
Camden

Norfolk
Island

km   0   500

73

Although soon shedding its connection with the private company, the colony did retain the desire to stay clear of convictism. It was strongly Nonconformist in religion, and this spirit of independence was reinforced by the introduction of German Lutheran settlers, who established themselves and a wine-making tradition in the Barossa Valley.

The discovery of gold in Victoria in 1851 at such sites as Bendigo and Ballarat had the predictable effect of raising immigration levels to new heights. Within one decade the population trebled in size to nearly 1.2 million. This was the last decade, however, in which population growth was attributable more to immigration than to the indigenous birth rate. The 'golden decade' put the finishing touches to transportation even in Van Diemen's Land. The one exception was Western Australia, which did not share the general prosperity and actually requested the introduction of transportation, which it maintained until 1868. What the discovery of gold emphasized most of all was the shift of political leverage from the country to the towns. The modern urban bias of Australian life had been firmly established. In all, it already seemed a distant day from those times when the sentence of transportation struck terror into the hearts of convicted prisoners.

New Zealand, 1840–1870

European involvement in New Zealand began in the early nineteenth century when sealers, whalers and traders, many of them from Australia, formed small shore establishments under the watchful eye of Maori chiefs. Missionaries arrived, keen to convert the Maoris, the Anglicans under Samuel Marsden in 1814 soon joined by rival Wesleyans and subsequently by Roman Catholics. In the late 1830s the colonizers of the New Zealand Company planned large-scale emigration, and their activities in London, together with increasing lawlessness on the spot, prompted the British government to annex New Zealand, claiming the South Island by right of discovery and the North Island by right of cession from the Maori chiefs under the Treaty of Waitangi in 1840. During the ensuing decade the company and subsidiary associations, acting on the theories of Edward Gibbon Wakefield, established settlements at Wellington and Nelson (1840), New Plymouth and Auckland (1841), Dunedin (1848) and Christchurch (1850). A federal constitution with six provincial councils and a general assembly meeting at Auckland was finally introduced in 1852, with local self-government conceded in principle four years later. In 1876 the provincial councils, then ten in number, were abolished, and New Zealand became a unitary state.

What delayed the practical enjoyment of full self-government, and hampered economic development on the North Island, was deteriorating relations between Europeans and Maoris, which led to intermittent but often bloody warfare between 1845 and 1872. The Treaty of Waitangi had not satisfactorily settled the contentious matters of sovereignty and land alienation. With scattered British communities still precarious coastal enclaves, the Maori tribes, though nominally British subjects, were left independent and in control of most of the North Island. Gradually the British sphere expanded through acquisition of Maori land, by either purchase or confiscation, and the initial economic co-operation between Europeans and Maoris was undermined by the settlers' land-hunger. Equally disruptive were the designs of governors George Grey and Thomas Gore Browne and their supporters who wanted to assert substantive, not nominal, sovereignty over the Maori tribes, and who were prepared to employ military force to impose British rule.

Fighting broke out at Kororareka and the Bay of Islands in the Northern War of 1845–6,

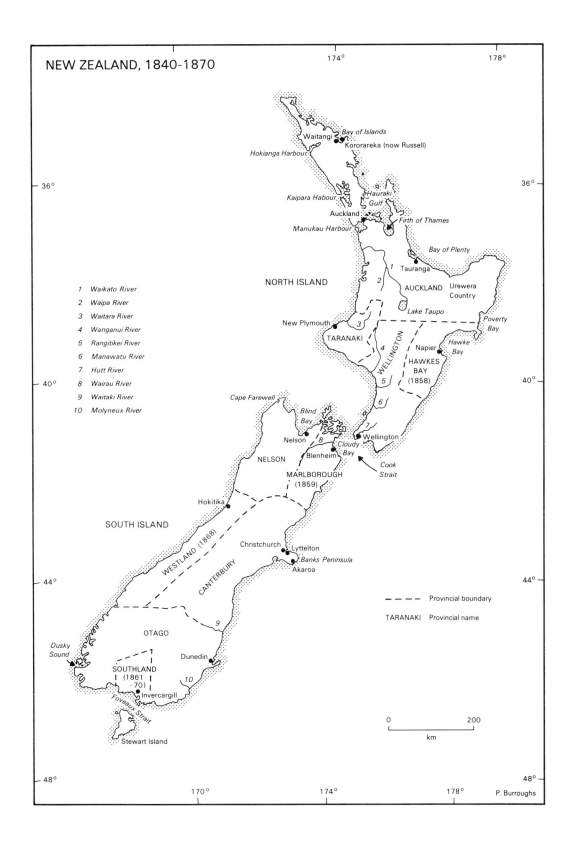

NEW ZEALAND, 1840-1870

174° 178°

Bay of Islands
Waitangi
Kororareka (now Russell)

Hokianga Harbour

36°   36°

Kaipara Habour
Hauraki Gulf
Auckland
Firth of Thames
Manukau Harbour

Bay of Plenty

NORTH ISLAND
Tauranga
AUCKLAND
Urewera Country

1   *Waikato River*
2   *Waipa River*
3   *Waitara River*
4   *Wanganui River*
5   *Rangitikei River*
6   *Manawatu River*
7   *Hutt River*
8   *Wairau River*
9   *Waitaki River*
10 *Molyneux River*

Lake Taupo
Poverty Bay
New Plymouth
TARANAKI
Napier
Hawke Bay
WELLINGTON
HAWKES BAY (1858)

40°   40°

Cape Farewell
Blind Bay
Nelson
Wellington
Cloudy Bay
Blenheim
Cook Strait
NELSON
MARLBOROUGH (1859)

Hokitika

SOUTH ISLAND
WESTLAND (1868)
CANTERBURY
Christchurch
Lyttelton
Banks Peninsula
Akaroa

44°   44°

– – – –   Provincial boundary

TARANAKI   Provincial name

OTAGO
9
Dusky Sound
Dunedin
SOUTHLAND (1861 -70)
10
Invercargill
Foveaux Strait

0   200
km

Stewart Island

48°   48°

170°   174°   178°   P. Burroughs

and in the Wellington region in 1846 and at Wanganui in 1847 in the Taranaki War. A period of peace and some renewal of collaboration then ensued, but the growing reluctance of Maori chiefs to sell land was reinforced in the late 1850s by the emergence of the King Movement, a loose confederation centred on the Tainui tribes of the Waikato region, with varying degrees of backing from other tribes. Clashes in the Taranaki and Waitara districts in 1860–1 were followed by others in the Waikato region in 1863–4. Then fighting spread across the whole North Island, focused particularly in Titokowaru's war in south Taranaki–Wanganui (1868–9) and Te Kooti's war on the east coast (1868–72). During those years governors assembled between 9,000 and 12,000 British regulars and up to 4,000 colonial troops, and cajoled the imperial authorities into lavishing men and money on protracted, sterile warfare until the British government eventually withdrew its troops in despair. Yet incontestable victory through a decisive battle eluded military commanders because of the stout resistance and shrewd strategy of smaller Maori forces; only in the long run, and then somewhat adventitiously, did superior numbers give the settlers victory of a kind. By that time the continued expansion of sheep farming and the discovery of gold had brought more European settlers and a temporary surge of prosperity, especially to the South Island whose economic growth had not been impeded by the conflict of race relations.

British exploration in Africa, 1770–1856

Little was known of the interior of Africa in late-eighteenth-century Britain. Such information as there was derived from an unreliable mixture of classical, Portuguese and Arabic sources. It was the coastline that was primarily known, together with the north-east of the continent and the mouths of some major rivers. A formidable array of barriers, not least that posed by disease, stood in the way of European penetration of Africa. However, this period was to see a growing British interest in African geography, partly out of scientific curiosity, partly because of imagined commercial benefits and partly because of the French wars and Napoleon's invasion of Egypt.

The main problems of African geography concerned the source of the Nile and the location of the Niger, about which virtually nothing was known. It was mainly Britons (or Germans in British employ) who were responsible for resolving these problems in this period, although other areas of Africa, particularly the southern part of the continent, saw significant work by Portuguese and Afrikaner travellers.

Initially the Nile attracted attention. James Bruce, who reached the source of the Blue Nile in 1770, W. G. Browne and Johann Burckhardt were to travel extensively in Egypt, Sudan and Abyssinia. In 1788, however, the establishment of the African Association focused geographical attention on the Niger, where it was to remain for sixty years. In 1795 Mungo Park was sent on his first expedition into Africa, reaching the Niger at Segu in 1796, the first Briton to do so. Hornemann's dispatch across the desert in 1798 by the association was to culminate in his death three years later.

Park's achievement answered one question, that the Niger flowed eastwards, but left the location of the Niger's mouth unresolved. Backed now by the government, as were all major expeditions thereafter, Park's second journey, to follow the Niger to the coast, was halted by his death near Bussa in 1806.

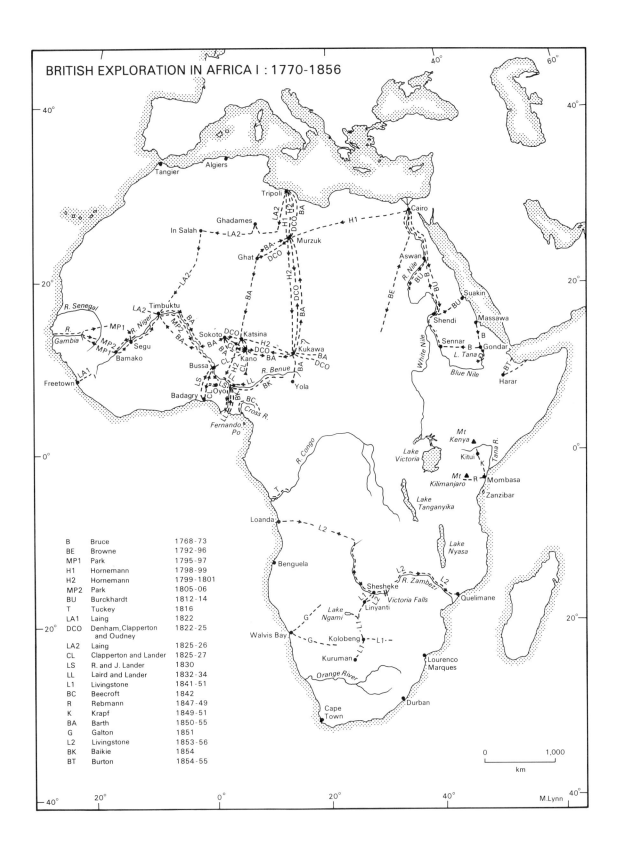

BRITISH EXPLORATION IN AFRICA I : 1770-1856

B	Bruce	1768-73
BE	Browne	1792-96
MP1	Park	1795-97
H1	Hornemann	1798-99
H2	Hornemann	1799-1801
MP2	Park	1805-06
BU	Burckhardt	1812-14
T	Tuckey	1816
LA1	Laing	1822
DCO	Denham, Clapperton and Oudney	1822-25
LA2	Laing	1825-26
CL	Clapperton and Lander	1825-27
LS	R. and J. Lander	1830
LL	Laird and Lander	1832-34
L1	Livingstone	1841-51
BC	Beecroft	1842
R	Rebmann	1847-49
K	Krapf	1849-51
BA	Barth	1850-55
G	Galton	1851
L2	Livingstone	1853-56
BK	Baikie	1854
BT	Burton	1854-55

M.Lynn

Tuckey's 1816 expedition to the Congo (a possible mouth of the Niger) was a failure, and attention shifted to the northern approach across the desert. The 'Bornu mission' of Denham, Clapperton and Oudney in 1822-5 was the first to cross the Sahara to the states of Hausaland and Bornu and return. Laing reached Timbuktu in 1825 and died nearby the following year; the Frenchman René Caillé, who visited Timbuktu in 1828, was the first European to return successfully.

Hugh Clapperton's expedition of 1825 marked a breakthrough. Clapperton and Richard Lander opened a southern route to the Niger from Badagry. Clapperton died in Sokoto in 1827, but Lander was to use the same route with his brother John in 1830 when he finally traced the Niger to the sea. The Landers' success was followed by Laird's use, in 1832, of the new technology of steamships to open the river to British commerce.

Heinrich Barth's government-sponsored expedition of 1850-5 brought this phase of geographical interest to an end. Barth travelled over much of the western Sudan, reached Timbuktu and made a major contribution to geographical knowledge. It was to contact Barth that Baikie's expedition was dispatched up the Niger and Benue in 1854, a voyage chiefly remarkable for proving quinine's value as a prophylactic against malaria, and marking an end to previous expeditions' grim mortality rates.

Barth's and Baikie's expeditions were the climax of British interest in the Niger. Developments were occurring elsewhere that were to point to the future. Krapf and Rebmann, two CMS missionaries, began a number of journeys into the East African interior after 1847; Rebmann was the first European to see Mount Kilimanjaro in 1848, and Krapf Mount Kenya in 1849. To the south, another missionary, David Livingstone, began his career in 1841. In 1851 he reached the Zambezi and between 1853-6 he crossed the continent. His work and the public acclaim it received in Britain were to inaugurate the second phase of British exploration in Africa.

British Exploration in Africa, 1856-1890

In the 1850s British interest turned to the geography of East and Central Africa. Stimulated by the earlier work of Krapf, Rebmann and Livingstone, the source of the Nile and the outline of the Great Lakes were to be the focus of attention in this phase. Geographical curiosity was to be allied, particularly in Livingstone's case, with evangelical concern and, in time, overt commercial and political ambitions.

It was primarily British travellers who were responsible for this, although from the 1860s, with the work of Rohlfs and then Nachtigal in North Africa, and later De Brazza and Binger in West Africa, important German and French contributions were made.

Two main thrusts were launched in the 1850s. The first was to locate the source of the Nile. Richard Burton and John Speke set out to Lake Tanganyika in 1857. During their return Speke reached Lake Victoria, and his belief that this was the Nile's source was to unleash fierce controversy in Britain. It was a controversy that was to continue even after his second expedition, with James Grant, which beat Samuel Baker's expedition from the north and finally located the Nile's source in Lake Victoria in July 1862.

The other thrust of British interest came in the form of the government's Zambezi Expedition of 1858-64 led by Livingstone. Livingstone's use of a steamer on the Zambezi, and later the Rovuma, as a means of bringing 'Christianity and commerce' into Central Africa came to little, though he did succeed in reaching Lake Nyasa by way of the Shire.

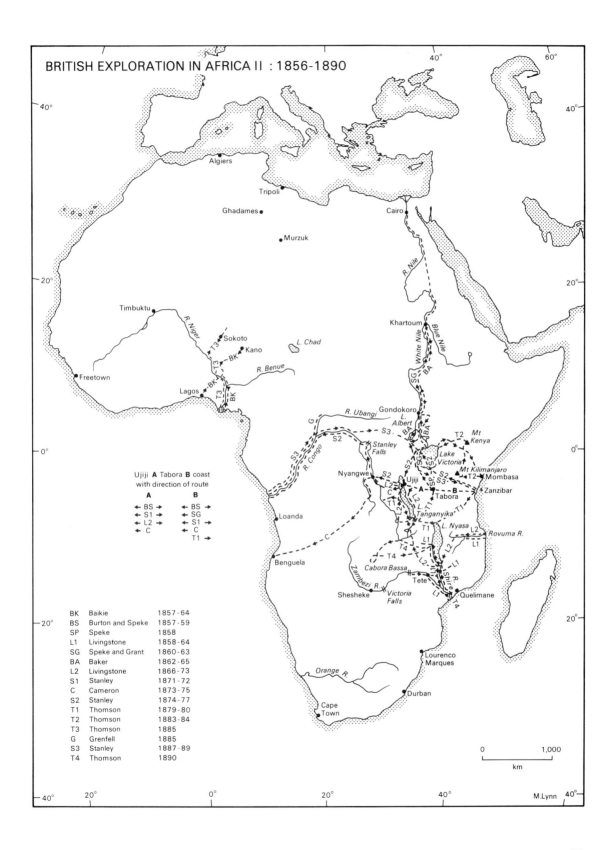

BRITISH EXPLORATION IN AFRICA II : 1856-1890

Ujiji **A** Tabora **B** coast
with direction of route

A	B
← BS →	← BS →
← S1 →	← SG →
← L2 →	← S1 →
← C	← C →
	T1 →

BK	Baikie	1857-64
BS	Burton and Speke	1857-59
SP	Speke	1858
L1	Livingstone	1858-64
SG	Speke and Grant	1860-63
BA	Baker	1862-65
L2	Livingstone	1866-73
S1	Stanley	1871-72
C	Cameron	1873-75
S2	Stanley	1874-77
T1	Thomson	1879-80
T2	Thomson	1883-84
T3	Thomson	1885
G	Grenfell	1885
S3	Stanley	1887-89
T4	Thomson	1890

M.Lynn

0   1,000
km

Livingstone's journey coincided with the Niger Expedition of 1857–64 led by Baikie; these were to be the last of the government-funded geographical expeditions.

Livingstone's work struck a chord in the British public, and the 1860s were to see further expeditions to map the Great Lakes, mainly sponsored by the Royal Geographical Society. In 1866 Livingstone set off on his last great journey, around Lakes Nyasa and Tanganyika. He was to be 'found' by Henry Stanley at Ujiji in 1871 and died, to the south of Lake Tanganyika, in 1873. V. L. Cameron, sent by the RGS to find Livingstone in 1873, mapped many of the rivers of Central Africa and became the first European to cross the continent from east to west.

By the mid-1870s much of the earlier British ignorance about the geography of Africa had been cleared. Subsequent expeditions were to take on an openly political role alongside their geographical intent. Joseph Thomson's journeys reflect this transition, with his early journeys for the RGS – to Lake Tanganyika in 1879–80 and to Lake Victoria in

1883–4 – being replaced by treaty-making journeys to Sokoto for the National African Company in 1885 and to the Zambezi area for the British South Africa Company in 1890. Similarly, Stanley travelled extensively in the Congo on behalf of King Leopold in the early 1880s, and his Emin Pasha Relief Expedition of 1887–9, to rescue the Egyptian-appointed Governor of the Upper Nile, was also aimed at staking claims to large parts of Central Africa.

The Relief Expedition was the last of the nineteenth-century expeditions to make a major contribution to geographical knowledge. By 1890 most of the geographical and medical problems which had restricted European penetration of the continent had been solved. In this sense British travellers of the eighteenth and nineteenth centuries were the necessary precursors of imperialism, even though their overt links were, in most cases, very limited. In the 1890s the routes of the geographical traveller and missionary came to be followed by the soldier and the military expedition.

The Cape of Good Hope, *c.* 1806

Britain's contacts with the Cape developed alongside her trade with India. Although during the eighteenth century the Cape was controlled by the Dutch East India Company, it was a vital staging-post for European shipping to and from the east. Between 1788 and 1792 approximately 170 ships per annum called at Cape ports, chiefly Cape Town, above all for fresh supplies, slightly more than 16 per cent being British. With the outbreak of Europe's Revolutionary Wars and France's invasion of the Netherlands in 1795, it was the Cape's strategic position which led the British to occupy it in September that year. Although temporarily restored to the new Batavian Republic by the Treaty of Amiens in 1802, renewed war with France provoked British reoccupation in January 1806. The peace

settlements of 1814–15 recognized the Cape as a British possession.

Although of mixed European origin, the white population taken over by the British increasingly shared a culture rooted in Calvinist religion and the Afrikaans language. Its most important constituents were the company personnel, mercantile or professional classes and artisans concentrated in Cape Town; the farming or stockbreeding families; and a much larger non-European population, notably slaves (nearly 30,000 in 1806), coloured or mixed-race groups, and the indigenous Khoikhoi and San peoples.

Britain's inheritance was an uneasy one, for Cape society was inherently expansive. Physical conditions, natural population growth, patterns of farm ownership and widespread

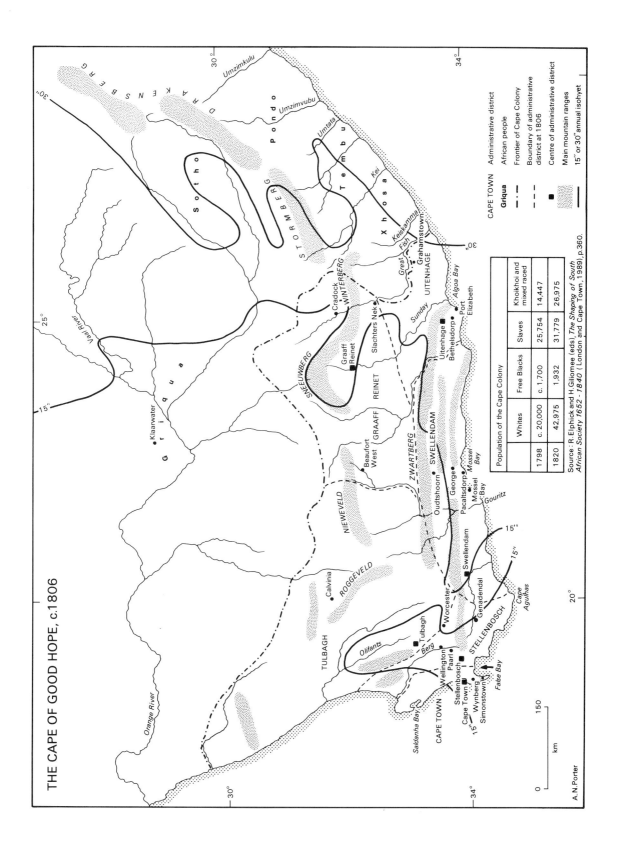

THE CAPE OF GOOD HOPE, c.1806

Population of the Cape Colony

	Whites	Free Blacks	Slaves	Khoikhoi and mixed raced
1798	c. 20,000	c. 1,700	25,754	14,447
1820	42,975	1,932	31,779	26,975

Source: R. Elphick and H.Giliomee (eds), *The Shaping of South African Society 1652 - 1840* (London and Cape Town, 1989), p.360.

CAPE TOWN   Administrative district

  African people

 ·—··— Frontier of Cape Colony

 ——— Boundary of administrative district at 1806

Griqua ——— Centre of administrative district at 1806

 ■ Centre of administrative district

  Main mountain ranges

  15" or 30" annual isohyet

A.N.Porter

81

pastoralism all made for territorial expansion. This was further fuelled by Cape Town's growth, by foreign demand for meat, wine, wheat and later wool and, as internal markets grew larger, by land speculation. Colonists moved east along the valleys of the Cape, rather than northwards across the difficult mountain ranges to the higher, drier Karoo plateau. By 1806, however, the limits to relatively easy eastward expansion had been reached. Not only was Xhosa, Pondo and Tembu territory well populated, but, pressed by marauders and refugees from upheavals further north, these peoples in turn were spreading southwards and increasingly resented white demands and competition.

Disputes over land, labour and cattle between white settlers and Xhosa (often allied with Khoikhoi) flared into war in 1779–81, 1793, 1799–1802 and 1811–12. Conflict between the Dutch authorities in Cape Town and settlers over land grants, taxation and frontier defence bred rebellion in Graaff Reinet in 1795; the British experienced similar revolts in 1799, 1801 and 1815. Under the Dutch expanding settlement had out-stripped effective control from Cape Town and even from administrative district cen-tres. Initially the British broadly accepted

Cape customs and institutions; thoughts of temporary occupation and wartime security made cautious, non-interventionist govern-ment advisable. After 1806, however, this changed as the likelihood of French recovery evaporated. In pursuit of peace, stable frontiers of white settlement and financial self-sufficiency, British governors such as Somerset, Cradock and Caledon tried to make administration more effective. The growth of both Britain's Cape trade and numbers of English-speaking merchants gave point to this. Poor communications, and the continued remoteness of much of the colony, made reform difficult. Nevertheless, new admini-strative districts and magistracies were estab-lished steadily, at George (1811), Cradock and Grahamstown (1812) and Beaufort West (1818). Population grew, and agricultural pro-duction expanded. For many the period after 1806 was one of growing prosperity. Trade values rose more than seven-fold between 1807 and 1815, aided partly by the large garrison of up to 6,500 troops. Nevertheless, many colonists disliked the authoritarian, newly-intrusive administration, with its growing tendency towards Anglicization, quite as much as they had its equally dictatorial but more ineffective predecessors.

South Africa: colonies and republics, 1820–1854

The Cape's history in this period can be inter-preted as that of the British failure either to contain or to reconcile local conflicts over resources. This was not for want of trying. When legislative Acts, backed up with insigni-ficant military or administrative force, failed to stabilize or 'close' the frontiers, imperial officials turned to closer settlement of frontier zones. Most significant was the experimental plantation in 1820 of 5,000 settlers in Albany district, designed not only to solve a South African problem but also to relieve Britain's own post-war economic crisis. Close settle-

ment proved a fiasco; the emigration only exacerbated the eastern frontier's difficulties – land-hunger, labour shortages and conflicts between black and white, Afrikaner and English-speaker. A similar but barely more successful experiment was tried with coloured smallholders in the Kat River Settlement from 1829.

This deepening impasse was broken by local initiatives. Confronted with unrespon-sive authorities committed to legislation (such as slave emancipation in 1833) widely regarded as inimical, some Afrikaners began to move

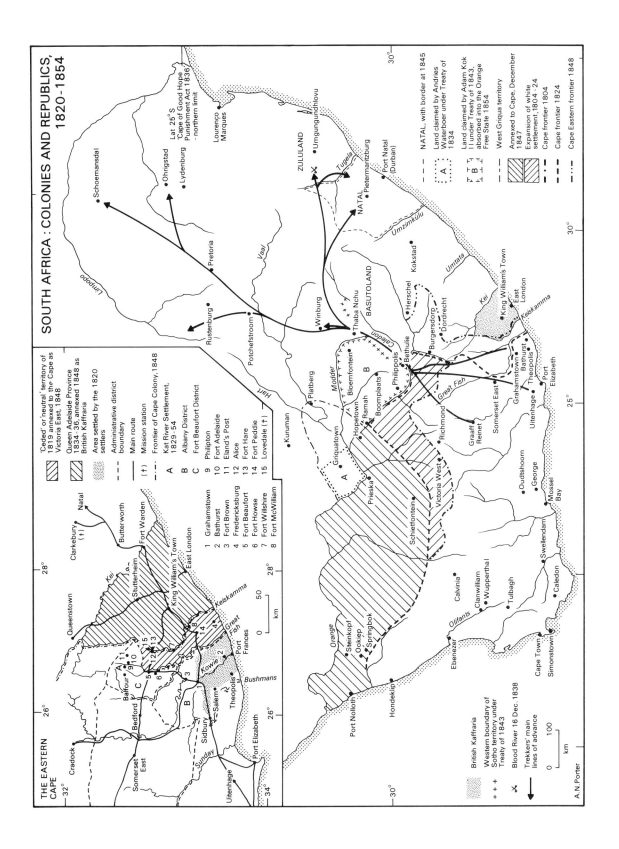

north out of the colony. When war on the eastern frontier in 1834 was followed by Lord Glenelg's insistence that Governor D'Urban withdraw his annexation of Queen Adelaide Province, resentment ran high. The gradual trickle of emigrants became the Great Trek across the Orange, beyond the Vaal and into Natal. This long migration did little to ease tensions in the Cape but greatly extended the area of conflict and competition.

Against a background of missionary and humanitarian protest, imperial authorities made half-hearted attempts to contain this expansion of white settlement. Treaties in 1834 with the West Griqua leader, Andries Waterboer, and in 1843 with both Adam Kok II and Mshweshwe, king of the Sotho, were aimed at consolidating authority and agreeing fixed territories in the north-east. The Cape of Good Hope Punishment Act (1836), although largely ignored, took the unprecedented step of unilaterally extending jurisdiction far beyond the colonial frontier. The appointment of a lieutenant-governor to the eastern Cape was not only a sop to local feeling but was intended to take a firmer grip on transfrontier affairs. More decisively in 1842, responding to Boer expansion after the Boers' defeat of the Zulu at Blood River (December 1839), pleas from local traders and worries about French ambitions, Britain annexed Natal. The costs and complications of such extensions of territory had always to be weighed against the dangers of failing to expand – losses of security, of local political support or of potential revenues from trade and land sales. Treaties with local rulers, like Governor Maitland's in 1844 with the Xhosas and Mpondo, were often preferable but rarely held firm when individuals on the spot ignored them.

Eventually, Governor Sir Harry Smith, with the new powers of high commissioner, attempted to take control by pushing the colony's frontier to the Orange and annexing the Orange River Sovereignty. This gamble on the outcome of extending formal imperial rule failed. Renewed war in the east, defeat of British forces by Mshweshwe's Sotho, and apprehension at Afrikaner intransigence destroyed Smith's credibility and convinced the British Cabinet that control north of the Orange was excessively wasteful. In the Sand River and Bloemfontein Conventions (1852 and 1854) imperial policy-makers recognized that the South African Republic and Orange Free State were their own best guardians, and could even serve Britain's remote interest in the northern interior.

Emigration from Britain, 1815–1914

The years after 1815 saw the growth of large-scale and sustained emigration from Britain. Many of the emigrants were driven overseas by pressures at home: the dislocation caused by industrialization, the decay of old trades and crafts, low wages or widespread unemployment in an expanding population, rural poverty, and famine in Ireland. Throughout the century there remained some correlation between years of great distress or unemployment and the peaks of emigration, but people were also positively attracted abroad by the prospects of wider opportunities, higher wages and standards of living, and ownership of land. The emigrants were predominantly working class, unskilled and poor, with a leavening of artisans and middle class, especially in the early 'selected' migration to New Zealand. Most were single males or young families, though schemes of child migration to Canada were popular in the later nineteenth century.

The majority of emigrants went to the United States, the land of golden opportunity.

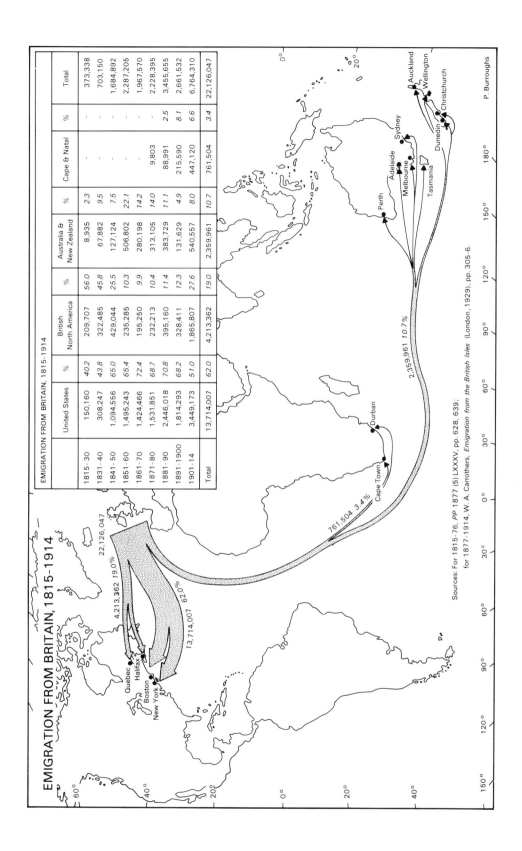

EMIGRATION FROM BRITAIN, 1815-1914

EMIGRATION FROM BRITAIN, 1815-1914									
	United States	%	British North America	%	Australia & New Zealand	%	Cape & Natal	%	Total
1815-30	150,160	40.2	209,707	56.0	8,935	2.3	-	-	373,338
1831-40	308,247	43.8	322,485	45.8	67,882	9.5	-	-	703,150
1841-50	1,094,556	65.0	429,044	25.5	127,124	7.5	-	-	1,684,892
1851-60	1,495,243	65.4	235,285	10.3	506,802	22.1	-	-	2,287,205
1861-70	1,424,466	72.4	195,250	9.9	280,198	14.2	-	-	1,967,570
1871-80	1,531,851	68.7	232,213	10.4	313,105	14.0	9,803	-	2,228,395
1881-90	2,446,018	70.8	395,160	11.4	383,729	11.1	88,991	2.5	3,455,655
1891-1900	1,814,293	68.2	328,411	12.3	131,629	4.9	215,590	8.1	2,661,532
1901-14	3,449,173	51.0	1,865,807	27.6	540,557	8.0	447,120	6.6	6,764,310
Total	13,714,007	62.0	4,213,362	19.0	2,359,961	10.7	761,504	3.4	22,126,047

Sources: For 1815-76, *PP* 1877 (5) LXXXV, pp. 628, 639;
for 1877-1914, W. A. Carrothers, *Emigration from the British Isles* (London, 1929), pp. 305-6.

P. Burroughs

Even many of those who travelled to British North America were lured into the republic by better wages and plenteous good land. Others were attracted by sheep farming in New Zealand, pastoral or urban life in Australia or the mid-century gold discoveries. A smaller number chose South Africa. The cheaper cost of transatlantic voyages was also a major determinant of destination, from the time when emigrants crowded into the returning Canadian timber vessels to the days of the faster steamships. The vast majority had to find the cost of passages from their own savings or the pockets of relatives, or occasionally from private associations, landlords at home or employers abroad. No public money was provided for the transatlantic trade, which the British government feared would prove an expensive and troublesome responsibility and thought best left to private enterprise and individual initiative. In the case of Australasia, the discouragement of distance was partially overcome by the provision of some assisted passages from such colonial funds as land revenues and the activities of colonizing agencies that diverted part of the exodus to New Zealand in the 1840s and beyond. Meanwhile the British government did become involved in exercising some supervision of the emigrant traffic through a series of Passenger Acts, designed to ensure minimum standards of safety and health on the ships. To protect individuals against the frauds and abuses inherent in the trade, emigration agents were appointed at the chief ports of embarkation: Liverpool, Bristol, London, Glasgow, Leith, Dublin, Cork, Belfast, Limerick, Sligo and Londonderry.

The official statistics given here represent total departures from British ports, foreigners as well as British subjects, a distinction first drawn by the authorities in 1853. If the figures were adjusted to include only British subjects for the period 1853–1914, total emigration for the century would be reduced to 16,920,443; Australasia with 2,285,435 or 13.5 per cent and British North America with 3,463,166 or 20.5 per cent would gain slightly at the expense of the United States with 9,570,146 or 56.6 per cent. The official statistics do not differentiate between Australia and New Zealand as destinations, but a few random figures in other sources suggest that New Zealand's share of the traffic was seldom more than 15 to 20 per cent. South Africa does not appear as a separate destination in the official returns until 1880, and earlier emigrants there were presumably included in the category 'Elsewhere', a small figure until the mid-century. Aside from clandestine emigration and unrecorded sailings, other migrants from Britain not included in these figures would be some 150,000 convicts transported, chiefly to Australia, and several thousand soldiers who settled overseas on discharge or desertion from the British Army.

Barbados, *c.* 1830

Barbados was the primary site of the 'sugar revolution' which transformed the British Caribbean in the seventeenth century. An island of only 166 square miles, its gently rolling landscape was almost entirely arable. The forest was rapidly removed, virtually all of the land having been cleared as early as 1665. Although some degree of agricultural diversification continued until the 1670s, sugar plantations spread quickly throughout the island to create the monocultural sugar colony *par excellence*.

The pattern of settlement established in Barbados by the 1670s persisted, in its essentials, into the twentieth century. The number of sugar plantations with mills remained constant, at about 350, from the later seventeenth century to the time of emancipation. Wind became the most common source of power, gradually displacing animals. In 1830

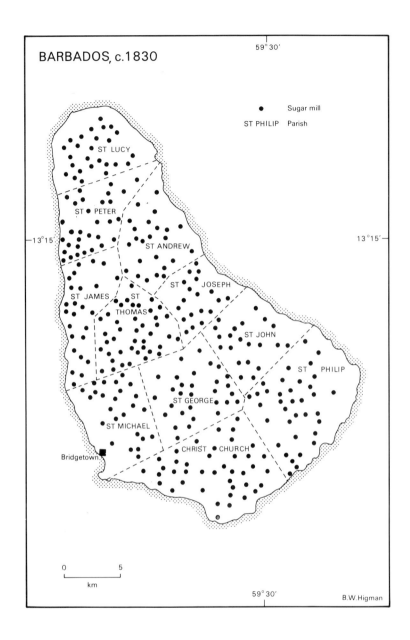

BARBADOS, c.1830

• Sugar mill
ST PHILIP Parish

ST LUCY

ST PETER

ST ANDREW

ST JOSEPH

ST JAMES   ST THOMAS

ST JOHN

ST PHILIP

ST GEORGE

ST MICHAEL

CHRIST CHURCH

Bridgetown

0   5
km

59°30'

13°15'   13°15'

59°30'

B.W.Higman

sugar mills were spread almost uniformly throughout the island, thinning only around the urban centre of Bridgetown and in the relatively rugged eastern parishes where the coral terraces were raised to create steep cliffs. At the same time, the concentration of the slave population in sugar production was at its maximum in the eastern parishes, with cotton and other agriculture relatively common in the leeward parishes, especially around Bridgetown.

In 1830 Barbados had a total population of about 102,000, with a density of 615 per square mile. This made it one of the most densely populated colonies of the Empire, a fact noted with local pride from the middle of the seventeenth century. The most densely populated parishes were St Michael and St George.

Approximately 78 per cent of the island's 82,000 slaves lived on sugar plantations, which were characterized by their relatively small scale, emphasis on food crop production and resident planter class. Cultivation techniques were highly labour intensive. Of the remaining slaves, half lived in towns and half on small plantations producing cotton, provisions, ginger and other minor crops.

Trinidad, *c.* 1850

Trinidad was one of the last Caribbean colonies established by the British, being taken from the Spanish in 1797. Rapid population growth and expansion of the plantation system followed, but the island's population was a mere 42,000 at the time of emancipation. Slaves accounted for 54 per cent of the total, freedmen 38 per cent and whites 8 per cent, an unusual mix for a British plantation colony.

Vast tracts of land remained unsettled in 1838, and the pattern of settlement changed relatively little until the 1860s. The slave population was confined to a narrow belt, ringing the Gulf of Paria and matching closely the distribution of the sugar industry. Between 1807 and 1834 slaves had been moved from the northern plantation region, around the town of Port of Spain, to the expanding sugar zone in the south. Cocoa expanded just as rapidly as sugar, but it was a smallholder's crop cultivated largely by the free coloured and free black population, making little use of slave labour. It was produced chiefly on the northern uplands, along with coffee and pro-

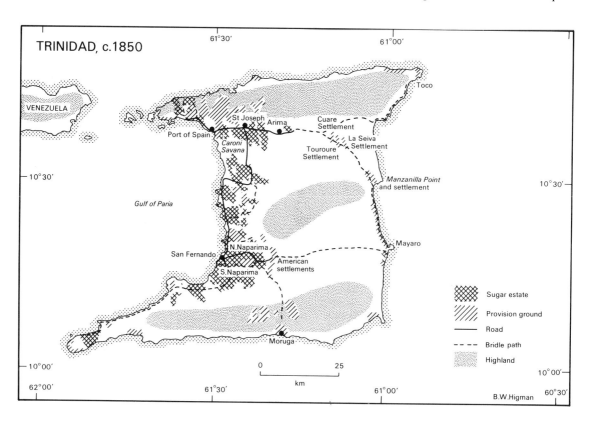

visions, while the south became a sugar monoculture.

After emancipation, many ex-slaves abandoned plantation labour for small farming. But they did not move very far from the existing areas of settlement, establishing villages near the towns of Port of Spain and San Fernando, and along the road to Arima. Sugar production languished in the 1840s but revived in the early 1850s as a result of Indian indentured immigration and the clearing of virgin soil. Cocoa experienced a similar revival.

The eastern marches were occupied by settlements created before emancipation. In the south, the 'American' settlements were established in 1816 for slaves liberated by the British during the war of 1812. In the north, demobilized soldiers of the West India Regiments were located in settlements between Arima and Manzanilla which were not integrated into the transportation system until the 1860s.

British expansion in India, 1805–1885

At Wellesley's departure in 1805 the British stake in India east of the Indus and the rivers of the Punjab was a powerful one (see p. 54). Most of the major entities which had emerged as regional successor states to the Mughal Empire had either been conquered or turned into subordinate allies. But 1805 was no more a stopping point in the process of expansion than 1765 had proved to be. Conquests continued, and those whom the British chose to treat as 'princes' without formal conquest were welded into a system of subordination to a 'paramount' British power. By the middle of the nineteenth century the political map of 'India' up to the mountains of Afghanistan was more or less complete; only to the east in Burma were further major annexations to be made.

Continuing British expansion is extremely difficult to fit into any overall framework of explanation or analysis. At the risk of oversimplification, however, a mass of individual acts of conquest or annexation can be related to certain phases. The map is intended to illustrate these phases.

The first phase followed with a certain logic from projects interrupted by Wellesley's departure. By 1805 he had succeeded in clamping British supremacy over most of peninsular India and over the Ganges and Jumna valleys. Had he been able to subjugate the Maratha chieftains, his system would have been complete. He was not, however, granted the time to do this; and, although badly mauled, the Marathas had kept some freedom of action. What Wellesley had intended the Marquess of Hastings completed in a series of wars from 1817 to 1819. Part of the price of Maratha defeat was loss of territory to the British. Annexations took place at the expense of the Bhonsles (A1), Holkar (A2), Sindhia (A3), Baroda (A4) and above all the Peshwa (A5), whose territorial power was extinguished.

The Peshwa apart, the Maratha chiefs remained in control of much territory, but the terms on which they survived as territorial powers marked an important stage in the evolution of British doctrine about the status of 'princes' and their 'states'. They were no longer to be even nominally the equal allies of the East India Company; they were its subordinates, subject to its 'paramountcy'. The doctrine of 'paramount' power was never very precisely formulated, but it was quickly made clear that the British reserved to themselves the right to bring to an end by annexation the limited autonomy enjoyed by the princes. This power to annex was used quite freely up to 1856 but much more sparingly thereafter. Historians have failed to detect any clearly enunciated policy of annexation, but

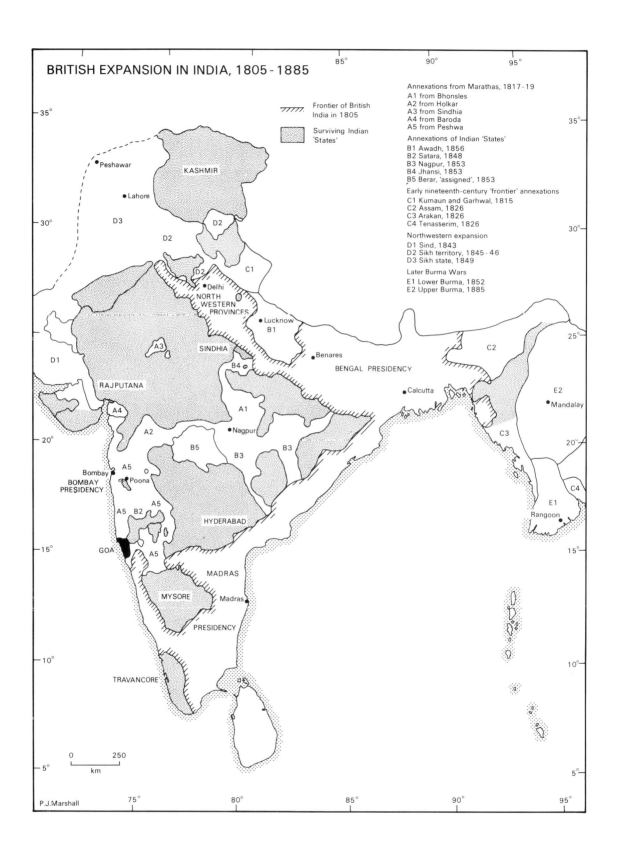

BRITISH EXPANSION IN INDIA, 1805 - 1885

Frontier of British
India in 1805

Surviving Indian
'States'

Annexations from Marathas, 1817 - 19
A1 from Bhonsles
A2 from Holkar
A3 from Sindhia
A4 from Baroda
A5 from Peshwa

Annexations of Indian 'States'
B1 Awadh, 1856
B2 Satara, 1848
B3 Nagpur, 1853
B4 Jhansi, 1853
B5 Berar, 'assigned', 1853

Early nineteenth-century 'frontier' annexations
C1 Kumaun and Garhwal, 1815
C2 Assam, 1826
C3 Arakan, 1826
C4 Tenasserim, 1826

Northwestern expansion
D1 Sind, 1843
D2 Sikh territory, 1845 - 46
D3 Sikh state, 1849

Later Burma Wars
E1 Lower Burma, 1852
E2 Upper Burma, 1885

35°

30°

Peshawar

KASHMIR

Lahore

D3

D2

D2

C1

Delhi

NORTH
WESTERN
PROVINCES

Lucknow
B1

A3

SINDHIA

Benares

BENGAL PRESIDENCY

C2

D1

RAJPUTANA

B4

Calcutta

E2
Mandalay

A4

A1

A5

Nagpur

B5

B3

B3

C3

Bombay
BOMBAY
PRESIDENCY

A5

Poona

A5

A2

E2

A5

B2

HYDERABAD

E1

GOA

A5

MADRAS

Rangoon

C4

MYSORE

Madras

PRESIDENCY

TRAVANCORE

0   250

km

P.J.Marshall

75°   80°   85°   90°   95°

inhibitions about using it were easily discounted at certain periods, most obviously in the governor-generalship of Lord Dalhousie (1848–56). On the pretext of chronic misrule, Dalhousie annexed Awadh in 1856 (B1); and on the grounds that adopted heirs could not be recognized, the Maratha states of Satara (B2), Nagpur (B3) and Jhansi (B4) were all taken over. Berar was 'assigned' to the Company by the Nizam for the repayment of debt (B5).

Annexations beyond what the British could regard as the heartland of India, secured between 1765 and 1819, were ostensibly prompted by concern for stable frontiers. In the early nineteenth century the British fought wars to chastise those who appeared to be threatening the security of the northern and eastern boundaries of the Bengal Presidency. In each case territory was taken to protect the frontier for the future. On the north, after the Gurkha War of 1814–16, Kumaun and Garhwal were annexed (C1). To the east, the British expelled the Burmese from the Assam valley (C2), keeping it for themselves, and took the Burmese provinces of Arakan (C3) and Tenasserim (C4) in 1826.

The stakes on the company's western frontier were in every sense high ones during the first half of the nineteenth century. Not only were rich lands with huge populations involved, but from the later 1820s frontier policy was coming to be made with an eye to the movements of a potential European rival, the Russians. Eventually Sind was to be conquered in 1843 (D1), and the British were to be drawn into the first of the most bitterly contested of all their Indian wars in 1845, when they took on the Sikh army of the Punjab state. The first Sikh War ended in limited annexations (D2) and an attempt to construct a client state for the rest of the Punjab. This attempt collapsed in another ferocious war, which ended in the full annexation of the Punjab in 1849 (D3). There is no clear consensus among historians about the dynamic behind this powerful thrust to the north-west in the 1840s. The need for a secure frontier against the Russians, fear that a disintegrating Punjab state would destabilize much of British India, the search for commercial gain and the ambitions of individuals are all canvassed as potential explanations.

Mastery of the Punjab gave the British a north-western frontier that was to involve them in a long and painful process of demarcation and attempted pacification. Further significant additions of territory in the west were, however, at an end. This was not the case in the east. Fresh inroads were made into Burma with the seizure in 1852 of what was termed 'lower' Burma (E1). In 1885 the rest of the Burmese kingdom was declared to be annexed in an episode in which domestic British political calculations seem, for the first and last time, to have played a prominent role in an Indian war (E2). After 1885 the rulers of British India continued to nurture imperial ambitions from time to time in the Middle East or in Africa, but the expansion of their own immediate territory was virtually complete.

Revolt in India, 1857–1858

During 1857–8 large tracts of northern India were in armed revolt against British rule. Outside a few beleaguered strongholds, effective British control was broken from Delhi in the west to Patna in the east. The revolts began with a series of mutinies by the Indian soldiers or sepoys of the Bengal Army, the largest of the three elements of the East India Company's forces. Deep-seated fears among the soldiers of the Bengal Army about recent trends in British policy which appeared to threaten them crystallized around rumours that they would be subjected to ritual defilement through the use of cartridges greased with animal fat. Once the

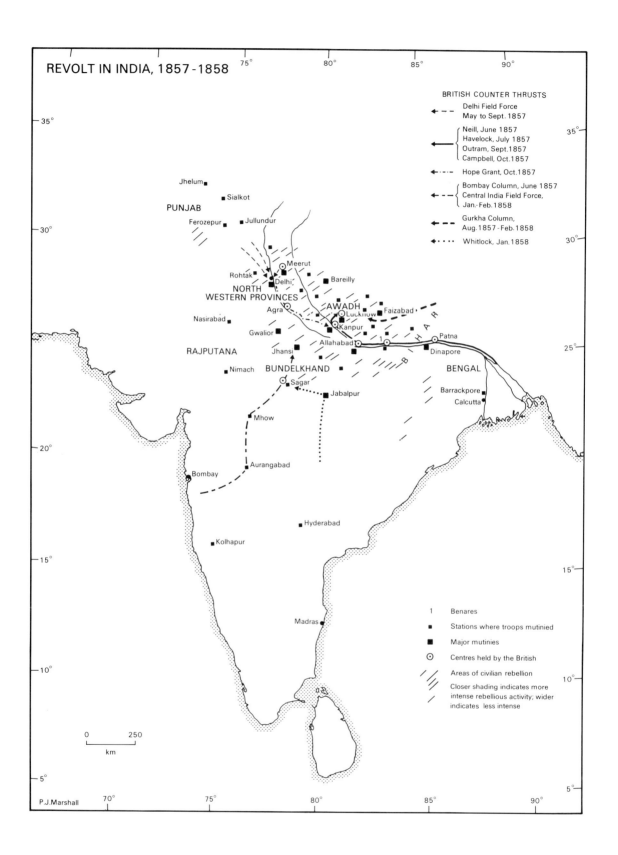

REVOLT IN INDIA, 1857-1858

BRITISH COUNTER THRUSTS

←--- Delhi Field Force
        May to Sept. 1857

←——— { Neill, June 1857
        Havelock, July 1857
        Outram, Sept. 1857
        Campbell, Oct. 1857

←-·-·- Hope Grant, Oct. 1857

←--- { Bombay Column, June 1857
        Central India Field Force,
        Jan.-Feb. 1858

←- - - Gurkha Column,
        Aug. 1857 - Feb. 1858

←···· Whitlock, Jan. 1858

Jhelum■

■ Sialkot

PUNJAB

Ferozepur■   ■ Jullundur

Rohtak■   ⊙ Meerut
        ◉ Delhi   ■ Bareilly

NORTH
WESTERN PROVINCES
            AWADH
Agra ⊙   ⊙ Lucknow   Faizabad
Nasirabad ■   ▲ Kanpur
    Gwalior ■   Allahabad ⊙   1   Patna ⊙
                                          Dinapore

RAJPUTANA
        Jhansi ⊙

■ Nimach   BUNDELKHAND   BENGAL

            Sagar ⊙
                    ···· Jabalpur   Barrackpore ■
                                      Calcutta ⊙

            ■ Mhow

                ■ Aurangabad

Bombay ●

            ■ Hyderabad

■ Kolhapur

                            1   Benares
                            ■   Stations where troops mutinied
                            ■   Major mutinies
                            ⊙   Centres held by the British
                            ///   Areas of civilian rebellion
                                     Closer shading indicates more
            Madras ●   intense rebellious activity; wider
                                     indicates less intense

0   250
└────┘
  km

P.J. Marshall

first major outbreak had taken place at Meerut in May 1857, mutinies spread throughout the cantonments of the Bengal Army, often, it would seem, in desperate attempts to pre-empt counteraction by the government.

In areas like the Punjab, where the soldiers got little support from the local population, mutiny was contained fairly easily. But in the belt between Delhi and Patna, large numbers of civilians joined in the uprising. The motives for civilian participation are now recognized to have been extremely complex. Often under some pressure, representatives of pre-British ruling dynasties, most significantly the imperial Mughal one, put themselves at the head of risings and became the symbols of the old order which the rebels sought to restore. At a lower level, landed notables disaffected towards the British were often important in sustaining revolt. Those civilians who actually took up arms against the government were for the most part the people of the countryside. In some places, like the recently annexed kingdom of Awadh, parts of western Bihar and areas in the north-western provinces, rural revolt was widespread. Those involved included groups who would resist any govern- ment when given the chance, the followers of disaffected leaders, men who came from the same areas and the same sections of society as the sepoys did, and a wide range of people with grievances against British rule. Generaliza- tions about a uniformly oppressive or reck- lessly modernizing regime which had alienated the great mass of its subjects have long ago been abandoned. Instead it is suggested that the impact of colonial rule had been uncertain and uneven. Some had gained from it, but many evidently felt that they had lost ground under the British. The military mutinies gave them the chance to try to recover what they believed that they had lost.

This chance did not last for long. With reinforcements of European troops, aided by contingents of the other armies from Bombay and Madras and by 'loyal' Sikhs from the Punjab and Gurkhas from Nepal, the British mounted their counter-attacks. At first, their main efforts were directed at recovering Delhi, the focus of the military revolt, and at relieving their garrison besieged in Lucknow, capital of Awadh. With the main rebel forces dis- persed, prolonged campaigns of 'pacification' followed.

The treaty ports of China and their opening to British trade, 1842–1860

Trading links with China were developed by the East India Company during the eighteenth century although they became confined to the port of Canton and were closely controlled by mandarin officials. China's tea and silk were the principal items of trade; British merchants sold woollens and later some cotton textiles in return, but throughout the century the Chinese required very little from Western industry. The expanding and highly lucrative trade in opium from Bengal to southern China after 1773, however, led by the 1830s to demands from the British trading houses for greater freedom in the China market and to the growth of a commercial lobby in London which pressed for a more assertive govern- ment policy on their behalf. When the Chinese authorities attempted to stamp out the drug trade by confiscating the cargoes of British merchants and demanding their withdrawal from Canton, the British government became drawn into a political dispute where inter- national reputation and domestic opinion prompted naval action. Defeat in the 'Opium Wars' of 1839–42 and 1856–60 forced China to open more of her ports to foreign traders and

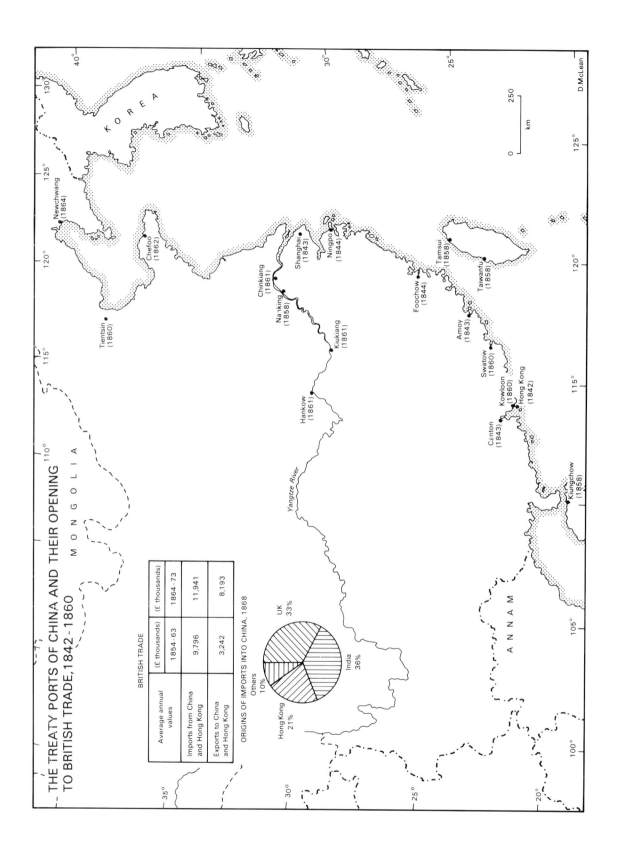

THE TREATY PORTS OF CHINA AND THEIR OPENING
TO BRITISH TRADE, 1842-1860

MONGOLIA

KOREA

ANNAM

Yangtze River

Newchwang (1864)

Chefoo (1862)

Tientsin (1860)

Chinkiang (1861)

Nanking (1858)

Shanghai (1843)

Ningpo (1844)

Tamsui (1858)

Taiwanfu (1858)

Foochow (1844)

Amoy (1843)

Kukiang (1861)

Hankow (1861)

Swatow (1860)

Kowloon (1860)

Hong Kong (1842)

Centon (1843)

Kiungchow (1858)

0   250   km

D.McLean

BRITISH TRADE

	(£ thousands) 1854-63	(£ thousands) 1864-73
Average annual values		
Imports from China and Hong Kong	9,796	11,941
Exports to China and Hong Kong	3,242	8,193

ORIGINS OF IMPORTS INTO CHINA, 1868

UK 33%

India 36%

Hong Kong 21%

Others 10%

to cede Hong Kong to Britain as a permanent trading base. Britain dominated the foreign trade of China in the nineteenth century, although, contrary to many expectations, China never became a major export market for British industries. In 1869, for example, £5 million worth of exports went to China out of a total British export value of £70 million; usually the ratio was less impressive. However, economic and naval power in the Far East gave Britain considerable political influence at the Chinese capital, Peking. Not until the 1880s and 1890s did the eastward expansion of Russia to the Pacific coast and the growth of trading competition from Germany, Japan and the United States cause any doubts to be raised about Britain's continued supremacy.

Britain's position in China, *c*. 1900

China's military defeat by Japan in 1895 revealed the extent of her decline and threw into question her ability to survive as a sovereign state. Alarmed by the possibility of a formal partition of the country between the foreign powers, the British government in 1898 agreed spheres of economic interest in China with her principal rivals, Russia and Germany, and thereby secured for British enterprise the prosperous Yangtze valley and most of southern China. In the late 1890s there was considerable competition among the European powers to acquire railway concessions from China as a means of confirming both political prestige and commercial preponderance. Although Britain's domi-nance in China was slowly declining in the decades before 1914, British shipping still carried the bulk of China's foreign trade over this period; British trade, via the thriving entrepôt of Hong Kong, remained important; and British financiers dominated the multinational banking consortia which financed bankrupt Chinese governments and ambitious railway schemes. China remained, however, of marginal importance to Britain's global economy. Only about 3 per cent of British exports went to China at the turn of the century, and approximately 4 per cent of the total British capital invested abroad by 1914 was invested in Chinese economic enterprise and China's international debt.

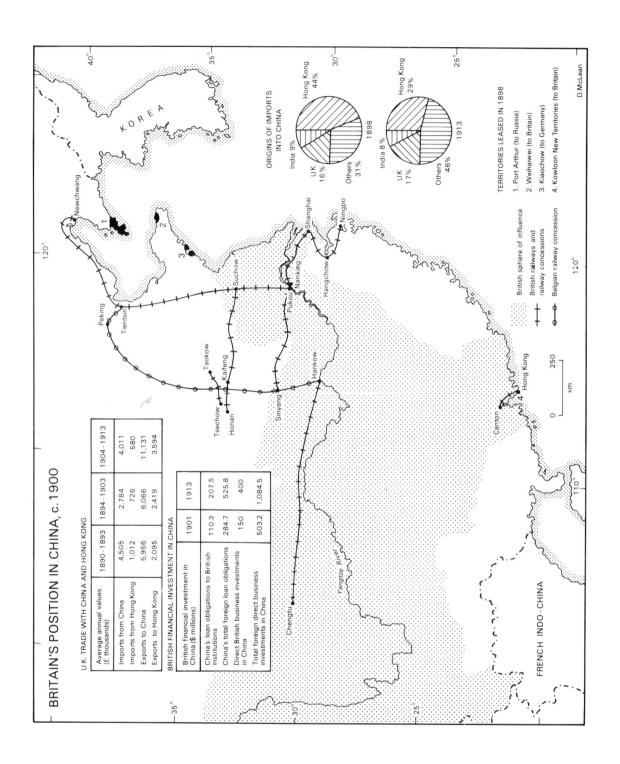

BRITAIN'S POSITION IN CHINA, c.1900

U.K. TRADE WITH CHINA AND HONG KONG

Average annual values (£ thousands)	1890-1893	1894-1903	1904-1913
Imports from China	4,505	2,784	4,011
Imports from Hong Kong	1,012	726	580
Exports to China	5,956	6,066	11,131
Exports to Hong Kong	2,095	2,419	3,594

BRITISH FINANCIAL INVESTMENT IN CHINA

British financial investment in China ($ millions)	1901	1913
China's loan obligations to British institutions	110.3	207.5
China's total foreign loan obligations	284.7	525.8
Direct British business investments in China	150	400
Total foreign direct business investments in China	503.2	1,084.5

ORIGINS OF IMPORTS INTO CHINA

Hong Kong 44%
India 9%
UK 16%
Others 31%
1898

Hong Kong 29%
India 8%
UK 17%
Others 46%
1913

TERRITORIES LEASED IN 1898
1. Port Arthur (to Russia)
2. Weihaiwei (to Britain)
3. Kiaochow (to Germany)
4. Kowloon New Territories (to Britain)

British sphere of influence
British railways and railway concessions
Belgian railway concession

KOREA

Newchwang
Peking
Tientsin
Taokow
Tsechow
Honan
Kaifeng
Suchow
Sinyang
Hankow
Chengtu
Yangtze River
Nanking
Pukou
Hangchow
Shanghai
Ningpo
Canton
Hong Kong

FRENCH INDO-CHINA

0   250
km

D.McLean

Britain in south-east Asia, 1824–1914

Early territorial advances in the region were largely determined by the needs of India and considerations of European diplomacy. The ill-defined frontier between Bengal and Burma aggravated Anglo-Burmese relations. War in 1824 led to the Treaty of Yandabo (1826) by which Burma ceded Arakan and Tenasserim, recognized East India Company control over Assam and Manipur and was required to pay a crippling indemnity (£1 million) and to exchange envoys with Calcutta. Continuing tension plus commercial pressure resulted in Dalhousie's war of 1852 by which Rangoon and the rice bowl of Lower Burma were added to company possessions. Like the kings of Siam, who were bending before the wind of western imperialism by concluding free trade treaties (e.g. the Bowring Treaty of 1855) and surrendering peripheral territories to the British and French, Mindon Min tried to retain the independence of 'Burma proper'. However, it could not long survive in its truncated form; British interest in teak, rubies and the route to south-west China, together with unease about French ambitions, led to the conquest of Mandalay (1885), deposition of King Thibaw, annexation of Upper Burma and the incongruous attachment of the whole country to the government of India in 1886 (see p. 90).

Meanwhile in the archipelago (see p. 101) the Company acquired Penang (1786) as a base for the China trade. Raffles's settlement of Singapore (1819) worried those who sought Dutch support in Europe against a French revival; but Singapore's rapid commercial progress convinced doubters of its value, and Anglo-Dutch differences were patched up by the Treaty of London (1824), whereby the Company exchanged Benkulen for Malacca and the region was partitioned into two spheres of influence. In 1826 Penang (with Province Wellesley), Malacca and Singapore became a single administrative unit, the Straits Settlements, but after the loss of its China trade monopoly (1833) the Company lost interest in the Straits. The resentful commercial community campaigned for the transfer of the Settlements from the government of India to the Colonial Office, which eventually occurred in 1867. Anxiety about the 'turbulent frontier' with the Malay states, interest in the tin-mining potential of the interior and, in particular, fear that another power might seize the opportunity to intervene in the British sphere all convinced the Liberal government of the need to pacify the west coast Malay states. By the Pangkor Engagement with Perak chiefs (January 1874) the 'advisory' or 'residential' system was introduced and subsequently spread to other sultanates. The inauguration of the Federated Malay States (1896) marked Britain's real control and also the area's economic importance, seen first in tin-mining and, from the mid-1890s, rubber cultivation. Wary of creeping centralization, the five states that later accepted British Advisers studiously avoided incorporation within the FMS.

In 1841 James Brooke, having assisted in the suppression of a rebellion in Sarawak, was appointed its governor by the Sultan of Brunei (see p. 98). Fully sovereign (or Raja) in 1846, James and his successor Charles (reigned 1868–1917) dug deeper into the withering Brunei kingdom, although their Sarawak regime was always financially precarious. Further north, the North Borneo Company won concessions from the sultans of Brunei and Sulu, and a charter from the crown (1881), and pursued a 'gambling style of government'. The island of Labuan was acquired as a coaling station by London in 1846, but the British government did not intervene further in the affairs of Borneo until concern lest freelance imperialism unsettle international relations induced London to establish protectorates over Brunei, North

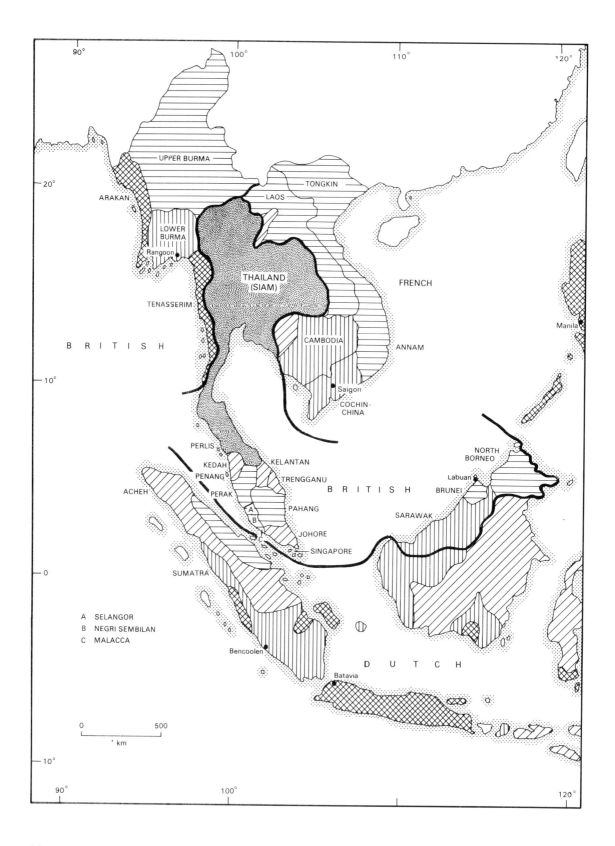

UPPER BURMA

ARAKAN

LOWER
BURMA

Rangoon

TENASSERIM

B R I T I S H

PERLIS

KEDAH
PENANG

PERAK

ACHEH

A SELANGOR
B NEGRI SEMBILAN
C MALACCA

SUMATRA

Bencoolen

Batavia

0   500

˙ km

LAOS

TONGKIN

THAILAND
(SIAM)

FRENCH

CAMBODIA

ANNAM

Saigon

COCHIN-
CHINA

KELANTAN

TRENGGANU

B R I T I S H

PAHANG

A
B

JOHORE

SINGAPORE

MANILA

Manila

NORTH
BORNEO

Labuan

BRUNEI

SARAWAK

D U T C H

90°   100°   110°   120°

20°

10°

0

10°

98

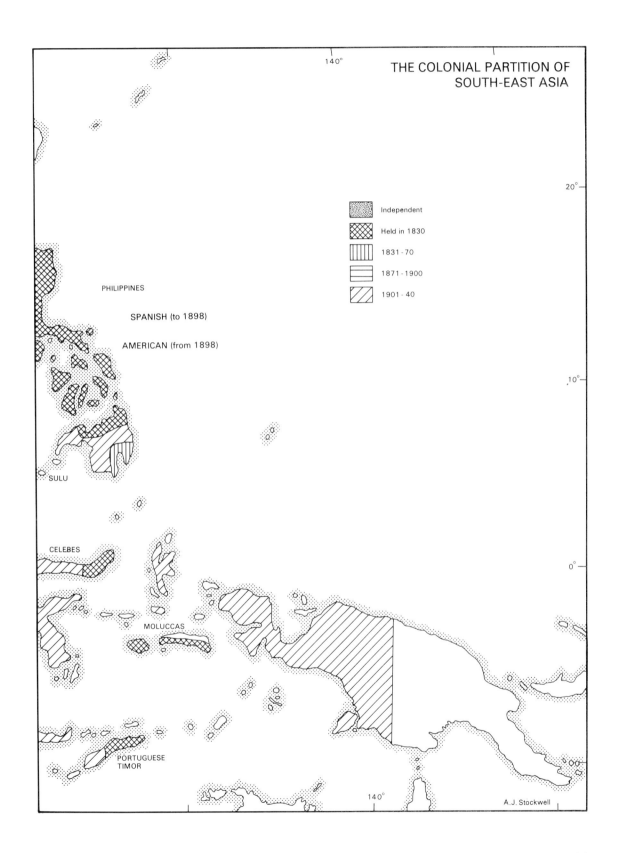

THE COLONIAL PARTITION OF
SOUTH-EAST ASIA

Independent

Held in 1830

1831 - 70

1871 - 1900

1901 - 40

PHILIPPINES

SPANISH (to 1898)

AMERICAN (from 1898)

SULU

CELEBES

MOLUCCAS

PORTUGUESE
TIMOR

140°

20°

10°

0°

140°

A.J. Stockwell

99

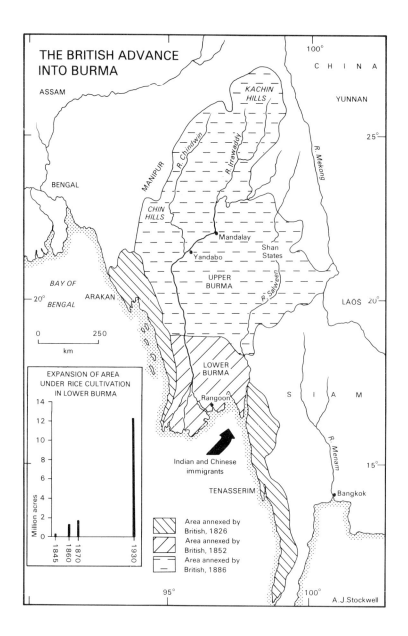

THE BRITISH ADVANCE
INTO BURMA

EXPANSION OF AREA
UNDER RICE CULTIVATION
IN LOWER BURMA

Area annexed by
British, 1826

Area annexed by
British, 1852

Area annexed by
British, 1886

A.J.Stockwell

Borneo and Sarawak (1888). Brunei's total
disappearance was prevented by the appointment of a British Resident there in 1906 and,
from the 1930s, the development of oil.

On the eve of the First World War, British
territorial responsibilities in south-east Asia
embraced Burma as part of the Indian empire
and a melange of dependencies in the Malay
world more or less under the control, or at least
supervision, of the governor/high commissioner in Singapore.

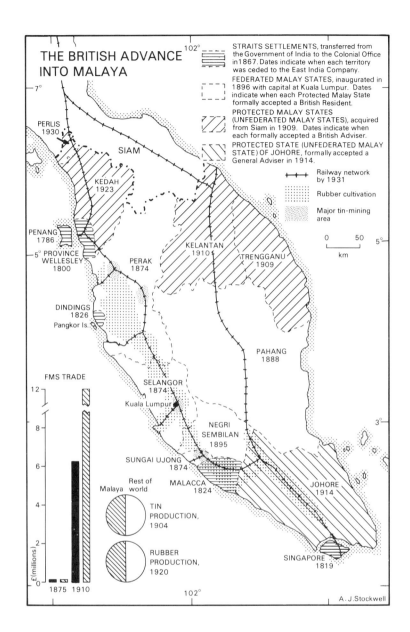

THE BRITISH ADVANCE INTO MALAYA

STRAITS SETTLEMENTS, transferred from the Government of India to the Colonial Office in 1867. Dates indicate when each territory was ceded to the East India Company.

FEDERATED MALAY STATES, inaugurated in 1896 with capital at Kuala Lumpur. Dates indicate when each Protected Malay State formally accepted a British Resident.

PROTECTED MALAY STATES (UNFEDERATED MALAY STATES), acquired from Siam in 1909. Dates indicate when each formally accepted a British Adviser.

PROTECTED STATE (UNFEDERATED MALAY STATE) OF JOHORE, formally accepted a General Adviser in 1914.

╫╫╫ Railway network by 1931

Rubber cultivation

Major tin-mining area

0   50
km

SIAM

PERLIS 1930
KEDAH 1923
PENANG 1786
PROVINCE WELLESLEY 1800
PERAK 1874
DINDINGS 1826
Pangkor Is.
KELANTAN 1910
TRENGGANU 1909
PAHANG 1888
SELANGOR 1874
Kuala Lumpur
NEGRI SEMBILAN 1895
SUNGAI UJONG 1874
MALACCA 1824
JOHORE 1914
SINGAPORE 1819

FMS TRADE

£(millions)
12
8
6
4
2
0
1875 1910

TIN PRODUCTION, 1904
Rest of
Malaya world

RUBBER PRODUCTION, 1920

A. J. Stockwell

Britain in the Middle East before 1914

Britain's interest in the Middle East was predominantly political. Afghanistan, Persia and the region of the Persian Gulf were viewed by British officials primarily as outer defences for the frontiers of India against the threat posed by Russia's territorial advance across central Asia in the late eighteenth and nineteenth centuries. Commercial interests existed, mostly in the Persian Gulf, but these were of negligible value when set in the context of Britain's

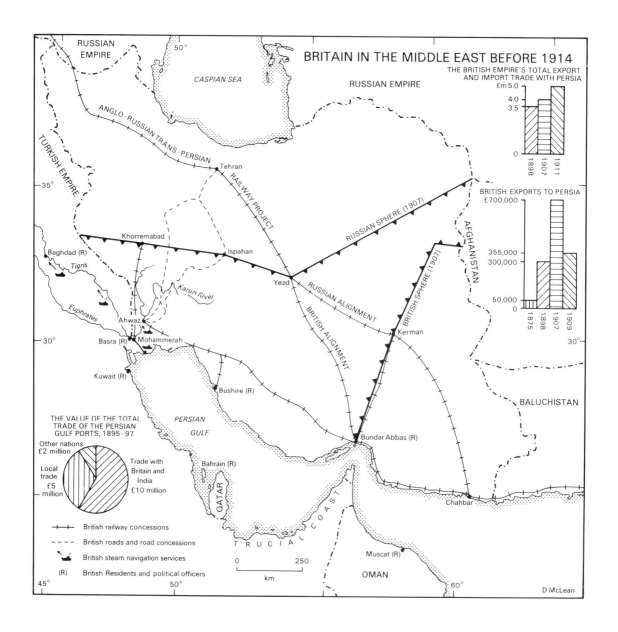

BRITAIN IN THE MIDDLE EAST BEFORE 1914

THE BRITISH EMPIRE'S TOTAL EXPORT
AND IMPORT TRADE WITH PERSIA
£m 5.0
4.0
3.5
0
1898 1907 1911

BRITISH EXPORTS TO PERSIA
£700,000

355,000
300,000

50,000
0
1875 1898 1907 1909

RUSSIAN EMPIRE

CASPIAN SEA

RUSSIAN EMPIRE

ANGLO-RUSSIAN TRANS-PERSIAN RAILWAY PROJECT

Tehran

TURKISH EMPIRE

RUSSIAN SPHERE (1907)

AFGHANISTAN

Baghdad (R)

Tigris

Khorremabad

Ispahan

Yezd RUSSIAN ALIGNMENT

BRITISH SPHERE (1907)

Karun River

Euphrates

BRITISH ALIGNMENT

Kerman

Ahwaz

Basra (R) Mohammerah

Kuwait (R)

Bushire (R)

BALUCHISTAN

PERSIAN GULF

Bundar Abbas (R)

THE VALUE OF THE TOTAL
TRADE OF THE PERSIAN
GULF PORTS, 1895-97

Other nations
£2 million

Local
trade
£5
million

Trade with
Britain and
India
£10 million

Bahrain (R)

QATAR

TRUCIAL COAST

Chahbar

Muscat (R)

OMAN

+—+—+ British railway concessions

- - - - British roads and road concessions

British steam navigation services

(R) British Residents and political officers

0   250
km

D.McLean

international trading system. In the Gulf, naval actions against pirates and close relations with the local Arab rulers kept the sea lanes clear for British commerce and maintained a visible political presence. By the end of the nineteenth century diplomatic tension between Britain and Russia increasingly focused on Persia, where the bankruptcy of the regime and its deteriorating political authority in the country led both powers to consider the consequences of its disintegration. After decades of international rivalry, in 1907 Britain and Russia agreed spheres of influence in Persia; this agreement gave the Indian authorities the security they needed in the southeast of the country. But British ambitions went further than that. Although it was acknowledged that the region around the Persian Gulf was militarily indefensible, the British and Indian governments tried to build up strong economic control in the south of Persia by supporting local road and rail concessions and subsidizing shipping services. These, it was hoped, could prevent any gradual penetration of the region by Russia and forestall the strategic disaster of a Russian foothold on the Persian Gulf. The British, in fact, were remarkably successful. The Gulf remained a British preserve; in 1902, for instance, 90 per cent of the shipping in its waters flew the British flag; British financial interests acquired virtually all economic concessions; and even Persia's customs revenues from its southern ports were tied to securing British loans to the government in Tehran. In 1908 a British syndicate struck oil in southern Persia, and a major new economic stake in the area rapidly developed. By 1914 thirty wells had been drilled, and the refineries at Abadan were exporting nearly 250,000 tons of oil per annum. The British government effectively prevented a joint Anglo-Russian trans-Persian railway project to which the Russian government, and some British financiers, attached importance. Protracted disagreement about the proposed route across southern Persia meant that no progress had been made by 1914, and the military authorities in India could therefore rest assured that any advance of Russian forces towards the Indian frontier would not be facilitated by modern lines of communication. In 1915 the Russian government conceded a free hand to Britain in central and southern Persia. (For Egypt, see p. 110.)

British expansion in West Africa: the Gambia and Sierra Leone, 1820–1914

Official British interest in the Windward Coast of West Africa centred originally on the campaign against the slave trade, following its abolition by Britain in 1807. Freetown, occupied in 1787, became a crown colony in 1808, and Sierra Leone was thereafter the centre of the Royal Navy's campaign against the slave trade in West Africa. The Isles de Los were occupied in 1818 as an anti-slaving base, while the settlement of liberated slaves into villages around Freetown led to the growth of Sierra Leone out of its original nucleus. The signing of anti-slaving treaties with interior rulers and attacks on slavers, like that in the Gallinas in 1840, entangled the British government deeply in the politics of the Sierra Leonian area.

Trade was the other, though lesser, motivation for British involvement on the coast. James Island, occupied by traders since 1618, and Bathurst, established in 1816, became the Colony of the Gambia in 1821, with its wax and hide trades the focus of British interest. MacCarthy's Island was added in 1823 and Albreda in 1857. The growth in the groundnut and palm-oil trades accompanied the spread of large numbers of Creole traders from Freetown along the coast and into the interior. Sherbro was annexed in 1861, while the activities of Sierra Leonian traders led to Bulama and the mouths of the Scarcies and Mellacourie being regarded as British spheres.

For all its increasing involvement, the British government remained reluctant to sanction expansion. Even the growth of the French colony in Senegal in the 1850s and 1860s – with the creation of a series of posts up the Senegal River and the establishment of a presence on the Mellacourie, Pongos and Nunez in 1865 – had little effect on British policy. In the 1860s the first of a number of proposals was considered to exchange the Gambia for French territory on the Ivory Coast.

This was to change in the mid-1870s as Anglo-French rivalry became more acute

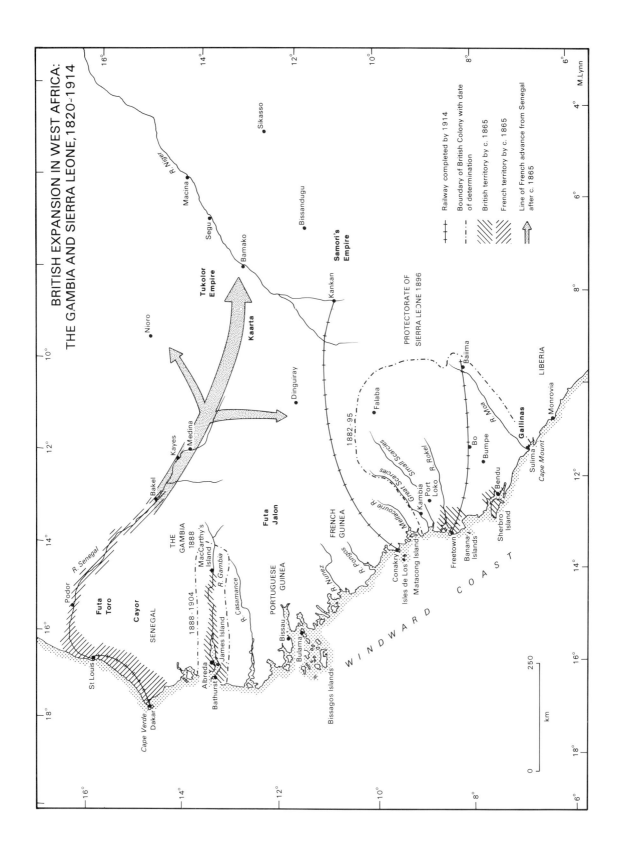

BRITISH EXPANSION IN WEST AFRICA:
THE GAMBIA AND SIERRA LEONE, 1820-1914

Railway completed by 1914
Boundary of British Colony with date
of determination
British territory by c. 1865
French territory by c. 1865
Line of French advance from Senegal
after c. 1865

M.Lynn

Sikasso

R. Niger

Macina

Bissandugu

Segu

Bamako

Kankan

Samori's
Empire

Tukolor
Empire

Kaarta

Nioro

PROTECTORATE OF
SIERRA LEONE 1896

Dinguiray

Baiima

1882-95

LIBERIA

Falaba

Kayes

Medina

R. Moa

Bakel

Bo

Bumpe

Kambia
Port
Loko

R. Rokel

Sulima

Cape Mount

Gallinas

Monrovia

R. Senegal

Futa
Jalon

Great Scarcies

Small Scarcies

Bendu

Sherbro
Island

Freetown

Banana
Islands

Podor

THE GAMBIA
1888

FRENCH
GUINEA

Mellacourie R.

Conakry

Isles de Los

Matacong Island

Futa
Toro

Cayor

MacCarthy's
Island

R. Gambia

R. Pongos

R. Nunez

SENEGAL

1888-1904

James Island

R. Casamance

St Louis

Albreda

Bathurst

PORTUGUESE
GUINEA

Bissau

Bulama

Cape Verde.

Dakar

Bissagos Islands

WINDWARD COAST

km

250

0

km

throughout West Africa. Disputes over river navigation rights, clashes over Matacong in 1877 and talk of a railway to link Senegal, the Niger and Algeria were allied to growing fears of French expansion on the Senegal and Upper Niger. Behind this lay increasing commercial tension, with a slump in commodity prices, internal unrest among the interior states disrupting trade to the coast, shifts in caravan routes following the emergence of Samori and fears of French tariffs, such as were imposed on the Mellacourie in 1880. The decline in customs revenue, consequent on the disruption in Sierra Leone's trade, loomed large in the calculations of local officials and provided a spur for expansion which Whitehall found difficult to resist.

French expansion after 1880 was dramatic. In 1883 Bamako was occupied and in 1887 Conakry. The years 1890–3 saw the conquest of the Tukolor Empire, and with the capture of Samori in 1898 most of the western Sudan had passed into French hands. The British response to this was essentially defensive, aiming to protect existing settlements rather than create new ones. The interior of the Gambia was occupied in 1887–8; a treaty with France in 1889 delineated the colony's boundaries. Similarly measures were taken to occupy the interior of Sierra Leone. In 1879 the Scarcies were occupied and the colony's western border settled in 1882; a treaty of 1886 settled the eastern border with Liberia. In the early 1890s British jurisdiction was slowly extended over the hinterland; in 1896 the Protectorate of Sierra Leone was declared and a railway from the coast begun. Resistance was strong, however, and it was only after the defeat of the 'Hut Tax Rising' of 1898 that British rule was established, with varying degrees of effectiveness, over the interior.

British expansion in West Africa: the Gold Coast and Nigeria, 1840–1914

Despite a brief period administering the Gold Coast trading forts (1821–8), the British government had no colonial possessions in this part of West Africa in 1840. Yet Britain was none the less becoming deeply involved in the area, partly because of its anti-slave-trade commitments and partly because of the economic importance of West Africa following the development of the palm-oil trade from the Niger delta. The campaign against the slave trade, with attacks on slaving areas, the signing and enforcement of anti-slave-trade treaties and the launching of the 1841 Niger expedition, took on a new emphasis after 1840. The problems of trading disputes, endemic in the oil trade, led to the appointment of a consul for the Bights of Benin and Biafra in 1849 and his subsequent involvement in the politics of the Niger coast. In 1851 Lagos was seized, and the resulting entanglement in the Yoruba wars of the interior led to its becoming a colony in 1861 and to its piecemeal expansion thereafter. On the Niger, government expeditions in 1854 and 1857 were followed by the creation of a consulate at Lokoja (1866–9). Throughout, the problem was that maintaining Britain's interests at a time of great transition in African society involved Britain more and more deeply in local politics.

Similar processes occurred on the Gold Coast. Problems over the extent of British jurisdiction led to the take-over of the British forts in 1843 and, through the signing of a series of agreements ('bonds'), to the establishment of a quasi-protectorate over the Fante: a commitment which brought Britain into conflict with the Asante. War with Asante in 1863 and 1873–4 led to the declaration of the Gold Coast Colony in 1874.

Proposals were repeatedly made to reduce

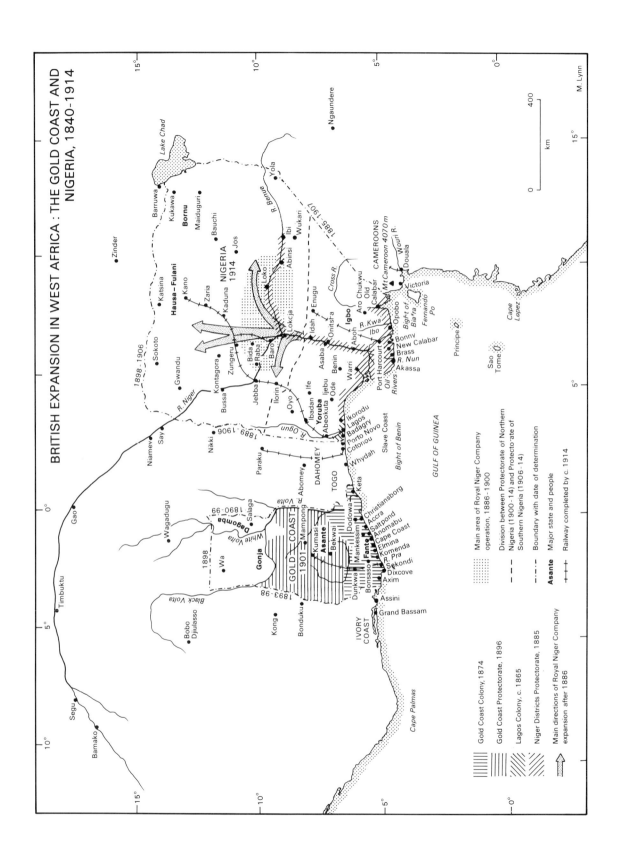

BRITISH EXPANSION IN WEST AFRICA : THE GOLD COAST AND
NIGERIA, 1840-1914

M. Lynn

Main area of Royal Niger Company
operation, 1886 - 1900

Division between Protectorate of Northern
Nigeria (1900 - 14) and Protectorate of
Southern Nigeria (1906 - 14)

Boundary with date of determination

Asante Major state and people

Railway completed by c. 1914

Gold Coast Colony, 1874

Gold Coast Protectorate, 1896

Lagos Colony, c. 1865

Niger Districts Protectorate, 1885

Main directions of Royal Niger Company
expansion after 1886

Britain's involvement in West Africa – most notably by a House of Commons committee in 1865 – but local circumstances meant that in practice Britain was too deeply entangled to withdraw. From the mid-1870s, indeed, new pressures to expand developed. Deteriorating Anglo-French relations, with clashes over the Slave Coast and lower Niger and fears about French expansion from Senegal, were to combine with increasing problems in the oil trade. Commodity price falls and clashes with delta middlemen led a number of British traders to urge government action. Following the German seizure of the Cameroons and Togo in 1884 and the subsequent Berlin West Africa Conference, the Niger Districts Protectorate was declared in 1885 (renamed Oil Rivers Protectorate from 1891, Niger Coast Protectorate from 1893). In 1886 the Royal Niger Company – an amalgam of several British trading companies – was established with a charter to defend British interests on the middle Niger.

For the British government it was hoped that this might mark an end to expansion in West Africa. However, expansion now had a momentum of its own. The threat posed by French expansion in the western Sudan after 1890 and in Dahomey in 1892, and continuing problems in Britain's political and trading relations with Asante, Yorubaland and the delta, meant that a further burst of expansion was to occur.

Britain occupied Asante in 1896 and, having crushed an Asante rising in 1900, annexed the Gold Coast in 1901. In 1893, as the Yoruba wars petered out, Yorubaland was taken over. In the delta, the removal of Jaja of Opobo in 1887 and Nana of the Itsekiri in 1894 marked a push to make British rule a reality, a move that culminated in the conquest of Benin in 1897. The Protectorate of Southern Nigeria was established in 1900, and with the Aro Chukwu expedition of 1901 the conquest of Igboland was begun.

An Anglo-French convention of 1898 completed the partitioning of West Africa. For the British, however, there still remained the conquest of the Sokoto caliphate, a process begun by the Royal Niger Company attacks on Ilorin and Bida in 1897. Following the government's take-over of the Company and the establishment of the Protectorate of Northern Nigeria in 1900, the caliphate was conquered by 1906. In 1914 the protectorates of Northern and Southern Nigeria were unified into the Protectorate of Nigeria.

British expansion in East Africa, c. 1840–c. 1900

British interest in East Africa initially centred on Zanzibar, which, with its growing slave trade, was both the entrepôt for a network of trading routes stretching deep into the African interior, and the focus of trade with the Persian Gulf and Bombay, much of it organized by Indian merchants, of whom many were British subjects. In 1841 a British consul was appointed to the island.

British interest in the mainland developed from the 1840s. Ludwig Krapf, from 1844, was the first of a number of missionaries and travellers pushing into the interior over the next thirty years. John Speke was the first European to reach Lake Victoria (1858) and the source of the White Nile (1862). From 1866 David Livingstone undertook the last of his great journeys – around Lakes Nyasa and Tanganyika – dying at Chitambo's in 1873. Other travellers like Stanley, Baker, Grant and Cameron successfully delineated the major features of the Great Lakes during the 1860s and 1870s (see p. 79).

For the British government, however, interest in the area began and ended in Zanzibar, with official policy committed to supporting

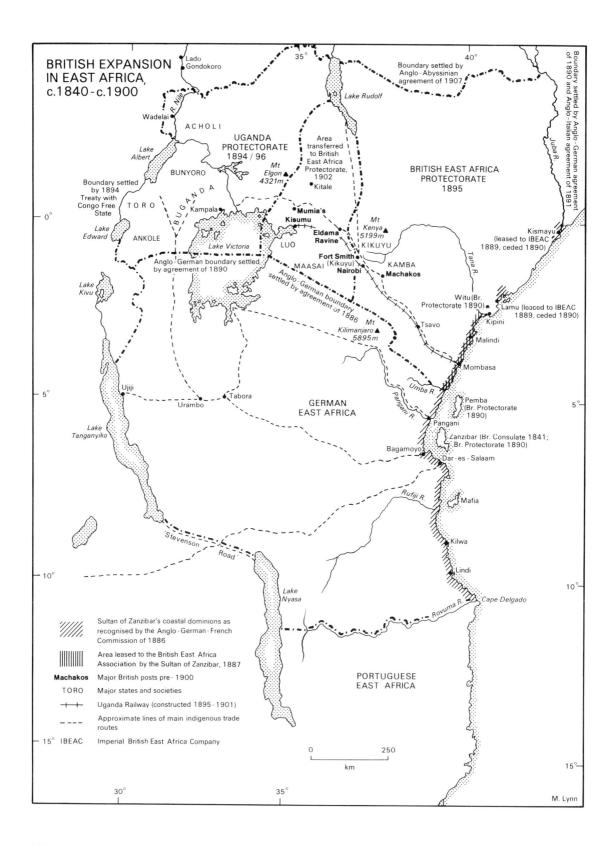

BRITISH EXPANSION
IN EAST AFRICA,
c.1840 - c.1900

Lado
Gondokoro

R. Nile
Wadelai
ACHOLI

Lake
Albert
BUNYORO
TORO

UGANDA
PROTECTORATE
1894/96

Boundary settled
by 1894
Treaty with
Congo Free
State

Lake
Edward
ANKOLE

BUGANDA
Kampala

Lake Victoria

Boundary settled by Anglo - Abyssinian
agreement of 1907

Lake Rudolf

Mt
Elgon
4321m
Kitale

Area
transferred
to British
East Africa
Protectorate,
1902

BRITISH EAST AFRICA
PROTECTORATE
1895

Boundary settled by Anglo - German agreement
of 1890 and Anglo - Italian agreement of 1891

Juba R.

Mumia's
Kisumu
Eldama
Ravine

LUO

Mt
Kenya
5199m
KIKUYU

Kismayu
(leased to IBEAC
1889, ceded 1890)

Anglo - German boundary settled
by agreement of 1890

Fort Smith
(Kikuyu)
Nairobi

MAASAI

Anglo - German boundary
settled by agreement of 1886

KAMBA
Machakos

Tana R.

Witu (Br.
Protectorate 1890)

Lamu (leased to IBEAC
1889, ceded 1890)
Kipini

Lake
Kivu

Mt
Kilimanjaro
5895m

Tsavo

Malindi

Umba R.

Mombasa

Lake
Kivu

Ujiji
Urambo

Tabora

GERMAN
EAST AFRICA

Pangani R.

Pemba
(Br. Protectorate
1890)

Pangani

Lake
Tanganyika

Bagamoyo

Zanzibar (Br. Consulate 1841;
Br. Protectorate 1890)

Dar - es - Salaam

Stevenson

Road

Rufiji R.

Mafia

Lake
Nyasa

Kilwa

Lindi

Rovuma R.
Cape Delgado

Sultan of Zanzibar's coastal dominions as
recognised by the Anglo - German - French
Commission of 1886

Area leased to the British East Africa
Association by the Sultan of Zanzibar, 1887

PORTUGUESE
EAST AFRICA

Machakos   Major British posts pre - 1900

TORO   Major states and societies

╫   Uganda Railway (constructed 1895 - 1901)

- - -   Approximate lines of main indigenous trade
routes

IBEAC   Imperial British East Africa Company

0   250
km

M. Lynn

108

the sultan's position in East Africa. It was only in the 1880s that this began to change when European diplomatic realignments, along with the British occupation of Egypt (1882), gave new urgency to control of the Nile and the East African interior. In 1884 the activities of Carl Peters and the Society for German Colonization, subsequently endorsed by Bismarck, raised the spectre of German intervention and a clash with British interests. In 1886, however, Britain and Germany settled their differences, signing an agreement which divided East Africa into two spheres of interest along a border drawn between the Umba River and Lake Victoria. In addition an Anglo-German-French commission delineated the Sultan of Zanzibar's mainland possessions along a ten-mile coastal strip.

Yet old attitudes died hard, for the British government still remained reluctant to become involved on the mainland. It was left to a private venture, Sir William Mackinnon's British East African Association, to occupy the British sphere. In 1887 Mackinnon obtained the lease of the sultan's coastal territories north of the Umba River; in 1888 the Association was granted a charter as the Imperial British East Africa Company.

It was the position of Buganda, ignored by the 1886 agreement, which ended the British government's reluctance to intervene inland. A complex mixture of missionary and business interests with European diplomatic considerations, and Britain's decision to continue her

occupation of Egypt, led to further activity in the area by Peters and to the Anglo-German agreement of July 1890. The partition of East Africa was completed. In return for Heligoland in the North Sea, Germany recognized a British protectorate over Zanzibar and the extension of the 1886 boundary due west across Lake Victoria, thereby giving Britain control over Buganda and the source of the Nile. In December, Captain Lugard, on behalf of Mackinnon's company, signed a treaty of protection with the Kabaka of Buganda.

The old British policy in East Africa was at an end, and the 1890s were to see Britain consolidating her position in the area. Buganda was still the key. When the Company collapsed, it was bought out, and a British protectorate over Buganda was declared in 1894; in 1896 this was extended to Buganda's neighbours. In order to sustain the new protectorate the Uganda Railway from Mombasa was begun in 1895 and the Protectorate of British East Africa established over the territory between Uganda and the sea. Large numbers of European settlers and Indian traders and labourers began to flock in with the railway. Yet in 1895, although partition had been completed, conquest had hardly begun. In the same year a widespread rising by the Mazrui of the coast occurred, and the full-scale 'pacification' of British East Africa was only to be completed in the decade after 1900.

Britain, Egypt and the Sudan, 1870–1914

British interest in Egypt sprang from pre-occupation with routes to India and from Britain's growing stake in Mediterranean and eastern trade; already marked by 1840, it grew especially after the Suez Canal opened in 1869. It was heightened by suspicion of Russian designs on Turkey and French ambition in North Africa and the Levant. After 1870 these

economic ties and strategic concerns became linked to political and territorial control.

Despite heavy investment, much of Egypt's economy remained inefficient and unproductive, and foreign loans were wasted on imperial fantasies, as Khedive Ismail tried to subdue the southern and western Sudan and Abyssinia. In 1875 Egypt was virtually

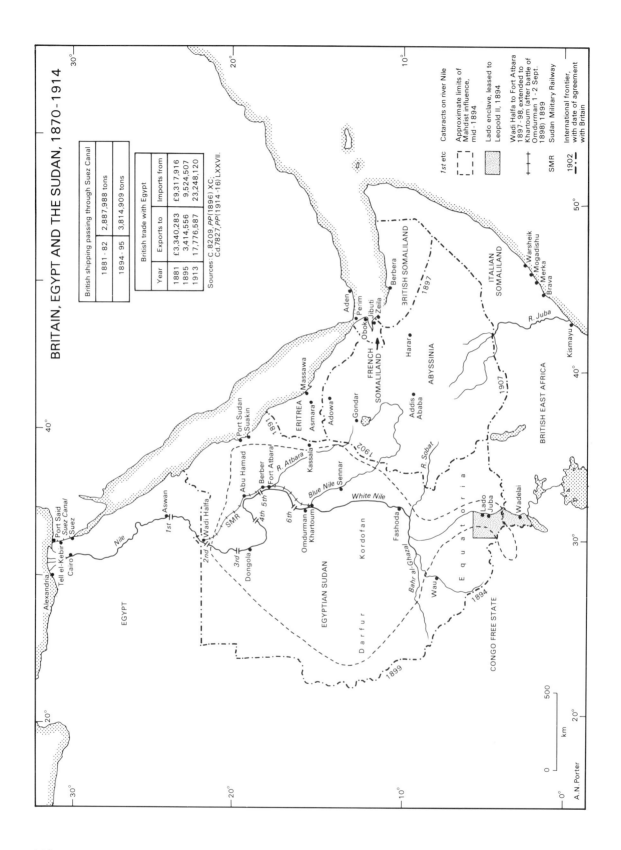

BRITAIN, EGYPT AND THE SUDAN, 1870-1914

British shipping passing through Suez Canal

| 1881-82 | 2,887,988 tons |
| 1894-95 | 3,814,909 tons |

British trade with Egypt

Year	Exports to	Imports from
1881	£3,340,283	£9,317,916
1895	3,414,556	9,524,507
1913	17,776,587	23,248,120

Sources: C.8209,*PP*(1896) XC;
Cd.7827,*PP*(1914-16) LXXVII.

1st etc	Cataracts on river Nile
	Approximate limits of Mahdist influence, mid-1894
	Lado enclave, leased to Leopold II, 1894
	Wadi Halfa to Fort Atbara 1897-98, extended to Khartoum (after battle of Omdurman 1-2 Sept. 1898) 1899
SMR	Sudan Military Railway
1902	International frontier, with date of agreement with Britain

A.N.Porter

bankrupt and deeply indebted to Britain and France; Disraeli took advantage of the Khedive's embarrassment to purchase his Suez Canal shares. During 1876, believing Egypt's collapse would benefit hardly anyone, Britain and France established international control over her finances to manage debt repayments and restore solvency. This intervention and internal economic crisis provoked unrest and political conflict, to which Britain finally responded by bombarding Alexandria (11 July 1882), invading the country and defeating the 'nationalists' under Urabi at Tell el-Kebir (13 September).

Gladstone's government intended to restore 'order' and retire gracefully, but events in the south made this impossible. From 1881 Sudanese revolt spread outwards from Kordofan, provoked by Egyptian rule and inflamed by the Islamic revivalism of the Mahdi. Sudanese defeat of an Egyptian army under Hicks at Omdurman in September 1883, and General Gordon's stubborn mishandling of withdrawal resulting in his death at Khartoum (26 January 1885), created the appearance of a rout. While economic necessity dictated Egypt's abandonment of the Sudan, the circumstances of withdrawal left her vulnerable to the confident, hostile Mahdist state.

Egyptian rulers remained legally self-governing, under the nominal suzerainty of the Turkish sultan at Constantinople. In reality they not only relied on British backing but endured the administrative supervision of Britain's consul-general (Sir Evelyn Baring, later Lord Cromer, 1883–1907) and numerous expatriate officials. Although solvency was restored by 1889, Egypt's political reliability still seemed far off to British governments. Withdrawal also became less likely after 1884 because France, resenting Britain's influence, along with Italy and Leopold's Congo developed expansionist ambitions in the east and south. Only Germany in 1890 recognized a British sphere of interest on the Upper Nile. Anglo-Italian and Anglo-Congolese agreements (March 1891 and May 1894) contributed little to fixing Sudanese frontiers; leasing the Lado enclave to Leopold II was proof of weakness rather than evidence of friendship. As the development of European alliances increased Britain's insecurity, Egypt's strategic importance to her grew. To forestall threats from the Upper Nile, Lord Salisbury's Cabinet, having already decided to build the Uganda Railway, reluctantly embarked in March 1896 on reconquering the Sudan. Italy was checked for forty years when Abyssinia overwhelmed her troops at Adowa (1 March 1896); after victory at Atbara (8 April 1898), Kitchener finally defeated the Mahdists at Omdurman (2 September 1898); and Britain's determined advance, linked to Salisbury's conciliation of Russia and Germany, persuaded France to retreat from Fashoda (October–November 1898) rather than face war.

Omdurman and Fashoda made possible an Anglo-Egyptian condominium over the Sudan. Frontiers were agreed, rapidly with France in the Anglo-French declaration of 21 March 1899, more slowly with Abyssinia (May 1902) and Leopold II (May 1906). Policy-making was dominated by British officials, but administrative control in the south was hardly more effective than Egypt's in the 1870s. In Egypt itself Britain's officials struggled to contain nationalist discontent. They eventually abandoned pretence in response to Turkey's declaration of war, by pronouncing Egypt a formal protectorate on 18 December 1914.

Britain and the partition of South Africa, 1854–1910

The settlements of 1852–4 (see p. 84) increased the independent white governments to four, and in 1859 Britain apparently confirmed its lack of interest in the interior by rejecting the Cape governor's federal plans. However, this was of no lasting significance. The idea that South Africa's future lay with a single political authority steadily gained ground in response to political and economic conflicts between the states, the growth of the regional economy and the intervention of foreign powers.

Colonial expansiveness was unabated, fed by the mixed motives of governments wanting saleable public lands and taxable resources, whites anxious for farms or land as a speculation, public works departments and private employers desperate at all times for African labour at ever lower wages, and a preoccupation with security arising from the resentments caused by such pressures on the black communities. In the south-east the colonial take-over proceeded as the Cape and Natal steadily claimed the territories between the Keiskamma and Umzimkulu rivers. Elsewhere, however, the imperial government was either unable or unwilling to stand aloof. The Free State's wars with the Sotho over eastern lands in the 1860s led to the imperial annexation of Basutoland in 1868, followed by an abortive period of Cape administration (1871–84) and finally imperial repossession. In 1871 the imperial high commissioner annexed Griqualand West, also coveted by the Free State both for its land and for the recently discovered diamond fields. Britain also acted in 1871, 1881 and 1884 to fix the Transvaal's westward boundary, where Boer settlers, either uncontrolled or tacitly encouraged by Pretoria, established new republics in Stellaland and Goshen, blocking Cape traders' and missionaries' 'road to the north'. When paper agreements failed in 1885, Britain saw no alternative to annexing British Bechuanaland and establishing a protectorate over the Tswana of northern Bechuanaland.

This reflected no indiscriminate hostility to Transvaal expansion, for the republic was allowed part of Zululand (1888) and to administer Swaziland (1894). It indicated rather the interdependence of imperial and colonial interests, especially those of the Cape as the region's strongest state. Cape anger at Britain's allowing German claims to South-West Africa (1884–5), despite its minerals and trading links with the colony, was considerable. Intervention in Bechuanaland offered compensation by protecting a Cape interest (not least land as security against colonial loans for railway construction), while serving imperial purposes by preventing the coalescence of Boer and German across the continent.

Britain's relationship with the Cape was nevertheless always uneasy. Not only was the Cape slow to incorporate territories acquired on its behalf. It refused to participate in confederation schemes pursued by the imperial government during 1874–8 as an answer to South Africa's need for investment and growth, Transvaal bankruptcy after a series of wars, African unrest and Britain's general wish to limit foreign interests in the region. Cape ministers rejected the tariff co-operation wanted by the interior republics. In resisting integration, however, Cape politicians put their own future at risk; the discovery of gold in the Transvaal (1883–6) turned the tables, bringing economic growth in the republic and the relative decline of the British colonies.

The Transvaal, having resisted British annexation (1877) in 1880–1, increasingly welcomed foreign contacts and exploited the influence provided by colonial dependence on its growing economy. Feeling the imperial connection threatened, Britain's answer was to reaffirm its backing for Natal and the Cape. The Cape's expansion northwards was

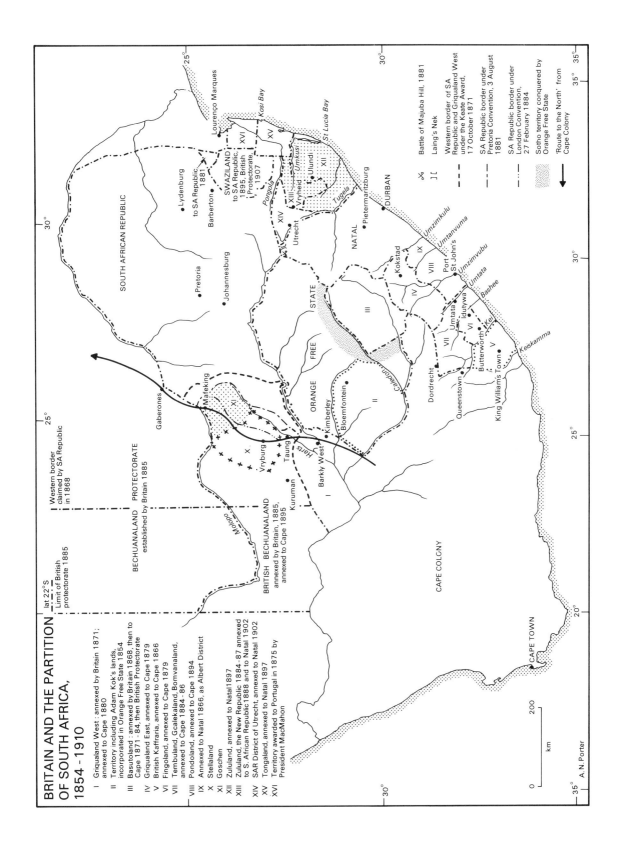

BRITAIN AND THE PARTITION OF SOUTH AFRICA, 1854 - 1910

I   Griqualand West: annexed by Britain 1871; annexed to Cape 1880
II   Territory including Adam Kok's lands, incorporated in Orange Free State 1854
III   Basutoland : annexed by Britain 1868, then to Cape 1871 - 84, then British Protectorate
IV   Griqualand East, annexed to Cape 1879
V   British Kaffraria, annexed to Cape 1866
VI   Fingoland, annexed to Cape 1879
VII   Tembuland, Gcalekaland, Bomvanaland, annexed to Cape 1884 - 86
VIII   Pondoland, annexed to Cape 1894
IX   Annexed to Natal 1866, as Albert District
X   Stellaland
XI   Goschen
XII   Zululand, annexed to Natal 1897
XIII   Zululand, the New Republic 1884 - 87 annexed to S. African Republic 1888 and to Natal 1902
XIV   SAR District of Utrecht, annexed to Natal 1902
XV   Tongaland, annexed to Natal 1897
XVI   Territory awarded to Portugal in 1875 by President MacMahon

lat 22°S
Limit of British protectorate 1885

Western border claimed by SA Republic in 1868

Battle of Majuba Hill, 1881
Laing's Nek
Western border of SA Republic and Griqualand West under the Keate Award, 17 October 1871
SA Republic border under Pretoria Convention, 3 August 1881
SA Republic border under London Convention, 27 February 1884
Sotho territory conquered by Orange Free State
'Route to the North' from Cape Colony

SOUTH AFRICAN REPUBLIC
BECHUANALAND PROTECTORATE established by Britain 1885
BRITISH BECHUANALAND annexed by Britain, 1885, annexed to Cape 1895
CAPE COLONY
ORANGE FREE STATE
NATAL

Lydenburg
to SA Republic
Barberton
SWAZILAND to SA Republic, 1895, British Protectorate, 1907
Lourenço Marques
Kosi Bay
St Lucia Bay
Umkusi
Pongola
Ulundi
Vryheid
Utrecht
Tugela
DURBAN
Pietermaritzburg
Pretoria
Johannesburg
Umzimkulu
Umtamvuma
Kokstad
Port St John's
Umzimvubu
Umtata
Bashee
Keiskamma
Idutywa
Umtata
Kei
Butterworth
Dordrecht
Queenstown
King Williams Town
Caledon
Mafeking
Gaberones
Vryburg
Taung
Haris
Barkly West
Kimberley
Bloemfontein
Kuruman
Molopo

CAPE TOWN

0   200
km

A.N. Porter

25°
30°
35°
20°
25°
30°
35°
30°
25°
20°
30°
35°

encouraged (see p. 115). Natal's long-standing designs, fostered by the Anglo-Zulu War (1879) and its aftermath, were fulfilled by annexation of Zululand, Tongaland and Utrecht district. The other arm of imperial policy, direct pressure on the Transvaal itself to accommodate a range of British interests, led finally to war (see p. 116). Conquest of the republics at last brought political realities more into line with the essential economic unity of South Africa, and paved the way for its political union in 1910.

Britain and the partition of Central Africa, 1875–1910

In the 1870s Central Africa attracted steady attention from Europe's businessmen and missionaries. The British, especially the Scots, were particularly involved. In 1875–6 the Free Church of Scotland established its Livingstonia mission, and the Church of Scotland based itself at Blantyre, both with financial assistance from prominent merchants. The London Missionary Society occupied Ujiji in 1878. The shipowner William Mackinnon, having failed to establish a chartered company, hoped to draw the lakes' trade northwards by building a road from Dar-es-Salaam. In the west, Manchester's merchants and promoters like the Duke of Sutherland were interested by Leopold II's new preoccupation with the Congo. Expansive visions, however, far outstripped realities; Anglo-Portuguese diplomatic accord and joint business ventures flourished intermittently until 1884 but achieved little.

Central Africa, however, could not escape concern with access to the interior generated by events elsewhere between 1882 and 1886. Outsiders advanced rapidly from two directions and came into collision in 1890–1. The Portuguese, anxious to make something of Angola and Mozambique and fearing loss of territory to powerful rivals, took steps to occupy effectively these hitherto ill-defined spheres. They restricted entry to the Zambezi, claimed Nyasaland for themselves, established the Mozambique Company to develop the region, took over the Delagoa Bay railway concession to the Transvaal and threatened to occupy Mashonaland. From the south, Cape interests represented by Cecil Rhodes and metropolitan capitalists organized by George Cawston eventually joined forces to open up 'Zambesia', hoping to exclude the Transvaal and seeking extensive mineral deposits. On the basis of an exclusive concession of mineral rights negotiated with Lobengula of the Ndebele by C. D. Rudd, they established the British South Africa (BSA) Company, bought out a host of rivals and obtained a charter from the British government.

Britain was interested chiefly in containment of the Transvaal (see p. 112) and in preventing international clashes over African issues. The charter granted to the BSA Company was intended to secure the first object, enabling government to avoid expense and responsibility. The second, however, required much diplomacy. The western border of Mozambique was only finally settled in June 1891, after difficult negotiations, an ultimatum to the Portuguese and the company's outrageous challenge to the original Anglo-Portuguese agreement (August 1890) for a larger sphere and secure access to Beira.

The company's 'Pioneer Column' of settlers left Bechuanaland in July 1890, reaching Fort Salisbury in September. Mashonaland rapidly proved disappointing, and the company therefore widened its search for minerals and turned to the possibilities of extensive settlement. Relations with the Ndebele consequently deteriorated, and they were manoeuvred by the company into war in October 1893. This heralded the internal partition between black and white of what by mid-1895 was

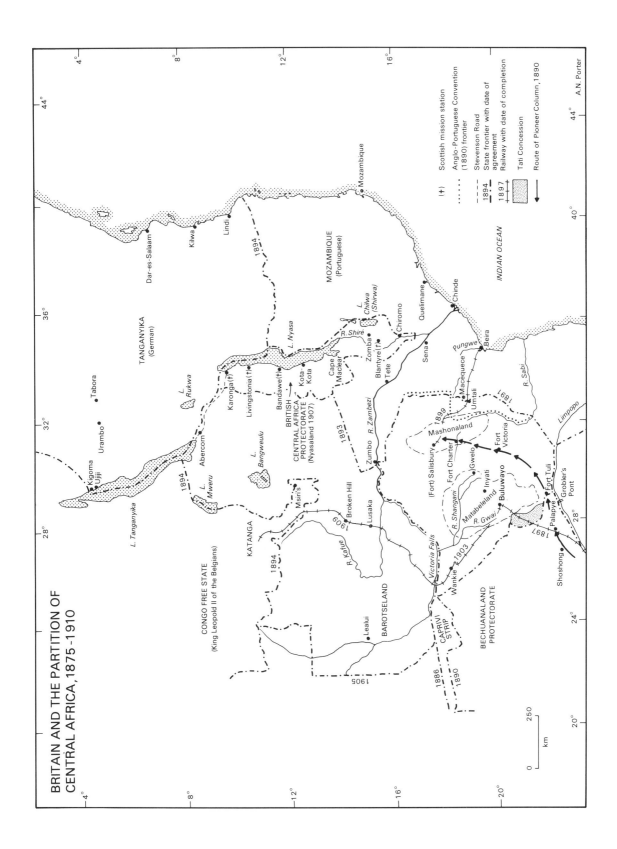

BRITAIN AND THE PARTITION OF
CENTRAL AFRICA, 1875-1910

A.N. Porter

Scottish mission station

(†)

Anglo-Portuguese Convention
(1890) frontier

.... Stevenson Road

━ ━ ━ State frontier with date of
1894 agreement

Railway with date of completion
1897

Tati Concession

Route of Pioneer Column, 1890

INDIAN OCEAN

TANGANYIKA
(German)

MOZAMBIQUE
(Portuguese)

CONGO FREE STATE
(King Leopold II of the Belgians)

KATANGA

BAROTSELAND

BRITISH
CENTRAL AFRICA
PROTECTORATE
(Nyasaland 1907)

BECHUANALAND
PROTECTORATE

CAPRIVI
STRIP

Mashonaland

Matabeleland

Dar-es-Salaam
Kilwa
Lindi
Mozambique

Tabora
Urambo
Kigoma
Ujiji

L. Tanganyika
L. Rukwa
L. Mweru
L. Bangweulu
L. Nyasa

Abercorn
Karonga (†)
Livingstonia (†)
Bandawe (†)
Kota Kota

Msiri's

Broken Hill
Lusaka
Lealui

R. Kafue

Victoria Falls
Wankie

Cape Maclear
Zomba
Blantyre (†)
Tete
L. Chilwa
(Shirwa)
R. Shiré
Chiromo
Quelimane
Chinde
Sena
Pungwe
Beira

Macequece
Umtali
R. Sabi
Fort Victoria
Gwelo
Fort Charter
(Fort) Salisbury

Zumbo
R. Zambezi
Limpopo

Inyati
Buluwayo
R. Shangani
R. Gwai

Shoshong
Palapye
Grobler's
Pont
Fort Tuli

1894
1893
1894
1894
1899
1897
1905
1886
1890
1897
1903
1909

km
0   250

becoming known as 'Rhodesia'. The inflow of settlers and harsh administration provoked a serious uprising by Ndebele and Shona in 1896–7.

Beyond the Zambezi, the company failed to establish effective claims to Katanga, and its Barotseland border was disputed with the Portuguese until 1905. The imperial government, however, was unwilling for political, religious and humanitarian reasons to see Nyasaland fall to Portugal. There again the BSA Company helped out. Anxious to keep open an option on this outlying territory, Rhodes took over the local African Lakes Company, and agreed to subsidize Foreign Office administration of the British Central Africa Protectorate, established in May 1891. BSA Company administration of the area further west to the Kafue River (designated Northern Rhodesia in 1897) was formally recognized in 1894, and the remaining independent chiefdoms were conquered by 1900. White settlement in both Northern Rhodesia and Nyasaland was slower and far smaller than in the south.

The South African War, 1899–1902

The South African War, which began with the expiry of the South African Republic's ultimatum to Britain on 11 October 1899 and ended with the Peace of Vereeniging on 31 May 1902, was fought on a scale incredible to most contemporaries. Hitherto imperial wars, such as the Ashanti campaigns of 1873–4 and 1895, had been small affairs. In South Africa too the comparative weakness of the Afrikaner republics led imperial authorities to think the Transvaal would make political concessions to the Uitlanders on the Rand in response to no more than diplomatic pressure and military threats. Britain's military planning was perfunctory; even if conflict should occur a British victory was expected to be swift and inevitable.

This confidence was seriously misplaced. Boer forces, totalling nearly 35,000 in October 1899, were well equipped, were ably and sometimes brilliantly led and knew the country well. Immediate thrusts into Natal, Cape Colony and Bechuanaland created panic, pinned down British troops, especially in the east, and gave the Boers control of large sectors of the railway system. By Christmas they had won impressive victories on all three fronts, exposing British military weaknesses, and ruining the reputation of generals Gatacre, Methuen and Buller. They were unable, however, to build on these early successes. The original British garrison of 20,000 was steadily reinforced; the imperial command was reconstructed under Lord Roberts and Lord Kitchener in December 1899; and continued British control of the ports enabled resources – Argentinian mules, Australian foodstuffs, Canadian volunteers – to be quickly deployed.

Lifting the Boers' siege of Kimberley and General Cronje's surrender with 4,000 troops at Paardeberg in February 1900 marked the turn in the war of formal military engagements. Roberts advanced up the railway, taking Bloemfontein in April and Pretoria in June. On both sides large numbers of Africans played important roles, as labourers, runners, scouts and even combatants. From April 1900, however, the war was transformed. Boer leaders (de Wet, de la Rey and Smuts) developed a highly mobile and effective guerrilla campaign. The Cape was invaded several times in 1900 and 1901, forcing the British to place virtually the whole colony under martial law. Yet there was no real hope of bringing the British to terms. Divisions within the Afrikaner communities as to the wisdom of fighting on, and widespread black support for the British side, restricted Boer operations. The systematic British response, directed by Kitchener, involved destroying Boer farms, moving their women and children and large numbers of black African refugees into

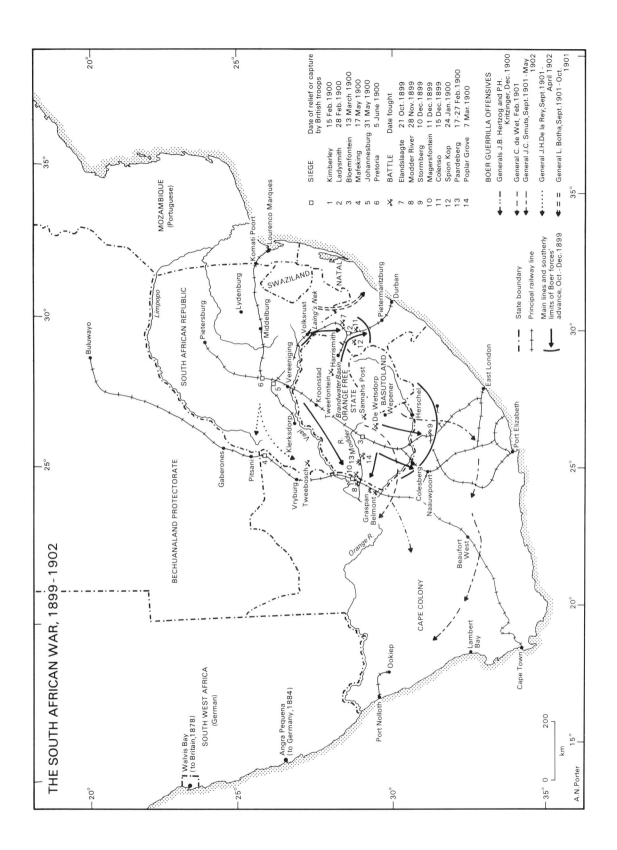

THE SOUTH AFRICAN WAR, 1899-1902

SIEGE		Date of relief or capture by British troops
□	1	Kimberley	15 Feb. 1900
	2	Ladysmith	28 Feb. 1900
	3	Bloemfontein	13 March 1900
	4	Mafeking	17 May 1900
	5	Johannesburg	31 May 1900
	6	Pretoria	5 June 1900

BATTLE		Date fought
✗	7	Elandslaagte	21 Oct. 1899
	8	Modder River	28 Nov. 1899
	9	Stormberg	10 Dec. 1899
	10	Magersfontein	11 Dec. 1899
	11	Colenso	15 Dec. 1899
	12	Spion Kop	24 Jan. 1900
	13	Paardeberg	17-27 Feb. 1900
	14	Poplar Grove	7 Mar. 1900

BOER GUERRILLA OFFENSIVES

- ·····> Generals J.B. Hertzog and P.H. Kritzinger, Dec. 1900
- – –> General C. de Wet, Feb. 1901
- ‒‒> General J.C. Smuts, Sept. 1901 - May 1902
- ······> General J.H. De la Rey, Sept. 1901 - April 1902
- ==> General L. Botha, Sept. 1901 - Oct. 1901

‒··‒ State boundary

‒+‒ Principal railway line

↓ Main lines and southerly limits of Boer forces' advance, Oct. - Dec. 1899

A.N. Porter

'concentration camps' strung out along the railway lines north of Bloemfontein, the cordoning-off of vast areas, notably in the Orange River Colony, and extensive sweeps to corner remaining Boer troops.

These tactics were extremely damaging, materially and politically. Almost 28,000 Boers – estimated at more than 10 per cent of the republic's population – died in the camps, chiefly from disease, as did a still larger proportion of the African inmates. Thirty thousand farms were ruined, creating immense problems of post-war reconstruction. Under the umbrella of martial law, another bitter civil struggle went on, as black and white exploited opportunities to denounce Afrikaners and pay off old scores.

The war cost Britain £250 million and employed in all some 400,000 troops. Its plentiful demonstrations of failure and incompetence contributed much to the pressure for reforms in Britain, notably in the organization and training of the army and in social welfare. It embittered political debate and, while prompting extreme manifestations of aggressive nationalistic enthusiasm or imperial sentimentality, also promoted serious reservations and concern about imperial commitments.

Imperial defence: army garrisons, 1848 and 1881

From the mid-eighteenth century Britain began stationing permanent military garrisons in her colonies, at first haphazardly and then routinely, as an adjunct to naval protection. Aside from threats of external aggression, British troops thus assumed responsibilities for internal security which had hitherto in peacetime been left to the colonists. As the Empire grew in size, diversity and geographical spread during and after the wars with France, so the military obligations expanded. Regiments remained in British North America to discourage the territorial ambitions of the United States, especially during the Canadian rebellions of 1837–8 and the American Civil War. The Mediterranean bases, too, served wider strategic purposes; and in India a substantial garrison of British regulars and even larger numbers of native troops of the East India Company were maintained for fear of possible Russian invasion, and meanwhile used as an instrument of territorial expansion and internal pacification. Following the Mutiny in 1857, the two forces were merged into one army, slightly smaller in size but comprising a higher proportion of European to native troops. In the West Indies the transition from slave to free societies seemed to demand the continued presence of scattered garrisons to forestall revolts by Negroes or whites; and in South Africa turbulent frontiers, stirred up by Bantu and Boers and British annexations, presented a continuous military obligation with periodic bursts of warfare. While Australia was undemanding except for guarding convicts, intermittent fighting in New Zealand during the Maori Wars between 1845 and the 1860s tied up between 10,000 and 12,000 British troops.

Even with the aid of native corps in the Caribbean, Africa and the Far East, global commitments and sudden crises kept the limited resources of the British Army constantly overstretched at a time when Parliament begrudged expenditure on a large standing army in years of European peace. Infantrymen, who provided the bulk of imperial garrisons, with small detachments of artillery and the occasional cavalry regiment, therefore spent long spells of duty overseas, often in unhealthy climates and primitive living conditions that produced high and costly rates of death, disease and invaliding. From Earl Grey's defence review as colonial secretary in 1846 to Edward Cardwell's military reforms over twenty years later, however, this

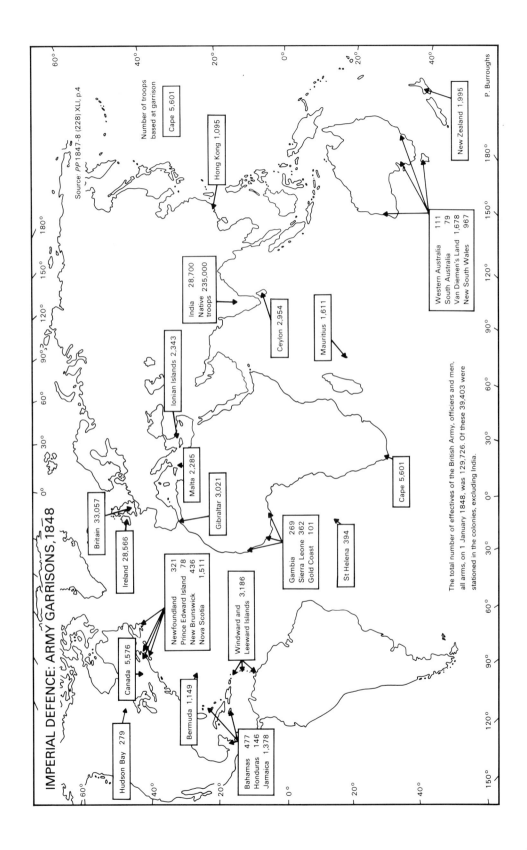

IMPERIAL DEFENCE: ARMY GARRISONS, 1848

Source: *PP* 1847-8 (228) XLI, p.4

Number of troops based at garrison

Cape 5,601

Hong Kong 1,095

New Zealand 1,995

P. Burroughs

Western Australia	111
South Australia	79
Van Diemen's Land	1,678
New South Wales	967

India 28,700
Native troops 235,000

Ceylon 2,954

Mauritius 1,611

Ionian Islands 2,343

Malta 2,285

Gibraltar 3,021

Britain 33,057

Ireland 28,566

Newfoundland	321
Prince Edward Island	78
New Brunswick	436
Nova Scotia	1,511

Windward and Leeward Islands 3,186

Gambia	269
Sierra Leone	362
Gold Coast	101

St Helena 394

Cape 5,601

Canada 5,576

Hudson Bay 279

Bermuda 1,149

Bahamas	477
Honduras	146
Jamaica	1,378

The total number of effectives of the British Army, officers and men, all arms, on 1 January 1848, was 129,726. Of these 39,403 were stationed in the colonies, excluding India.

119

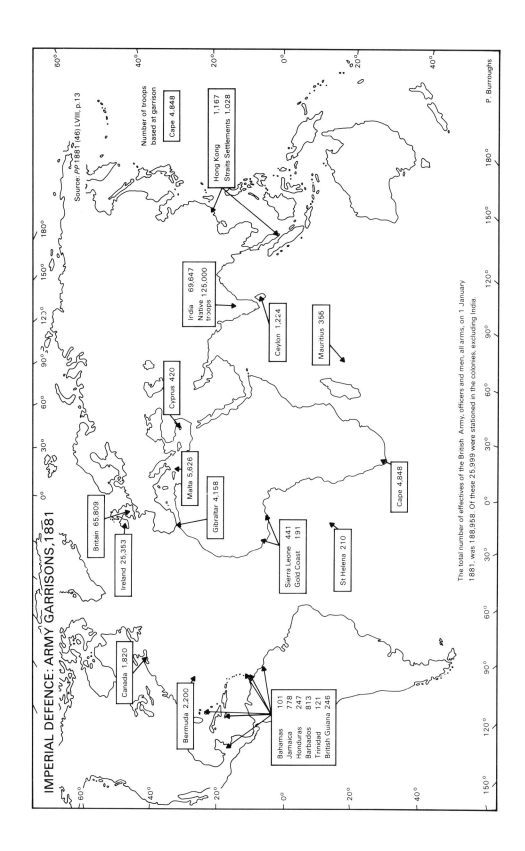

IMPERIAL DEFENCE: ARMY GARRISONS, 1881

Source: *PP* 1881 (46) LVIII, p.13

Number of troops based at garrison

| Cape | 4,848 |

| Hong Kong | 1,167 |
| Straits Settlements | 1,028 |

| India | 69,647 |
| Native troops | 125,000 |

| Ceylon | 1,224 |

| Mauritius | 355 |

| Cyprus | 420 |

| Malta | 5,626 |

| Gibraltar | 4,158 |

| Britain | 65,809 |

| Ireland | 25,353 |

| Sierra Leone | 441 |
| Gold Coast | 191 |

| St Helena | 210 |

| Cape | 4,848 |

| Canada | 1,820 |

| Bermuda | 2,200 |

Bahamas	101
Jamaica	778
Honduras	247
Barbados	813
Trinidad	121
British Guiana	246

The total number of effectives of the British Army, officers and men, all arms, on 1 January 1881, was 188,958. Of these 25,999 were stationed in the colonies, excluding India.

P. Burroughs

whole strategy was gradually altered. Instead of spreading scarce manpower thinly across the Empire, Grey and his successors sought to scale down and withdraw permanent colonial garrisons as and when opportunity offered and to station a larger proportion of the army in Britain to strengthen home defence. In an age of improved communications and as yet unchallenged naval superiority, regiments could be speedily dispatched to trouble-spots abroad as emergencies arose. Such a redeployment also facilitated overdue improvements in the terms and conditions of military service, including short-term enlistment, in a bid to enhance the attractions of army life and the quality and morale of soldiers. The new strategy was intended to be cheaper. Reverting to an older pattern of local self-reliance, the routine duties of policing and internal security were transferred to settlement colonies, where self-defence became the corollary of self-government.

These diverse aims were never fully realized. Frequent colonial wars during the years of mounting international competition after 1870 repeatedly called for British expeditionary forces which, together with the massive burden of India, created acute shortages of troops even though the army steadily rose from 160,000 in 1876 to 195,000 in 1898. As supporters and critics alike recognized, defence of the Empire had become the army's primary responsibility as well as the decisive determinant of its character and institutions.

Imperial defence: naval stations, 1848, 1875 and 1898

After the French wars the Royal Navy was scaled down to a peace establishment far below the 214 ships of the line and 792 smaller vessels in 1815. With Parliament and the political nation demanding retrenchment, it was impossible to maintain a large navy and also unnecessary in the absence of rival fleets. The number of ships of the line fit for service therefore fell from 80 in 1817 to the lowest point of 58 in 1835, as did naval estimates at £4.4 million. At the same time the navy found, as did the army, that the number and diversity of its commitments steadily increased in all parts of the globe with the expansion of Britain's commerce and empire. In a mutually reinforcing, triangular relationship, the navy supplied an essential network of protection for world-wide trade routes, secured by strategic bases which afforded harbour and refreshment facilities, focal centres of power and often commercial entrepôts. What Admiral Fisher later described as the 'keys' that locked up the globe were provided at various times by such bases as Heligoland, Gibraltar, Malta, the Ionian Islands, Cyprus; Gambia, Sierra Leone, Lagos, Ascension; Halifax, Bermuda, St Lucia, Trinidad, Falkland Islands; the Cape, Mauritius, Zanzibar, Mombasa, Aden, Seychelles, Ceylon; Singapore, Malacca, Hong Kong. In addition to the general duty of protecting maritime commerce, the navy defended British interests overseas and acted as an instrument of foreign policy with the occasional punitive expedition or display of gunboat diplomacy; it sought to suppress slave trading and piracy; it surveyed coastlines and charted oceans all over the world.

Between 1815 and 1835 Britain enjoyed effortless naval supremacy, in part because potential rivals lacked the capabilities and the desire to mount a serious challenge. In the following two decades fears of French and Russian naval ambitions, a series of invasion scares and deficiencies exposed by the Crimean War prompted higher levels of naval spending on ships and manpower. In naval as in military strategy, the British government showed an awareness of the extent to which the navy's global commitments had weakened defence in home waters and the emphasis on

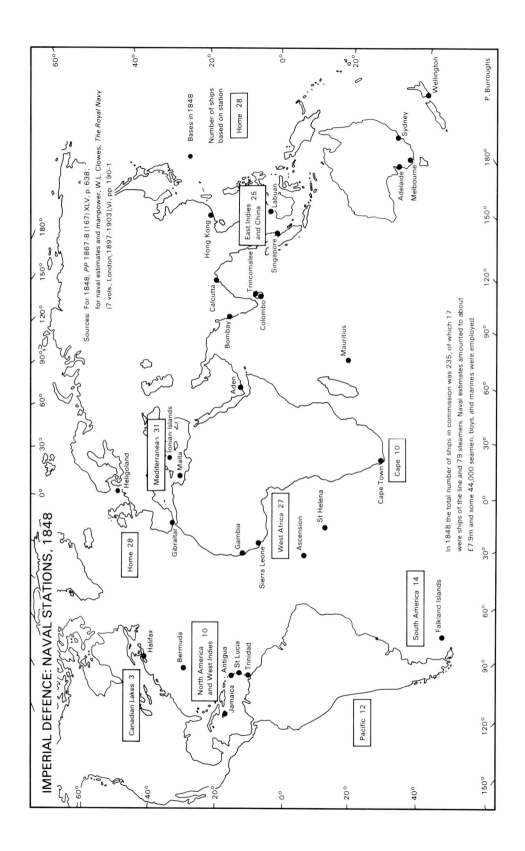

IMPERIAL DEFENCE: NAVAL STATIONS, 1848

Sources: For 1848, *PP* 1867-8 (167) XLV, p. 638; for naval estimates and manpower, W. L. Clowes, *The Royal Navy* (7 vols., London, 1897-1903), VI, pp. 190-1

Bases in 1848

Number of ships based on station

Home 28

East Indies and China 25

Labuan

Hong Kong

Trincomalee

Singapore

Calcutta

Colombo

Bombay

Mauritius

Aden

Mediterranean 31

Ionian Islands

Malta

Heligoland

Cape 10

Cape Town

Gibraltar

St Helena

West Africa 27

Gambia

Ascension

Sierra Leone

Home 28

Sydney

Adelaide

Melbourne

Wellington

South America 14

Falkland Islands

Bermuda

North America and West Indies 10

Antigua

St Lucia

Trinidad

Jamaica

Halifax

Canadian Lakes 3

Pacific 12

In 1848 the total number of ships in commission was 235, of which 17 were ships of the line and 79 steamers. Naval estimates amounted to about £7.9m and some 44,000 seamen, boys, and marines were employed.

P. Burroughs

122

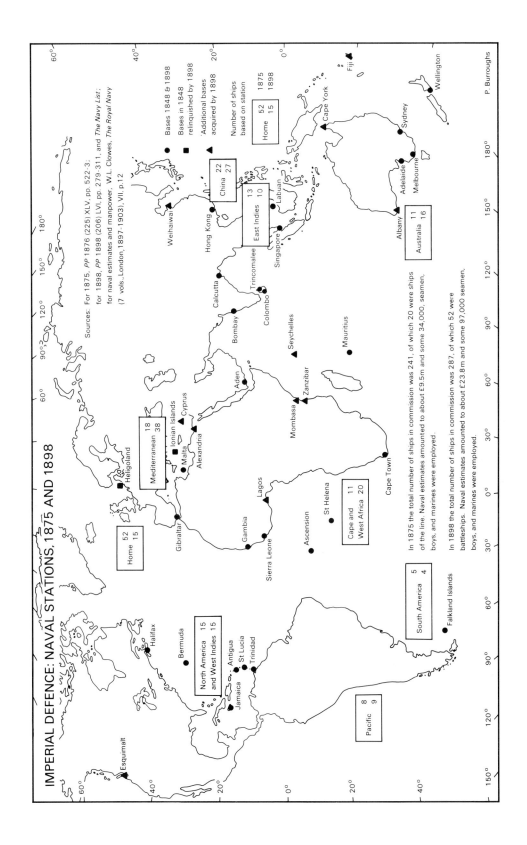

IMPERIAL DEFENCE: NAVAL STATIONS, 1875 AND 1898

Sources: For 1875, *PP* 1876 (225) XLV, pp. 522-3;
for 1898, *PP* 1898 (206) LVI, pp. 279-311, and *The Navy List*;
for naval estimates and manpower, W.L. Clowes, *The Royal Navy*
(7 vols., London, 1897-1903), VII, p.12

● Bases 1848 & 1898

■ Bases in 1848
  relinquished by 1898

▲ Additional bases
  acquired by 1898

Number of ships
based on station

	1875	1898
Home	52	15

China	22	27

East Indies	13	10

Australia	11	16

Mediterranean	18	38

Home	52	15

| Cape and | 11 | 20 |
| West Africa | | |

South America	5	4

| North America | 15 | 15 |
| and West Indies | | |

Pacific	8	9

In 1875 the total number of ships in commission was 241, of which 20 were ships of the line. Naval estimates amounted to about £9.5m and some 34,000, seamen, boys, and marines were employed.

In 1898 the total number of ships in commission was 287, of which 52 were battleships. Naval estimates amounted to about £23.8m and some 97,000 seamen, boys, and marines were employed.

123

the smaller classes of vessels at the expense of warships had diminished the battle strength of the fleet. By the mid-1860s, however, complacency about British naval mastery had returned, and the development of iron-clad steamships gave industrial Britain a further competitive edge over other powers. For some twenty years it was again possible to combine naval superiority with decreasing expenditure.

This happy interlude came to an abrupt end in 1884, when disturbing revelations of British naval weaknesses and ambitious French shipbuilding heightened public disquiet already aroused by the rise of foreign rivalry to Britain's commercial and colonial pre-eminence. Popular clamour forced the government in 1889 to declare its intention to maintain a two-power naval standard and embark on a costly programme of new construction, including ten battleships. Thereafter anxiety about the French and Russian challenges remained (until 1905), as did the pressure to spend ever more money on the fleet. As advances in technology and weaponry caused the expense of constructing vessels to mount, so the naval estimates rapidly escalated in the years to the First World War. This feverish expenditure helped to hide from most contemporaries the slow but steady decline in British naval supremacy and in the effectiveness of sea power in general.

Protestant missionaries and the Anglican Church overseas, 1780–1914

Before the late eighteenth century, colonial ecclesiastical organization and missionary work overseas was sporadic and haphazard. Among Anglicans, the Society for the Promotion of Christian Knowledge (formed in 1698–9) assisted Danish missionaries and in 1728 started its own South India mission, using continental Lutherans in the absence of English volunteers. Under the auspices of the Society for the Propagation of the Gospel (1701) or the East India Company, individual clergy and chaplains – like John Wesley in Georgia (February 1736 to December 1737) – sometimes worked voluntarily with slaves, free blacks or native Indians, in addition to their formal responsibilities for settler congregations or other expatriates. There being no colonial bishops, colonial clergy and congregations were conventionally subject to the jurisdiction of the Bishop of London. Baptists, Congregationalists and other dissenters operated in similar fashion in the Thirteen Colonies and the West Indies.

A more systematic extension overseas of the Church of England's hierarchy and the rapid growth of missionary enterprise followed the loss of the American colonies. To superintend Anglicans in the newly independent territories, Bishop Seabury of Connecticut was consecrated in 1784, albeit without the temporal powers normally held by bishops at home. Simultaneously in Canada the dioceses of Nova Scotia (1787) and Quebec (1793) were established with endowments, jurisdiction and political influence fitting for bishops who were intended, as in Britain itself, to be important supports for government. By contrast, missionary expansion initially received little backing from leading politicians or church dignitaries. It reflected the enthusiasms of many comparatively modest people caught up in the extensive religious revival after 1760, notably those ardent laymen who founded the voluntary lay societies of the 1790s – the Baptist Missionary Society (1792), the Anglican Church Missionary Society (1799) and the London Missionary Society (1795). Subsequently the Wesleyan Methodists (in 1818) and the Church of Scotland (in 1825) organized the expanding overseas missions of

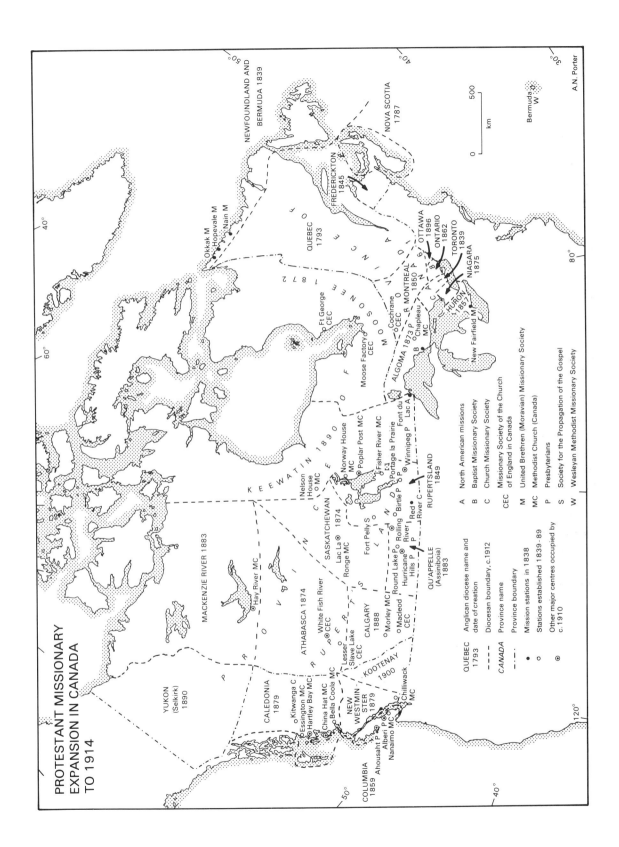

PROTESTANT MISSIONARY
EXPANSION IN CANADA
TO 1914

NEWFOUNDLAND AND
BERMUDA 1839

NOVA SCOTIA
1787

FREDERICKTON
1845

QUEBEC
1793

Okkak M
Hopevale M
Nain M

OTTAWA
1896
ONTARIO
1862
TORONTO
1839
NIAGARA
1875

MONTREAL
1850 P

Cochrane
CEC

ALGOMA 1873 P

Chapleau
MC

HURON
1857

New Fairfield M

Ft George
CEC

Moose Factory
CEC

Font du
Lac A

B

MACKENZIE RIVER 1883

KEEWATIN 1890

Nelson
House
MC

Norway House
MC

Poplar Post MC

Fisher River MC

Portage la Prairie

Winnipeg P

Birtle P

Red P

RUPERTSLAND
1849

Hay River MC

White Fish River

SASKATCHEWAN
1890

Lac La
Ronge MC

Fort Pelly S

Round Lake P
Rolling
River I
River C

Hurricane
Hills P

QU'APPELLE
(Assiniboia)
1883

ATHABASCA 1874

Lesser
Slave Lake
CEC

CALGARY
1888

Morley MC

Macleod
CEC

YUKON
(Selkirk)
1890

CALEDONIA
1879

Essington C
Kitwanga C
Hartley Bay MC
China Hat MC
Bella Coola MC

NEW
WESTMIN-
STER 1879

KOOTENAY
1900

Chilliwack
MC

COLUMBIA
1859

Ahousaht P
Albert P
Nanaimo MC

A   North American missions
B   Baptist Missionary Society
C   Church Missionary Society
CEC Missionary Society of the Church
     of England in Canada
M   United Brethren (Moravian) Missionary Society
MC   Methodist Church (Canada)
P   Presbyterians
S   Society for the Propagation of the Gospel
W   Wesleyan Methodist Missionary Society

QUEBEC   Anglican diocese name and
1793   date of creation

---   Diocesan boundary, c.1912

CANADA   Province name

–·–·–   Province boundary

●   Mission stations in 1838

○   Stations established 1839-89

◉   Other major centres occupied by
         c.1910

Bermuda
W

500
0   km

A.N. Porter

125

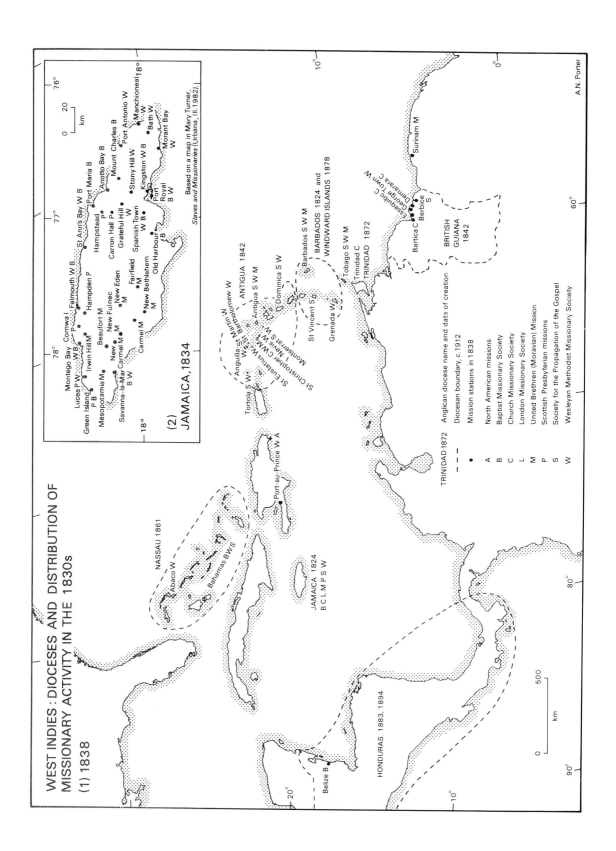

WEST INDIES : DIOCESES AND DISTRIBUTION OF
MISSIONARY ACTIVITY IN THE 1830s

(1) 1838

(2) JAMAICA, 1834

Based on a map in Mary Turner,
Slaves and Missionaries (Urbana, Ill.1982).

TRINIDAD 1872   Anglican diocese name and date of creation

- - - - -   Diocesan boundary, c.1912

•   Mission stations in 1838

A   North American missions
B   Baptist Missionary Society
C   Church Missionary Society
L   London Missionary Society
M   United Brethren (Moravian) Mission
P   Scottish Presbyterian missions
S   Society for the Propagation of the Gospel
W   Wesleyan Methodist Missionary Society

A.N. Porter

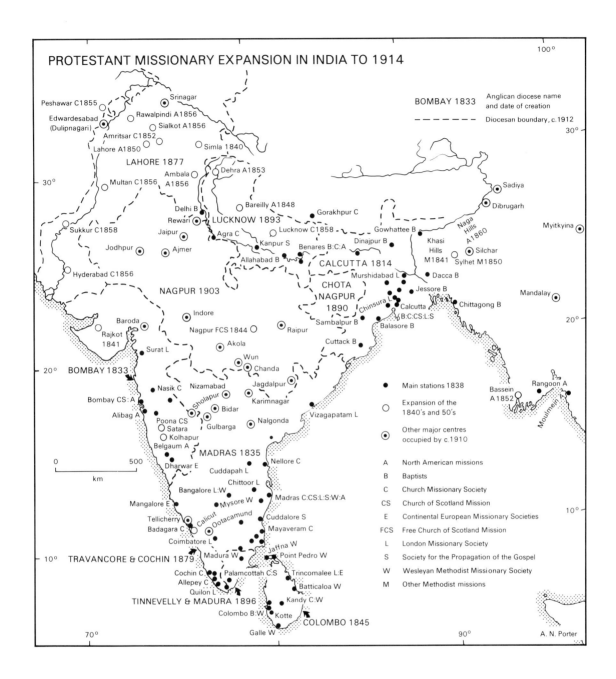

PROTESTANT MISSIONARY EXPANSION IN INDIA TO 1914

BOMBAY 1833 — Anglican diocese name and date of creation

- - - - - - - Diocesan boundary, c.1912

Peshawar C1855
Edwardesabad (Dulipnagari)
Amritsar C1852
Lahore A1850
LAHORE 1877
Srinagar
Rawalpindi A1856
Sialkot A1856
Simla 1840
Ambala A1856
Dehra A1853
Multan C1856
Delhi B
Rewari
LUCKNOW 1893
Agra C
Bareilly A1848
Gorakhpur C
Lucknow C1858
Jaipur
Kanpur S
Benares B:C:A
Dinajpur B
Gowhattee B
Sadiya
Dibrugarh
Naga Hills A1860
Khasi Hills M1841
Silchar
Sylhet M1850
Myitkyina
Sukkur C1858
Jodhpur
Ajmer
Allahabad B
CALCUTTA 1814
NAGPUR 1903
Hyderabad C1856
CHOTA NAGPUR 1890
Murshidabad L
Dacca B
Mandalay
Baroda
Rajkot 1841
Indore
Nagpur FCS 1844
Raipur
Chinsura
Sambalpur B
Calcutta B:C:CS:L:S
Balasore B
Chittagong B
Surat L
Akola
Cuttack B
BOMBAY 1833
Wun
Chanda
Nasik C
Nizamabad
Jagdalpur
Bombay CS:A
Sholapur
Karimnagar
Bassein A1852
Rangoon A
Alibag A
Poona CS
Bidar
Satara
Gulbarga
Nalgonda
Vizagapatam L
Kolhapur
Belgaum A
MADRAS 1835
Nellore C
Dharwar E
Cuddapah L
Bangalore L:W
Chittoor L
Mangalore E
Mysore W
Madras C:CS:L:S:W:A
Tellicherry
Calicut
Ootacamund
Cuddalore S
Badagara C
Mayaveram C
Coimbatore L
Jaffna W
TRAVANCORE & COCHIN 1879
Madura W
Point Pedro W
Cochin C
Palamcottah C:S
Trincomalee L:E
Allepey C
Batticaloa W
Quilon L
TINNEVELLY & MADURA 1896
Kandy C:W
Colombo B:W
Kotte
COLOMBO 1845
Galle W
Moulmein
A. N. Porter

● Main stations 1838
○ Expansion of the 1840's and 50's
◉ Other major centres occupied by c.1910

A North American missions
B Baptists
C Church Missionary Society
CS Church of Scotland Mission
E Continental European Missionary Societies
FCS Free Church of Scotland Mission
L London Missionary Society
S Society for the Propagation of the Gospel
W Wesleyan Methodist Missionary Society
M Other Methodist missions

0   500 km

their members as the direct responsibility of the church itself. All saw themselves as part of an extensive evangelical community, embracing with equal readiness Protestants in continental Europe and the United States; their task they saw in global rather than British colonial terms.

The earliest prominent spheres of missionary activity were the Pacific, Bengal, Cape Colony, the West Indies and Sierra Leone. In each area problems of either colonial or ecclesiastical order rapidly arose which were to become perennial. In India, for example, social snobbery and dislike of missionaries'

127

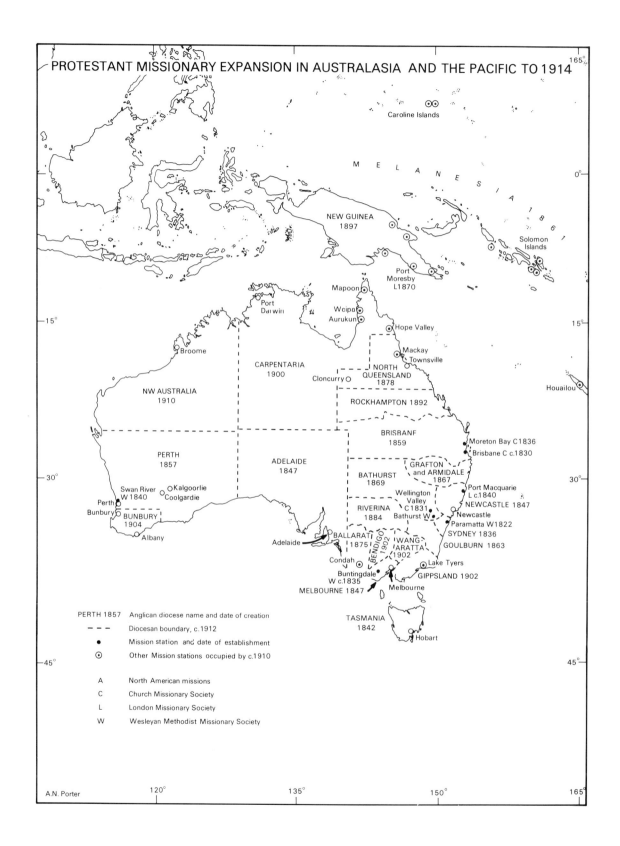

PROTESTANT MISSIONARY EXPANSION IN AUSTRALASIA AND THE PACIFIC TO 1914

Caroline Islands

MELANESIA

NEW GUINEA
1897

Solomon
Islands

Port
Moresby
L1870

Mapoon

Port
Darwin

Weipa
Aurukun

Hope Valley

Houailou

Broome

CARPENTARIA
1900

Mackay
Townsville

NORTH
QUEENSLAND
1878

NW AUSTRALIA
1910

Cloncurry

ROCKHAMPTON 1892

BRISBANE
1859

Moreton Bay C1836
Brisbane C c.1830

PERTH
1857

ADELAIDE
1847

GRAFTON
and ARMIDALE
1867

BATHURST
1869

Port Macquarie
L c.1840

Swan River
W 1840

Kalgoorlie
Coolgardie

Wellington
Valley
C1831

NEWCASTLE 1847

Perth
Bunbury

BUNBURY
1904

RIVERINA
1884

Bathurst W

Newcastle

Paramatta W1822
SYDNEY 1836

Albany

BALLARAT
1875

WANG
ARATTA
1902

GOULBURN 1863

Adelaide

BENDIGO
1902

Lake Tyers

Condah

GIPPSLAND 1902

Buntingdale
W c.1835

Melbourne

MELBOURNE 1847

PERTH 1857   Anglican diocese name and date of creation

- - -   Diocesan boundary, c.1912

●   Mission station and date of establishment

⊙   Other Mission stations occupied by c.1910

TASMANIA
1842

Hobart

A   North American missions
C   Church Missionary Society
L   London Missionary Society
W   Wesleyan Methodist Missionary Society

A.N. Porter

120°   135°   150°   165°

128

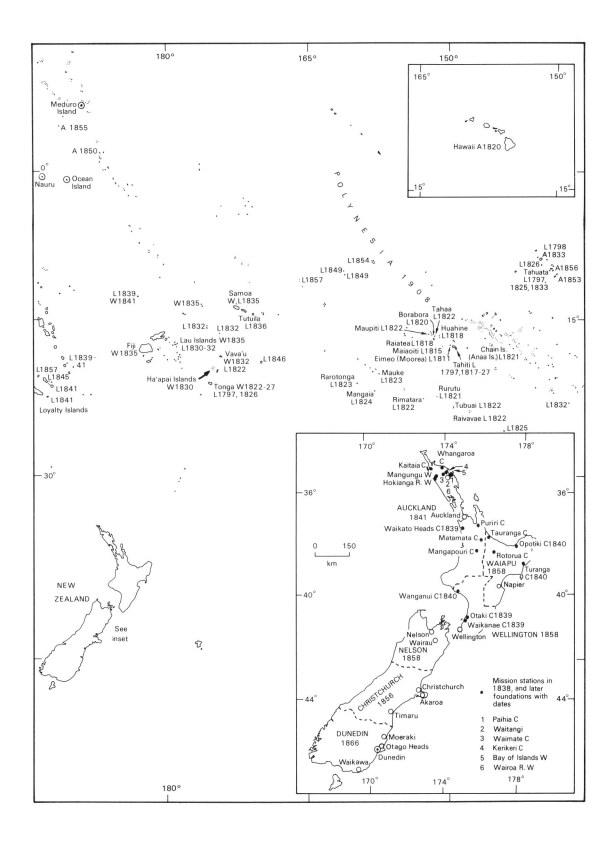

Meduro Island
·A 1855

A 1850

0°
Nauru Ocean Island

30°

NEW ZEALAND

See inset

POLYNESIA 1908

Hawaii A1820

165°   150°
165°   150°

15°

15°

L1839 W1841

W1835

Samoa W,L1835
Tutuila

L1832: L1832 L1836

Lau Islands W1835
L1830-32

Fiji W1835

Vava'u
W1832   L1846
L1822

Ha'apai Islands
W1830

Tonga W1822-27
L1797, 1826

L1857
L1845
L1841
L1841

L1839· ·41

Loyalty Islands

L1854
L1849   L1849
L1857

Borabora
L1820

Maupiti L1822

Tahaa
L1822

Huahine
L1818

Raiatea L1818
Maiaoiti L1815
Eimeo (Moorea) L1811

Chain Is.
(Anaa Is.)L1821

Tahiti L
1797,1817-27

Rarotonga
L1823

Mauke
L1823

Mangaia
L1824

Rimatara
L1822

Rururu
·L1821

Tubuai L1822

Raivavae L1822

L1798
A1833

L1826
Tahuata
L1797,
1825, 1833

A1856
A1853

15°

L1832·

L1825

170°   174°   178°

Whangaroa

Kaitaia C   C
Mangungu W   3 2 1
Hokianga R. W   6

4
5

AUCKLAND
1841

Auckland

Puriri C

Waikato Heads C1839
Matamata C

Mangapouri C

Tauranga C
Opotiki C1840

Rotorua C

WAIAPU
1858

Turanga
C1840

Napier

Wanganui C1840

Otaki C1839
Waikanae C1839
Wellington

WELLINGTON 1858

Nelson
Wairau

NELSON
1858

CHRISTCHURCH
1856

Christchurch
Akaroa

Timaru

Moeraki
Otago Heads
Dunedin

Waikawa

DUNEDIN
1866

36°

40°

44°

0   150

km

Mission stations in
1838, and later
foundations with
dates

1 Paihia C
2 Waitangi
3 Waimate C
4 Kerikeri C
5 Bay of Islands W
6 Wairoa R. W

170°   174°   178°

180°

165°

150°

30°

36°

15°

40°

44°

180°   170°   174°   178°

129

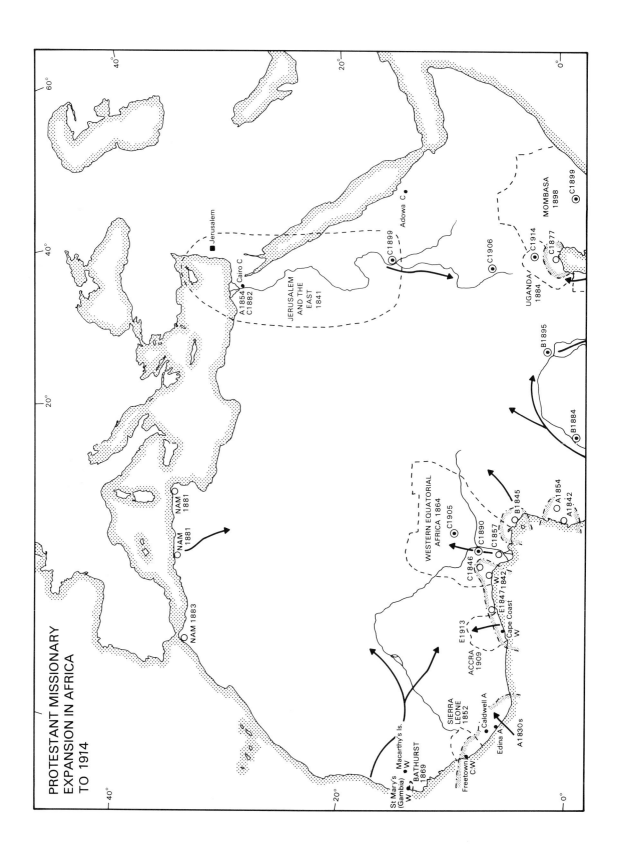

PROTESTANT MISSIONARY
EXPANSION IN AFRICA
TO 1914

St Mary's
(Gambia) • Macarthy's Is.
W • W
BATHURST
1869

SIERRA
LEONE
1852

Freetown
C•W
• Caldwell A
Edina A •
• A1830s

ACCRA
1909

E1913
Cape Coast
W

E1847 1842
W

C1846
C1857
C1890
• B1845
WESTERN EQUATORIAL
AFRICA 1864
C1905

A1854
A1842

NAM
1881

NAM
1881

NAM 1883

JERUSALEM
AND THE
EAST
1841

■ Jerusalem

Cairo C
A1854
C1882

Adowa C
C1899

C1906

C1914
UGANDA
1884
C1877

MOMBASA
1898
C1899

B1895

B1884

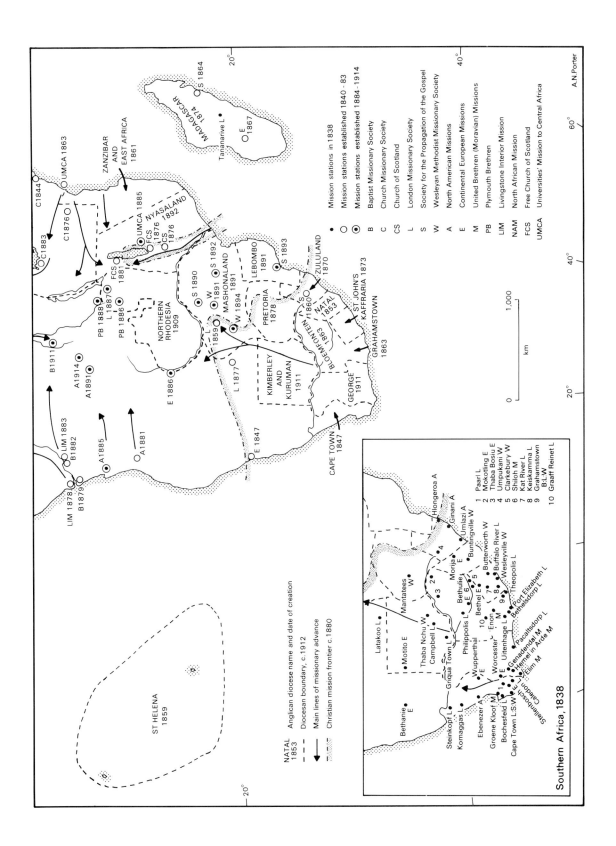

A.N.Porter

	Mission stations in 1838	•	○
	Mission stations established 1840 - 83		
	Mission stations established 1884 - 1914		⊙
B	Baptist Missionary Society
C	Church Missionary Society
CS	Church of Scotland
L	London Missionary Society
S	Society for the Propagation of the Gospel
W	Wesleyan Methodist Missionary Society
A	North American Missions
E	Continental European Missions
M	United Brethren (Moravian) Missions
PB	Plymouth Brethren
LIM	Livingstone Interior Mission
NAM	North African Mission
FCS	Free Church of Scotland
UMCA	Universities' Mission to Central Africa

NATAL 1853 — Anglican diocese name and date of creation
------- Diocesan boundary, c. 1912
→ Main lines of missionary advance
Christian mission frontier c. 1880

ST HELENA 1859

ZANZIBAR AND EAST AFRICA 1861

MADAGASCAR

S 1864
E 1867
Tananarive L 1874

C 1844
UMCA 1863
C 1876
C 1883

UMCA 1885
FCS 1876
CS 1876
NYASALAND 1892
FCS 1881

NORTHERN RHODESIA 1909

PB 1888
L 1887
PB 1886

E 1886

B 1911

A 1914
A 1891

LIM 1883
B 1882
A 1885
A 1881

LIM 1878
B 1879

E 1847

S 1890
S 1891
MASHONALAND 1891
W 1894
W 1892

LEBOMBO 1891
PRETORIA 1878
ZULULAND 1870
S 1893

L 1859
BLOEMFONTEIN 1863
NATAL 1853
ST JOHN'S KAFFRARIA 1873
GRAHAMSTOWN 1863

L 1877

KIMBERLEY AND KURUMAN 1911

GEORGE 1911

CAPE TOWN 1847

0   km   1,000

Southern Africa, 1838

Bethanie E
Steinkopf L
Komaggas L
Ebenezer A

Latakoo L
Motito E
Thaba Nchu W
Campbell L

Mantatees W
Griqua Town L

Wupperthal E
Groene Kloof M
Worcester E
Bochesfeld L·S·W
Cape Town L·S·W
Steilenbosch
Caledon E

Philippolis L
Bethulie E
Bethel E
Uitenhage L
Genadendal M
Hemel in Arde M
Elim M
Pacaltsdorp L

Hlongeroa A
Ginani A
Umlazi A
Buntingville W

Morija E
Butterworth W
Buffalo River L
Wesleyville W
Theopolis L
Port Elizabeth L
Bethelsdorp L

1 Paarl L
2 Mokotling E
3 Thaba Bosiu E
4 Umpukani W
5 Clarkebury W
6 Shiloh M
7 Kat River L
8 Keiskamma L
9 Grahamstown B·L·W
10 Graaff Reinet L

131

supposedly radical leanings were allied to fears lest Christian teaching provoke Muslim and Hindu hostility to East India Company rule. Parliament approved the establishment of the diocese of Calcutta (1814) in order to serve both secular and ecclesiastical interests in part by licensing, ordaining and disciplining the growing number of Anglican missionaries and their converts. While this helped erode suspicion of missionaries, it opened the recurrent and often debilitating debate as to the respective powers of bishops and home societies over their missionaries in the field. The missions only won unrestricted freedom of entry to British India as a result of the Company's charter renewals of 1813 and 1833, by which time the educational work in which most societies were involved was seen by government as a chief means both to attach significant Indian social groups to British rule and to promote India's 'progress'. While Indian missionaries in general were torn between irritation at government's 'neutrality' in religious matters and appreciation of growing official support for their schools and colleges, the picture to the 1850s was nevertheless one of improving relations between missions and colonial government.

A very different pattern emerged in West Indian colonies like Jamaica and in the Cape Colony. Many planters and settlers resented missionary preaching or teaching and the growth of self-sufficient communities of converts as subversive of white authority and contrary to whites' interest in cheap labour. In such circumstances, despite constant injunctions not to meddle in politics, missionaries often found themselves ranged against colonial rulers in defence of civil rights and liberties for non-Europeans. The struggles in the 1820s of John Smith in Demarara and Dr John Philip in South Africa were testimony not only to the extreme conflicts which could arise between missionary and colonial interests, but to the persistent links between the anti-slavery or humanitarian movement and missionary enterprise.

In Sierra Leone, however, from 1808

onwards Christian missionary education apparently held out the only promise of creating a coherent community from the chaotic mixture of ethnic groups among the slaves freed there by the west coast naval squadron. Colonial governors and Anglican and Wesleyan missionaries worked closely together in a setting where the demarcation lines between colonial administration, education and missionary attempts at conversion were uncommonly blurred.

The relation between colonial rule and missionary work was thus clearly a complex one. In circumstances where colonial or indigenous governments failed them, missionaries were inclined to turn to the imperial government in London. From the West Indies they pressed the Colonial Office and Parliament to override colonial assemblies' rights of self-government in the interests of the slaves. Philip urged the expansion of direct imperial control beyond the Cape's existing frontier as a means to protect Africans from white settler expansion, war and dispossession. Missionary evidence on behalf of the Maori contributed to the British government's attempt with the Treaty of Waitangi to halt deteriorating relations and to forestall large-scale commercial settlement in New Zealand. In practice, most missionaries would have welcomed government support except for the fact that it was rarely to be had on their own terms. Thus, although in general an Anglican society like the Church Missionary Society was more deferential towards colonial or imperial authorities than one with a strongly Nonconformist tradition like the Baptists, neither the support of missionary societies nor that of individual missionaries could automatically be taken for granted.

Colonial governments and the Anglican Church also reshaped their relationship between 1830 and 1870. Although in New South Wales the creation of the Church and School Corporation in the mid-1820s, endowed with one-seventh of the colony's land to support an Anglican establishment, suggested that eighteenth-century precedents were still influential, there was little future for such links between church and state. In the white colonies the pressure from religiously pluralist or indifferent immigrant populations for all churches to be placed on an equal footing was irresistible. Compromises, like New South Wales's decision in 1836 to provide state grants-in-aid to all major denominations, were short lived. By the 1870s state support was available only for secular education, and religious voluntarism – in any case normal among non-Anglicans – was the norm, even in a colony like New Zealand with its strong denominational groups. London's withdrawal from religious and ecclesiastical matters was an inescapable feature of developing colonial self-government; separation of church and state in the white colonies was legally complete by 1865, and had proceeded much more rapidly than in Britain itself.

This development provoked a vigorous response from many who were working after 1830 for a reformed and revitalized metropolitan Anglicanism. The foundation of the Colonial Church Society (1838) and the Colonial Bishoprics Fund (1841) was a sign of determination among both low and high churchmen not to surrender the colonies to either irreligion or sectarian rivals. These initiatives went together with mounting demands for the co-ordination and control of all Anglican missionary work by the church, not only within the colonies but beyond them, and for the consecration of missionary bishops to lead that expansion. The numbers of emigrants from Britain to the colonies of white settlement were growing rapidly, and it was felt not only by Anglican leaders but also by other denominations that ecclesiastical provision should be made for them just as it was being increased for Britain's own rising population. At the same time hopes grew that colonial churches would come to assume responsibility for their own missionary enterprise, releasing home societies' funds for new work.

For contemporaries such ambitions both threatened an increase in religious factional-ism or competition at home and abroad, and jeopardized amicable relations between bishops and missionary societies. For historians they re-emphasize the need when examining the ties between religion and empire to look beyond the boundaries of colonial rule and society. No more than traders and commerce were evangelists and Christianity to be confined within the formal Empire. Indeed, the extent to which the patterns of British mercantile activity and those of missionary enterprise coincide is both striking and in need of further study. Missionaries always looked ahead to the conversion or (more commonly in the late nineteenth century) evangelization of the whole world. As the LMS venture into the Pacific in the wake of the late-eighteenth-century explorations or David Livingstone's later travels illustrate, the urge to expand their work to 'the regions beyond' was always strong.

The late 1830s and 1840s witnessed the second of the major waves of modern missionary expansion; not only were many existing operations reinforced, but new missionary frontiers were opened up. In West Africa, Methodists, Anglicans and Presbyterians all moved forward on the Gold Coast, as well as inland from Lagos and up the Niger River. New bishoprics in Hong Kong and Rupert's Land provided support for the CMS in extending its work. Expansion was steadily reinforced by other nineteenth-century developments, such as periodic metropolitan revivalism, the growth in numbers and migrations of converts, mounting pessimism as to the damaging impact of western culture and trade on non-European societies and the expansion of rivals such as Islam or, for Protestant missionaries, Roman Catholicism. After 1860 the remotest of places appeared increasingly attractive to Anglicans and Nonconformists alike. In 1865 Hudson Taylor formed his immensely influential and non-denominational China Inland Mission; Baptists, Plymouth Brethren and the Livingstone Inland Mission subsequently headed deep into the Congo basin. Missionary bishops like

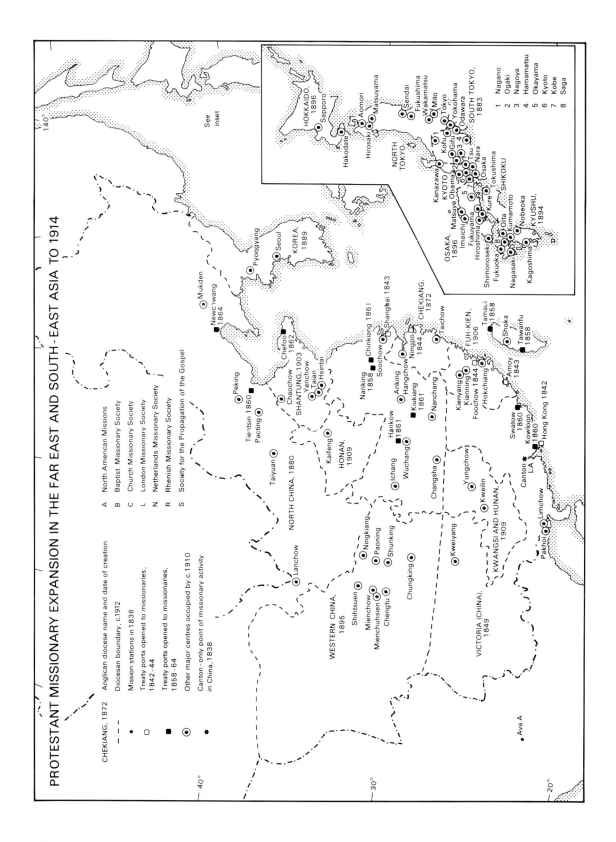

PROTESTANT MISSIONARY EXPANSION IN THE FAR EAST AND SOUTH-EAST ASIA TO 1914

CHEKIANG, 1872   Anglican diocese name and date of creation

– – –   Diocesan boundary, c.1912

•   Mission stations in 1838

□   Treaty ports opened to missionaries, 1842-44

■   Treaty ports opened to missionaries, 1858-64

⊙   Other major centres occupied by c.1910

✶   Canton – only point of missionary activity in China, 1838

A   North American Missions
B   Baptist Missionary Society
C   Church Missionary Society
L   London Missionary Society
N   Netherlands Missionary Society
R   Rhenish Missionary Society
S   Society for the Propagation of the Gospel

1   Nagano
2   Ogaki
3   Nagoya
4   Hamamatsu
5   Okayama
6   Kyoto
7   Kobe
8   Saga

HOKKAIDO, 1896   Sapporo   Hakodate

NORTH TOKYO,   Aomori   Matsuyama   Sendai   Fukushima   Wakamatsu
Hirosaki   Mito   Tokyo   Yokohama   Odawara   SOUTH TOKYO, 1883

Kanazawa   Kofu   Gifu   Tsu   Nara   Osaka
KYOTO   Matsuye   Obama   Tokushima   SHIKOKU
OSAKA, 1896   Imaichi   Fukuyama   Kure   Kumamoto   KYUSHU, 1894
Hiroshima   Oita   Nobeoka
Shimonoseki   Fukuoka   Nagasaki   Kagoshima

Mukden   Newchwang 1864   Pyongyang   Seoul   KOREA, 1889

Peking   Tientsin 1860   Pacting   Chefoo   Chaochow   SHANTUNG, 1903   Yenchow   Taian   Hsintai

Taiyuan   Kaifeng   HONAN, 1909   Nanking 1858   Soochow   Shanghai 1843   Chinkiang 1861   CHEKIANG, 1872
Ningpo 1844   Taichow   FUH-KIEN, 1906   Tamsui 1858   Shoka   Taiwanfu 1858

NORTH CHINA, 1880   Anking   Hankow 1861   Hangchow   Kienyang   Kienning   Foochow 1844   (Hokchiang)   Amoy 1843

Lanchow   Ichang   Wuchang   Kiukiang 1861   Nanchang   Swatow 1860   Kowloon 1860   Hong Kong 1842

Changsha   Yungchow   Kweilin   Canton   Limchow   Pakhoi
L. A

Ningkiang   Paoning   Shunking   Kweiyang   KWANGSI AND HUNAN, 1909

WESTERN CHINA, 1895   Shihtsuen   Mienchow   Mienchuhsien   Chengtu   Chungking   VICTORIA (CHINA), 1849

Ava A

134

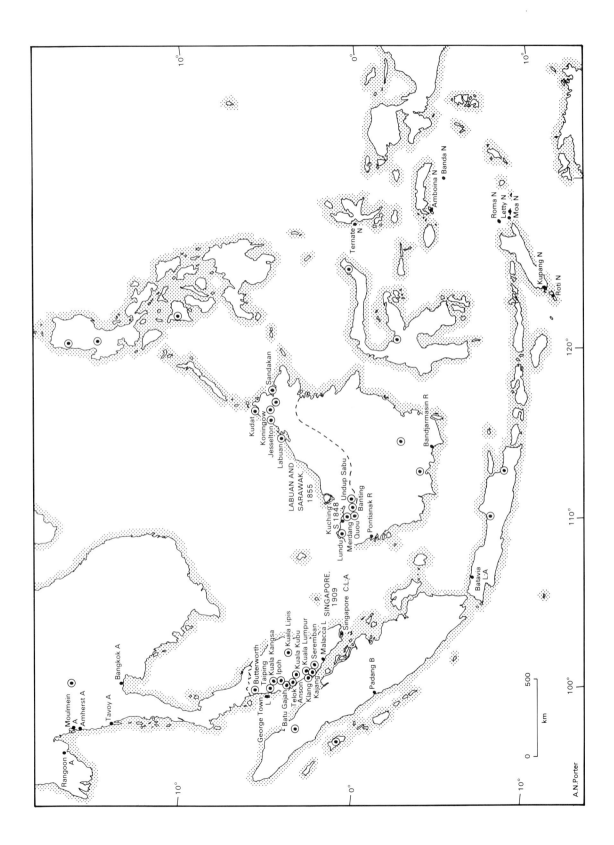

Rangoon ●
Moulmein ⊙
A
Amherst A ●
Tavoy A ●
Bangkok A ●

George Town ●
Butterworth ⊙
Taiping ⊙
Kuala Kangsa ⊙
Batu Gajah ⊙
Ipoh ⊙
Telok ⊙
Anson ⊙
Klang ⊙
Kajang ⊙
Kuala Kubu ⊙
Kuala Lumpur ⊙
Seremban ⊙
Kuala Lipis ⊙
Malacca L ●
Singapore C.L.A.

SINGAPORE, 1909

Padang B ●

Kudat ●
Koningow ⊙
Jesselton ⊙
Sandakan ⊙
Labuan ⊙

LABUAN AND
SARAWAK,
1855

Kuching S 1848
Lundu ⊙
Merdang ⊙
Quou ⊙
Banting ⊙
Undup Sabu
Pontianak R ●

Bandjarmasin R ●

Batavia L.A. ●

Ternate N ●

Amboina N ●
Banda N ●

Roma N ●
Letty N ⊙
Moa N ⊙

Kupang N
Roti N ●

500

km

0

A.N.Porter

Patteson in Melanesia (1861-71) and Mackenzie, heading the Universities Mission to Central Africa (1861-2), carried on the example of Bishop Selwyn from New Zealand. The first modern African bishop, Samuel Ajayi Crowther, was posted to the Niger in 1864.

Such forward movement, of course, hinged not only on metropolitan ambitions, institutions or finance, but on the willingness of non-Europeans to assist it. In many cases missions were actively courted, to some extent perhaps for their religion but most often, it appears, for other reasons. To many African rulers, missionaries held out prospects above all of trade, of education, of protection against rivals internal or external and of assistance in their dealings with Europeans. Missions frequently also attracted the misfits, the outcast or criminal, runaway slaves, the poor, oppressed and deprived. In late-nineteenth-century India, for example, upsurges in conversions among Hindu society's depressed classes were associated with critical problems of famine, land shortage and debt; sceptical comment about 'famine Christians' was common.

Recorded numbers of converts – always small in absolute terms and often unreliable – are therefore by themselves poor indicators of the missionary impact. Of great importance was the role of missions as effective solvents of non-European societies; they acted as channels for the inflow of western knowledge and values, calling into question traditional authority and institutions, challenging customary ideas, for example about marriage or the status of women, and influencing patterns of local political influence or power. Missionaries were usually few in number and seemingly vulnerable, but their influence was in practice difficult for indigenous authorities to control. Contemporaries recognized this well. A British administrator like Harry Johnston in Central Africa welcomed missionary outposts as in each case 'an essay in colonization', paving the way for British influence and control. For the same reason, local rulers from China to Yorubaland often tried to restrict missionaries' access or exclude them altogether.

At this point missions and governments again often began to co-operate. The period 1880-1914 saw by far the greatest increases yet in the scale and geographical extent of missionary endeavours. Involvement with the imperial government or its local representatives was at times virtually inevitable, especially in the insecure conditions of Africa during the 1880s and 1890s. Anxious to protect themselves or their converts, or wishing to break down the resistance of local societies where they had long been unsuccessful, missionaries often emerged as supporters either of coercion or of formal imperial expansion, estimating their future as more promising under British rule. This was not of course new; in the mid-century they secured access to China with the backing of western governments under the peace treaties of 1842 and 1858-60. Now British missionaries played a significant role in the establishment of imperial claims to Uganda, Nyasaland and Southern Rhodesia (now Zimbabwe), and applauded the reconquest of the Sudan in 1898.

These alliances with the secular arms of British authority, however, were rarely more than temporary. The consolidation of formal imperial administration, for example in Africa following the continent's partition, re-created tensions between church and state akin to those earlier conflicts already mentioned. In Egypt and Nigeria administrators angered missionaries by restricting their operations in the interests of peace and security. Colonial officials frequently found inter-missionary disputes over territorial spheres irritating if not incomprehensible, while missionaries themselves resented official deference to indigenous allies on a host of issues from domestic slavery to property rights.

The rise and fall of co-operation between missions and government at the end of the nineteenth century in areas of expanding imperial control were affected partly by the changing nature of the missionary movement itself. Not only had the status and professionalism of missionaries risen markedly during the century, but after 1880 large numbers of public-school and university volunteers came forward. Specialists such as trained doctors were recruited on a growing scale. On the one hand, this brought into the field many more missionaries capable of bridging the gap between the predominant evangelical opinion of 'provincial' Britain and those who ran imperial and colonial government. On the other, the new missionaries more commonly had the confidence, upbringing and contacts which enabled them to be effective critics of empire if and when they chose.

These same qualities, especially when allied as they often were with the evangelical revivalist's heightened sensitivity to spiritual or ethical shortcomings, also had serious implications for converts. As numbers grew, missionaries had to face the question when and in what manner they might withdraw, leaving non-Europeans to take over their own churches. By the 1860s British missionaries broadly agreed that this goal required converts able to finance themselves, laity and ministers capable of disciplined self-government and clear evidence of indigenous missionary activity. In all denominations, however, and notwithstanding pressures from organizers at home, missionaries on the ground found it hard before 1914 to agree that these conditions were being met or that local ecclesiastical prospects looked secure enough to justify any withdrawal. Crowther's episcopate at his death in 1891 was widely seen as a disaster, necessitating a white successor; V. S. Azariah, the first Indian bishop, was appointed only in 1912 and then in the face of much criticism and resistance.

While insensitivity to indigenous ambitions and reluctance to accommodate them thus had the short-term effect of prolonging and intensifying colonial controls, they nevertheless stimulated developments ultimately inimical to alien rule. This was very strikingly illustrated in Britain's West and South African possessions, where those disenchanted with the missionary-led bodies often left *en masse* to set up their own 'independent' churches. There and elsewhere many who had received a missionary education used it to challenge colonial control in both church and state. At the same time some missionaries began slowly to revise their ideas, partly in the interest of retaining the allegiance of articulate converts, partly out of genuine disquiet, for example at the excesses of 'pacification' or of whites intent on turning the powers of colonial government to their own advantage. By 1910, when the World Missionary Conference was held in Edinburgh, something of the interdenominational co-operation, the genuinely global perspective, the detachment from government and the relative absence of condescension which had characterized late-eighteenth-century attitudes towards converts was beginning to be recovered.

Canada, 1867–1949

The passing of the British North America Act in 1867 by the British Parliament was an exercise in state-building which contrasted with contemporary European examples where nationalism was the driving force. It was the Reformers in Canada West who became increasingly frustrated by the compromises with the Francophones of Canada East which the Act of Union (1841) seemingly required. They were also casting covetous eyes upon the lands of the west. Their success came in 1863 when the Conservative leaders, John A. Macdonald and George E. Cartier, sensed the dangers of inertia in the face of American hostility and expansion. The result was a coalition pledged to bring about a wider

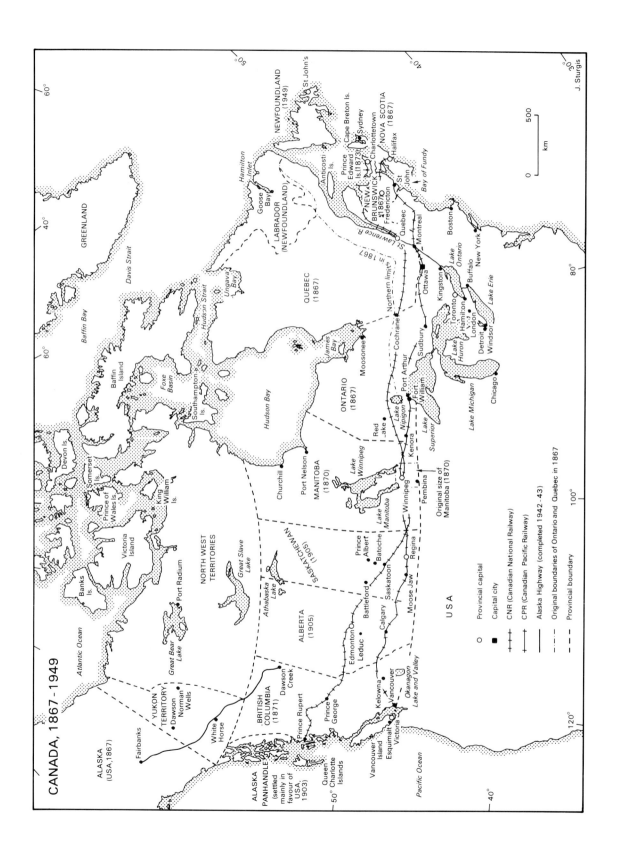

CANADA, 1867 - 1949

GREENLAND

ALASKA
(USA, 1867)

Fairbanks

YUKON
TERRITORY

Dawson

Norman
Wells

White
Horse

BRITISH
COLUMBIA
(1871)

Dawson
Creek

Prince Rupert

Prince
George

Kelowna

Okanagan
Lake and Valley

Vancouver
Island

Esquimalt
Victoria

Vancouver

Queen
Charlotte
Islands

ALASKA
PANHANDLE
(settled
mainly in
favour of
USA,
1903)

50°

Pacific Ocean

Port Radium

Great Bear
Lake

Banks
Is.

Victoria
Island

Prince of
Wales Is.

King
William
Is.

Somerset
Is.

Devon Is

Baffin Bay

Baffin
Island

Davis Strait

Atlantic Ocean

60°

40°

NORTH WEST
TERRITORIES

Great Slave
Lake

Athabaska
Lake

SASKATCHEWAN (1905)

ALBERTA
(1905)

Edmonton

Leduc

Calgary

Battleford

Prince
Albert

Batoche

Saskatoon

Moose Jaw

Regina

Foxe
Basin

Southampton
Is.

Hudson Strait

Ungava
Bay

Hudson Bay

Churchill

Port Nelson

MANITOBA
(1870)

Lake
Winnipeg

Lake
Manitoba

Winnipeg

Pembina

Original size of
Manitoba (1870)

Red
Lake

Lake
Nipigon

Kenora

Port Arthur

Fort
William

Lake
Superior

Chicago

Lake Michigan

QUEBEC
(1867)

James
Bay

Moosonee

ONTARIO
(1867)

Cochrane

Sudbury

Lake
Huron

Lake
Ontario

Lake Erie

Windsor
Detroit

London

Hamilton
Toronto

Buffalo

New York

Boston

Kingston

Ottawa

Montreal

Quebec

St Lawrence R.

Northern limit in 1867

LABRADOR
(NEWFOUNDLAND)

Goose
Bay

Hamilton
Inlet

Anticosti
Is.

NEWFOUNDLAND
(1949)

St John's

Cape Breton Is.

Sydney

Prince
Edward
Is. (1873)

Charlottetown

NOVA SCOTIA
(1867)

Halifax

St
John

Fredericton

NEW
BRUNSWICK
1867

Bay of Fundy

USA

50°

40°

30°

80°

100°

120°

40°

60°

60°

40°

J. Sturgis

500

0

km

○ Provincial capital

■ Capital city

╫╫ CNR (Canadian National Railway)

╫╫ CPR (Canadian Pacific Railway)

── Alaska Highway (completed 1942-43)

─ · ─ Original boundaries of Ontario and Quebec in 1867

─ ─ ─ Provincial boundary

union within British North America. The task proved to be both time-consuming and exceedingly difficult. Only the emergence of forceful local leadership in the persons of Leonard Tilley and Charles Tupper, combined with the foolhardy attacks of the Fenians, made possible the inclusion of New Brunswick and Nova Scotia. In the latter province the feeling persisted, reasserting itself forcibly in the 1880s and 1920s, that it had been unfairly bundled into an ill-considered marriage. Price Edward Island remained aloof at first but changed its mind in 1873 when Canadian financial help for railway debts and the buying out of absentee landlords proved to be sufficient bait.

The real prize, however, was the west. The condition attached to British Columbia's inclusion was the building of a connecting railway. Frequently, before the completion of the Canadian Pacific Railway in 1885, the burden imposed by its costs threatened to dissolve the vision of a country from sea to sea. The last injection of capital, in fact, came about as a fortuitous by-product of a tragedy unfolding in the region formerly controlled by the Hudson's Bay Company. Without any consideration for the rights or the way of life of the *métis* or Indians, the Canadian government in 1869 blithely began to negotiate with the company for the release of its vast territories. The desire to stamp its claim to the territory by attracting settlers alarmed the *métis*. Under the leadership of Louis Riel, a provisional government was set up in the Red River which eventually won concessions on land and language in 1870 within the postage-stamp-sized province of Manitoba. However, it also committed the blunder of executing a Canadian prisoner, thus ensuring a lack of sympathy from English-speaking and Protestant Canada when the traditional economy,

based on the buffalo hunt, was breathing its last in the Saskatchewan River region in the mid-1880s. Summoned once again as leader, Riel, increasingly out of touch with reality, gambled on military victory and lost. No better demonstration of the Canadian Pacific Railway's usefulness than the quick dispatch of troops could have been devised. The trickle of settlers in the 1870s became a flood by the 1890s. Population was sufficient by 1905 to allow the creation of the two new provinces of Saskatchewan and Alberta. The belated entry of Newfoundland into confederation in 1949 can be explained mainly as a result of the Depression of the 1930s. Insolvency forced the abandonment of responsible government and its replacement by a commission government appointed by Britain. Aided considerably by the building of numerous military and air bases, the commission was successful in getting the colony out of debt. After the war the future constitutional direction of the island was decided by referendum, wherein by a slim majority the decision was to join Canada.

The processes involved in the making of a nation which defied continentalism led to the adoption of economic policies which aroused sectional and regional opposition. Upon such tensions were superimposed the inherent strains resulting from Anglophone and Francophone sensibilities. Just as Quebec could be angered by the hanging of Riel in 1885 or the imposition of conscription in 1917 and 1944, so could the west be exasperated by protectionist policies, seen as favouring Ontario. By 1949 there were signs, such as the promise of wealth from oil in Alberta and the stirrings in Quebec, that more of the high ground held by the fathers of confederation concerning the desirability of a strong central government would have to be conceded.

Australia and federation, 1901

Australia as a federal nation came into being on 1 January 1901. When one considers the relatively homogeneous population of the Australian colonies, all with similar forms of government and five of them occupying an island continent, it was perhaps surprising that such a development had not occurred earlier. The explanation is that each colony had evolved its own particularist culture and its own in-built loyalties. New South Wales, its economy based on exports, had always had a free-trade outlook, while Victoria had deliberately created a manufacturing economy behind tariff walls. Bitter rivalry existed between Sydney and Melbourne. South Australia, the 'paradise of dissent', had its own superiority complex which others found insufferable. Tasmania (formerly Van Diemen's Land), despite its convict past, became the most Anglophile and conservative of all the colonies. Queensland, its population still composed of nearly 50 per cent immigrants, had a tropical economy which led it to make repeated attempts to procure non-European labour that put it at cross-purposes with the traditions of the rest. Until the mineral discoveries of the 1890s, Western Australia had always been the distant and poor cousin of the others. Thus each colony luxuriated in its own distinctiveness, a tendency enhanced by the winning of responsible government in the 1850s. When the third Earl Grey (colonial secretary, 1846–52) put forward proposals for federation in the late 1840s, they elicited no nationalistic response at all. During the next three decades each colony was preoccupied with the development of its own economy.

What kind of shock to the system was required to jolt the colonies into more of a common outlook? The first came in the 1880s with the realization that Australia was part of a larger world of imperialistic rivalries and ambitions. Certain politicians such as Sir Henry Parkes and Alfred Deakin sensed the dangers of isolation. An eye-opener for colonists was Britain's failure to grasp the seriousness of foreign encroachment in the Pacific. This was felt most acutely when Britain refused to uphold Queensland's annexation of New Guinea. There were those who thought that only a united Australia could awaken Britain to the threat posed by French and German expansion.

For most Australians, however, the crucial turning-point was the economic slump of the 1890s. No longer could it be assumed that prosperity was increasing on a never-ending upward curve. Mercantile and business interests were now attuned to the need for change. To the fore came the Australian Natives' Association, formed as long ago as 1871 at the very time when native-born Australians began to outnumber immigrants. Important as its contribution was, it would be a mistake, however, to read too much into the claims that federation was the result of nationalist sentiment or the egalitarian ethos of the outback. In fact, the labour movement was, of all interest groups, the most opposed to federation. Rather, federation was backed by middle-class Anglophiles who were seeking the means by which to effect a return to prosperity and progress. Even then, it was to take nearly ten years of agitation before their efforts were crowned with success. One important reason for this delay was the democratic method by which it was achieved. The fullest explanation of federation involves one in a panoply of grass-roots activities such as petitions, conferences and referenda. To this extent Australians were true to a democratic tradition which had been carefully nurtured by radicals in the past. But in making their calculations as to how to vote, each individual may have been following the same kind of logic which had motivated squatters, bush-rangers and gold diggers of an earlier age.

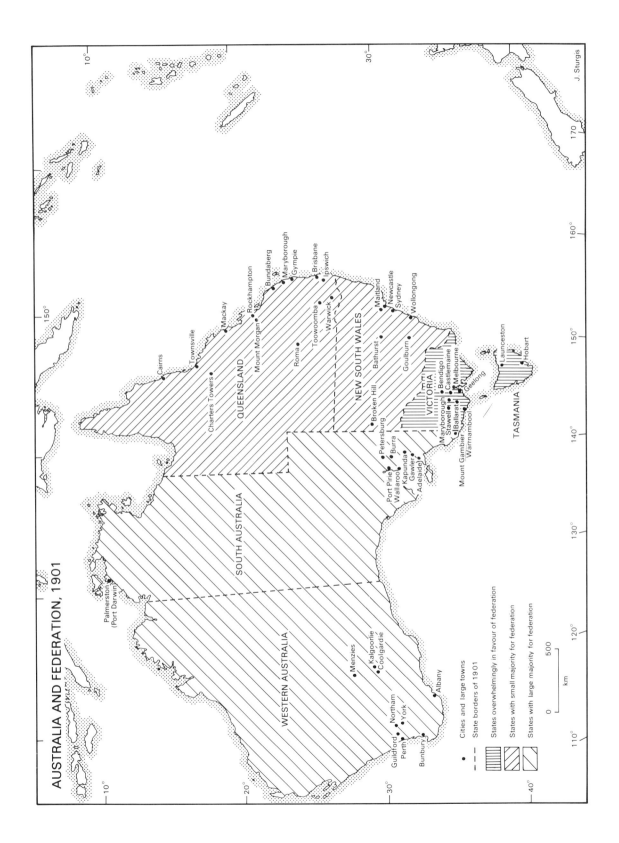

AUSTRALIA AND FEDERATION, 1901

WESTERN AUSTRALIA

SOUTH AUSTRALIA

QUEENSLAND

NEW SOUTH WALES

VICTORIA

TASMANIA

Palmerston (Port Darwin)

Guildford
Perth
Bunbury
Northam
York
Albany

Menzies
Kalgoorlie
Coolgardie

Port Pirie
Wallaroo
Kapunda
Gawler
Adelaide
Burra
Petersburg

Mount Gambier
Warrnambool
Maryborough
Stawell
Ballarat
Bendigo
Castlemaine
Melbourne
Geelong

Broken Hill

Cairns
Townsville
Charters Towers
Mackay
Rockhampton
Mount Morgan
Bundaberg
Maryborough
Gympie
Brisbane
Ipswich
Toowoomba
Warwick
Roma

Bathurst
Maitland
Newcastle
Sydney
Wollongong
Goulburn

Launceston
Hobart

J. Sturgis

Cities and large towns

State borders of 1901

States overwhelmingly in favour of federation

States with small majority for federation

States with large majority for federation

km

0   500

10°
20°
30°
40°

110° 120° 130° 140° 150° 160° 170°

10°
30°

150° 160° 170°

141

Britain and the Pacific

European explorers in the Pacific (see p. 57) were followed first by missionaries (see p. 128–9) and then by traders, whalers, deserters, escaped convicts and others on the make or on the run from settlements in Australia and New Zealand (see pp. 70–6). Fruit, vegetables, salted pork and sandalwood were exchanged for European textiles, hardware, arms and spirits. Land was sold or leased to settlers who established themselves in Fiji and New Caledonia (French) but were less evident elsewhere and scarcely at all in Tonga or the Cook Islands. Sugar, copra and sea island cotton were developments of the second half of the nineteenth century. Unbridled adventurism created a lawlessness in the islands that was only increased from the 1860s by the demand for cheap labour both within and beyond the South Pacific. Islanders suffered the fatal impact of European greed and diseases; labourers (particularly from the southern Solomons, the New Hebrides and the Gilbert and Ellice groups) were trafficked between the islands or transported into the virtual slavery of Queensland and Peru, while 'a new form of slavery' brought in Indians, notably to Fiji where the Asian population (Chinese as well as Indians) came to outnumber Fijians in the twentieth century.

The extension of political control was partly an attempt to restrain rash individuals and partly a response to the ambitions of other powers. When British settlers grabbed Fiji, the British government concluded a treaty with Chief Cakobau by which the islands (some 300 of them of which only about 100 were inhabited) were ceded to the crown (1874). Three years later the High Commission of the Western Pacific was set up, in the first instance to control Britons involved in labour recruitment and other often unsavoury activities elsewhere in the Pacific. Meanwhile, the ocean was partitioned between the powers. In the 1840s and 1850s the French established themselves in Tahiti, the Marquesas Islands and New Caledonia, and they annexed the Loyalty Islands in 1864. Germany and the USA joined the scramble in the 1880s. In 1884 eastern New Guinea (western New Guinea having been part of the Netherlands East Indies since the 1820s) was divided between Britain (the southeast) and Germany (the north-east), while Germany also took the Bismarck Archipelago. In 1890 Samoa was shared by Germany and the USA after an earlier tripartite arrangement involving Britain had failed. The USA acquired Hawaii in 1898, and Germany purchased the Marianas and Palau (Caroline) Islands from Spain in 1899. Britain's position in Tonga (or Friendly Islands) was recognized by an Anglo-German agreement of 1899 (British protected state 1900), and in 1906 an Anglo-French convention set up joint control (or condominium) over the New Hebrides. After the First World War, New Zealand, which had already gained the Cook Islands from Britain (1901), took on the former German colony of Western Samoa as a League of Nations mandate; while Australia, to which Britain had earlier transferred British New Guinea (1902–6), administered the mandates of German New Guinea (with the Bismarck Archipelago) and the phosphate island of Nauru. At the same time the Japanese took possession of the German island colonies north of the equator (Marianas, Carolines and Marshalls). The naval treaty concluded between the powers at the Washington Conference (1922) included an engagement to maintain the status quo with regard to fortifications and naval bases in the Pacific.

As British responsibilities in the Pacific increased in the late nineteenth century, so the High Commission of the Western Pacific extended its jurisdiction over a pattern of islands not otherwise administered by Fiji, Australia, New Zealand or other powers. Thus, although the constitutional status of territories changed from time to time (for

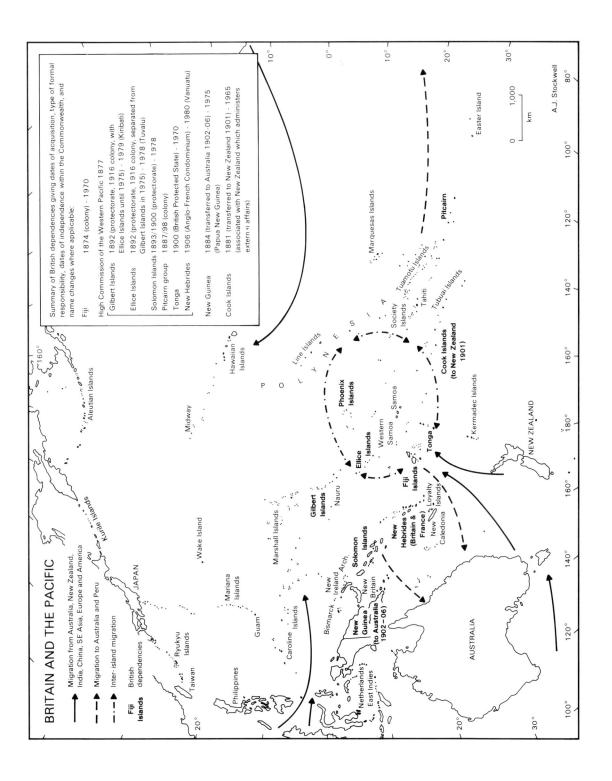

BRITAIN AND THE PACIFIC

→ Migration from Australia, New Zealand, India, China, SE Asia, Europe and America

▲ - - Migration to Australia and Peru

▲ - · - Inter-island migration

Fiji Islands British dependencies

Summary of British dependencies giving dates of acquisition, type of formal responsibility, dates of independence within the Commonwealth, and name changes where applicable:

Fiji   1874 (colony) - 1970

High Commission of the Western Pacific 1877

Gilbert Islands   1892 (protectorate, 1916 colony, with Ellice Islands until 1975) - 1979 (Kiribati)

Ellice Islands   1892 (protectorate, 1916 colony, separated from Gilbert Islands in 1975) - 1978 (Tuvalu)

Solomon Islands 1893/1900 (protectorate) - 1978

Pitcairn group   1887/98 (colony)

Tonga   1900 (British Protected State) - 1970

New Hebrides   1906 (Anglo-French Condominium) - 1980 (Vanuatu)

New Guinea   1884 (transferred to Australia 1902-06) - 1975 (Papua New Guinea)

Cook Islands   1881 (transferred to New Zealand 1901) - 1965 (associated with New Zealand which administers external affairs)

A.J. Stockwell

143

example, the Gilbert and Ellice group was a protectorate in 1892 but a crown colony from 1916), the High Commission came to embrace the Solomons, Gilbert and Ellice Islands (including the Northern Line and Phoenix Islands), Pitcairn (including the Southern Line group), New Hebrides (shared with France) and Tonga (for which jurisdiction was transferred from the high commission to Fiji in 1952).

Communications: principal steamer routes and coaling stations, 1889

The vital supports of Britain's nineteenth-century supremacy included not only her foreign trade and overseas investment but her shipping. British shipowners and shipbuilders adjusted successfully to rising demands and did much to develop new technologies – steam, compound engines, iron and steel materials; with highly skilled workers, they produced better and cheaper ships than anyone else. Consequently between 1860 and 1914 Britain owned roughly one-third of the world's tonnage; from 1890 to 1914 she built two-thirds of the world's ships and carried approximately 50 per cent of its sea-borne trade. Income from shipping and associated activities such as insurance contributed significantly to her invisible earnings. Although her merchantmen faced powerful competition from Scandinavians and Americans before 1850, thereafter Britain's leading position was virtually unchallenged; only Germany was a generally significant competitor between 1890 and 1914. Even such rivalry as existed was restricted, to the chagrin of shippers, by the organization especially after 1880 of the shipping conferences or 'rings', which variously fixed rates, pooled earnings and divided traffic among the participating lines.

Technical advances assisted sail as well as steam shipping; the former remained profitable on long-distance routes, to Australia or North and South American Pacific ports, until the 1890s. Steam made steady headway on shorter routes, for example dominating the Mediterranean by the early 1860s, but expansion elsewhere depended on developing efficient engines, so lowering running costs and releasing coal space for cargo. A major breakthrough came with Alfred Holt's Ocean Steam Ship Company in 1865, which competed successfully in the China trade. In 1869 the opening of the Suez Canal greatly shortened the distances involved, and steam rapidly captured the trade in high-value commodities such as tea. Simultaneously steam drew ahead in the North Atlantic. Although steamships long remained equipped with sails, from 1870 onwards new sailing tonnage fell rapidly behind steam.

Government took an early interest in steam, sensing its significance for the national economy, naval defence and imperial communications. From about 1840, on Palmerston's initiative, substantial subsidies in the form of mail contracts were provided to strategically placed companies such as Cunard, running to the USA, and P&O, which served the Far East. These lines not only set standards for others and encouraged technical development, but also provided the Admiralty with a pool of first-class vessels in time of emergency. The growth of steamship companies also gradually altered the structure of commerce, quickening and regularizing supplies, intensifying competition, in part through improved information, and contributing to the sustained late-nineteenth-century fall in prices of goods.

The implications of expansion for imperial defence were only slowly understood at the Admiralty and in other government quarters. After a long period in which Britain's maritime supremacy had been taken for granted, trade protection became a fashionable topic in the mid-1870s. The war scare of 1877–8

Coaling stations, 1889 (see map on pp. 146-7)

Names used are taken from the Admiralty map 'Principal coaling stations with 500 tons and more, for shipping purposes', dated 8 August 1889, British Library Map Collection Sec. 1 (1188).

1 Oterranai	54 Bangkok	107 Montevideo
2 Hakodate	55 Rangoon	108 Buenos Aires
3 Akishi Bay	56 Calcutta	109 Punta Arenas
4 Yokohama	57 Madras	110 Lota and Coronel
5 Kobe	58 Trincomali	111 Valparaiso
6 Nagasaki	59 Colombo	112 Coquimbo
7 Vladivostok	60 Point de Galle	113 P. Taltal
8 Ching Wang Tao	61 Bombay	114 P. Iquique
9 Chifu	62 Karachi	115 Callao
10 Shanghai	63 Muscat	116 Colon
11 Ningpo	64 Bushire	117 Curacao
12 Amoy	65 Basra	118 Trinidad
13 Swatow	66 Aden	119 Demarara
14 Hong Kong	67 Perim Island	120 Para
15 Haiphong	68 Jibuti	121 Maranham
16 Kelung	69 Zanzibar	122 Port Royal
17 Tourane	70 Dar-es-Salaam	123 Grenada
18 Saigon	71 Diego Suarez	124 Barbados
19 Singapore	72 Nosi Be	125 St Lucia
20 Penang	73 Mayotte	126 St Thomas
21 Labuan	74 St Mary	127 Havana
22 Batavia	75 Mozambique	128 Santiago
23 Surabaya	76 Delagoa Bay	129 Sitka
24 Banjuwangi	77 Port Natal	130 Esquimault
25 Broome	78 East London	131 P. Angeles
26 Fremantle	79 Port Elizabeth	132 Seattle
27 King George Sound	80 Simon's Bay	133 San Francisco
28 Adelaide	81 Cape Town	134 San Buenventura
29 Melbourne	82 Port Nolloth	135 San Diego
30 Hobart	83 St Helena	136 Mazatlan
31 Port Kembla	84 Ascension Island	137 Acapulco
32 Sydney	85 St Paul de Loanda	138 Corinto
33 Newcastle	86 Akassa	139 Limon
34 Brisbane	87 Sierra Leone	140 Vera Cruz
35 Maryborough	88 Dakar	141 Tampico
36 Townsville	89 St Louis	142 Nassau
37 Bay of Islands	90 Port Louis	143 Galveston
38 Whangarei	91 Mahe	144 New Orleans
39 Auckland	92 Tenerife	145 Mobile
40 Wellington	93 Las Palmas	146 Charleston
41 Nelson	94 Gibraltar	147 Quebec
42 Westport	95 Lisbon	148 St John's
43 Greymouth	96 Malta	149 Halifax
44 Port Lyttelton	97 Alexandria	150 Yarmouth
45 Oamaru	98 Port Said	151 Lunenburg
46 Otago Harbour	99 Suez	152 Miramichi
47 Napier	100 Massawa	153 Bermuda
48 Gavvtu	101 S. Vincent (C. de Verde)	154 Port Basque
49 Suva	102 Pernambuco	155 St John
50 Noumea	103 Bahia	156 Azores (Fayal, Terceira and S. Miguel)
51 Padang	104 Rio de Janeiro	157 Honolulu
52 Acheh Head	105 Santos	
53 Pulo Bras	106 Santa Catharina	

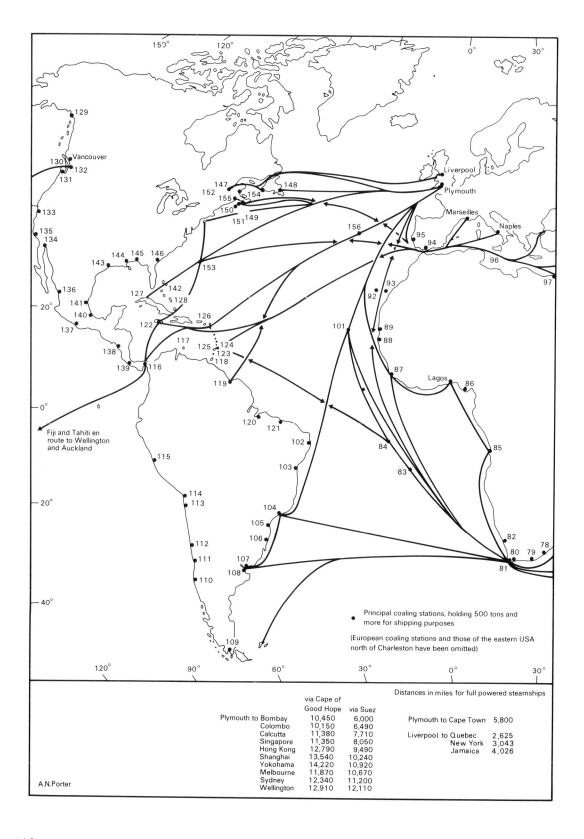

Fiji and Tahiti en route to Wellington and Auckland

Liverpool
Plymouth
Marseilles
Naples
Vancouver
Lagos

Principal coaling stations, holding 500 tons and more for shipping purposes

(European coaling stations and those of the eastern USA north of Charleston have been omitted)

Distances in miles for full powered steamships

	via Cape of Good Hope	via Suez
Plymouth to Bombay	10,450	6,000
Colombo	10,150	6,490
Calcutta	11,380	7,710
Singapore	11,350	8,050
Hong Kong	12,790	9,490
Shanghai	13,540	10,240
Yokohama	14,220	10,920
Melbourne	11,870	10,670
Sydney	12,340	11,200
Wellington	12,910	12,110

Plymouth to Cape Town	5,800
Liverpool to Quebec	2,625
New York	3,043
Jamaica	4,026

A.N.Porter

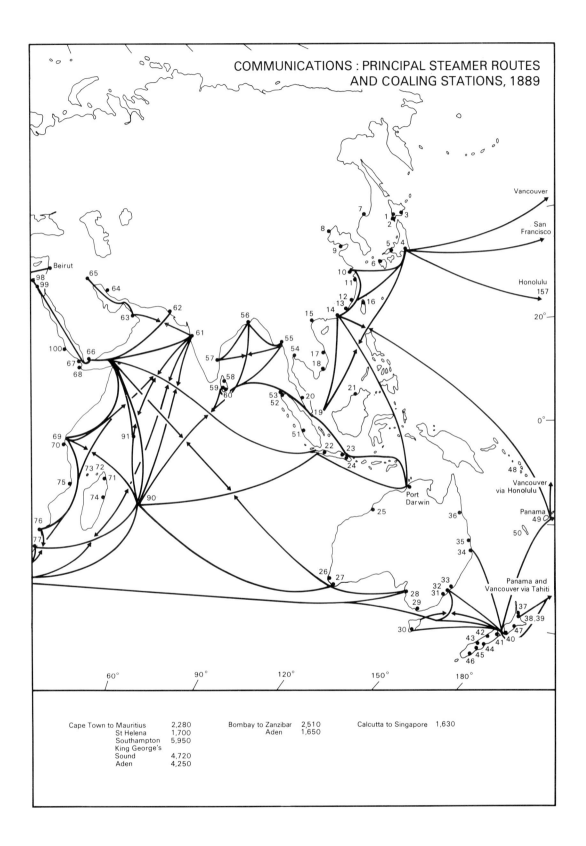

COMMUNICATIONS : PRINCIPAL STEAMER ROUTES
AND COALING STATIONS, 1889

Vancouver

San
Francisco

Honolulu
157

20°

Beirut

Vancouver
via Honolulu

Panama
49

50

Port
Darwin

Panama and
Vancouver via Tahiti

0°

60°   90°   120°   150°   180°

Cape Town to Mauritius	2,280	Bombay to Zanzibar	2,510	Calcutta to Singapore	1,630
	St Helena	1,700		Aden	1,650		
	Southampton	5,950					
	King George's						
	Sound	4,720					
	Aden	4,250					

produced flurries of concern about the state of colonial defence and the availability of coaling stations for British ships. The Carnarvon Commission of 1879 produced three major reports (1881–2) stressing the need for secure bases to provide world-wide mobility for the Royal Navy. Development of this network of coaling and repair facilities along the principal shipping lanes as the means to obtain command of the seas was central to naval planning until about 1905. In response to the growth of Britain's trade and mercantile marine, there thus developed a global concept of effectively integrated 'Imperial' defence. This partly replaced the older fragmented provision of home and colonial facilities until the shifting relations of the great powers caused Britain to concentrate afresh on north-western Europe and the North Sea from 1905 to 1914.

Communications: telegraphs, 1865–1914

Land lines were slowly developed during the 1830s and 1840s, but the first successful submarine telegraph was only laid in 1851, crossing the English Channel. Even then many technical problems in laying, repairing and maintaining cable still remained unsolved. The first transatlantic cable from Valentia to Placentia Bay functioned only briefly in 1858, but other far shorter cables (Malta to Sardinia and Corfu 1857–61, Suez to Aden and Karachi 1859–60) were hardly more successful. Initial support came from financial and commercial interests in Liverpool, Manchester, Glasgow and London and, to a lesser extent, from governments concerned to improve communications with India. With the eventual success of the Government of India's Persian Gulf line in 1863 and two Atlantic cables in 1866, submarine telegraphy was firmly established. The late 1860s saw a burst of company formation and rapid expansion of the system until 1876, when Australia and New Zealand were first linked. In a second phase from 1879 to 1889 the principal African submarine telegraphs were laid. By 1898 Britain owned approximately 60 per cent of the world's cables, as well as the giant among operators, the Eastern Telegraph Company. Formed in 1872 by amalgamation of the four operators on the direct route to India, the ETC with its numerous associated companies dominated everywhere but the North Atlantic.

Although written correspondence remained immensely important, submarine telegraphs revolutionized commerce by making available much more recent information about commodity prices and market conditions. Competition of all kinds increased, and contributed to the late-nineteenth-century fall in world prices. Merchants were encouraged to specialize and, by maintaining smaller stocks, tied up less capital. The impact of telegraphs on imperial government was far more ambiguous; the advantages of more frequent news were offset by problems with greater volumes of business, and control of imperial officials from London was not made noticeably easier. Cables nevertheless had major implications for defence planning, facilitating the movement of troops or fleets around the world as well as creating defence problems by their very existence. While less vulnerable than land lines, shallow water cables and landing stations were obvious targets, and interference with vital communications was likely where foreign governments controlled the cables.

In 1867, hoping to channel the new telegraphic enthusiasm, Lord Derby's ministry drew up a public list of lines government might encourage as 'most called for by imperial and commercial interests'. This furthered the movement towards the extensive subsidizing of British telegraph companies by the imperial and colonial governments. Increasingly

Telegraphs, 1865–1914 (see map on pp. 150–1)

1	Port Arthur	53	Suakin	105	Cherbourg
2	Taku	54	Perim	106	Rotterdam
3	Chefoo	55	Obok	107	Goteborg
4	Tsingtao	56	Aden	108	Nystad
5	Shanghai	57	Mombasa	109	Farsund
6	Nagasaki	58	Zanzibar	110	Peterhead
7	Koyi	59	Seychelles	111	Azores
8	Amami	60	Mozambique	112	Hearts Content/Placentia
9	Nafa (Okinawa)	61	Mojanga	113	Halifax
10	Pachung San (Miyako)	62	Delagoa Bay	114	Portsmouth
11	Kelung	63	Durban	115	Boston
12	Hong Kong	64	Simon's Bay	116	New York
13	Manila	65	Cape Town	117	Bermuda
14	Haiphong	66	Swakopmund	118	Nassau
15	Hue	67	Mossamedes	119	Havana
16	Saigon	68	Benguela	120	Port Royal
17	Penang	69	St Paul de Loanda	121	San Juan
18	Labuan	70	Gabon	122	St Thomas
19	Sandakan	71	Duala (Cameroon)	123	Barbados
20	Sarawak	72	Bonny/Brass	124	Trinidad
21	Singapore	73	Lagos	125	Para
22	Batavia	74	Cotonou	126	Maranhao
23	Banjuwangi	75	Accra	127	Ceara
24	Port Darwin	76	Grand Bassam	128	Pernambuco
25	Thursday Island	77	Sierra Leone	129	Bahia
26	Roebuck Bay (Broome)	78	Conakry	130	Rio de Janeiro
27	Perth	79	Bissao	131	Santos
28	Adelaide	80	Bathurst	132	Montevideo
29	Melbourne	81	Dakar	133	Talcahuano
30	Sydney	82	St Louis	134	Valparaiso
31	Brisbane	83	St Vincent	135	Coquimbo
32	Bundaberg	84	Tenerife	136	Antofagasta
33	Norfolk Island	85	Las Palmas	137	Iquique
34	Fiji	86	Funchal	138	Arica
35	Nelson	87	Gibraltar	139	Mollendo
36	Cocos Island	88	Algiers	140	Chorillos
37	Galle	89	Malta	141	Paita
38	Madras	90	Tripoli	142	Santa Elena
39	Bombay	91	Crete	143	Buenaventura
40	Karachi	92	Athens	144	Panama
41	Gwadar	93	Corfu	145	Colon
42	Jask	94	Trieste	146	San Juan del Sur
43	Bushire	95	Livorno	147	La Libertad
44	Fao	96	Civitavecchia	148	San Jose
45	Kerman	97	Naples	149	Salina Cruz
46	Tehran	98	Palermo	150	Coatzacoalcos
47	Odessa	99	Nice	151	Vera Cruz
48	Constantinople	100	Marseilles	152	Tampico
49	Cyprus	101	Lisbon	153	Galveston
50	Port Said	102	Vigo	154	Esquimault/Vancouver
51	Alexandria	103	Bilbao	155	Ascension Island
52	Jedda	104	Brest		

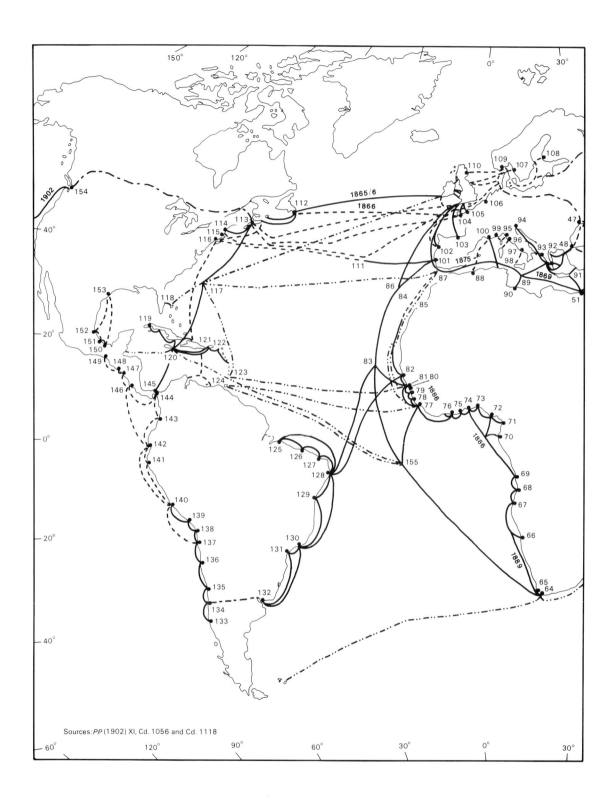

Sources: *PP* (1902) XI, Cd. 1056 and Cd. 1118

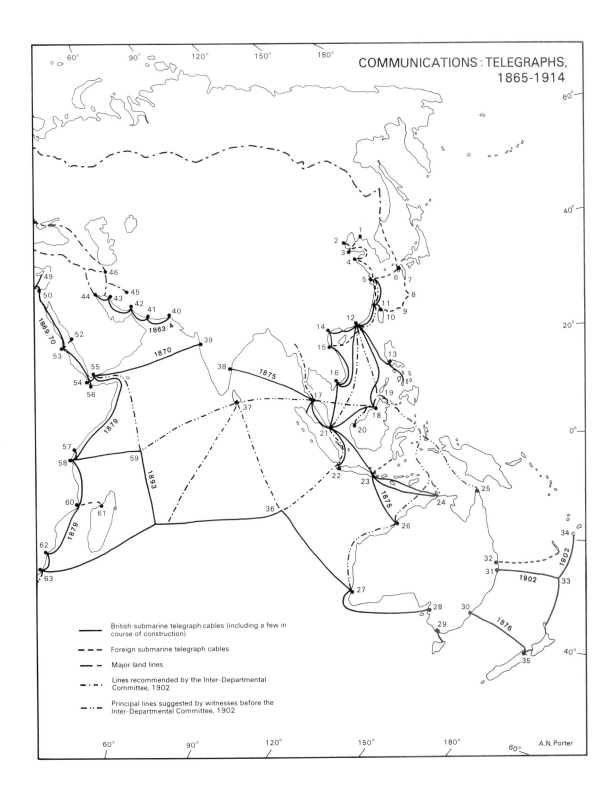

COMMUNICATIONS : TELEGRAPHS,
1865-1914

British submarine telegraph cables (including a few in
course of construction)

Foreign submarine telegraph cables

Major land lines

Lines recommended by the Inter-Departmental
Committee, 1902

Principal lines suggested by witnesses before the
Inter-Departmental Committee, 1902

A.N.Porter

subsidies were provided for strategic rather than other purposes, like the £55,000 per annum paid for twenty years from 1879 to the ETC's line from Aden to Cape Town. Between 1900 and 1914, in response to changing international conditions, importance was widely attached to 'all-British' cable routes and the maintenance of a comprehensive network for imperial defence. 'Imperial' cables were extolled, albeit somewhat fancifully, as contributing to imperial unity; and, as with British shipping, fears were current that American-inspired take-overs of telegraph companies might jeopardize national security. Nevertheless, except for the all-British Pacific cable (1902), governments remained satisfied with contractual obligations tied to subsidies and a government director of telegraphs on subsidized companies' boards. Widespread criticism of 'excessive' rates charged by telegraph 'pools' resulted in parliamentary investigation but little government action, paralleling the case of the shipping 'conferences'. Good dividends for ETC shareholders were a small price for a generally reliable service. Neither government nor private enterprise could make safe unavoidably insecure lines, such as Malta to Bombay, and by 1910 it was possible to anticipate a solution in the development of wireless or radio telegraphy.

The First World War, 1914–1918: East Africa

In 1914 Britain's imperial possessions in East Africa consisted of Uganda, the East African Protectorate (known as Kenya after 1920) and the islands of Zanzibar and Pemba. A small number of white settlers farmed land alienated from Africans in the area of central Kenya that became known as the 'White Highlands'. An Indian settler community, mainly labourers and traders, outnumbered the whites. In German East Africa (renamed Tanganyika Territory in 1920) a few white settlers had established plantations in the southern and central highland areas.

Germany's African possessions of Togo and Kamerun as well as South-West Africa were all conquered by early 1916. In German East Africa, the largest and most populous colony, the Germans fought until the armistice was declared in Europe. Initial attempts by the Germans to keep the African colonies neutral were rejected by the Allied powers. The wireless station at Dar-es-Salaam endangered the Cape route, as did a continued German presence on the Indian Ocean.

From the start of the war the British had control of the seas and effectively blockaded the German colony. Both sides had weak local military forces, but the British were able to draw on Indian, South African and West African troops, as well as on the support of the Belgians and later the Portuguese. The Allies employed nearly 100,000 men against German forces of never more than 15,000.

The British secured naval control of the lakes, but their attack on Tanga in November 1914 failed. There was stiff fighting east of Kilimanjaro, and German flying columns attacked the Uganda Railway. By early 1916 the Germans retreated south towards the central railway line. They avoided an attempt to entrap them and continued a tactical guerrilla retreat into the southern regions of the colony and also into neighbouring Portuguese East Africa. In this way the Germans tied down large numbers of Allied troops. Both the Allies and the Germans conscripted thousands of carriers and labourers for war service. Some of the heaviest recruitment was among the Luo and Kikuyu of west and central Kenya, and also in Nyasaland. The total figure is unknown but was in excess of one million. Possibly 10 per cent of the carriers died, mainly from

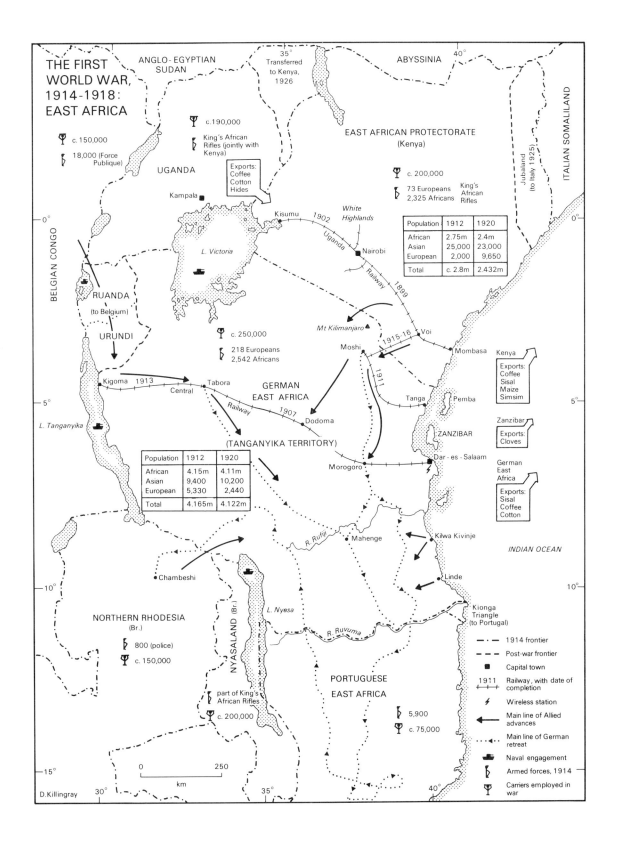

THE FIRST
WORLD WAR,
1914-1918:
EAST AFRICA

ANGLO- EGYPTIAN
SUDAN

35°
Transferred
to Kenya,
1926

ABYSSINIA

40°

c.150,000

18,000 (Force
Publique)

c.190,000

King's African
Rifles (jointly with
Kenya)

EAST AFRICAN PROTECTORATE
(Kenya)

UGANDA

Exports:
Coffee
Cotton
Hides

c. 200,000

73 Europeans
2,325 Africans

King's
African
Rifles

Jubaland
(to Italy 1925)

ITALIAN SOMALILAND

Kampala

BELGIAN CONGO

Kisumu

1902

White
Highlands

Uganda

Nairobi

0°

0°

L. Victoria

Railway

1899

Population	1912	1920
African	2.75m	2.4m
Asian	25,000	23,000
European	2,000	9,650
Total	c. 2.8m	2.432m

RUANDA
(to Belgium)

URUNDI

c. 250,000

218 Europeans
2,542 Africans

Mt Kilimanjaro

1915-16

Voi

Moshi

Mombasa

Kenya

Exports:
Coffee
Sisal
Maize
Simsim

Kigoma

1913

Tabora

Central

GERMAN
EAST AFRICA

1911

5°

5°

L. Tanganyika

Railway

1907

Dodoma

Tanga

Pemba

Zanzibar

Exports:
Cloves

ZANZIBAR

(TANGANYIKA TERRITORY)

Population	1912	1920
African	4.15m	4.11m
Asian	9,400	10,200
European	5,330	2,440
Total	4.165m	4.122m

Morogoro

Dar - es - Salaam

German
East
Africa

Exports:
Sisal
Coffee
Cotton

R. Rufiji

Mahenge

Kilwa Kivinje

INDIAN OCEAN

Chambeshi

Linde

10°

10°

NORTHERN RHODESIA
(Br.)

800 (police)

c. 150,000

L. Nyasa

NYASALAND (Br.)

R. Ruvuma

Kionga
Triangle
(to Portugal)

part of King's
African Rifles

c. 200,000

PORTUGUESE
EAST AFRICA

5,900

c. 75,000

1914 frontier

Post-war frontier

Capital town

1911 Railway, with date of
completion

Wireless station

Main line of Allied
advances

Main line of German
retreat

Naval engagement

Armed forces, 1914

Carriers employed in
war

0   250

km

D.Killingray

30°

35°

40°

153

diseases and famine. The result of the war, especially in Tanganyika, was widespread destruction and disease. The German commander, von Lettow Vorbeck, finally surrendered his force in Northern Rhodesia in November 1918.

The British favoured annexation of Tanganyika for economic and political reasons. Control of the territory would help to safeguard imperial routes in the Indian Ocean and also provide continuous British territory from the Cape to Cairo. At the peace settlement Tanganyika became a 'C'-class mandate entrusted to Britain by the League of Nations; Belgium had a similar mandate for Ruanda and Urundi. The Portuguese received the small area of the Kionga triangle. Italy had entered the war against the Central Powers in spring 1915 with the promise of compensatory territory in Africa if the Allies extended their possessions at German expense. In 1925 the arid region of Jubaland was ceded by Britain to Italy as part of that settlement.

As a result of the war, labour conscription and disease, the economic position of Africans was weakened. By contrast the war helped to strengthen the economic power of white settlers, particularly in Kenya, where they gained further land concessions and greater control over labour. In the immediate post-war years white settlers attempted to increase their political control in Kenya while strongly opposing increased electoral rights for the more numerous Indian community. At the same time Africans protested against land alienation, labour exaction, increased taxation and the continuation of the wartime pass system. African political opposition, mainly among the Kikuyu, was easily broken and diverted. Indians were also denied equality with whites. However, white settlers failed to consolidate their economic and political power over Kenya while the British government, by the Devonshire Declaration of 1923, reasserted its continued control over the colony and trusteeship of the African population.

The First World War, 1914–1918: South-West Africa

German control over South-West Africa was achieved by a series of bloody and brutal wars. The long-drawn-out resistance by the Nama and Herero was finally crushed in 1907 with great loss of life. The victorious Germans reserved large areas of South-West Africa for white settlement. In 1914 the colony had 15,000 white settlers, mainly Germans farming the more fertile central areas, a good railway system and a growing export trade in diamonds and copper. Over 80 per cent of trade was with Germany. A small European military force guarded internal security and the lengthy frontiers.

When Britain declared war on Germany in August 1914 the wireless stations in South-West Africa, linked to Berlin and German warships, seriously threatened British imperial strategic and commercial interests in the South Atlantic and on the Cape route. Certain imperial and local politicians also saw war as an opportunity to extend further British control over Southern Africa. The Union government's support for the war bitterly divided Afrikaners. A small-scale rebellion by Afrikaner republicans in 1914–15 opposed intervention in South-West Africa. It was suppressed but effectively tied down 30,000 troops of the South African Defence Force (SADF) needed for the campaign against the Germans.

In September and December 1914 the British and South Africans captured Lüderitz and Swakopmund, destroyed the wireless stations and isolated the German forces from coastal supplies. The Germans who had occupied Walvis Bay withdrew. During early

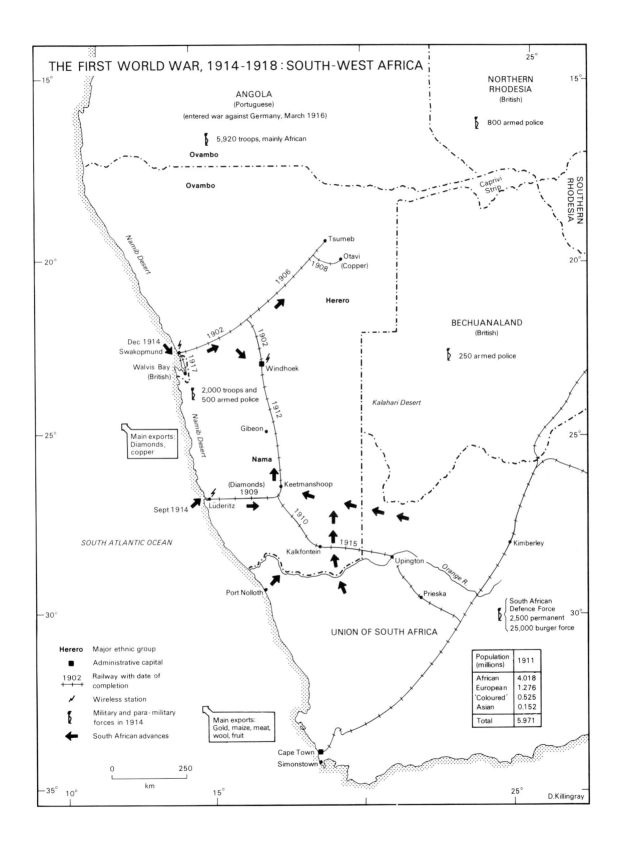

THE FIRST WORLD WAR, 1914-1918: SOUTH-WEST AFRICA

ANGOLA
(Portuguese)
(entered war against Germany, March 1916)

5,920 troops, mainly African

Ovambo

Ovambo

NORTHERN RHODESIA
(British)

800 armed police

Caprivi Strip

SOUTHERN RHODESIA

Namib Desert

Tsumeb

1906

1908

Otavi (Copper)

1902

Herero

1902

BECHUANALAND
(British)

250 armed police

Dec 1914
Swakopmund

Walvis Bay
(British)

1917

Windhoek

2,000 troops and
500 armed police

1912

Main exports:
Diamonds,
copper

Gibeon

Namib Desert

Kalahari Desert

Nama

(Diamonds)
1909

Keetmanshoop

Sept 1914

Lüderitz

1910

Kimberley

SOUTH ATLANTIC OCEAN

Kalkfontein

1915

Upington

Orange R.

Port Nolloth

Prieska

South African
Defence Force
2,500 permanent
25,000 burger force

UNION OF SOUTH AFRICA

Population (millions)	1911
African	4.018
European	1.276
'Coloured'	0.525
Asian	0.152
Total	5.971

Herero   Major ethnic group

■   Administrative capital

1902   Railway with date of completion

⤪   Wireless station

   Military and para-military forces in 1914

←   South African advances

Main exports:
Gold, maize, meat,
wool, fruit

Cape Town
Simonstown

0   250
km

D.Killingray

155

1915 three columns of white South African troops, supported by 35,000 African labourers, advanced from the coast and from the Union against the Germans. The German force of a few thousand men was greatly outnumbered. Defeated at Gibeon, it retreated northwards and finally surrendered at Tsumeb in July 1915. The advancing South Africans built new railways to link Walvis Bay and South Africa with the German network. In the north of the colony South African control was consolidated with the defeat of Ovambo resistance, crushed in 1915–17 with co-operation from the Portuguese.

During the war South Africa's agricultural exports to Britain and other Allies greatly increased, especially sales of meat, wool, fruit and maize. A consolidated Union tariff, introduced in 1914, provided protection for state-organized import substitution and expanding industries. Wartime co-operation with Britain led to the Royal Navy gaining a base at Simonstown by the 1921 agreement. At the end of the war South-West Africa became a

'C'-class mandate of the League of Nations administered by South Africa. Smuts, South Africa's premier, failed to extend South African control over the British High Commission Territories (Basutoland, Bechuanaland, Swaziland), and a link with Southern Rhodesia was rebuffed by the white electorate there, but he successfully incorporated South-West Africa with its valuable mineral resources into the Union as virtually a fifth province. The racial segregation policies of South Africa were extended to the territory and its economy and trade tied to South Africa. Many Germans remained to become naturalized South Africans, while white farmers and ranchers from South Africa moved into the eastern areas of the mandate in the early 1920s.

In 1946 the South-West Africa mandate was transferred to the United Nations. South Africa refused to recognize this, and for a long time the status of the territory, known as Namibia, was contested. Namibia eventually became independent in 1990, although Walvis Bay has remained part of the Republic of South Africa.

The First World War, 1914–1918: the Middle East

The Ottoman Empire's entry into the war as an ally of the Central Powers challenged Britain's strategic interests in the Middle East: her presence in Egypt, nominally a Turkish province, which safeguarded the lower Nile valley and the vital Suez Canal route to India and east Asia; and her newly acquired interests in the oil-producing areas of southern Persia.

Britain's war against Turkey was fought on three major fronts. The Sinai campaign began in 1914. Turkish attacks on the Suez Canal were repelled, and by early 1918 Allenby's forces had invaded Palestine. Operations in Mesopotamia, up the valleys of the rivers Tigris and Euphrates, went disastrously wrong, and an Indian force had to surrender at Kut in April 1916. A few months earlier an attempt to seize the Straits (the Gallipoli

campaign), to knock Turkey out of the war, swing the Balkan states to the Allied side and relieve the pressure on Russia, had to be abandoned as a costly failure. As a result the war against Turkey continued until her collapse and surrender in October 1918.

During the war Britain attempted both to contain and to exploit a rising tide of nationalism in the Middle East. Egyptian nationalism, already strident before 1914, was exacerbated by Britain's declaration of a protectorate (18 December 1914) as well as by her wartime economic and labour policies, and finally broke into open revolt in 1919–21. A nominal independence was conceded to Egypt in 1922 with the Suez Canal remaining securely under British military control. The British aided an Arab revolt in Hejaz against

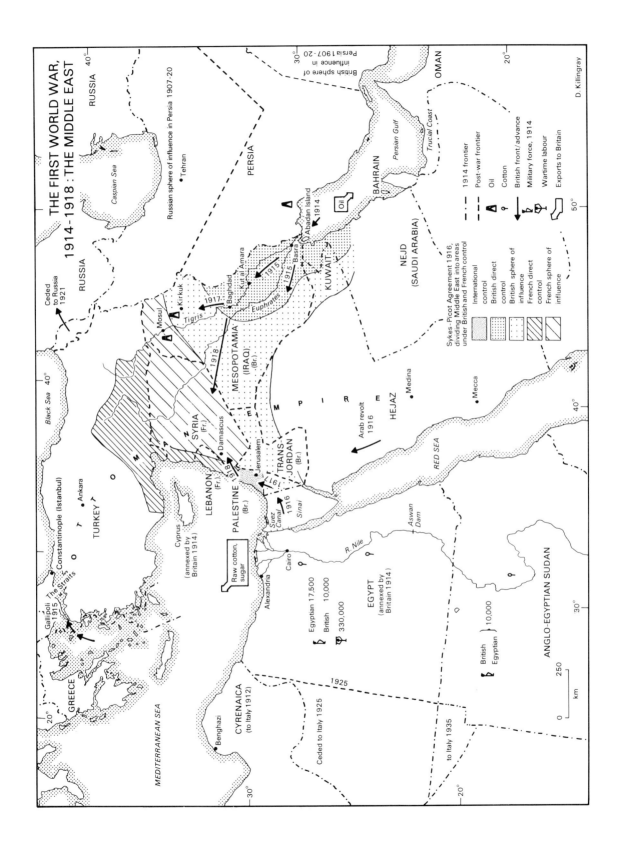

THE FIRST WORLD WAR,
1914–1918 : THE MIDDLE EAST

Russian sphere of influence in Persia 1907–20

British sphere of
influence in
Persia 1907-20

D. Killingray

RUSSIA

RUSSIA

RUSSIA

Ceded
to Russia
1921

Caspian Sea

Black Sea

PERSIA

Tehran

Constantinople (Istanbul)
The Straits

Ankara

TURKEY

GREECE

Gallipoli
1915

Cyprus
(annexed by
Britain 1914)

Mosul

Kirkuk

1917

Baghdad

Tigris

1918

Kut al Amara

1915

1915

Euphrates

Basra

Abadan Island
1914

Oil

BAHRAIN

Persian Gulf

Trucial Coast

OMAN

MESOPOTAMIA
(IRAQ)
(Br.)

KUWAIT

NEJD
(SAUDI ARABIA)

SYRIA
(Fr.)

Damascus

1918

LEBANON
(Fr.)

Jerusalem

PALESTINE
(Br.)

TRANS-
JORDAN
(Br.)

E   M   P   I   R   E

Arab revolt
1916

HEJAZ

Medina

Mecca

1916

Sinai

Suez
Canal

Raw cotton,
sugar

RED SEA

MEDITERRANEAN SEA

Alexandria

Cairo

R. Nile

Aswan
Dam

EGYPT
(annexed by
Britain 1914)

Egyptian 17,500
British 10,000

330,000

British
Egyptian } 10,000

ANGLO-EGYPTIAN SUDAN

Benghazi

CYRENAICA
(to Italy 1912)

Ceded to Italy 1925

1925

to Italy 1935

0   250
km

Sykes-Picot Agreement 1916,
dividing Middle East into areas
under British and French control

International
control

British direct
control

British sphere of
influence

French direct
control

French sphere of
influence

1914 frontier

Post-war frontier

Oil

Cotton

British front / advance

Military force, 1914

Wartime labour

Exports to Britain

157

the Turks in mid-1916, declaring that they would 'recognize and support the independence of the Arabs'. These political promises, couched in contradictory language, ran counter to two other British policies. First, in an attempt to resolve Franco-British rivalry in the region, the secret Sykes–Picot Agreement (March 1916) between the two powers planned the division of the Middle East into colonial spheres of influence and control. Second, by the Balfour Declaration of November 1917 Britain pledged support for a 'Jewish national home' in Palestine. Her object in this was to secure a permanent British presence in Palestine and also to gain international Jewish support for the war.

The collapse of the Ottoman Empire in late 1918 created a power vacuum in south-western Asia which the British and the French tried to fill. Britain's main aim was to consolidate her position in the Middle East by controlling the land bridge between the Mediterranean and the Persian Gulf, and safeguarding the vital oil supply areas of Persia and Mesopotamia (Iraq). She also continued her traditional policy of excluding Russia from the area, a task made more difficult by increased Russian unpredictability following the Bolshevik Revolution. At the same time manpower short-

ages, domestic political pressures, global imperial crises and American economic influence all imposed restraints on Britain's military power to act against revived Turkish nationalism on the Straits.

By the Treaty of San Remo (April 1920) the conquered Ottoman territories were divided into League of Nations mandates, with Britain controlling Palestine, Transjordan and Iraq, and the French taking Syria and Lebanon. This satisfied neither the fragmented Arab nationalists, who demanded an independent greater Syria and Iraq, nor the Zionist settlers, and the British faced serious revolt in Iraq (1920–1) and a long period of communal strife in Palestine. The rapid expansion of post-war imperial control imposed heavy burdens on Britain; she had gained large territorial possessions but lacked the means and will to maintain that control. As a result 'independence' for Egypt was paralleled by acceptance of national governments in Iraq and Transjordan. Britain relinquished direct political control over Persia but kept a firm hold on the strategic Persian Gulf and the oil supply route. In the inter-war years Britain exercised an informal empire over a large area of the Middle East.

Britain and the Middle East after the Treaty of Lausanne, 1923

Britain emerged from the First World War as the foremost power in the Middle East (see p. 157). Her troops were dispersed throughout the Levant, the Tigris–Euphrates floodplain and metropolitan Turkey, as well as concentrated in the great Suez base. These advances in the orient were treasured as the United Kingdom's main strategic recompense for her recent war effort. Between 1919 and the culmination of the Middle Eastern 'settlement' at the Lausanne conference in July 1923, however, the British proved incapable of sustaining either the full extent or the unbridled

character of this new imperium, although they none the less retained a sufficient stake in the region for it to be thereafter a major pivot of the United Kingdom's overseas power.

In the immediate aftermath of the war it was assumed that the twin protectorates of Egypt and Mesopotamia would provide the hard core of Britain's regional authority. In both countries, however, this intrusiveness sparked off nationalist revolts as soon as the pressure of war lifted, breaking out along the Upper Nile in 1919, and across the flatlands of Mesopotamia in 1920. At first the British government's

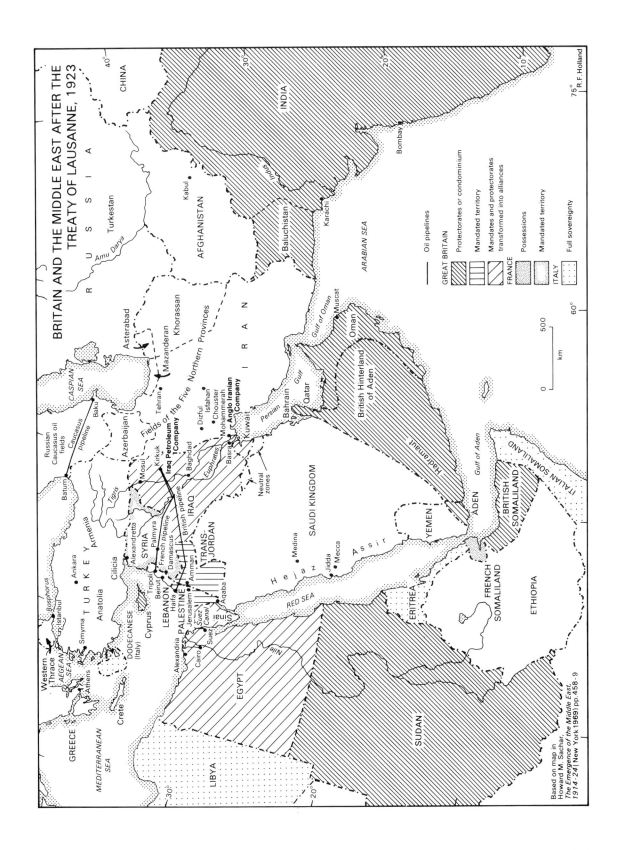

BRITAIN AND THE MIDDLE EAST AFTER THE TREATY OF LAUSANNE, 1923

GREAT BRITAIN

Oil pipelines

Protectorates or condominium

Mandated territory

Mandates and protectorates transformed into alliances

FRANCE

Possessions

Mandated territory

ITALY

Full sovereignty

R.F. Holland

Based on map in
Howard M. Sachar,
*The Emergence of the Middle East,
1914–24* (New York 1969) pp. 458–9

CHINA

R U S S I A

Turkestan

Amu Darya

AFGHANISTAN

Kabul

Baluchistan

Karachi

INDIA

Bombay

ARABIAN SEA

Asterabad

Khorassan

(Mazanderan

Tehran

Fields of the Five Northern Provinces

I R A N

Anglo Iranian Company

Dizful

Isfahan

Chouster

Mohammerah

Baku

Azerbaijan

Caspian Pipeline

CASPIAN SEA

Russian Caucasus oil fields

Caucasus Pipeline

Batum

Armenia

Kirkuk

Mosul

Iraq Petroleum Company

Baghdad

Euphrates

Tigris

IRAQ

Basra

Kuwait

Bahrain

Qatar

Persian Gulf

Gulf of Oman

Muscat

Oman

British Hinterland of Aden

Neutral zones

SAUDI KINGDOM

Medina

Mecca

Jidda

Hejaz

Assir

Hadramaut

Gulf of Aden

ADEN

BRITISH SOMALILAND

ITALIAN SOMALILAND

FRENCH SOMALILAND

ERITREA

ETHIOPIA

YEMEN

RED SEA

SUDAN

EGYPT

Nile

Cairo

Alexandria

Suez

Suez Canal

Sinai

Aqaba

Jerusalem

PALESTINE

TRANS-JORDAN

Amman

Damascus

British pipeline

French pipeline

Palmyra

SYRIA

LEBANON

Haifa

Beirut

Tripoli

Alexandretta

Cilicia

Ankara

T U R K E Y

Anatolia

Smyrna

Istanbul

Bosphorus

Crete

Athens

GREECE

Western Thrace

AEGEAN SEA

MEDITERRANEAN SEA

Cyprus

DODECANESE (Italy)

LIBYA

0   500
km

159

response was one of military repression, but financial constraints soon necessitated cheaper, more flexible solutions in the shape of treaties reserving special privileges for Britain. This approach was heralded at the Cairo conference of responsible British officials in March 1921. Hence the following year Egypt was granted her independence subject to appropriate financial, military and diplomatic qualifications, and in 1924 a similar agreement was finally arrived at with Iraq (as Mesopotamia was now called). This 'empire by treaty' was not at all what the British had aspired to in the heady days of 1917–18, but it served essential purposes well enough until the onset of another world war.

In the Levant, too, inflated expectations had to be scaled down. Adventurist British opinion dreamed of a greater Syria under the auspices of a British-controlled Hashemite dynasty. Certainly at the Paris peace conference it was easily agreed that Turkey should be stripped of all her Arab provinces. Reluctantly, however, the authorities in London were compelled to recognize the claims of France to Syria based on the 1916 Sykes–Picot Agreement. Thus by the San Remo accords of April 1920 the Levant was partitioned between France and Britain, the latter having to stand by afterwards when the local nationalists, who had fought at the side of Allenby, were bombed out of Damascus. It was to secure at least one British-cum-Arab state in the area, and to provide a royal vacancy for the itinerant Emir Abdullah, that Transjordan's severance from Palestine proper was subsequently confirmed. For many years ahead this sandy waste, created by British fiat and sustained by British money, was to afford at least one wholly reliable partner in Arab affairs. Meanwhile in 'coastal' Palestine British military administration had been replaced with civilian rule, the position of which, however, was made increasingly tiresome by the fury of Jewish settlers at the curtailment both of Palestine's boundaries and of its absorption of immigrants, and by the rising anger of the Arab denizens at the discrimination and dispossession to which they were subject.

Persia, whose wartime neutrality had not precluded creeping British occupation, was also brought within the United Kingdom's 'treaty sway' in August 1919. In this way Curzon, for whom that country represented the mobile frontier of British imperialism, sought to exploit the collapse of Russia and so extend British domination from its old haunts in the southern provinces far to the north – including Tehran. Here, too, however, the result was nationalist reaction, so that the treaty was never ratified by the *majlis* (or parliament), and the pro-British shah was swept away by Reza Khan in February 1921. The United Kingdom did eventually persuade the latter to sign a treaty in 1928, but British prestige was never stable thereafter, and fell back on its localized stronghold surrounding the installations of the Anglo-Iranian Oil Company in the Gulf headlands.

It was in the peace-making with respect to Turkey proper, however, that post-war British aspirations were most comprehensively thwarted. Under the Mudros Armistice, British troops had been accorded military access throughout the country. When Italy, smarting from her failure to secure her Anatolian claims at the Paris peace conference, began to infiltrate troops into the Smyrna region, it was largely under Prime Minister Lloyd George's inspiration that the excuse was seized for Greek armies to pour into western Anatolia, laying waste as they went. Under the direct aegis of British bayonets in Constantinople, and their Greek proxies in the Turkish interior, the Sultan was forced to sign the Treaty of Sèvres (August 1920), the main thrust of which was to make Turkey into a compliant partner in a British Mediterranean empire.

This vista was swiftly foreshortened by the secularist national resistance of Kemal Ataturk with its centre of gravity in Ankara, by the evaporation of Franco-Italian acquiescence and by the crushing failure of Greek arms. In Britain support for a new war to shore up the broken system of Sèvres disappeared once the

Kemalist forces closed in on the British 'lines' at Chanak bordering the Straits, and subsequently the new Conservative government negotiated a less draconian peace with Turkey at Lausanne. Under this, while the Ataturk regime accepted the alienation of its non-Turkish patrimony, it regained its own metropolitan substance, including the greater part of Western Thrace. By 1924, then, the British were in possession of what, compared to the visions of 1917–18, was a 'minimalist' version of Middle Eastern empire both in extent and more often than not in its *modus operandi*. Subsequently they were all the more determined to defend what they held.

The partition of Ireland,
1914–1922

It was the Irish Question, not the rivalries of European politics, which dominated British politics as 1914 dawned. The Liberal government was pushing a Home Rule Bill through the Houses of Parliament, while many Tory leaders, increasingly orchestrated by the Orange factions of Ulster, were threatening to thwart this departure by paramilitary action. Incipient civil war in Britain was thereafter conveniently averted by the outbreak of general war in Europe. The Irish Question was speedily wound down, with Home Rule finally being put on the statute book with the royal assent, but immediately suspended from operation for the duration of the war – and possibly beyond. This tactic ('now you see it, now you don't') suited English expediencies but not Irish emotions, and the credibility of traditional Irish Catholic nationalism was fatally damaged. The initiative passed to revolutionary elements, who staged a 'rising' against British authority in Dublin during Easter 1916. Though forlorn in its immediate chances of success, the brutality with which the rebellion was put down by General Maxwell extinguished the flickering attachments to the Union remaining among Irish people.

Any chance of reversing this Anglo-Irish alienation disappeared in 1917–18 under the shadow of conscription. When the First World War began, more Irish Catholics had rushed to join the British colours than was the case with their Protestant compatriots, many of whom were more interested in the opportunity to impose Orange rule in Ulster than with events elsewhere. Catholics therefore deeply resented the British government's intention in 1918 to obtain manpower by applying compulsion to Ireland, especially when this compulsion was quite clearly to be aimed against Catholic, not Protestant, males. In the end Germany collapsed before English squaddies stormed once more through the saloon bars of Dublin, but the fear and loathing that surrounded this issue marked the final breach between the 'Nationalist' and 'Loyalist' communities in Ireland.

At the general election of late 1918 in Ireland, outside Ulster the old-style Nationalists were swept aside by triumphant Sinn Fein ('Our Freedom') candidates, who proceeded to boycott Westminster and set up their own assembly (or 'Dail') in Dublin. This constitutional stand-off deteriorated in July 1919 when an inspector of the Royal Irish Constabulary was assassinated in Thurles, County Tipperary; this was the start of the gun war. The following year Lloyd George's coalition government presided over the passage of a Government of Ireland Act which allowed for the devolution of certain powers to separate and subordinate legislatures in Belfast – thus confirming Orange dominion in the north – and Dublin. The latter assembly, however, never met, since the time had long since passed when constitutional unionism, even of a qualified and autonomist sort, could be yoked to modern Irish nationalism. Throughout 1920

161

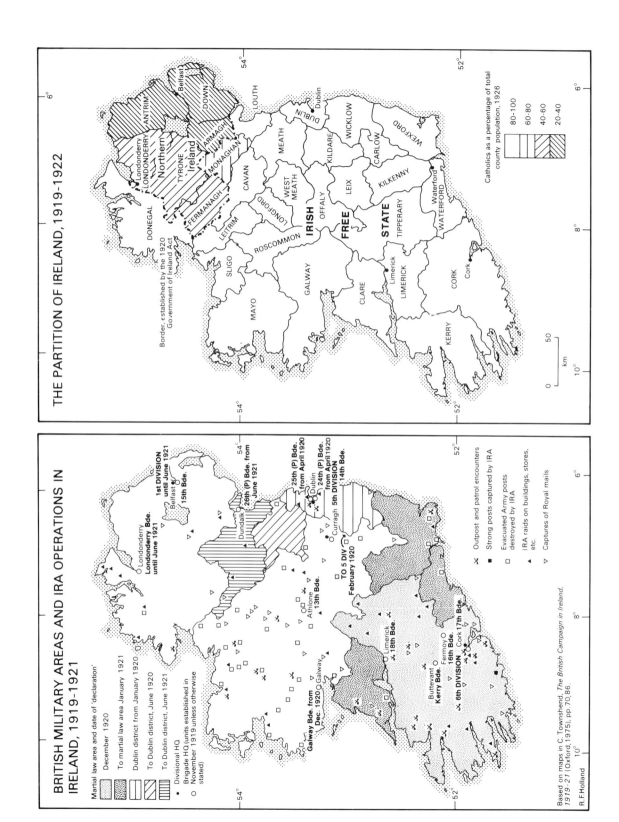

THE PARTITION OF IRELAND, 1919-1922

Border, established by the 1920
Government of Ireland Act

Catholics as a percentage of total
county population, 1926

80-100
60-80
40-60
20-40

km
0   50

BRITISH MILITARY AREAS AND IRA OPERATIONS IN IRELAND, 1919-1921

Martial law area and date of 'declaration'

December 1920

To martial law area January 1921

Dublin district from January 1920

To Dublin district, June 1920

To Dublin district, June 1921

● Divisional HQ
○ Brigade HQ (units established in
November 1919 unless otherwise
stated)

1st DIVISION
until June 1921

15th Bde.

Londonderry
Londonderry Bde.
until June 1921

26th (P) Bde. from
June 1921

25th (P) Bde.
from April 1920

24th (P) Bde.
from April 1920

Dundalk

Dublin

5th DIVISION
14th Bde.

Curragh

TO 5 DIV
February 1920

Athlone
13th Bde.

Galway Bde. from
Dec. 1920 ○ Galway

Limerick
18th Bde.

Buttevant
Kerry Bde.

Fermoy
16th Bde.

Cork 17th Bde.

6th DIVISION

Outpost and patrol encounters ✕

Strong posts captured by IRA ■

Evacuated Army posts ☐
destroyed by IRA

IRA raids on buildings, stores, ▲
etc.

Captures of Royal mails ▽

Based on maps in C. Townshend, *The British Campaign in Ireland,*
1919-21 (Oxford, 1975), pp.70,86.

R.F.Holland

162

guerrilla warfare spread through many of the Catholic counties, pursued – usually too late – by British troops and edicts of martial law (see p. 162).

The regular British Army, used to the set-pieces of the western front, resented being made responsible for such a dispersed and ramshackle war, in which soldiers were more likely to be shot in the back than from the front. It was to circumvent this fastidiousness that – inspired principally by Winston Churchill as Minister for War – the 'Black and Tans' were introduced, a force formed from the less salubrious and employable 'demobs' in England, who subsequently toured Ireland in their motorized units trying 'to get murder by the throat'– usually by murdering people. Certainly after the early months of 1921 there were signs that what had become the Irish Republican Army was close to being intimidated out of action, if not existence.

By then, however, politics had replaced guns, if only because the British public had tired of a war in their 'back yard' which was both sickening and expensive. It is also conventionally believed that, in turning to negotiations, Lloyd George was eager to please the Americans. Whatever the governing motives, clandestine talks followed the announcement of a 'military truce' in June 1921, and climaxed in the 'Treaty' signed by the British Prime Minister and an Irish delegation at 10 Downing Street on 6 December 1921. The British conceded effective Irish self-rule in the form of dominion status on the Canadian model, without overriding safeguards respecting fiscal or diplomatic affairs. The Irish negotiators, however, had conceded the fact of Ulster's right of separation, the sovereignty of the British crown and the use of Irish ports by the Royal Navy. It was, at bottom, an attempt to solve the Irish question through the modulations of Commonwealth membership.

This treaty, however, was deeply controversial among Irish people. Eamonn de Valera, as President of the Irish Republic, characterized it as betrayal. After a general election in 1922 was won by the 'Treaty' government of Patrick Cosgrave, civil war erupted. The regime survived, albeit only with British military assistance. Meanwhile the Ulster government was able to entrench its authority within the supposedly temporary frontiers of the 1920 Act, even in those counties of Fermanagh and Tyrone where the Catholic population was large and sporadically in the majority. In 1924, contrary to the 1921 treaty, these boundaries were confirmed as permanent. Although thereafter Eamonn de Valera and his political party, Fianna Fail, accepted the constraints of constitutionalism, they never recognized the legitimacy of dominion status; hence in 1937 Eire became to all intents and purposes a republic, and in 1949 seceded from the British Commonwealth. Since that time the historic British Isles have been partitioned against themselves.

Communications: imperial airways, 1918–1950

Before 1914 flying was largely a matter for individual enthusiasts and an object of scepticism. However, during the First World War airmen's training and air technology developed rapidly, and the commercial and military potential of flying was confirmed. The Royal Air Force was established in 1918, following the use of aircraft in limited operations on the western front. Air power's attractions lay in speed and mobility, which offered an escape from the lumbering defensiveness of contemporary warfare, and in its cheapness relative to other forces. Territorial over-extension and financial pressures led Britain from 1919 to rely increasingly on the RAF in the Middle East.

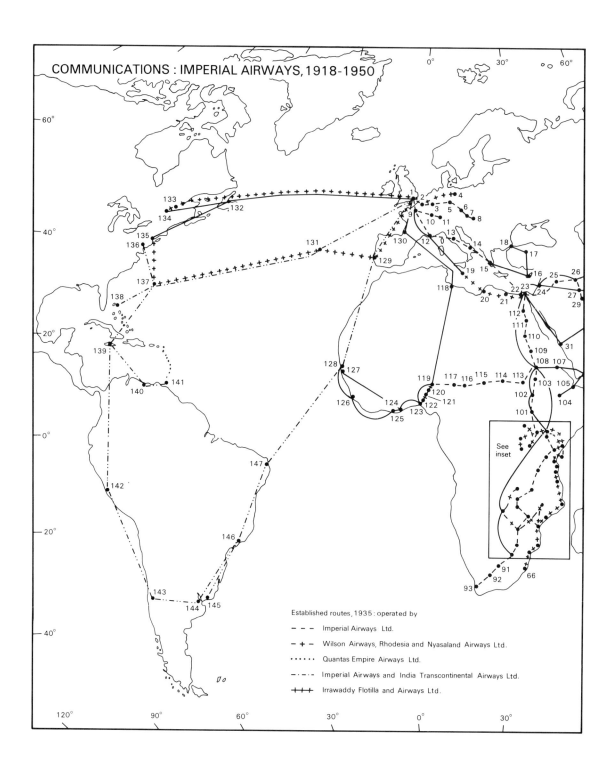

COMMUNICATIONS : IMPERIAL AIRWAYS, 1918-1950

Established routes, 1935 : operated by

- – – – Imperial Airways Ltd.
- –+– – Wilson Airways, Rhodesia and Nyasaland Airways Ltd.
- · · · · · · Quantas Empire Airways Ltd.
- –·–·– Imperial Airways and India Transcontinental Airways Ltd.
- +++ Irrawaddy Flotilla and Airways Ltd.

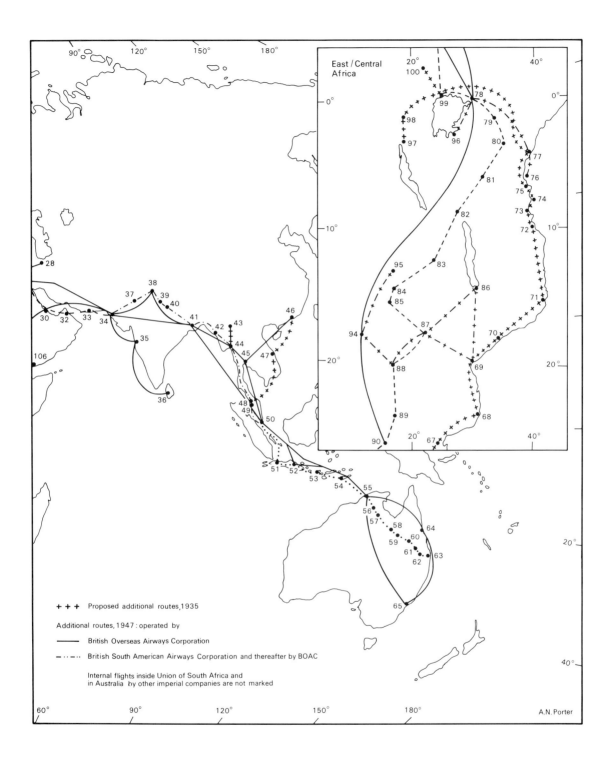

East / Central
Africa

+ + +   Proposed additional routes,1935

Additional routes, 1947 : operated by

————   British Overseas Airways Corporation

–·–·–·–   British South American Airways Corporation and thereafter by BOAC

Internal flights inside Union of South Africa and
in Australia by other imperial companies are not marked

A.N.Porter

165

Imperial Airways, 1918–50 (see map on pp. 164–5)

1 London	50 Singapore	99 Kampala
2 Brussels	51 Batavia (Djakarta)	100 Kasemy
3 Cologne	52 Surabaya	101 Juba
4 Berlin	53 Rambang	102 Malakal
5 Leipzig	54 Kupang	103 Kosti
6 Prague	55 Darwin	104 Addis Ababa
7 Vienna	56 Daly Waters	105 Hargeisa
8 Budapest	57 Newcastle Waters	106 Aden
9 Paris	58 Camooweal	107 Asmara
10 Basle	59 Cloncurry	108 Khartoum
11 Zurich	60 Winton	109 Kareima
12 Marseilles	61 Blackall	110 Wadi Halfa
13 Rome	62 Charleville	111 Luxor
14 Brindisi	63 Brisbane	112 Asyut
15 Athens	64 Bowen	113 El Obeid
16 Nicosia	65 Sydney	114 El Fasher
17 Ankara	66 Durban	115 Abeche
18 Istanbul	67 Lourenco Marques	116 Fort Lamy
19 Malta	68 Inhambane	117 Maiduguri
20 Benghazi	69 Beira	118 Castel Benito
21 Matruh	70 Quelimane	119 Kano
22 Alexandria	71 Mozambique	120 Kaduna
23 Cairo	72 Lindi	121 Minna
24 Lydda	73 Kilwa	122 Oshogbo
25 Rutba	74 Mafia	123 Lagos
26 Baghdad	75 Dar-es-Salaam	124 Accra
27 Basra	76 Zanzibar	125 Takoradi
28 Tehran	77 Mombasa	126 Freetown
29 Kuwait	78 Kisumu	127 Bathurst
30 Bahrain	79 Nairobi	128 Dakar
31 Jiddah	80 Moshi	129 Lisbon
32 Sharja	81 Dodoma	130 Bordeaux
33 Gwadar	82 Mbeya	131 Azores
34 Karachi	83 Mpika	132 Gander
35 Bombay	84 Broken Hill	133 Quebec
36 Negombo	85 Lusaka	134 Montreal
37 Jodhpur	86 Chelika	135 New York
38 Delhi	87 Salisbury	136 Baltimore
39 Kanpur	88 Bulawayo	137 Bermuda
40 Allahabad	89 Pietersburg	138 Nassau
41 Calcutta	90 Johannesburg	139 Kingston
42 Akyab	91 Kimberley	140 Caracas
43 Mandalay	92 Victoria West	141 Port of Spain
44 Rangoon	93 Cape Town	142 Lima
45 Bangkok	94 Livingstone/Victoria Falls	143 Santiago
46 Hong Kong	95 Ndola	144 Buenos Aires
47 Hue	96 Mwanza	145 Montevideo
48 Alor Star	97 Usumbura	146 Rio de Janeiro
49 Penang	98 Ngoma	147 Natal

Journey time in days taken from London in 1936:

Adelaide 14.0	Brisbane 12.0	Khartoum 3.5
Alexandria 2.5	Buluwayo 7.75	Rangoon 7.0
Baghdad 3.5	Calcutta 6.5	Singapore 8.5
Bahrain 4.0	Cape Town 9.0	Zanzibar 6.0
Bombay 5.5	Johannesburg 8.25	

Vigorous international commercial competition began in 1919–20 on the short cross-Channel routes. Britain first imitated France and Belgium, subsidizing private companies in return for government controls over choice of routes and frequency of service. Following the report of its Civil Air Transport Subsidy Committee (1923), the British government encouraged formation of a single company to develop the principal imperial routes. Imperial Airways Ltd was thus born of a multiple merger in 1924, with a capital of £1 million, two government directors on its board of ten and £1 million in subsidies promised over ten years. Governments were no more willing to risk foreign domination of imperial air communications than of earlier steamship and telegraphic links.

Expansion followed telegraphic precedents, moving first eastwards, then south. The RAF established a regular public mail to the Middle East in 1921; in November 1925 Imperial Airways contracted for passengers and mails fortnightly to Karachi, but completion beyond Basra was delayed by the Persian government, with the result that Karachi and Delhi were only reached during 1929. Successful return flights to Cape Town and Melbourne were first completed in 1926. Imperial Airways' plans for Cape Town were made in 1929–30, and the first regular airmail began in 1931. By 1932 disasters had eliminated airships as serious competitors. Imperial Airways steadily extended its weekly services, to Cape Town (1932), Brisbane (1934) and Hong Kong and Nigeria (1936). Duplication then followed.

Progress was inevitably slow. Frequent stops were essential, and the comfort and competitiveness of shipping for most passengers and freight were unchallenged. Airstrips were not built in a day, and the negotiation of overflying rights was protracted. At the further reaches of the network, the 1930s saw Imperial Airways increasing its financial interest in linked operators such as Wilson Airways, assisting the establishment of Quantas Empire Airways (1934) and lending personnel to local companies such as Irrawaddy Flotilla and Airways. Until 1945 British civil aviation developed above all in an imperial setting. British companies were long excluded from the USA just as Americans found it difficult to break into British spheres. Links between London, Canada and the USA via Bermuda were only negotiated in the late 1930s; direct passenger flights between London and New York only began in July 1946 and then on a reciprocal basis.

The Second World War fundamentally changed the aviation world. Technical advances reinforced the importance attached to global air warfare and bases overseas, and brought national airlines into more direct competition. Expanding demand and challenges especially from the USA were met by government action. Under the Civil Aviation Act (1946), the Air Ministry retained responsibility only for air defence; a new Ministry of Civil Aviation supervised the co-ordination of Britain's world-wide interests. Imperial Airways, reconstructed in March 1940 as the British Overseas Airways Corporation, was again reshaped, and services to Europe came under a new British European Airways Corporation. South American routes were very briefly (1947–9) the responsibility of a British South American Airways Corporation.

Britain in India, to 1939

The more Britain leaned upon India as a supplier of materials, a market for her manufactures, an area for investment and a 'barrack-room in the eastern seas', so she required and Indians requested increasing participation of locals in the running of the Raj. Landmarks in the constitutional evolution of India in the half-century after the foundation of the Indian National Congress (1885) were as follows:

(i) the Indian Councils Act of 1892 which enlarged legislative councils to include non-official European and Indian members;

(ii) the Morley–Minto Reforms of 1909 which further expanded the legislative councils, providing elected majorities in six provincial councils and separate electorates for Muslims (the 'communal roll');

(iii) the Montagu Declaration, 20 August 1917, announcing a policy of developing self-governing institutions with a view to the introduction of responsible government;

(iv) the Montagu–Chelmsford Reforms, 1919, which introduced 'dyarchy' in the provinces whereby 'reserved subjects' (like finance and police) were retained in British hands while others (such as agriculture, education and sanitation) were transferred to Indian ministers answerable to provincial legislatures that were 70 per cent elective according to a property franchise;

(v) the Government of India Act of 1935, which, coming at the end of a long process of inquiry and negotiation from the Simon Commission (1927) through three round-table conferences (1930–2) to a parliamentary joint committee (1933–4), legislated for (a) the grant of virtual autonomy and complete self-government in the eleven provinces, (b) the introduction of 'dyarchy' in central government, (c) the creation of an All-India Federation (i.e.

embracing the provinces and princely states, the latter not having experienced direct British rule) and (d) the separation of Aden and Burma from the Government of India.

These developments have been variously interpreted; as a controlled and magisterial exercise in the transfer of power; as a retreat before the mounting forces of nationalism (which was provoked by such incidents as the Amritsar massacre on 13 April 1919 and inspired by Gandhi's non-co-operation movement, by the Khilafatists or by the Pakistan concept); or as pragmatic administrative devices whereby the British, having moved from 'salutary neglect' to overrule, sought to win the co-operation of significant elites in the management of the colonial state while simultaneously distracting and dividing potential opponents by manipulation of the constitution and encouragement of communal politics. To conclude that in the 1930s Britain was being forced out of India by the overwhelming power of Congress would be grossly to exaggerate the weakness of the one and the strength of the other; all the same, India was now a less reliable dependency than it had been fifty years earlier. Indian demands and British concessions (some of which were contradictory) had restricted Britain's room for manoeuvre. Moreover, British interests in the subcontinent were on the wane, relative both to the growth there of the trade and investments of others and to Britain's overseas commerce and investments as a whole.

The 1935 legislation met opposition from Tory diehards, Indian princes and Congress politicians. The Tories found it dangerously progressive; princes were anxious about their future within an all-India federation; and Congress objected to the endorsement of separate communal electorates. Because a majority of the princes refused to join the projected federation, this part of the constitution was not implemented. As regards the provincial

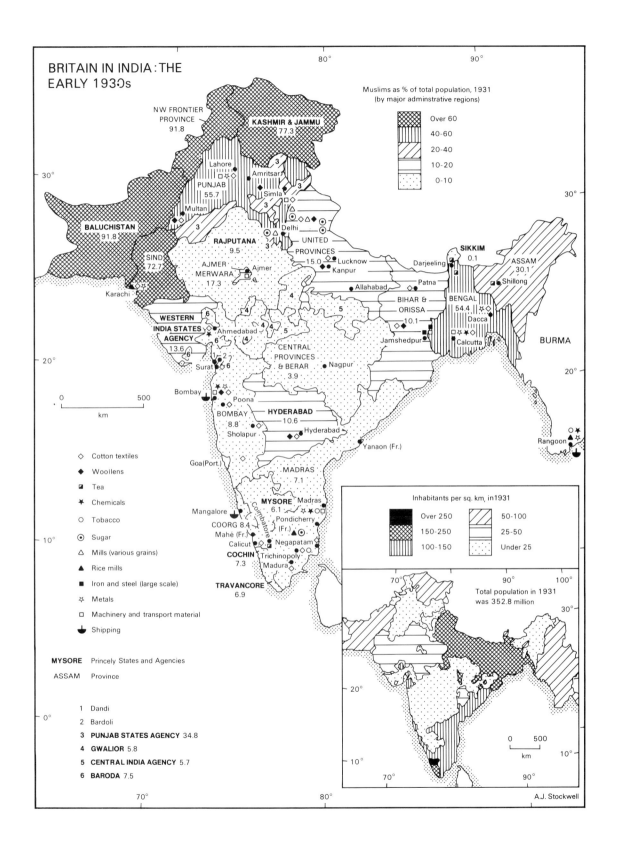

BRITAIN IN INDIA : THE EARLY 1930s

Muslims as % of total population, 1931
(by major administrative regions)

Over 60
40-60
20-40
10-20
0-10

NW FRONTIER
PROVINCE
91.8

KASHMIR & JAMMU
77.3

Lahore
PUNJAB
55.7
Amritsar
Simla
Multan
Delhi

BALUCHISTAN
91.8

SIND
72.7

RAJPUTANA
9.5

AJMER
MERWARA
17.3
Ajmer

UNITED
PROVINCES
15.0 Lucknow
Kanpur
Allahabad

Darjeeling

SIKKIM
0.1

ASSAM
30.1
Shillong

BIHAR &
ORISSA
10.1

Patna

BENGAL
54.4
Dacca
Jamshedpur
Calcutta

BURMA

WESTERN
INDIA STATES
AGENCY
13.6

Ahmedabad

CENTRAL
PROVINCES
& BERAR
3.9

Nagpur

Surat

Bombay

Poona
BOMBAY
8.8
Sholapur

HYDERABAD
10.6
Hyderabad

Yanaon (Fr.)

Rangoon

Symbol	Industry
◇	Cotton textiles
◆	Woollens
▨	Tea
✳	Chemicals
○	Tobacco
⊙	Sugar
△	Mills (various grains)
▲	Rice mills
■	Iron and steel (large scale)
☆	Metals
□	Machinery and transport material
⚓	Shipping

Goa (Port.)

MADRAS
7.1

MYSORE Madras
6.1
Pondicherry
(Fr.)

Mangalore
COORG 8.4
Mahé (Fr.)
Calicut
Negapatam
COCHIN
7.3
Trichinopoly
Madura

TRAVANCORE
6.9

0   500
km

MYSORE Princely States and Agencies
ASSAM Province

1 Dandi
2 Bardoli
3 PUNJAB STATES AGENCY 34.8
4 GWALIOR 5.8
5 CENTRAL INDIA AGENCY 5.7
6 BARODA 7.5

Inhabitants per sq. km, in 1931

Over 250
150-250
100-150
50-100
25-50
Under 25

Total population in 1931
was 352.8 million

0   500
km

A.J. Stockwell

169

measures, Congress eventually agreed to participate in the elections of January and February 1937. It won absolute majorities in six of the eleven provinces and was the largest single party in two others. By July 1937 Congress had formed ministries in seven provinces. By contrast, the Muslim League, originally formed (1906) to protect the Muslim minority of the United Provinces, failed to secure the support of Muslims living in the Muslim-majority provinces. The League's dismal performance, together with post-election Congress taunts, launched its leader, M.A. Jinnah, upon his campaign to establish himself as the sole spokesman for the Muslims of India.

Britain and the war in the Mediterranean, 1942–1945

For Britain's political and military leadership the Second World War was in its essentials and ideals a Mediterranean affair. In the crisis of 1940 surplus tanks were immediately dispatched to the Middle East, rather than used to reinforce the home front still threatened with invasion. At first the campaign in North Africa went well, and the Italian forces – which had crossed the Egypt–Libya border in early September 1939 – were not only evicted, but thrust back beyond Benghazi. Once a German army arrived under the able leadership of General Rommel in February 1941, however, the sequence was reversed, not least because British and Commonwealth troops were syphoned off into a disastrous campaign in Greece. Not only was this latter contingent defeated, and Greece lost, but the Eighth (or 'Desert') Army in North Africa was beaten back on to its Egyptian lines. The United States' entry into the war (December 1941) did not alter the balance of power in the Mediterranean, and on 20 June 1942 the surrender of the besieged garrison at Tobruk marked one of the nadirs of the war for Britain. This shock led the Americans to 'save' the British position in Egypt by sending large consignments of Sherman tanks; the consequent advantage in metal, and an overwhelming superiority in numbers allowed the recently appointed field commander, General Bernard Montgomery, to launch a smashing offensive at El Alamein on 23 October 1942 – the only distinctive triumph of British and Commonwealth forces against (admittedly very inferior) German opponents between 1939 and 1945.

The map illustrates the broad sweep of Mediterranean strategy in the aftermath of El Alamein. It was a strategy with which the Americans felt little sympathy, viewing it as a cloak for Britain's incorrigible imperialism. Only the need to 'blood' American troops and much British special pleading persuaded President Roosevelt to authorize the Anglo-American landings in north-west Africa ('Operation Torch') in November 1942. Even so, the resistance of the Axis forces was not broken until the fall of Tunis in May 1943. Subsequently much United States opinion would have preferred a single-minded concentration on the reinvasion of northern Europe. It was largely at British insistence that the Mediterranean fighting was continued with the attack on Sicily in July, and the momentum then sustained by the landings on the Neapolitan mainland during the following September, by which time Marshal Badoglio had succeeded Mussolini to power in Rome.

The Italian campaign proved, however, only a mixed Allied blessing. The German 'Gustav Line' was reinforced and for long proved impassable – the attempt to outflank this position after January 1944 by renewed landings at Anzio was a costly failure. It was not until the delayed capture of Monte Cassino (18 May 1944) that the way was open to Rome, and even then the laurel of the Eternal City fell to an American, not a British, commander

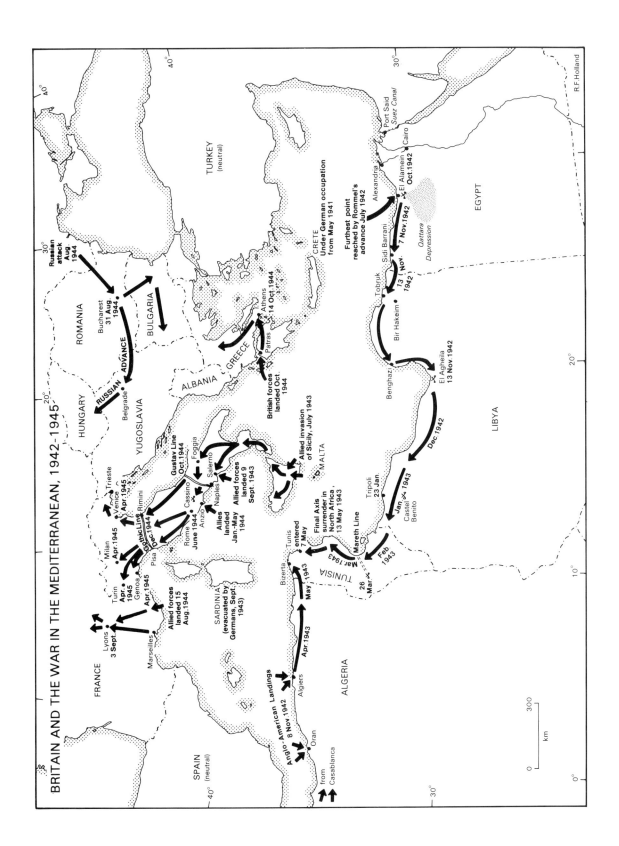

BRITAIN AND THE WAR IN THE MEDITERRANEAN, 1942–1945

R.F.Holland

SPAIN (neutral)

FRANCE

Lyons
Marseilles

Allied forces landed 15 Aug.1944

Turin Apr. 1945
Milan Apr.1945
Genoa Apr.1945
Pisa
Venice Apr.1945
Trieste
Rimini
Gothic Line Dec.1944

Rome June 1944
Anzio
Allies landed Jan.-May 1944
Cassino
Naples
Allied forces landed 9 Sept.1943
Salerno
Foggia
Gustav Line Oct.1944

SARDINIA (evacuated by Germans, Sept. 1943)

MALTA

Allied invasion of Sicily, July 1943

Anglo-American Landings 8 Nov.1942

Oran
from Casablanca
Algiers

ALGERIA

Apr. 1943

May 1943
Bizerta
Tunis
entered
7 May
Final Axis surrender in North Africa, 13 May 1943

TUNISIA
26 Mar.
Mar.1943
Mareth Line
Feb 1943
Jan.
Castel Benito
Tripoli 23 Jan.
Jan. 1943

Dec.1942

LIBYA

Benghazi
El Agheila 13 Nov. 1942

Bir Hakeim
Tobruk
13 Nov. 1942
Sidi Barrani
7 Nov.1942
El Alamein Oct.1942

Furthest point reached by Rommel's advance July 1942

Qattara Depression

EGYPT

Alexandria
Cairo
Port Said
Suez Canal

CRETE Under German occupation from May 1941

GREECE
Athens 14 Oct.1944
Patras
British forces landed Oct. 1944

ALBANIA

YUGOSLAVIA

Belgrade

RUSSIAN ADVANCE

HUNGARY

ROMANIA
Bucharest 31 Aug. 1944

Russian attack Aug. 1944

BULGARIA

TURKEY (neutral)

km
0   300

(Mark C. Clark). Subsequently, however, the Pisa–Rimini ('Gothic') Line blocked Allied progress northwards. By this time the Americans, the overwhelmingly dominant member of the Grand Alliance, were mostly interested in shutting down Italian operations, of whose utility they had not only doubts but suspicions. When the 'Gothic Line' was eventually breached and northern Italy occupied after April 1945, the British made much noise about a hypothetical march on Vienna and beyond, but in reality they were more interested in securing Trieste as a point of Balkan leverage.

By this stage in the war the landings in Normandy (6 June 1944) had finally demoted the Mediterranean in Alliance strategy. Nevertheless, the British continued to exhibit their bias towards operations along the Balkan and east Mediterranean littoral. They bitterly opposed, for example, the invasion of southern France ('Operation Anvil') and pressed for United States agreement to some initiative in the Aegean. Churchill became plagued with anxiety that Russian advances through the Balkans would soon deprive the United Kingdom of primacy in the only region where the war had expanded, rather than curtailed, her power. When the civil war which had broken out in Greece lapped at the gates of Athens, the British acted unilaterally of the Americans in landing troops to restore 'order'. Churchill spent Christmas 1944, not poring over maps of Europe, but personally supervising the pacification of the Greek capital. When the war finally ended in 1945, as in 1918, the British Army was scarcely a dominating presence on the continent of Europe, but it was dispersed in strength along great fringes of the Mediterranean shoreline. In this way the British leadership secured its single coherent war aim. After 1945, however, as after 1918, to sustain these territorial advantages was to prove well beyond Britain's capacity.

The war against Japan, 1941–1946

On 7–8 December 1941 the Japanese, enjoying superiority in land, sea and air forces and grossly underestimated by the Americans and British, bombed Pearl Harbor and invaded British Malaya. The 'impregnable' Singapore surrendered on 15 February 1942, and the rest of south-east Asia lay at Japan's feet. The Japanese now possessed a huge and enormously wealthy region whose loss posed grave problems for the Allied conduct of the war. However, the USA had been catapulted into the fighting, and the counter-offensive was swift. Victory at the Coral Sea (May 1942) blocked Japan's southward advance; the battle of Midway (June 1942) weakened Japan's naval strength; the recapture of Guadalcanal in the Solomons (February 1943) marked the start of MacArthur's 'island-hopping' strategy through the south-west Pacific and into the Philippines (October 1944 to February 1945), while Nimitz advanced across the Central Pacific through the Marshall and Gilbert islands to join MacArthur in victory at Leyte Gulf (October 1944). Meanwhile, Allied efforts were co-ordinated within the South-East Asia Command (SEAC – under Lord Mountbatten in Delhi from August 1943, and Kandy from April 1944), and Slim's Fourteenth Army fought through Burma to enter Rangoon in May 1945. The USSR declared war on Japan on 8 August 1945 and advanced into Manchuria, Korea, the Kurile Islands and Sakhalin; but it was bombing raids on Japanese cities, culminating in the atomic bombs dropped upon Hiroshima and Nagasaki, that brought about the emperor's rapid capitulation (14–15 August 1945). Japanese forces surrendered to MacArthur in Tokyo Bay on 2 September and to Mountbatten in Singapore on 12 September.

With Singapore Mountbatten's new headquarters, SEAC was charged with the reoccu-

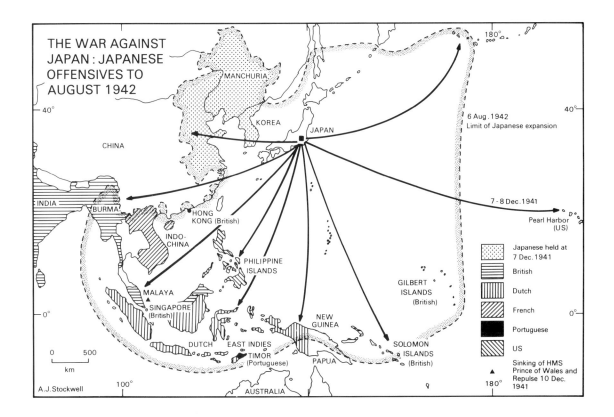

THE WAR AGAINST JAPAN: JAPANESE OFFENSIVES TO AUGUST 1942

40°

MANCHURIA
KOREA
CHINA
JAPAN

6 Aug.1942
Limit of Japanese expansion

40°

180°

INDIA
BURMA
HONG KONG (British)
INDO-CHINA

7-8 Dec.1941

Pearl Harbor (US)

PHILIPPINE ISLANDS

MALAYA
SINGAPORE (British)

GILBERT ISLANDS (British)

0°

DUTCH EAST INDIES
TIMOR (Portuguese)

NEW GUINEA

PAPUA

SOLOMON ISLANDS (British)

0°

Japanese held at 7 Dec.1941

British

Dutch

French

Portuguese

US

Sinking of HMS Prince of Wales and Repulse 10 Dec. 1941

0   500
km

A.J.Stockwell

100°

AUSTRALIA

180°

pation of Dutch and French colonies as well as Britain's lost territories in south-east Asia. Between September 1945 and May 1946 it was hard pressed to re-establish colonial control in the face of the Indonesian revolution (Sukarno declared independence on 17 August) and the Vietminh, let alone revive the trade in rice which was desperately needed within and beyond the region (especially in Bengal).

The war against Japan marked a turning-point in the history of colonial empires in Asia. The exposure of European vulnerability, Japanese atrocities and wartime shortages contributed to the political awakening of subject peoples. The Japanese encouraged displays of anti-western nationalism, delegated administration to local collaborators (like Dr Ba Maw, who became President of 'independent' Burma on 1 August 1943) or drove others (like the Chinese-dominated Malayan People's Anti-Japanese Army) into resistance. From early 1943, as they started to

plan for the post-war world, it became clear to the British, if not to the Dutch or French, that they could not return to the *status quo ante*. Indeed, as the Americans toyed with notions of post-war international trusteeship for former colonies, it seemed for a time that Britain might have to sacrifice Hong Kong and even Malaya as the price of a special relationship with Washington. Colonial Burma's government-in-exile in Simla devised a more progressive constitution for Burma in an ultimately vain attempt to contain nationalist demands for independence. In London a radical scheme for responsibilities in the archipelago was devised, consisting of a Malayan Union for the peninsula and separate crown colony governments for Singapore, Sarawak and North Borneo for the better administration, defence and economic rehabilitation of the area. The Japanese occupation had repercussions beyond south-east Asia too: Indian nationalists were encouraged in their

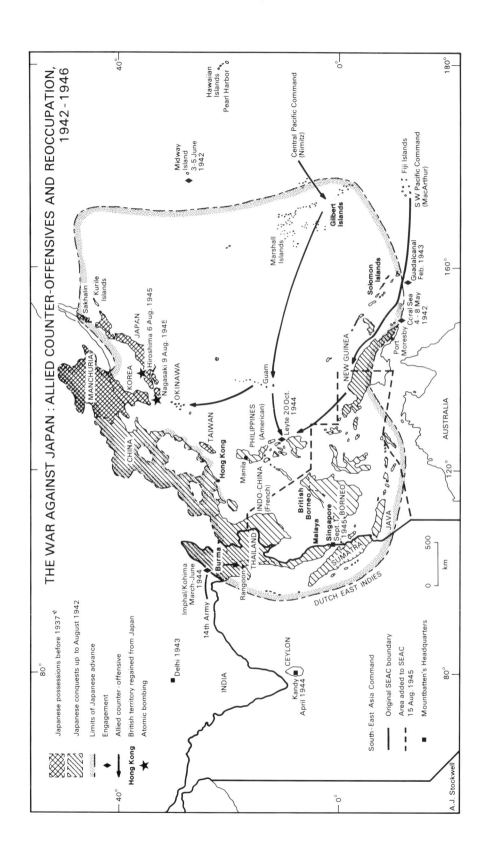

THE WAR AGAINST JAPAN : ALLIED COUNTER-OFFENSIVES AND REOCCUPATION, 1942 - 1946

Japanese possessions before 1937
Japanese conquests up to August 1942
Limits of Japanese advance
Engagement
Allied counter-offensive
British territory regained from Japan
Atomic bombing

Hong Kong

South-East Asia Command
Original SEAC boundary
Area added to SEAC 15 Aug. 1945
Mountbatten's Headquarters

A.J. Stockwell

demands (e.g. 'Quit India', August 1942); Australians, disappointed in their reliance upon the Royal Navy, turned to the USA for protection; and Africans were called upon to make good economic losses suffered in the east.

The partition of India

The Second World War revived Britain's need for the resources of India; the subcontinent's men and materials were mobilized, and India accumulated vast sterling balances in London. War also aggravated the problems of colonial control; when Viceroy Linlithgow declared war on behalf of India without consulting Indian political leaders, Congress reactivated non-co-operation. As the Japanese advanced upon the Indian empire early in 1942, Churchill dispatched Stafford Cripps on a mission to break the political deadlock. Cripps's offer of independence after the war in return for Congress collaboration during it was not taken up. Instead Congress embarked upon the 'Quit India' movement which failed to rock the Raj but did allow the Muslim League to slip into the vacuum (at least in part) created by the resignation of Congress provincial administrations. The Cripps offer of an Indian constituent assembly to devise a constitution for a successor state (or states) remained the basis for subsequent wartime and post-war attempts to arbitrate between Congress and League. However, Jinnah, with his eye on a Muslim future within India rather than outside it, so manipulated the demand for Pakistan that Viceroy Wavell's conference at Simla in June 1945 collapsed on Jinnah's insistence that Leaguers alone should represent Muslims in the proposed interim government. The next month Labour came to power; committed to Indian independence, Attlee directed that elections be held in India as a step towards this goal, but these only served to demonstrate the communal polarization that had occurred since 1937. In a bid to satisfy Congress and League without jeopardizing the essential unity of the subcontinent, the Cabinet Mission (Pethick-Lawrence, Cripps and A.V. Alexander) visited India (March to June 1946). Failing to heal Indian differences, the mission itself devised a three-tier structure providing a union of provinces and princely states, a measure of provincial autonomy and an intermediate tier of groups of provinces for certain common matters. The three proposed groups (or sections) were (A) Hindu-majority provinces, (B) Muslim-majority provinces and (C) Bengal and Assam where there was a balance between 'general' (Hindu) and Muslim representation. Congress and League grudgingly accepted the plan. Congress demanded independence in advance of the creation of provincial groups, while the League insisted upon communal guarantees before the transfer of power took place. But, after the departure of the mission, communalism became increasingly vicious (e.g. the Calcutta riots in August), and Wavell drew up a 'breakdown plan' for British evacuation. By the end of the year Attlee had lost confidence in Wavell's political ability and decided that 'a change in the batting' was necessary.

The announcement (20 February 1947) of Mountbatten's appointment and a date for independence ('not later than June 1948') was a bold move at a bleak time. The new viceroy first tried to win the acquiescence of Congress and the League to an all-India federation of the type that the British had been working for in the Government of India Act (1935) and the Cabinet Mission plan (1946). Believing he had succeeded, Mountbatten secured Cabinet approval, only to encounter Nehru's opposition on grounds that it would 'Balkanize' India. Hastily cobbling together an alternative, Mountbatten fell back on partition as the least unacceptable way out of the impasse

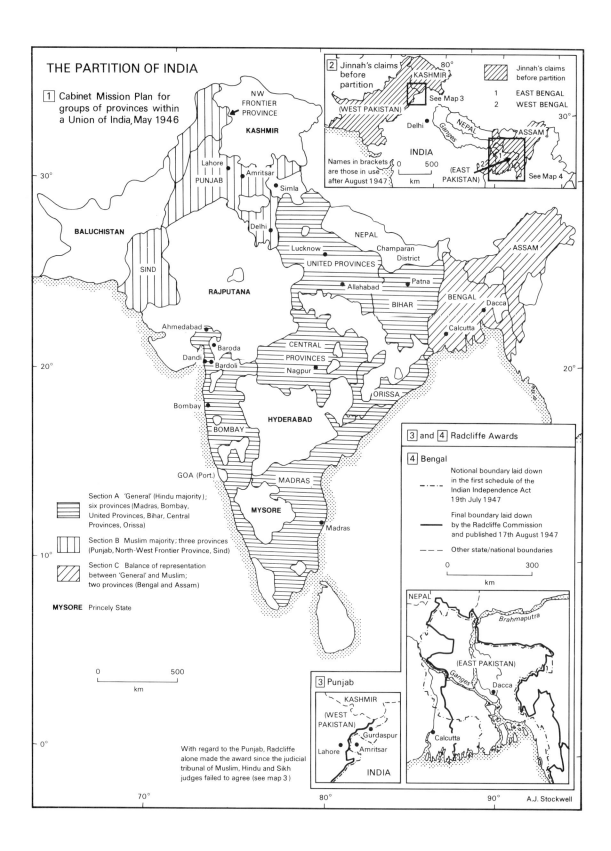

THE PARTITION OF INDIA

1 Cabinet Mission Plan for groups of provinces within a Union of India, May 1946

2 Jinnah's claims before partition

Jinnah's claims before partition

1 EAST BENGAL
2 WEST BENGAL

Names in brackets are those in use after August 1947

See Map 3
See Map 4

KASHMIR
(WEST PAKISTAN)
Delhi
INDIA
NEPAL
ASSAM
(EAST PAKISTAN)

0   500
km

NW FRONTIER PROVINCE
KASHMIR
BALUCHISTAN
Lahore
PUNJAB
Amritsar
Simla
SIND
Delhi
RAJPUTANA
Lucknow
Champaran District
UNITED PROVINCES
NEPAL
Patna
Allahabad
BIHAR
ASSAM
BENGAL
Dacca
Calcutta
Ahmedabad
Baroda
Dandi
Bardoli
CENTRAL PROVINCES
Nagpur
Bombay
ORISSA
HYDERABAD
BOMBAY
GOA (Port.)
MADRAS
MYSORE
Madras

Section A 'General' (Hindu majority); six provinces (Madras, Bombay, United Provinces, Bihar, Central Provinces, Orissa)

Section B Muslim majority; three provinces (Punjab, North-West Frontier Province, Sind)

Section C Balance of representation between 'General' and Muslim; two provinces (Bengal and Assam)

MYSORE Princely State

0   500
km

3 and 4 Radcliffe Awards

4 Bengal

Notional boundary laid down in the first schedule of the Indian Independence Act 19th July 1947

Final boundary laid down by the Radcliffe Commission and published 17th August 1947

Other state/national boundaries

0   300
km

NEPAL
Brahmaputra
(EAST PAKISTAN)
Ganges
Dacca
Calcutta

3 Punjab

KASHMIR
(WEST PAKISTAN)
Gurdaspur
Lahore
Amritsar
INDIA

With regard to the Punjab, Radcliffe alone made the award since the judicial tribunal of Muslim, Hindu and Sikh judges failed to agree (see map 3)

A.J. Stockwell

for the three major participants. Cabinet hoped that the 'dominion formula', whereby India and Pakistan would remain within the Commonwealth, held out the prospect of co-operation on defence and ultimate reunification, while Congress saw itself as heir to the core of the Raj and looked forward to enjoying power at the centre. As for the League, even assuming that its leaders actually wanted Pakistan (which is debatable), partition gave them but the 'husk' of a nation-state. However, with time running out they were in no position to wait for an improved offer. Once agreement had been reached, the pace of decolonization gathered momentum; the date of independence was brought forward to midnight on 14–15 August 1947; legislation was passed through Parliament in July; the army was divided; and the Radcliffe Commission defined the new states' boundaries. In all this the interests of minorities, notably the Sikhs,

were subordinated to the main purposes of sustaining the consent of Congress and League and of transferring power at minimum cost to Britain's dwindling resources. The 500 or so princes, who may have hoped for a continuing special relationship with Britain, were given no choice but to join one or the other successor state. The transfer of power was hailed at the time, and later, as a triumph of trusteeship which converted empire into commonwealth; the implementation of partition, however, was a messy business involving the displacement and migration of millions of Asians and half a million deaths in communal clashes. Integration of the princely states was also accompanied by upheaval; Indian forces invaded Hyderabad in September 1948, and the state of Kashmir became a battleground between India and Pakistan, with the United Nations mediating between them in 1949.

Britain in the Middle East, to 1954

Following the Treaty of Lausanne (see p. 158), embodying Britain's practical accommodation with Turkish metropolitan nationalism, it was hoped in London that the delayed post-war settlement in the Middle East would soon settle down. The determination to enforce this outcome showed in the firm response to subsequent challenges. When Sir Lee Stack, Sirdar of the Egyptian Army, was assassinated in Cairo during 1924, the opportunity was taken to downgrade further the condominium over the Sudan and enhance sole British control. In Cyprus, a crown colony, riots in 1931 were immediately followed by the abolition of representative government – a situation essentially unchanged two decades later. Meanwhile Jordan emerged as one of the most reliable pillars of British influence, the ruler being bound to the United Kingdom by a security treaty in 1928. In Egypt 'treaty politics' proved rather more convoluted, and the Wafd Party continued to agitate for

revisions of the 1922 agreement on which national independence was based. A new security arrangement was finally negotiated in 1936 under the terms of which the British military presence was largely restricted to the – admittedly huge – Suez base. In Palestine the Wailing Wall riots during 1930 dashed hopes that Jewish–Arab relations could be harmonized within the British mandate, and in 1936 an Arab revolt broke out. Nevertheless, this was efficiently repressed by the British Army, and politically Arab nationalism in Palestine remained incurably fragmented. British 'Arabists' were already warning of the potentially corrosive effects of the Palestine question on Britain's regional primacy, but to most people by 1939 Britain's moment in the Middle East seemed anything but passing.

Superficially, at least, the Second World War only confirmed British predominance. Initial defeats by the Italians in Somaliland

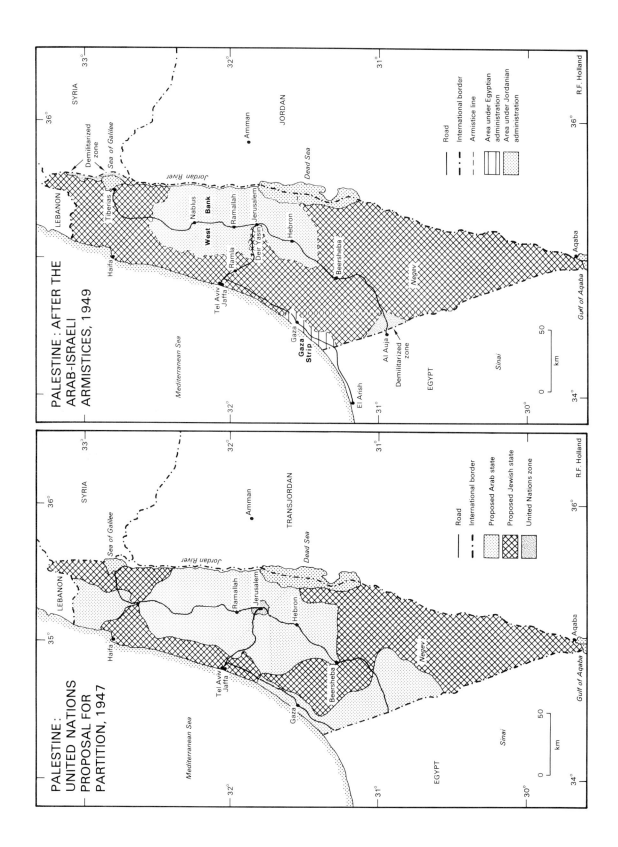

PALESTINE : AFTER THE ARAB-ISRAELI ARMISTICES, 1949

Road
International border
Armistice line
Area under Egyptian administration
Area under Jordanian administration

SYRIA

Demilitarized zone

Sea of Galilee

Jordan River

JORDAN

Amman

Dead Sea

R.F. Holland

LEBANON

Tiberias

Nablus

West Bank

Ramallah

Jerusalem

Haifa

Ramla

Deir Yasin

Hebron

Beersheba

Negev

Aqaba

Tel Aviv

Jaffa

Gaza

Gaza Strip

Al Auja

Demilitarized zone

Mediterranean Sea

El Arish

EGYPT

Sinai

Gulf of Aqaba

0   50
km

PALESTINE : UNITED NATIONS PROPOSAL FOR PARTITION, 1947

Road
International border
Proposed Arab state
Proposed Jewish state
United Nations zone

SYRIA

Sea of Galilee

Jordan River

TRANSJORDAN

Amman

Dead Sea

R.F. Holland

LEBANON

Haifa

Ramallah

Jerusalem

Hebron

Tel Aviv

Jaffa

Beersheba

Negev

Aqaba

Gaza

Mediterranean Sea

EGYPT

Sinai

Gulf of Aqaba

0   50
km

and Ethiopia were quickly reversed. A pro-German coup in Iraq was quashed. After the battle of El Alamein (November 1942) the threat of General Rommel's Afrika Korps to Egypt was lifted, after which – even more than before – Lord Lampson, as high commissioner, treated local politicians and the young King Farouk alike with a Cromerian hand. As in the First World War, and with the usual spate of strategic explanations, the British took the chance to place much of their traditional diplomatic 'sphere' on a military basis. In this spirit, and in harness with the Soviet Union, much of Iran was occupied, and by autumn 1944 – having been evicted by the Germans three years before – British soldiers returned to Greece, tightening their grip on Athens and the Peloponnesus. Hence in 1945, as in 1918, Britain emerged from a great war with her most tangible rewards gained in the east Mediterranean and Middle Eastern worlds.

Yet the war also inspired sentiments and forces which were soon to push the British on to the defensive. By 1945 British heavy-handedness had become so unpopular that no moderate Egyptian regime could negotiate with them and hope to survive. By 1947 the attempted Anglo-Greek design proved beyond British capacities, and they had to give way to the Americans. It was, however, in, or rather through, Palestine that British imperialism in the wider region became fatally weakened, despite the ambiguous stance of Britain towards Zionism during the war, and the Labour government's more pronounced attempts to deflect Zionist claims after 1945. When America's pro-Zionist pressure made British equivocation unsustainable, the Labour government tried to limit the damage by simply renouncing the mandate, which officially ended on 15 May 1948. To Arabs, however, British complicity in the emergence of Israel was transparent, and starkly confirmed by her neutrality during the Arab–Jewish War of 1948–9. Even in conservative Iraq, British standing began to waver. It was not, however, the Arabs, but the Iranians who struck the first major blow at Britain's exposed Middle Eastern flank; the nationalist regime of Mohammed Musaddiq nationalized the Anglo-Iranian Oil Company. This was the first anti-British coup in the region (outside metropolitan Turkey) not to meet with effective retribution since the reconquest of the Sudan in 1898. The repercussions were felt from Egypt, where the revolution of July 1952 intensified guerrilla harassment of the Suez base, to the Gulf, where Saudi Arabia stepped up her frontier claims upon the British-protected Trucial States.

By 1954, therefore, Britain's Middle Eastern position was imperilled from several quarters. Anthony Eden, as Conservative Foreign Secretary, did achieve a fresh treaty with Egypt (October 1954), and in so doing agreed to evacuate the Suez base, the strategic role of which was now defunct; but, as in 1936, these signatures hardly resolved the underlying question as to how far Egypt's freedom of manoeuvre actually extended. Most disturbing, perhaps, was that English predominance even in its safest haunts seemed now to be at stake. In the Sudan pro-Egyptian elements were coming to the fore; in Jordan, Arab nationalism was gaining a lodgement; and in Cyprus – where Anglophobia took pro-Greek rather than pro-Arab form – the campaign for *enosis*, or union with Greece, was gathering speed. By 1955, therefore, the question of Britain's problematical place among the great powers – with the rancorous divisions it had triggered within as much as without the United Kingdom – had come largely to focus on the Middle East.

Decolonization in south-east Asia: the Malayan Emergency, 1948–1960

Some have seen the Communist insurrection in Malaya as part of a Moscow-directed world revolution launched in Asia at the Calcutta Conference (February 1948). However, despite the rash of risings in south-east Asia later that year (see below), it would appear that the Malayan Communist Party (MCP) decided to fight the British largely in response to Malayan circumstances. Founded in 1930, the Chinese-dominated MCP practised insurgency (through the Malayan People's Anti-Japanese Army) during the Japanese occupation when it laid the Min Yuen network for the extraction of food and information from rural squatters. The MPAJA were also supplied by the British Force 136 with arms, some of which they retained for later use against the British. After the Japanese surrender the MPAJA briefly assumed control in many areas but held back from a coup. Indeed, for the next two years the Communists concentrated on the penetration of political parties and strikes; it was only when police action and trade union reform frustrated their advance that, under the leadership of Chin Peng (secretary-general from 1947), they resorted to large-scale violence. Intimidation of workers and attacks on planters (notably the murders of three Europeans at Sungci Siput) caused the federal government to declare a state of emergency on 18 June 1948 (see p. 181).

During the next three years the authorities suffered increasing casualties and material losses without the prospect of total victory.

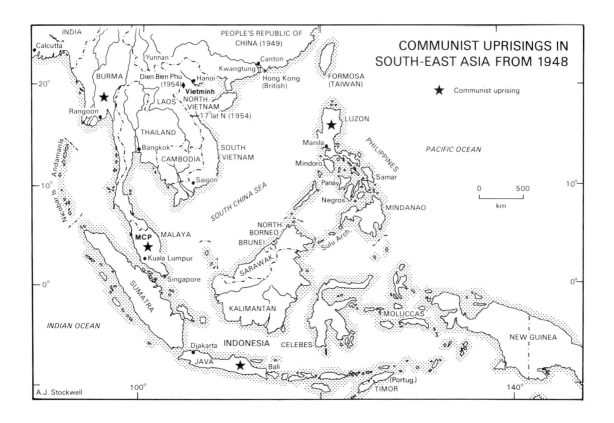

COMMUNIST UPRISINGS IN SOUTH-EAST ASIA FROM 1948

★ Communist uprising

A.J. Stockwell

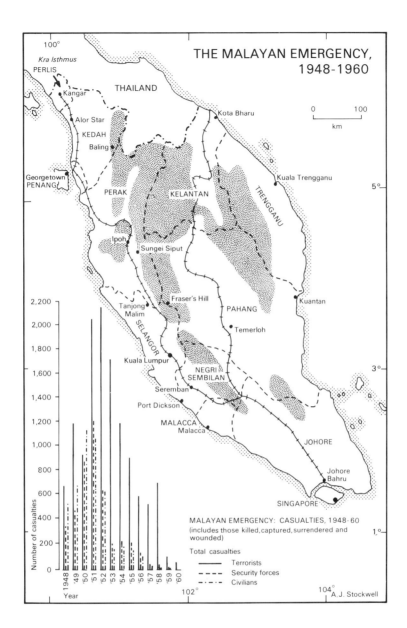

THE MALAYAN EMERGENCY,
1948-1960

MALAYAN EMERGENCY: CASUALTIES, 1948-60
(includes those killed, captured, surrendered and wounded)

Total casualties

——————— Terrorists
- - - - - - Security forces
-·-·-·- Civilians

A. J. Stockwell

British fortunes reached their lowest point when High Commissioner Gurney (1948–51) was assassinated *en route* to Fraser's Hill (6 October 1951); but in February 1952, after Secretary of State Lyttelton had examined the situation for himself, General Templer was appointed both high commissioner and director of operations (1952–4). While much of Templer's success was founded on the work of predecessors (such as the Briggs plan for the resettlement of some 500,000 squatters or Gurney's quasi-ministerial member system), none the less he overhauled the organization of counter-insurgency, reformed the systems of intelligence and public relations and revitalized morale. Although some of his actions (like the punitive curfew imposed on Tanjong Malim, March and April 1952) aroused criticism, Templer was committed to winning 'the hearts and minds' of Malayans.

In view of the precarious balance of Indo-chinese dominoes, the Cabinet defence committee decided (January 1953) that, were Thailand to fall to the Communists, British forces should cross the frontier and occupy the Kra Isthmus. The French were defeated by the Vietminh at Dien Bien Phu (May 1954), and Vietnam was partitioned at the seventeenth parallel (July 1954). Thailand, however, survived, while the authorities strengthened their hold upon Malaya and in September 1953 declared the first 'white area' (in Malacca) where improved security warranted relaxation of emergency restrictions. Thereafter more and more Communist terrorists surrendered and informed on comrades as the hard core retreated to the least accessible jungle near the Thai border.

Unlike the Vietminh, the MCP lacked significant assistance from outside Malaya. More importantly it failed to win the support of the Malays (apart from the guerrillas' Tenth Regiment which was active in Temerloh in 1949). To prevent the conflict escalating to communalism of Palestinian proportions, the British wooed uncommitted Chinese as well as the traditionally co-operative Malays, hence British interest in the Malayan Chinese Association. In December 1955 Tunku Abdul Rahman, Malay chief minister of the Alliance government, met Chin Peng at Baling. Chin Peng demanded political recognition but the Tunku insisted on the MCP's unconditional surrender. Chin Peng returned to the jungle empty-handed; the Tunku won the reputation of a 'statesmanlike' nationalist, achieving Malayan independence less than two years later. The state of emergency was declared at an end on 31 July 1960.

Decolonization in south-east Asia: the Union of Burma, and Malaysia

The White Paper of 17 May 1945, which promised Burma dominion status after the war, was swiftly overtaken by events in liberated Burma where Mountbatten reached an accord (September 1945) with Aung San, leader of the Anti-Fascist People's Freedom League and former Japanese collaborator. However, political stalemate ensued under Governor Dorman-Smith, and Attlee replaced him by Sir Hubert Rance (August 1946). Following Attlee's public declaration (20 December) in favour of early self-government for Burma, London talks resulted in an Anglo-Burmese agreement (27 January 1947) for the election of a constituent assembly. Aung San's AFPFL won an overwhelming victory in the April elections, and in June the constituent assembly resolved in favour of an independent sovereign republic outside the Commonwealth and to be known as the Union of Burma. On 19 July, Aung San and several members of his provisional government were assassinated, but this did not hold up Burma's advance to independence. Rance appointed Thakin Nu (vice-president of AFPFL) to lead a new government; the constituent assembly adopted the independence constitution on 24 September; and the Union of Burma was inaugurated on 4 January 1948 with Thakin Nu continuing as Prime Minister.

Pre-colonial differences between 'Burma proper' and the frontier areas of the Chins, Kachins, Karens and Shans had presented the constituent assembly with major problems. The Union constitution established three autonomous states (for the Shans, Kachins and Karenni) and a special division for the Chins (see p. 183). The question of a Karen state remained a piece of unfinished business at independence, and in August 1948 the Karens rebelled, thereby aggravating the Union's existing difficulties with Communist insurgency and general lawlessness. Burma's decolonization had kept in step with events in

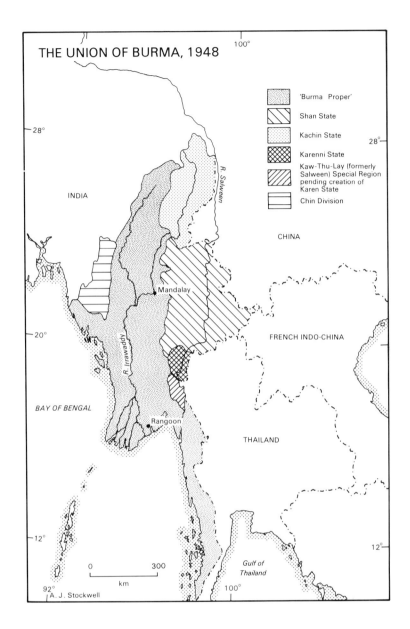

THE UNION OF BURMA, 1948

'Burma Proper'

Shan State

Kachin State

Karenni State

Kaw-Thu-Lay (formerly Salween) Special Region pending creation of Karen State

Chin Division

INDIA

CHINA

R. Salween

Mandalay

FRENCH INDO-CHINA

R. Irrawaddy

BAY OF BENGAL

Rangoon

THAILAND

Gulf of Thailand

0   300

km

A. J. Stockwell

India. Indeed, Burma's value to the British had lain in trade with the Raj and the security of Bengal; and, with Indian independence in the offing, there seemed little purpose in hanging on to Burma. The Labour government, regretting the nationalists' decision to sever ties with the Commonwealth, still hoped to sustain a special relationship with the Union. But, as Burma became wracked with insurrection and secession and retreated into historic isolation, British influence in the country faded.

Malaya and Singapore, by contrast, acquired fresh economic and strategic value to Britain after 1945. Hoping eventually to create a 'Dominion of South-East Asia', the British established direct control over a Malayan Union (of the nine peninsular Malay states plus Penang and Malacca), Singapore, North Borneo and Sarawak, and from 1948

183

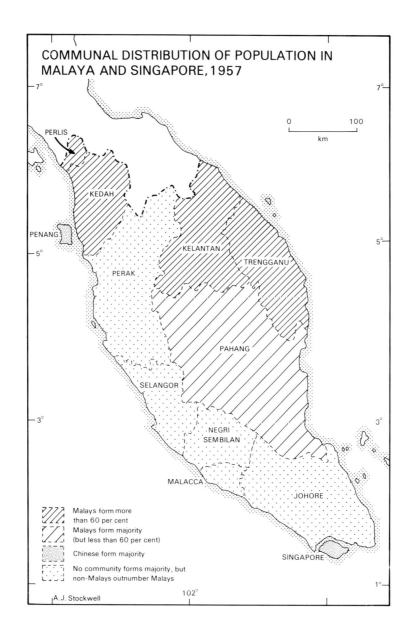

COMMUNAL DISTRIBUTION OF POPULATION IN
MALAYA AND SINGAPORE, 1957

	Malays form more than 60 per cent
	Malays form majority (but less than 60 per cent)
	Chinese form majority
	No community forms majority, but non-Malays outnumber Malays

A.J. Stockwell

co-ordinated regional policies through the commissioner-general in south-east Asia. However, the Malayan Union (1946), which offered citizenship to non-Malays, provoked such Malay opposition that the British were forced to replace it with the Federation of Malaya (1 February 1948). Thereafter, communal politics and Communist insurrection (see pp. 180–2) distracted the British from the early integration of all dependencies in the region. Instead of 'genuine multiracialism', the Alliance (of the dominant United Malays National Organization, Malayan Chinese Association and Malayan Indian Congress) emerged to win 51 of 52 elected seats on the federal council (July 1955) and form a government under Tunku Abdul Rahman. The Reid Commission (of Commonwealth jurists)

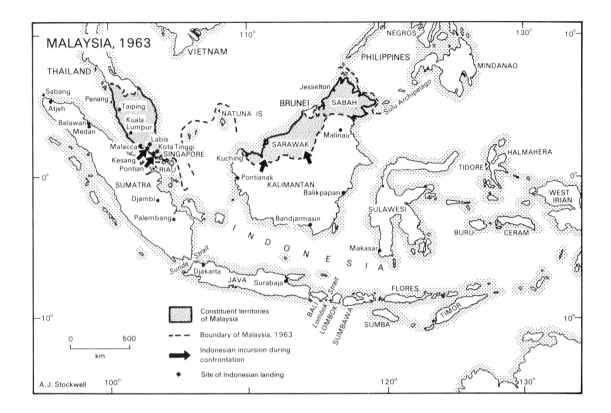

MALAYSIA, 1963

Constituent territories of Malaysia

- - - Boundary of Malaysia, 1963

➜ Indonesian incursion during confrontation

✳ Site of Indonesian landing

A. J. Stockwell

drafted an independence constitution providing a single nationality yet also guaranteeing Malay privileges. After independence (31 August 1957) Malaya remained within the Commonwealth and concluded a defence agreement with Britain but refused to join SEATO (see pp. 191–3). The future security of Singapore, which achieved internal self-government in 1959, persuaded Tunku Abdul Rahman to revive (and Britain and Lee Kuan Yew to accept) the idea of a Malaya–Singapore merger, while the Tunku also drew in Sarawak and Sabah (North Borneo) to offset Singapore's Chinese population. Malaysia

was inaugurated on 16 September 1963 but encountered opposition (see above): the Philippines claimed Sabah; Indonesia militarily 'confronted' Malaysian, British and Commonwealth forces on the borders of the new state from 1963 to 1966; and Singapore seceded to become an independent republic on 9 September 1965. For a number of reasons, notably its oil wealth, Brunei decided against joining Malaysia, and the sultanate remained under British protection until attaining full independence within the Commonwealth in January 1984.

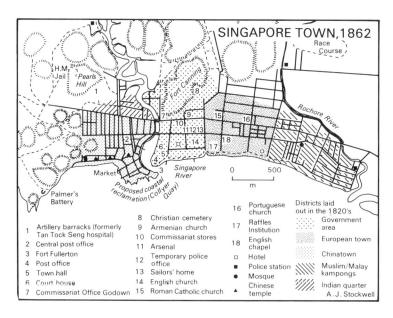

SINGAPORE TOWN, 1862

Race Course

H.M. Jail

Pearl's Hill
1

Fort Canning

Rochore River

7
9
15
16
10
11 12 13
2
6
5
4
14
18
17
3

Market

Singapore River

Palmer's Battery

Proposed coastal reclamation (Collyer Quay)

0   500
m

1   Artillery barracks (formerly Tan Tock Seng hospital)
2   Central post office
3   Fort Fullerton
4   Post office
5   Town hall
6   Court house
7   Commissariat Office Godown
8   Christian cemetery
9   Armenian church
10 Commissariat stores
11 Arsenal
12 Temporary police office
13 Sailors' home
14 English church
15 Roman Catholic church
16 Portuguese church
17 Raffles Institution
18 English chapel

□   Hotel
■   Police station
●   Mosque
▲   Chinese temple

Districts laid out in the 1820's

Government area

European town

Chinatown

Muslim/Malay kampongs

Indian quarter

A.J. Stockwell

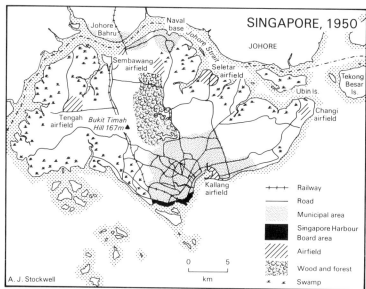

SINGAPORE, 1950

Johore Bahru

Naval base

Johore Strait

JOHORE

Sembawang airfield

Seletar airfield

Ubin Is.

Tekong Besar Is.

Tengah airfield

Bukit Timah Hill 167m ▲

Changi airfield

Kallang airfield

0   5
km

A.J. Stockwell

Railway
Road
Municipal area
Singapore Harbour Board area
Airfield
Wood and forest
Swamp

Singapore

At the crossroads of Indian Ocean and Far Eastern traffic, the settlement of Singapore (founded by Raffles in 1819) thrived on free trade and soon outstripped Penang and Malacca in entrepôt and regional commerce. Immigrants from the Malay states, India and especially China boosted the population from about 200 in 1819 to some 5,000 by 1821; a century later it totalled 350,000 of whom 72 per cent were Chinese. Urban development followed essentially plans of Raffles (1822) by which government, commercial and residential areas were separated and the latter divided into ethnic quarters. In 1832 Singapore became the capital of the Straits Settlements which were transferred from the Government of India to the Colonial Office in 1867. After the First World War the imperial government decided to construct a naval base to the north of the island for the defence of the Far East. It was opened in 1938, but Singapore surrendered to Japan on 15 February 1942. After 1945 it resumed its role in British strategy east of Suez; and, although it became part of Malaysia in 1963 (seceding as an independent republic within the Commonwealth in 1965), British forces remained until 1971.

The resources and products of the Commonwealth, 1952

When Joseph Chamberlain set out in the early 1900s to enunciate a doctrine of the British Empire as a great economic unit, he and his fellow tariff reformers looked upon overseas possessions principally as markets for the United Kingdom's hard-pressed industry. It was during the First World War that one of the distinctive appeals of imperial economic ideas came to lie in their emphasis on the Empire as a rich storehouse of natural resources which would help fend off the pinch of shortage. Such notions continued to thrive after 1918, when a disturbing sense of how the war had reduced British wealth and power relative to America's was palliated by a proprietary interest in an empire whose natural riches – and hence potential development – were more than equal to those of the USA.

During the Second World War the commodity resources of the Empire naturally had a significant place in British thinking. Thus when Singapore and Malaya were overrun by Japan, rubber production for the Allied war effort was successfully switched to British West Africa. Yet what we may term the 'empire of commodities' was much less important at a time when American currency, credit and materials were – from 1940 onwards – so freely on tap. After 1945, when United States Lend–Lease aid was promptly cut off, and the resuscitation of demand was frustrated by endemic shortages of supply, the Empire came back into the foreground of British economic calculations.

This imperial focus became especially intense when the prolonged economic crisis of 1947 – climaxing in the débâcle of sterling convertibility during the summer – badly undermined British confidence. The Labour Government of the day clutched at the conception of organizing production and exchange within the sterling area in a world divided, not only strategically between east and west, but between the dollar and non-dollar zones. It was Africa, in particular, with its many minerals and latent fertility which came to exert a fascination in Whitehall and the prospective development of which afforded Ernest Bevin, the Foreign Secretary, the characteristic hope that the United Kingdom 'might have the Americans eating out of our hands in five years'.

Thereafter each incremental growth in what, at bottom, was a new 'sterling problem' was matched by imperial reassurances to keep up the flagging spirits of ministers, officials and the great (and increasingly hungry) British public. This psychological process peaked in the aftermath of the first post-war devaluation of sterling in September 1949, when the currency's value was massively cut by 30 per cent, and stabilization necessitated renewed doses of austerity administered by the Chancellor of the Exchequer, Sir Stafford Cripps. The period was therefore marked by the production of many officially inspired maps such as the ones here, which encouraged the British people to believe that, whatever the travails

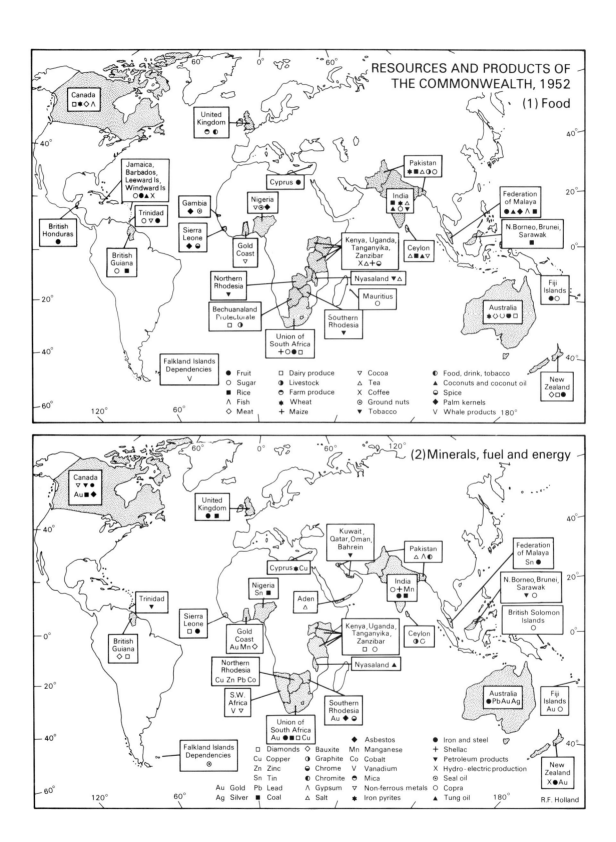

RESOURCES AND PRODUCTS OF
THE COMMONWEALTH, 1952

(1) Food

Canada
□✹◇∧

United
Kingdom
◉ ◑ ◐

Jamaica,
Barbados,
Leeward Is,
Windward Is
○●▲✕

Cyprus ●

Gambia
◆ ◉

Nigeria
▽◉●

Pakistan
✹■△○◑○

India
■ ◉ △
○ ○ ▼

Federation
of Malaya
● ▲ ◆ ∧ ■

British
Honduras
●

Trinidad
○ ▽ ●

Sierra
Leone
◆ ●

Gold
Coast
▽

British
Guiana
○ ■

Kenya, Uganda,
Tanganyika,
Zanzibar
✕△+◉

Ceylon
△■▲▽

N.Borneo, Brunei,
Sarawak
■

Northern
Rhodesia
▼

Nyasaland ▼△

Mauritius
○

Fiji
Islands
●○

Bechuanaland
Protectorate
□ ◑

Southern
Rhodesia
▼

Australia
✹◇∪●□

Falkland Islands
Dependencies
∨

Union of
South Africa
+○●□

New
Zealand
◇□●

● Fruit	□ Dairy produce	▽ Cocoa	◑ Food, drink, tobacco
○ Sugar	◑ Livestock	△ Tea	▲ Coconuts and coconut oil
■ Rice	◐ Farm produce	✕ Coffee	◉ Spice
∧ Fish	✹ Wheat	◉ Ground nuts	◆ Palm kernels
◇ Meat	+ Maize	▼ Tobacco	∨ Whale products

(2) Minerals, fuel and energy

Canada
▽ ▼ ●
Au ■ ◆

United
Kingdom
● ■

Kuwait,
Qatar, Oman,
Bahrein

Pakistan
△ ∧◑

Federation
of Malaya
Sn ●

Cyprus ✹Cu

Nigeria
Sn ■

Aden
△

India
○ + Mn
● ■

N.Borneo, Brunei,
Sarawak
▼ ○

Trinidad
▼

Sierra
Leone
□ ●

Gold
Coast
Au Mn ◇

Kenya, Uganda,
Tanganyika,
Zanzibar
□ ○

Ceylon
◑ ◐

British Solomon
Islands
○

British
Guiana
◇ □

Nyasaland ▲

Northern
Rhodesia
Cu Zn Pb Co

S.W.
Africa
∨ ▽

Southern
Rhodesia
Au ◆ ◉

Australia
● Pb Au Ag

Fiji
Islands
Au ○

Falkland Islands
Dependencies
◉

Union of
South Africa
Au ● ■ □ Cu

New
Zealand
✕ ● Au

□ Diamonds	◇ Bauxite	Mn Manganese	● Iron and steel
Cu Copper	◐ Graphite	Co Cobalt	+ Shellac
Zn Zinc	◐ Chrome	V Vanadium	▼ Petroleum products
Sn Tin	◑ Chromite	◉ Mica	✕ Hydro-electric production
Au Gold	Pb Lead	∧ Gypsum	▽ Non-ferrous metals	○ Copra
Ag Silver	■ Coal	△ Salt	✹ Iron pyrites	▲ Tung oil

R.F. Holland

188

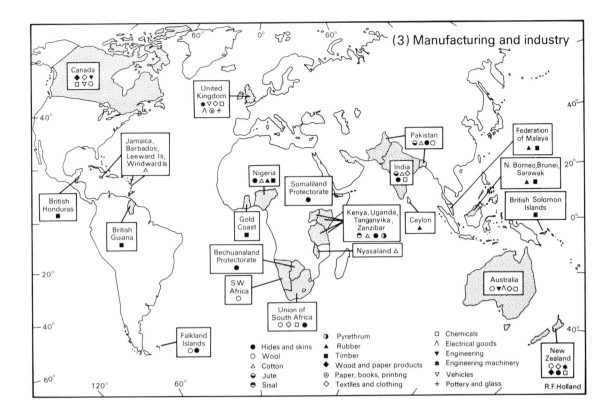

(3) Manufacturing and industry

Canada ◆ ◇ ▼ □ ▽ ○ ⊙

United Kingdom ✱ ▽ ◇ □ ∧ ⊙ +

Pakistan ⊖ ▲ ● ○

India ⊖ ▲ ◇ ● □

Federation of Malaya ▲ ▪

N. Borneo, Brunei, Sarawak ▪ ▲ ▪

Jamaica, Barbados, Leeward Is, Windward Is △

Nigeria ● ▲ ▲ ▪

Somaliland Protectorate ●

Ceylon ▲

British Solomon Islands

British Honduras ▪

Gold Coast ▪

Kenya, Uganda, Tanganyika, Zanzibar ⊖ △ ● ●

British Guiana ▪

Bechuanaland Protectorate

Nyasaland △

Australia ○ ▼ ∧ ◇ □

S W Africa ○

Union of South Africa ○ ◇ □ ●

Falkland Islands ○ ●

New Zealand ○ ◇ ✱ ◆ ● □

● Hides and skins	⊙ Pyrethrum	□ Chemicals
○ Wool	▲ Rubber	∧ Electrical goods
△ Cotton	▪ Timber	▼ Engineering
⊖ Jute	◆ Wood and paper products	✱ Engineering machinery
⊖ Sisal	⊙ Paper, books, printing	▽ Vehicles
	◇ Textiles and clothing	+ Pottery and glass

R.F.Holland

of the moment, the Empire/Commonwealth guaranteed future prosperity to all its citizens.

The last, rosy flush of these essentially propagandist ideas came in 1952, when the dislocating effects of the Korean War seemed to put at risk whatever modest economic advances had been made on the back of the previous devaluation. In fact very soon afterwards the Empire/Commonwealth faded as a category within which British governments considered economic policy. It did so because the other sterling countries had already reached the limits of their own preparedness to reduce imports and so divert gold and dollar income into the vaults of the Bank of England. Here, indeed, was the exposure of the fraudulence – inherently political rather than economic – of imperial economic doctrine: that the British public had some proprietary stake in Northern Rhodesian copper, Gold Coast cocoa or Australian wool which could be translated into the ready supply of such goods when a tight corner was entered. As the mid-1950s dawned, such shams could not conceal that the United Kingdom's position relative to her main competitors had, not least through manifest neglect, become distinctly weak. Before long, indeed, it became fashionable to blame this state of affairs on the imperial and Commonwealth connection for 'feather-bedding' British management and workers. By the end of the decade 'red on the map', in its economic as well as its purely territorial format, took on a sadly ironic air, where very shortly before it had seemingly opened up a vista where security and affluence could at last be enjoyed together.

189

Resources and products of the Commonwealth,
1952 (see maps on pp. 188–9)

Wheat

Canada	18.4 million tons
Australia	5.2 million tons
India	6.0 million tons
	29.6 million tons
World total	162.4 million tons
% main Commonwealth producers 18.2	

Rice

India	35.2 million tons
Pakistan	12.3 million tons
	47.5 million tons
World total	159.1 million tons
% main Commonwealth producers 29.8	

Tea

India	278,000 tons
Ceylon	142,000 tons
	420,000 tons
World Total	581,000 tons
% main Commonwealth producers 72.0	

Jute

Pakistan	1,222,000 tons
India	952,000 tons
	2,174,000 tons
World total	2,250,000 tons
% main Commonwealth producers 96.2	

Sheep

Australia	118 million
New Zealand	35 million
United Kingdom	22 million
Pakistan	7 million
Sudan	6 million
Kenya	3 million
	191 million
World total	781 million
% main Commonwealth producers 24.5	

Rubber

Malaya	585,000 tons
Ceylon	97,000 tons
	682,000 tons
World total	1,700,000 tons
% main Commonwealth producers 40.1	

Cocoa

Gold Coast	248,000 tons
Nigeria	109,000 tons
	357,000 tons
World total	741,000 tons
% main Commonwealth producers 48.1	

Manganese

India	685,000 tons
Gold Coast	406,000 tons
South Africa	346,000 tons
	1,437,000 tons
World total	2,760,000 tons
% main Commonwealth producers 52.0	

Tin

Malaya	57,000 tons
Nigeria	13,900 tons
	70,900 tons
World total	171,000 tons
% main Commonwealth producers 41.4	

Gold

South Africa	809 tons
Canada	307 tons
Australia	67 tons
Gold Coast	48 tons
Southern Rhodesia	34 tons
	1,265 tons
World total	1,672 tons
% main Commonwealth producers 75.6	

Diamonds

South Africa	2,383 tons
Gold Coast	2,059 tons
Sierra Leone	453 tons
Tanganyika	331 tons
British Guiana	35 tons
	5,261 tons
World total	18,694 tons
% main Commonwealth producers 28.1	

Britain and the South-East Asia Treaty Organization, 1954

During the Second World War the British had maintained only a marginal commitment to the Far East. After the war, United Kingdom governments modestly aimed to retain the patchwork of Britain's existing colonial, commercial and diplomatic interests in east Asia, but otherwise had no ambitions in an area which mattered far less to them than the Middle East. This low-key approach seemed well suited to a situation where the completeness of Japan's military defeat by the United States in 1945 held out the prospect of stability for the foreseeable future. This outlook was drastically changed by the Communist take-over in China during April 1949.

Thereafter British and American policies were always somewhat at odds, initially evidenced by the fact that the former immediately recognized Mao Tse-tung's regime, while the latter refused to do so. The Americans wanted their closest NATO ally to commit herself to a distinctive anti-Communist stance, while the British 'ideal' was a more piecemeal arrangement whereby they could call on the United States to subdue any threat to Britain's residual stake in the region. These contrasting aims were not easily reconciled, especially when Britain's contribution to the Korean War (which broke out in June 1950) fell considerably below Washington's expectations. Against this background the United States entered into a Pacific pact with Australia and New Zealand by signing the ANZUS Treaty in September 1951, insisting meanwhile on the exclusion of the United Kingdom from it.

The end of the fighting in Korea temporarily eased these disagreements; but they flared up yet more powerfully when France, which – with much American help – was at war with Communist (or Vietminh) 'rebels' in Indo-China, signified in early 1954 that her military position was now untenable. The United States demanded 'united action' among western allies to throw back this immi-nent Communist advance. Anthony Eden, the British Foreign Secretary, however, refused involvement, and was subsequently a moving spirit behind the Geneva Conference of June and July 1954 (essentially boycotted by the United States) which 'settled' Indo-China by creating two Vietnams and neutralizing Laos and Cambodia.

To palliate the United States's resentment over these events the British government participated in the negotiations which led to the Manila Treaty of September 1954, and the establishment of the South-East Asia Treaty Organization. Under its terms, the eight signatories (the United States, Britain, France, Australia, New Zealand, Siam, the Philippines and Pakistan) agreed to consult together if the security of the south-east Asia territories of any of these powers, or of Laos, Cambodia or South Vietnam, appeared to be in danger. What such consultation should mean, however, and what might constitute 'danger', was left undefined. Difference also arose during negotiations over whether or not the 'aggression' which the Organization should look to repel should be explicitly defined as (and limited to) Communism. Eventually the Americans signed such a declaratory appendix on their own, but even this was enough for neutralist India to refuse to join a body which so clearly betrayed its factional alignments.

Subsequently the British government, which shared many of the Indian reservations, was mainly intent on evading any commitments which SEATO membership might bring all too suddenly in its wake. Conversely, the United States for a while sought to channel much of its regional diplomacy and military planning through SEATO, hoping thereby to secure maximum allied support. After 1959, in particular, the organization's viability and purpose were tested in Laos, the deteriorating internal security of which the United States

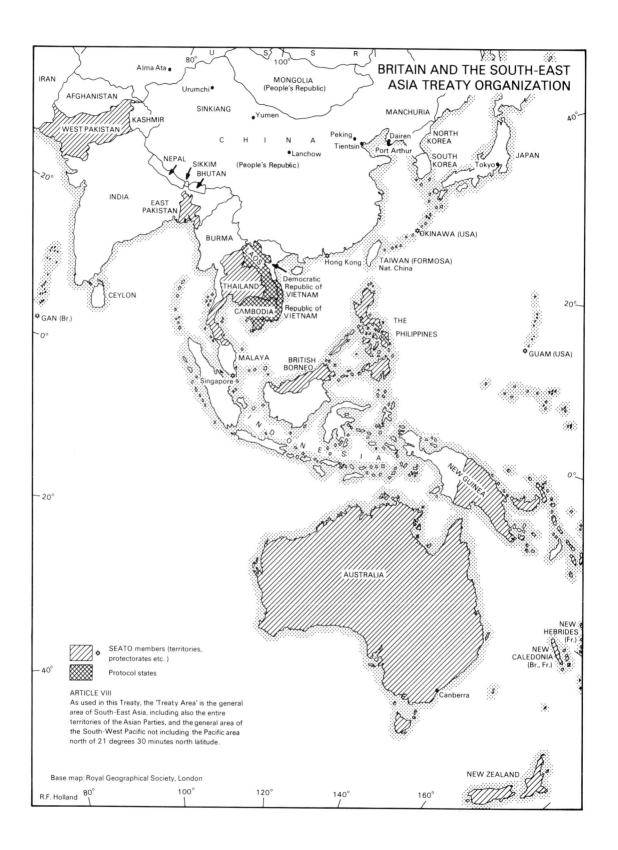

BRITAIN AND THE SOUTH-EAST
ASIA TREATY ORGANIZATION

U S S R

IRAN

AFGHANISTAN

MONGOLIA
(People's Republic)

Alma Ata

Urumchi

SINKIANG

Yumen

MANCHURIA

KASHMIR

WEST PAKISTAN

C H I N A

Peking
Tientsin

Dairen
Port Arthur

NORTH
KOREA

NEPAL

SIKKIM
BHUTAN

(People's Republic)

Lanchow

SOUTH
KOREA

JAPAN

Tokyo

INDIA

EAST
PAKISTAN

BURMA

OKINAWA (USA)

CEYLON

LAOS

THAILAND

CAMBODIA

Hong Kong

TAIWAN (FORMOSA)
Nat. China

Democratic
Republic of
VIETNAM

Republic of
VIETNAM

THE
PHILIPPINES

GAN (Br.)

MALAYA

BRITISH
BORNEO

GUAM (USA)

Singapore

I N D O N E S I A

NEW GUINEA

AUSTRALIA

Canberra

NEW
HEBRIDES
(Fr.)

NEW
CALEDONIA
(Br., Fr.)

SEATO members (territories,
protectorates etc.)

Protocol states

ARTICLE VIII
As used in this Treaty, the 'Treaty Area' is the general
area of South-East Asia, including also the entire
territories of the Asian Parties, and the general area of
the South-West Pacific not including the Pacific area
north of 21 degrees 30 minutes north latitude.

Base map: Royal Geographical Society, London

R.F. Holland

NEW ZEALAND

held clearly to be within its remit, but which Britain (and France) considered not to constitute an 'international' concern. With the subsequent crystallization of the crisis in South Vietnam, the United States ceased to count on any help from her European allies. As a result, SEATO's always problematical significance drained away; only Australia and New Zealand fought alongside America after the 'escalation' in Vietnam during 1963. By then Britain's withdrawal from the Far East was almost complete, although she had continued to assist Malaysia in her local confrontation with Indonesia, and to have a symbolic commitment to Hong Kong. In essence, SEATO represented for Britain a final episode in her long-term attempt (beginning in 1902 with the Anglo-Japanese treaty) to abdicate the responsibilities, and dangers, of being an east Asian power, without simultaneously forfeiting her more general aspiration to remain what in the 1950s was termed a 'top-table' nation.

The Baghdad Pact, 1955

By 1950–1 the possibilities of shoring up the United Kingdom's Middle Eastern position by the old treaty method had virtually disappeared. At the same time the Korean War had made all the western powers deeply afraid of similar Communist initiatives in other parts of the world. The British were particularly sensitive in the Middle East to the Soviet threat, because the Russians had always shown a subtle understanding of their vulnerability there. To meet their dilemma the British subsequently developed the idea of a Middle Eastern Defence Organization (or MEDO). Ideally, the apparent equality among its members would satisfy nationalist opinion, while not preventing effective British leadership. It would have a secretariat providing lucrative jobs for locals, the absence of which 'spoils' had always been a weakness of the old treaties. Perhaps most important, it was hoped that the Americans might be persuaded to underwrite MEDO where they had previously been unwilling to guarantee anything which smacked of a transparent British primacy in the region. Yet despite intense British lobbying MEDO never materialized, partly because the Americans refused these pleas, and partly because Nasser would have nothing to do with a project which so ill consorted with the image of a revolutionary leader.

The British therefore decided to reduce drastically their 'investment' in Egypt, especially as the development of the United Kingdom's atomic programme substantially reduced the purely strategic significance of the Suez base. Anthony Eden negotiated the Anglo-Egyptian treaty of 1954, and prepared to adopt more of an American version of regional security, in which Turkey (a NATO member after 1952) rather than Egypt was a paramount player. This blending of British and United States purposes, in which the former acted as a proxy for the latter, developed a step further in February 1955 when Iraq and Turkey signed a formal defence treaty in Baghdad, in which they invited other states concerned with Middle Eastern affairs to join. The so-called 'northern tier' was extended shortly afterwards when Pakistan and Iran also agreed to participate, as did the United Kingdom itself. Thus the revolutionary regime in Cairo was, it seemed, successfully isolated.

The Baghdad Pact, however, was not itself wholly satisfactory from a British vantage-point, since, with the exception of Iraq, the 'northern tier' was neither Arab nor particularly pro-British; Pakistan, for example, looked increasingly to the United States for great-power patronage and, more particularly, arms purchases. In London the hope therefore prevailed that the pact's membership could be expanded to take on a more Arab complexion. Above all, it was considered vital

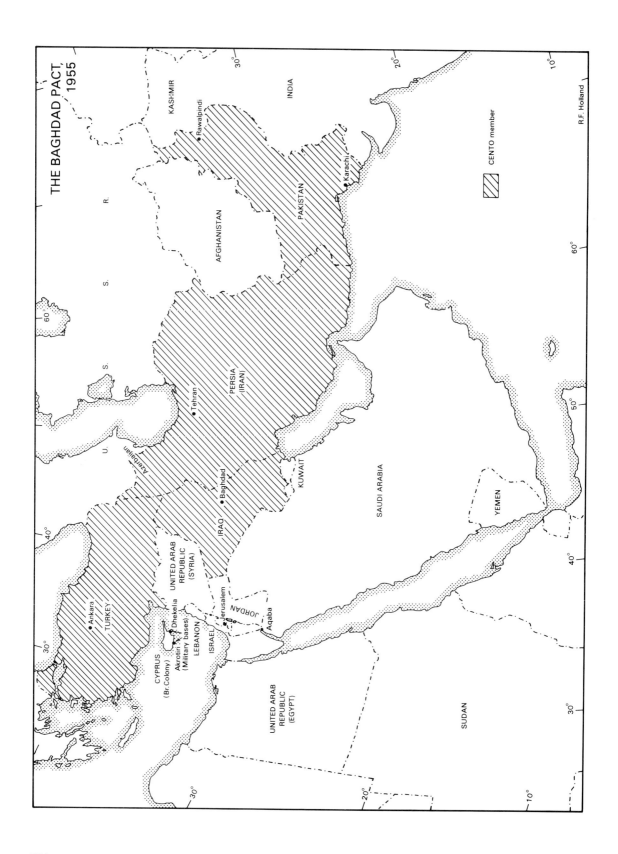

THE BAGHDAD PACT, 1955

CENTO member

194

to include Transjordan, but British pressure on the young King Hussein to accede to the pact only succeeded in stimulating riots in Amman during early 1956. When in their aftermath Transjordan moved away from Britain and (tentatively at least, since Hussein well knew that pan-Arab radicals were enemies of his dynasty) towards Egypt, the chances of the pact developing into the British dream of an updated Anglo-Arab Commonwealth began to disintegrate rapidly.

Britain's evident determination to reduce Egypt's status as a Middle Eastern power had only intensified Nasser's proclivity to promote himself and his country as the leading force in pan-Arab politics (a tendency which the Suez crisis, p. 198, later also served to confirm). The mutual defence agreement signed between Egypt and Syria in October 1955 constituted, in effect, a riposte to London and its allegedly 'reactionary' satellites; this in many ways surprising alignment between historic rivals in the Fertile Crescent steadily blossomed into the full constitutional union of the two countries known as the United Arab Republic (UAR).

It is usually held that after the Suez crisis the United States, while never becoming a member of the Baghdad Pact proper, became supportive of it, a tendency inherent in the 'Eisenhower doctrine' whereby the Americans finally assumed responsibility for the security of western interests in the Middle East. Certainly the conjoint American and British actions during the twin crises of July 1958, when the former intervened in the Lebanon and the latter in Jordan, underlined an entirely new harmony between London and Washington in Middle Eastern matters. But it would be truer to say that such direct methods of supervising western interests only served to confirm the bankruptcy of the Baghdad Pact as a genuinely regional institution. Iraq's membership of it, far from helping to maintain in power its Hashemite, pro-British monarchy, ironically hastened the end of such a compromised regime; the July 1958 crisis in the region, indeed, was first triggered by the bloody coup in the Iraqi capital which gave birth to a republic under the erratic leadership of General Kassem. Thus was terminated the United Kingdom's last significant toe-hold in the mainstream of Arab affairs. The Pact of 1955, bereft of its Arab façade, subsequently had its offices (and jobs) moved to Ankara, where it was renamed – with a drab formality which became it – the Central Treaty Organization (or CENTO). In fact the troubles besetting the UAR prevented that fragile entity from exploiting the resulting vacuum. These derived from Syrian resentment of Nasser's evident intention to bend the union to essentially Egyptian purposes, prompting the revolt by Syrian army officers on 28 September 1961 which both brought the UAR experiment to an abrupt halt and irreparably damaged Nasser's regime. The only beneficiaries of these various upsets were Israel and those American strategists who saw the latter as the only firm basis for western influence in the Middle East.

The Cyprus revolt, 1955–1959

Cyprus first passed beneath British sway as a protectorate under the Anglo-Turkish Convention of 1878. Having been transmuted into a crown colony in 1925, the island was accorded a representative constitution, but this was suspended in 1931 following popular disturbances. Direct rule by the colonial administration prevailed thereafter in a possession where the population was overwhelmingly European (80 per cent Greek and 20 per cent Turkish). Local opposition to the status quo took the form of a demand to be united with the motherland of Greece – *enosis*. Greek teachers predominated in the schools; Greek

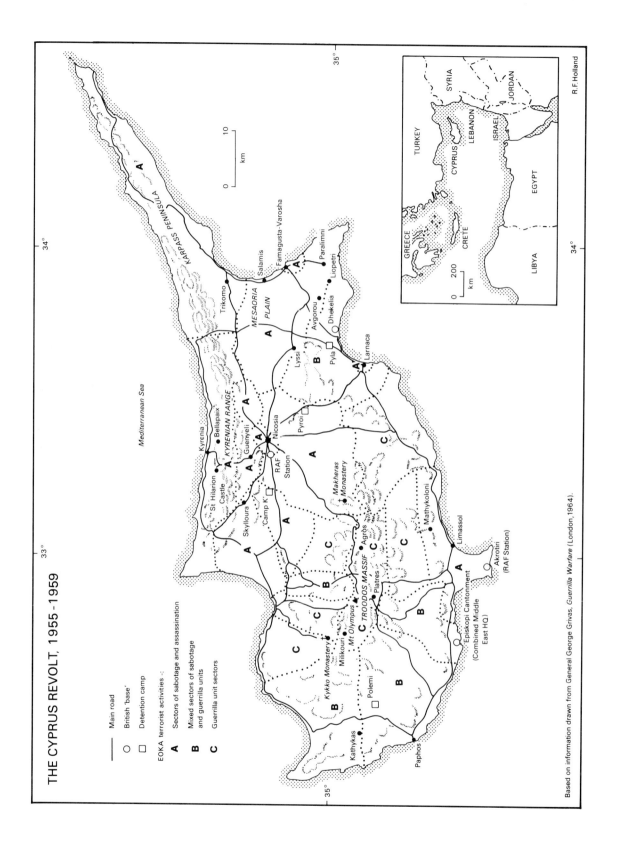

THE CYPRUS REVOLT, 1955 - 1959

Main road
○ British 'base'
□ Detention camp

EOKA terrorist activities :-
A Sectors of sabotage and assassination
B Mixed sectors of sabotage and guerrilla units
C Guerrilla unit sectors

KARPASS PENINSULA

Mediterranean Sea

Trikomo
Salamis
Famagusta-Varosha
Paralimni
Liopetri
Avgorou
Dhekelia
Larnaca
Pyla
Lyssi
MESAORIA PLAIN
Kyrenia
Bellapaix
Guenyeli
KYRENIAN RANGE
St Hilarion
Castle
Nicosia
Pyroi
RAF Station
'Camp K'
Skylloura
Makheras Monastery
Mathykoloni
Limassol
Agrós
Platres
TROODOS MASSIF
Mt Olympus
Kykko Monastery
Milikouri
Polemi
Episkopi Cantonment
(Combined Middle East HQ)
Akrotiri
(RAF Station)
Kathykas
Paphos

km 0 10

TURKEY
SYRIA
LEBANON
ISRAEL
JORDAN
EGYPT
CYPRUS
CRETE
GREECE
LIBYA

km 0 200

R.F.Holland

35°
34°
33°
34°

Based on information drawn from General George Grivas, *Guerrilla Warfare* (London, 1964).

196

flags were waved on days of celebration; and Greek was the main medium of the press. Hence *enosis* and self-determination were held to be synonymous. After 1945, however, even when an Asian island such as Ceylon was granted 'freedom', Cyprus was offered only the most qualified form of municipal government. Enosist passions rose and were voiced by the Orthodox Church, led after 1952 by the young patriarch Archbishop Makarios II. At this point, however, *enosis* also became the chief aim of a right-wing military nationalist from the Greek mainland, General George Grivas. On 1 April 1955, after Grivas himself had clandestinely moved to Cyprus and laid the foundations of a subversive organization known as EOKA, the explosion of several bombs in central Nicosia heralded the start of the Cyprus revolt.

The EOKA campaign which ensued did not seek to defeat the British forces in combat, but to reduce them to impotence by proving their vulnerability at every point. Guerrilla groups – rarely more than five or six fighters – operated in the mountainous areas of Troodos and the Kyrenia range, but sabotage and murder in the towns were just as important in Grivas's 'general plan'. Indeed, the most dangerous area for British personnel (and for Turks) was the arid Mesaoria plain (known as the 'death zone' to EOKA operatives). The high degree to which the civil service and police were penetrated by EOKA sympathizers militated against effective British responses, even when a leading soldier, General Harding, was made governor of the island. Desperate for some tangible success, Harding's tenure was characterized by a series of big sweeps in the mountains to capture the elusive Grivas, but he was never located (having quickly moved to a hiding-place in the suburbs of Nicosia).

Frustrated militarily, the British required a political weapon to discipline the Greek Cypriots; the only one available was to involve the Turkish government and tacitly raise the spectre of partition. Thus Turkey, along with Greece, was invited in 1955 to the fruitless tripartite conference in London; subsequently the British plaint was that self-determination could not be given to Cyprus without consideration being given to Turkish claims. While this was not, perhaps, the sole cause for the communal ill feeling which rapidly developed after 1956, it made an important contribution to it. EOKA set up a separate command structure to hit Turkish Cypriots; and the latter organized themselves for protection. In 1958 bitter Greek–Turkish riots broke out in Nicosia, and the communities in the island capital were subsequently divided by barbed wire, British patrols and mutual hatred.

After the Suez War, however, the entanglement in Cyprus became an embarrassment to Britain. Even the soldiers accepted what critics of the British government's policy had said throughout the revolt – that the United Kingdom's only prerequisite was access to designated bases, not control over the whole island. The problem therefore became one of finding a means of withdrawal from a situation which was infinitely more convoluted than it had been at the outset of the troubles. Since Archbishop Makarios had been exiled to the Seychelles in 1956 the *enosis* campaign had become more than ever dominated by the militant Grivas; and although Makarios was afterwards released it was only slowly that he succeeded in drawing the tactical initiative back into clerical hands. By 1959, however, the islanders of both communities were eager for an end to bloodshed and curfew, and the politicians were able to start talking. This led to Cyprus becoming an independent republic, with Makarios as President, in August 1960, and power-sharing arrangements which ensured a measure of Turkish influence (the Deputy President was always to be Turkish). The United Kingdom retained sovereign bases at Akrotiri and Dhekelia, a concession, ironically, both the main communities were happy to make since it held out the prospect of British protection against their mutual depredations. The bases have lasted; the equipoise between Greek and Turk within a single Cypriot state has not.

The Suez crisis, 1956

Superficially, the new Anglo-Egyptian treaty of October 1954 might seem to have heralded less stormy relations between London and Cairo. In fact, such a beneficent outcome was never likely. In agreeing to evacuate from the Suez base and Canal zone (see map, inset), the British government's intention was henceforth to channel its diplomacy through more pliable partners in the region, and so demote Egypt. In contrast, by abandoning its claim to the Sudan (see p. 179), the Egyptian revolutionary regime was freeing its hands for a more assertive role in the Arab Middle East. This direct clash of aims and ambitions was almost certain, sooner or later, to bring a fresh spate of Anglo-Egyptian troubles.

Gamul Abdul Nasser's chief preoccupation after 1954 was to develop a foreign policy outside 'British' constraints. Territorially, the focus of this competition lay at first in the Transjordan, whose expanded frontiers of 1949 had carried with them an angry Palestinian citizenry of uncertain loyalties. By exploiting these discontents, Nasser's purpose was to hustle the young King Hussein out of the British orbit – with its petty subsidies and fusty 'advisers' – into a nationalist front led by Egypt. This intrigue met with success when the Amman riots of March 1956 frightened Hussein into dismissing the *éminence grise* of Anglo-Jordanian relations, General Glubb, from his military post (see p. 195). Anthony Eden, who had at last succeeded Churchill as Prime Minister in April 1955, was determined to 'get Nasser' from this point on. In duelling with Eden, Nasser was alert to the necessity of driving a wedge between London and Washington. His arms deal with Czechoslovakia in September 1955 was, for example, a timely reminder to the Americans that Egypt was being driven by reactionary British diplomacy to defect from its western orientation. Given Eden's fragile relations with the United States Secretary of State, John Foster Dulles, such tactics had plenty of scope, and whenever the

Americans saw fit to kick Egypt, the latter's Pavlovian response was always to retaliate against Britain. Thus it was that when the United States announced its refusal to fund the Aswan Dam project, Nasser responded on 26 July by nationalizing the Suez Canal Company, an action which had few transparent implications for the United States, but plenty for the United Kingdom. Eden's immediate response was to call up 20,000 reservists and authorize preparations for a possible invasion of Egypt.

The British government expected such 'sabre rattling' would bring the Egyptians to heel. While its echo was being heard, the British were happy to sit through an essentially hidebound conference of maritime users in London, an attempt at Australian arbitration and much confabulating at the United Nations. Once it became clear, however, to Eden's embittered dismay, that the Americans were out to undermine the United Kingdom's role in the Middle East by an artful display of innocent neutrality, the Prime Minister had to decide whether the sabre rattling should or could be converted into overt force.

Many observers thought the logistical difficulties of invading Egypt would leave Eden little choice but to back down. After all, by 1956 the British Army was attaching itself to life alongside the Rhine, not the Nile. Fortuitously, however, at this juncture both the French, who held Nasser responsible for sustaining the insurgents against their rule in Algeria, and the Israelis, determined to punish Egypt for her harassments along the Gaza frontier, were also contemplating similar military action. Eden gambled on a *tour de force* – later castigated as 'collusion' – in which the British were fitted into a Franco-Israeli plan, timed to coincide with the United States presidential election, and so present the Americans with a European *fait accompli* in the Middle East.

Thus on 29 October, Israel invaded Egypt,

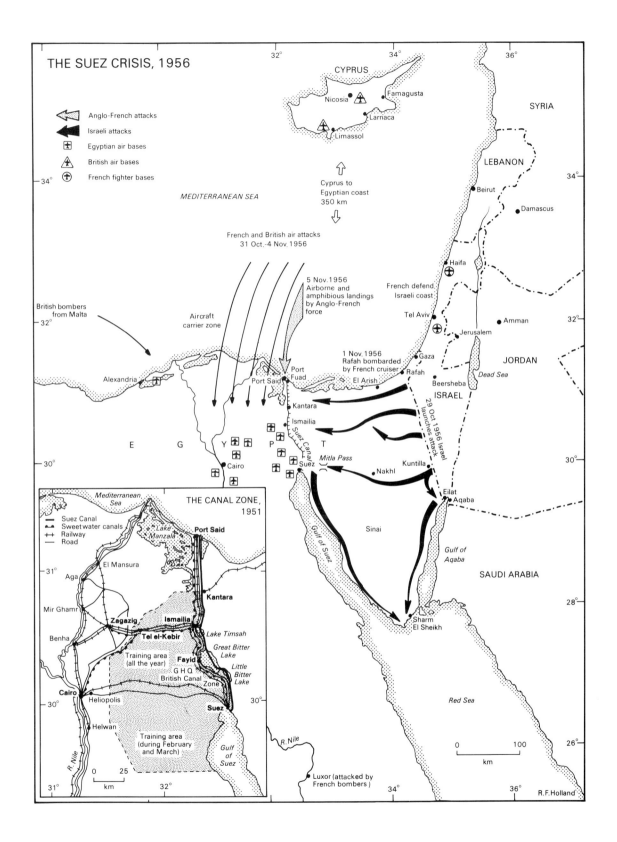

THE SUEZ CRISIS, 1956

Anglo-French attacks
Israeli attacks
Egyptian air bases
British air bases
French fighter bases

MEDITERRANEAN SEA

CYPRUS
Nicosia
Famagusta
Larnaca
Limassol

SYRIA

LEBANON
Beirut
Damascus

Cyprus to
Egyptian coast
350 km

French and British air attacks
31 Oct.-4 Nov. 1956

5 Nov. 1956
Airborne and
amphibious landings
by Anglo-French
force

Aircraft
carrier zone

British bombers
from Malta

French defend
Israeli coast

Haifa

Tel Aviv

Amman

Jerusalem

1 Nov. 1956
Rafah bombarded
by French cruiser

Alexandria

Port Fuad
Port Said

El Arish

Gaza
Rafah

Beersheba

Dead Sea

JORDAN

ISRAEL

Kantara

Ismailia

Suez Canal

29 Oct 1956 Israel launches attack

E   G   Y   P   T

Cairo

Mitla Pass

Suez

Nakhl

Kuntilla

Eilat
Aqaba

Sinai

Gulf of Suez

Gulf of Aqaba

SAUDI ARABIA

Sharm
El Sheikh

Red Sea

0   100
km

THE CANAL ZONE, 1951

Mediterranean Sea

Suez Canal
Sweetwater canals
Railway
Road

Lake Manzala

Port Said

El Mansura

Aga

Kantara

Mir Ghamr

Zagazig

Ismailia

Benha

Tel el-Kebir

Lake Timsah

Training area
(all the year)

Great Bitter
Lake

Fayid

G H Q
British Canal Zone

Little
Bitter
Lake

Cairo

Heliopolis

Suez

Helwan

Training area
(during February
and March)

Gulf
of
Suez

R. Nile

0   25
km

R. Nile

Luxor (attacked by
French bombers)

R.F.Holland

199

smashing the opposition in the Sinai passes and advancing upon the Canal. Britain and France, after a short but discreet interval to permit these successes, announced their intention to occupy the Canal Zone in order to minimize 'damage'. When Egypt refused to withdraw behind a ten-mile perimeter, her airfields were strafed by Anglo-French bombers to avert counter-strikes against Israeli targets, and the main invasion got under way. But the airborne landings were followed up only after a somewhat muddled delay by the sea-borne forces from Cyprus. The less-than-brilliant Anglo-French advance down the Canal therefore gave time for loud protestations in the United Nations, exemplified – not to say orchestrated – by the outraged United States administration, which throughout the crucial days had been denied any solid information about developments, a status hardly redolent of superpowerdom. These excitements were soon communicated to the money markets, where sterling, with its reserve currency role, was shown to be vulnerable in a way the franc was not. It was, therefore, the British who in the end decided on a withdrawal. By early December the evacuation was begun, although the Canal – which had been blocked – took some months to return to normality. In its aftermath Anthony Eden ceased to be Prime Minister, and Anglo-French relations deteriorated, while those with the United States were retrieved – at a price. But most significant was the demise of that Middle Eastern imperium which had been the acme of British overseas aspirations since the First World War.

British decolonization in Africa, 1956–1970

By the beginning of the 1950s, while British governments had accepted the inevitability of political change in Africa, such transition was still thought of in London as taking place over decades rather than years. It was also assumed that different territories and regions within British colonial Africa would evolve, not according to a single formula, but in a more polyglot fashion reflecting the great range of prevailing conditions. The most important such variable was white settlement. Where economic settlement by Europeans had not progressed very far – in what were known as 'native states' in the heyday of empire – the way was considered open for a staged but relatively unhindered approach to self-government. This was the case in British West Africa. Where, however, European interests – farming, mining or commercial – had been long entrenched, it was contemplated that a different principle would apply, whereby checks to African preponderance would be a natural complement to constitutional advance.

In varying degrees this prevision was held with regard to East, Central and Southern Africa. It was in these latter areas that the most distinctive conception of African colonial change developed by the British at this time – 'multiracialism' – was relevant. According to this rule, racial differences between black and white would before long be reconciled through the agency of economic growth and rising prosperity, and so provide the essential condition for smooth and gradual political development.

Over the second half of the 1950s the confidence which lay behind these metropolitan beliefs faltered. While rates of economic growth in British Africa reached historic peaks, the effects, both in encouraging the formation of a local middle class and in damping down anti-colonial nationalism, remained fitful. The Gold Coast (renamed Ghana) in 1957 became the first independent black African state south of the Sahara, but even in this relatively uncomplicated case the passage had

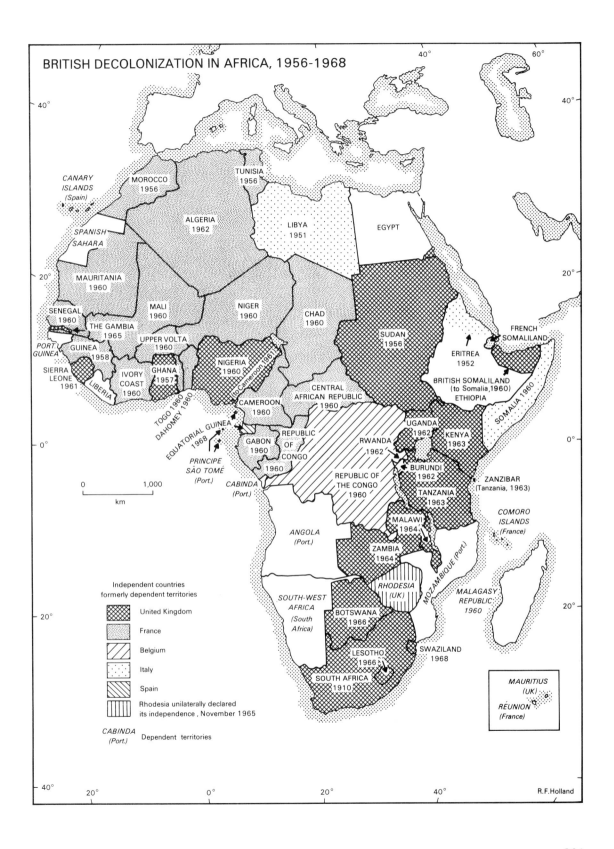

BRITISH DECOLONIZATION IN AFRICA, 1956-1968

CANARY
ISLANDS
(Spain)

MOROCCO
1956

TUNISIA
1956

ALGERIA
1962

LIBYA
1951

EGYPT

SPANISH
SAHARA

MAURITANIA
1960

MALI
1960

NIGER
1960

CHAD
1960

SUDAN
1956

ERITREA
1952

FRENCH
SOMALILAND

SENEGAL
1960

THE GAMBIA
1965

UPPER VOLTA
1960

NIGERIA
1960

(to Cameroon 1961)

CENTRAL
AFRICAN REPUBLIC
1960

BRITISH SOMALILAND
(to Somalia,1960)
ETHIOPIA

PORT.
GUINEA

GUINEA
1958

GHANA
1957

SOMALIA 1960

SIERRA
LEONE
1961

LIBERIA

IVORY
COAST
1960

CAMEROON
1960

UGANDA
1962

KENYA
1963

TOGO 1960

DAHOMEY 1960.

EQUATORIAL GUINEA
1968

GABON
1960

REPUBLIC
OF
CONGO
1960

RWANDA
1962

ZANZIBAR
(Tanzania, 1963)

PRINCIPE
SÃO TOMÉ
(Port.)

CABINDA
(Port.)

REPUBLIC OF
THE CONGO
1960

BURUNDI
1962

TANZANIA
1963

COMORO
ISLANDS
(France)

MALAWI
1964

ANGOLA
(Port.)

ZAMBIA
1964

MOZAMBIQUE (Port.)

MALAGASY
REPUBLIC
1960

RHODESIA
(UK)

SOUTH-WEST
AFRICA
(South
Africa)

BOTSWANA
1966

LESOTHO
1966

SWAZILAND
1968

SOUTH AFRICA
1910

0   1,000
km

Independent countries
formerly dependent territories

United Kingdom

France

Belgium

Italy

Spain

Rhodesia unilaterally declared
its independence , November 1965

CABINDA
(Port.)   Dependent territories

MAURITIUS
(UK)

RÉUNION
(France)

R.F.Holland

201

not proved easy as different groups had vied for advantage. An uneasy awareness grew that the risks of staying outweighed the risks of going. This calculation, however, would probably have taken longer to become pronounced had not the new French Fifth Republic under President de Gaulle moved so quickly after 1958 to introduce self-government to its African empire. The year 1960 was to be the *annus mirabilis* of the new states of Africa, but most of them were Francophone. The fear felt by a Conservative government in Britain of being outflanked in the African independence stakes by an equally conservative regime in France was not the least significant factor shaping Harold Macmillan's 'wind of change' policy following his victory in the 1959 general election. Since the decolonization timetables of the various European powers in Africa profoundly influenced each other (with the exception of Portugal, where the process was delayed until the 1970s), the map shows the relevant dates for the independence of all African countries prior to 1969.

The accelerated move to independence in British-ruled Africa after 1959 necessarily implied the more or less uniform application of what became known as 'African majority rule'. It followed that in practice the chief threat to the British government's policy ceased to be primarily that of discontented African nationalists, and became that of 'betrayed' white settlers and their political allies in Westminster. In fact in Kenya, always an important test-case, the whites proved too few and too economically differentiated to kick against the metropolitan pricks. The provision of an independence constitution for Northern Rhodesia in 1962, however, came very close to triggering the fatal combination of a trans-territorial white rebellion in British Africa and a Tory backlash in London. The moment passed, and by the time the white-dominated Southern Rhodesian government did issue its unilateral declaration of independence in November 1965, it did so isolated from any support other than that of South Africa and a bevy of sanctions-busters. The British drive to disengagement from Africa effectively peaked in 1968, when Botswana, the last of the three 'high commission territories', was finally shuffled off into a half-reluctant independence where (as with Lesotho and Swaziland) the reality was always certain to be recurrent intervention from Pretoria. Subsequently only the rebel regime based in Salisbury survived as an embarrassing token of the United Kingdom's past imperialism in Africa; not until the emergence of Zimbabwe in 1980 was this finally removed.

Decolonization: the Gold Coast

In 1946 it was widely recognized that indirect rule was no longer an adequate technique of government in British colonial Africa, and new constitutions were introduced into Nigeria and the Gold Coast, Britain's largest West African possessions. Both in the metropole, and even more among local colonial officials, however, the development of African self-government was still viewed in restricted terms of local and municipal administration. The riots in Accra, capital of the Gold Coast, during February 1948, stimulated by shortages of goods and consequent inflation, transformed this situation and led to the contemplation of more far-reaching democratic changes. A new governor, Sir Charles Arden-Clarke, was sent out to the Gold Coast with the instruction to 'save' the colony for the Empire.

The result was the 1951 Coussey Constitution (so named after the chairman of the committee whose recommendation it was) which introduced modern politics to the Gold Coast. In the elections which followed, victory went to a new radical 'youngmen's party' (the Convention People's Party, or CPP) led by Kwame Nkrumah. The latter had, in fact, to

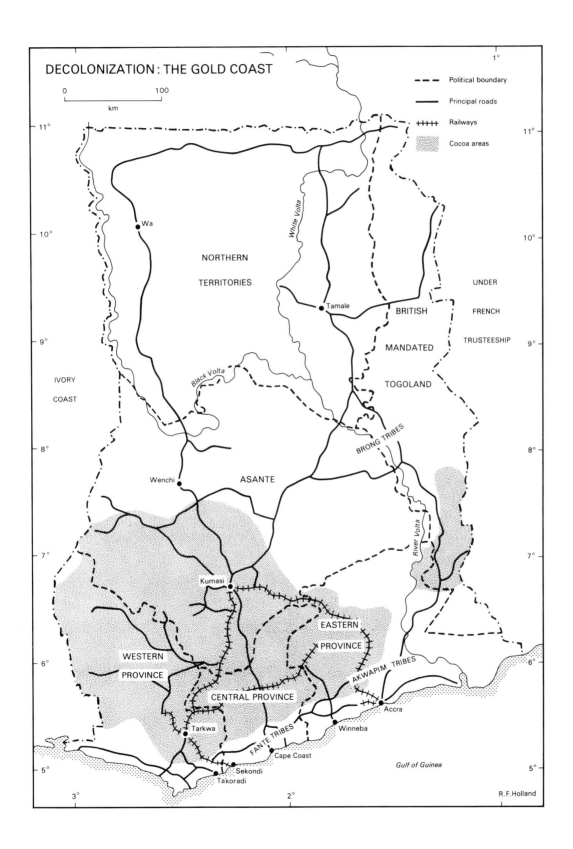

DECOLONIZATION: THE GOLD COAST

0   100
km

Political boundary
Principal roads
Railways
Cocoa areas

1°

11°   11°

Wa

10°   10°

NORTHERN

TERRITORIES

UNDER

White Volta

Tamale

BRITISH

FRENCH

9°   MANDATED   TRUSTEESHIP   9°

IVORY

COAST

Black Volta

TOGOLAND

8°   8°

Wenchi

ASANTE

BRONG TRIBES

River Volta

7°   7°

Kumasi

EASTERN

PROVINCE

WESTERN

PROVINCE

6°   6°

AKWAPIM TRIBES

CENTRAL PROVINCE

Accra

Tarkwa

Winneba

FANTE TRIBES

Cape Coast

Gulf of Guinea

5°   5°

Sekondi
Takoradi

3°   2°

R.F.Holland

203

be freed from prison to take up his position as leader of government business. One striking aspect thereafter of decolonization in the Gold Coast was the special relationship between Arden-Clarke and the young Nkrumah, both men interested in charting a stable, uneventful and relatively rapid path towards independence. Indeed, so symbiotic was the connection between governor and politician, and more broadly between old imperialism and new nationalism, that the colonial administration was soon being used for registering voters in precisely those areas where the CPP was bound to be chief beneficiary.

The Gold Coast, indeed, seemingly fulfilled the pressing need felt by the British government after 1952 (not least when elsewhere in Africa it was uncomfortably identified with the consolidation of white privilege) for a 'model' devolution of power to an African majority. In going down this road, however, it was important that the particular local politicians whom the British selected as their partners should be able to maintain their legitimacy as representing the colony's masses. Here the departing imperialists had to strike a very delicate balance, subjecting Nkrumah and the CPP to electoral processes sufficiently rigorous to establish their credentials both in the territory itself and in the eyes of 'world opinion', while ensuring that the fences thus erected were not so formidable as to bring down their protégés. Arden-Clarke and his London masters hoped that after a second general election, scheduled for 1954, the transfer of power could go ahead without further complications. In the run-up to those elections, however, the fragility of Nkrumah's pretensions to be the undisputed voice of African freedom in the Gold Coast became evident. The CPP's geographical heartland lay in the southern and coastal fringes of the colony, especially among the Fante tribes. In social terms, Nkrumah's chief support lay among those (often described as the 'Standard VII boys') with a smattering of school knowledge and a tenuous hold on employment in the lower reaches of government administration and business. In the agricultural hinterland, however, and especially the great cocoa-producing regions centred on Asante, loyalties were more volatile. At first the speeding up of political change to the evident advantage of Nkrumah and the CPP had not aroused great anxiety; but, once the centre and north realized that independence was close, an opposition began to take shape. It was sharpened, too, by Nkrumah's association with marketing legislation designed to divert cocoa farmers' surplus into the pockets of the administration; here was the shape of much mulcting to come. At the 1954 elections, therefore, although the CPP won a majority, there soon emerged an alternative coalition in the National Liberation Movement of Asante and the Northern People's Party (NPP), which also embraced the burgeoning Ewe nationalism in mandated Togoland.

This was highly embarrassing to Britain, especially since the NPP appealed for equity directly to London. In the colony, too, there were differences between district officials and Arden-Clarke; the former felt the latter – in his eagerness to promote Nkrumah – was diverging from the impartial traditions of the service. In the end a new commission under a British judge delivered a suitably bland report allowing the administration to pursue its aims unchecked. Nevertheless, extensive opposition did force Nkrumah to subject himself to a third and final pre-independence election. An astute tactician, he was active in identifying allies with whose help he could gain at least a proportion of the seats in and around Asante. Thus he exploited the kaleidoscopic rivalries always present in Kumasi, and teamed up with the Brong chieftaincies which had long been at odds with the kings and nobles of Asante. Much strong-arm behaviour was involved in these manoeuvrings. When the election was finally held in July 1956 Nkrumah duly won a majority of seventy-one seats, which the British government held to be a credible basis for the grant of full self-government. London nevertheless insisted that the independence constitution assume a federal form and so give some protection to those who felt uneasy about the future. This proviso Nkrumah was happy to accept because it could so easily be torn up after independence, as indeed happened. On 6 March 1957, therefore, the Gold Coast (renamed Ghana after an ancient empire in the area) became the first African colony south of the Sahara to become fully self-governing. Arden-Clarke and Kwame Nkrumah, the twin pivots of British strategy in this exemplary decolonization, thus presided over a transition in which the potential local divisions were damped down sufficiently for both the United Kingdom to withdraw gracefully and a group of moderate nationalists to enter into the political kingdom. Later on Nkrumah was to belie this accommodating and pliable image, but by then the British had much less at stake.

Decolonization: Kenya

The pace of decolonization in Kenya was not only rapid but also far faster than was generally anticipated until very shortly before independence in December 1963. Britain's East African colonies were thought much less developed than their West African counterparts and therefore likely to make political progress more slowly. Even in 1959 East African governors anticipated Kenya's achievement of full self-government only in 1975 or later. Several calculations underpinned this long-drawn-out perspective. After 1945 the imperial authorities in London were reluctant to hand over power to a white minority government, but also felt there were few Africans capable of running a modern state or democratic system of government by themselves. Officials were committed by the Devonshire Declaration of 1923 to the view that Africans' interests were to be 'paramount', but also feared white resistance to any erosion of their own influence. They therefore favoured the piecemeal development of multiracial politics in which the political and civil rights of all races would slowly be equalized and those of the minority communities – Europeans, Asians and Arabs – be safeguarded.

Few of Kenya's inhabitants agreed with this outlook. With their influence and often their wealth greatly enhanced by the war, many whites pressed for a degree of self-government like that already existing in Southern Rhodesia. Many Africans, particularly among the Kikuyu and others in central Kenya, were anxious to forestall this development but were ill organized and deeply divided. African resistance to state authority mounted, and sporadic violence increased from 1948, culminating in the outbreak of the Mau Mau rebellion and declaration of a state of emergency by the new governor, Sir Evelyn Baring, in October 1952.

This local disarray greatly strengthened the power of the imperial government to intervene in the colony's affairs, and gradually a three-pronged policy emerged. Military offensives under General Sir George Erskine against the insurgents, and detention of large numbers suspected of involvement with Mau Mau, had largely restored order by 1957; extensive land reforms were introduced to tackle the serious problems of poverty and deteriorating conditions in the heavily populated African reserves; and constitutional reforms in 1954 and 1958 were aimed at shaping both white and black political ambitions into patterns of multiracial co-operation.

These political initiatives met little success, partly because animosities were deeply entrenched but also because developments elsewhere in British colonial Africa reinforced the logic of African claims to majority rule. At a constitutional conference at Lancaster House, London, held in January 1960, the British government publicly accepted independence as its goal for Kenya. It also agreed to finance a policy of land purchase intended to satisfy African ambitions, to disarm white farmers' resistance to extended African ownership,

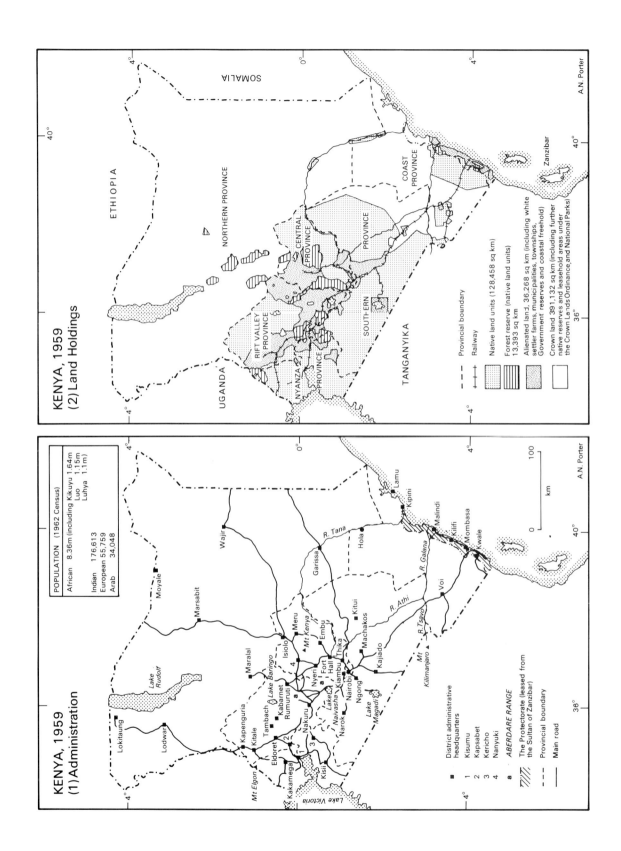

KENYA, 1959
(2) Land Holdings

ETHIOPIA

SOMALIA

UGANDA

NORTHERN PROVINCE

RIFT VALLEY
PROVINCE

CENTRAL
PROVINCE

NYANZA
PROVINCE

SOUTH-
ERN
PROVINCE

COAST
PROVINCE

TANGANYIKA

Zanzibar

- - - Provincial boundary

╫ Railway

Native land units (128,458 sq km)

Forest reserve (native land units)
13,393 sq km

Alienated land, 36,268 sq km (including white
settler farms, municipalities, townships,
Government reserves and coastal freehold)

Crown land 391,132 sq km (including further
native reserves and leasehold areas under
the Crown Lands Ordinance, and National Parks)

A.N. Porter

KENYA, 1959
(1) Administration

POPULATION (1962 Census)

African 8.36m (including Kikuyu 1.64m
Luo 1.15m
Luhya 1.1m)

Indian 176,613
European 55,759
Arab 34,048

ETHIOPIA

UGANDA

SOMALIA

Lokitaung

Lodwar

Lake
Rudolf

Moyale

Marsabit

Kapenguria

Kitale

Mt Elgon

Eldoret

Kakamega

Kisii

Lake Victoria

Tambach

Kabarnet

Rumuruti

Nakuru

Lake
Naivasha

Narok

Lake
Magadi

Ngong

Maralal

Lake Baringo

Isiolo

Nyeri

Fort
Hall

Kiambu

Nairobi

Kajiado

Meru

Mt Kenya

Embu

Thika

Machakos

Kitui

ABERDARE RANGE

Mt
Kilimanjaro

Voi

R. Athi

R. Tsavo

R. Galana

Hola

Garissa

R. Tana

Wajir

Lamu

Kipini

Malindi

Kilifi

Mombasa

Kwale

Zanzibar

District administrative
headquarters

1 Kisumu
2 Kapsabet
3 Kericho
4 Nanyuki

ABERDARE RANGE

The Protectorate (leased from
the Sultan of Zanzibar)

- - - Provincial boundary

Main road

0   100
km

A.N. Porter

206

especially in the so-called 'White Highlands', and to help stabilize the colony's economic and political future. The imperial authorities nevertheless continued to pursue their multiracial policies through support for the Kenya African Democratic Union, with its backing from minority communities and its 'regional government' plans, against the Kenya African National Union, which was committed to unitary government and immediate independence. Only in the summer of 1963 was this strategy belatedly abandoned and the electoral evidence of overwhelming support for KANU accepted.

Britain's defence commitments east of Suez, 1957–1971

'East of Suez' was the most characteristic refrain running through British defence debates in the 1960s. It denoted the complex of responsibilities, possessions and bases around the rim of the Indian Ocean. As a strategic concept, it was essentially invented in the aftermath of the 1957 Defence White Paper. Attempting to deduce the lessons of the failure of the Suez war, this statement put a newly heightened emphasis on the national nuclear deterrent. Such an emphasis, however, was allied to the provision of a mobile, non-nuclear arm for overseas emergencies. The armed services, which had a great stake in the continuance of conventional priorities, naturally wished to see the latter role amplified as much as possible. This tenacious conventionalism, however, required a theatre definition to support its claims, which 'east of Suez' duly provided.

The 'east of Suez' doctrine focused on the necessity for Britain to maintain the capability of projecting military power over large distances. This argument seemed particularly apposite in an age of decolonization, when fragile new states were considered likely to require assistance from a dispassionate mentor against internal or external threats. The crisis in Kuwait during 1961, when British forces intervened to protect the newly independent sheikhdom against an alleged threat from Iraq, provided an early opportunity to exhibit the feasibility and timeliness of such actions. The plethora of crises in this broadly defined region during these years – the army mutinies in East Africa during 1964, for example, and the 'confrontation' between Indonesia and Malaysia, when British troops again played a 'law and order' role – gave credibility to the 'east of Suez' notion when the Ministry of Defence was lodging its growing claims against the Exchequer.

The resilience of the strategy also partially arose from the encouragement given it by the United States, not least because it was linked to a more active interpretation of obligations under SEATO (see p. 191) than London had hitherto been prepared to accept. While the United Kingdom's 'east of Suez' never extended to participation in the Vietnam War, policing the Indian Ocean, and more especially the Persian Gulf, still represented a tacit contribution to America's strained responsibilities. Against this background it is not surprising that the Labour government elected in 1964 did not reverse the policy. Indeed, Harold Wilson as Prime Minister soon expressed the opinion that 'Britain's frontiers are on the Himalayas', and floated the possibility of providing India with a nuclear guarantee (the latter having recently engaged in a frontier clash with China). Preservation of the 'world role' became a leading motif of Wilson's leadership in 1965–6, mindful, perhaps, of the electoral fruits of blending labourism with big-power patriotism (Labour won the 1966 general election).

The Achilles' heel of the 'east of Suez' project was that it required a large platform

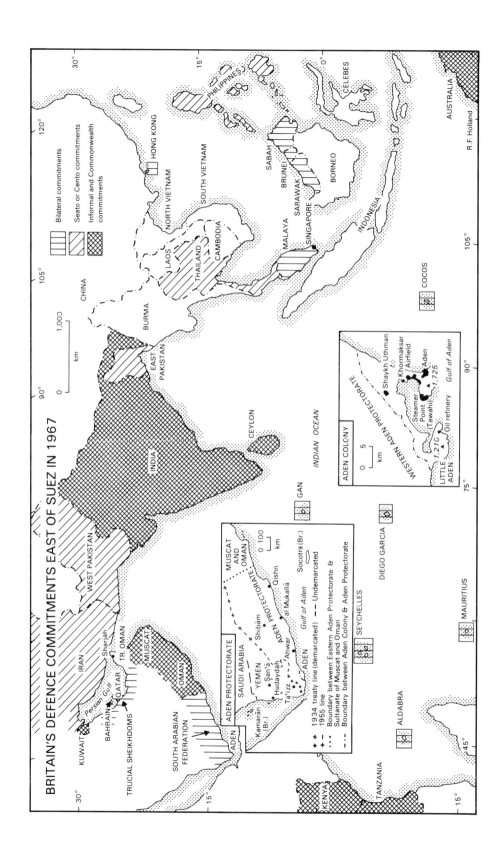

BRITAIN'S DEFENCE COMMITMENTS EAST OF SUEZ IN 1967

Bilateral commitments

Seato or Cento commitments

Informal and Commonwealth commitments

somewhere in the region. After 1958 large garrison facilities were built in Kenya, only for them to become defunct when that country was advanced rapidly to independence. Similar investments were then made in Aden, only to be made unusable as civil war in South Arabia spread from the interior to the coastal colony. Pushed from pillar to post, the viability of 'east of Suez' became more dependent on British sea power in the area, and above all on an adequate aircraft-carrier fleet, than on a land base – although Sharjah shone brightly for a while in the eyes of some army planners.

In the end the future of the policy was fought around the escalating cost of a new carrier, until the outcome was decided by *force majeure* in the form of the devaluation of sterling in November 1967. In the financial and strategic rationalization which followed, the Labour government ruled out carrier modernization and announced the decision to leave the Gulf in 1971. This was a decision which the succeeding Conservative government led by Edward Heath did not, in practice, reverse, despite the criticisms of withdrawal that party had levied during the 1970 election campaign.

Britain and the Falkland Islands, including the Falklands War of 1982

Situated in the South Atlantic Ocean some 300 miles from the South American mainland, the Falkland Islands cover an area of 4,700 square miles (12,173 sq km). The largest islands are East and West Falkland. During 1983 the Falklands, one of the few remaining British dependent territories, celebrated 150 years of British rule in spite of a long-standing Argentine claim to the islands (known as the Islas Malvinas in Argentina) and the rapid post-1945 process of decolonization.

Britain's interests in the islands date back to alleged discoveries in the 1590s, but it was not until 1765 that John Byron established a settlement at Port Egmont on Saunders Island. The ensuing diplomatic difficulties with France and Spain nearly escalated into a war during 1770–1. Naval economies resulted in the evacuation of the settlement in 1774, when a plaque was deposited to record British rights, which were employed to justify Britain's return in January 1833.

However, it was not until the 1840s that effective colonial control was implemented. The first governor was appointed in 1841, and these developments were accompanied by the transfer of the capital from Port Louis to

Stanley. As the nineteenth century progressed, the Falklands' strategic value was reinforced by the development of sheep rearing for the export of wool, thereby giving the economy a monocultural character. The population increased to a peak of 2,392 in 1931.

The 1976 and 1982 Shackleton Reports highlighted a recent process of economic and demographic decline (the 1980 population was 1,813). The post-1982 period witnessed an apparent reversal of these trends, partly because of the £31 million allocated to implement the economic recommendations of the 1982 Shackleton Report. The introduction of a fishing zone in 1987 fostered a radical economic transformation, since the revenue from fishing licences trebled the national income in one year (1986: £9.89 million; 1987: £30.7 million), enabled infrastructure improvements (e.g. housing and telecommunications) and facilitated the adoption of a long-term development strategy. The population (excluding the garrison) increased slightly to 1,916.

The 1982 Falklands War highlighted the centrality of the Anglo-Argentine relationship in the history of the islands. Sovereignty

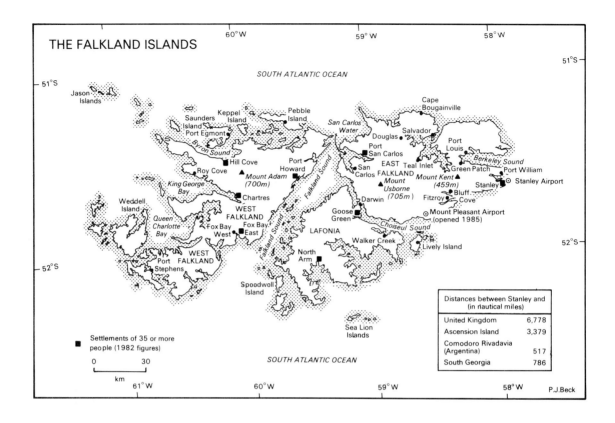

THE FALKLAND ISLANDS

SOUTH ATLANTIC OCEAN

Distances between Stanley and (in nautical miles)	
United Kingdom	6,778
Ascension Island	3,379
Comodoro Rivadavia (Argentina)	517
South Georgia	786

■ Settlements of 35 or more people (1982 figures)

0   30
km

SOUTH ATLANTIC OCEAN

P.J.Beck

has been disputed since 1833, when Argentina complained about the expulsion of its 'legitimate' settlement established in the 1820s upon the basis of rights dating back to the sixteenth century. This dispute culminated in the Argentine invasion of the Falklands and South Georgia during April 1982. British landings at San Carlos in May prepared the way for the recapture of Stanley in June. The war restored British control over the islands, but failed to resolve the root cause of the conflict, that is, the sovereignty problem. Argentina, though democratized and chastened by defeat, has not gone away, and its continuing challenge and relative proximity to the islands preoccupy British defence planning, as evidenced by the garrison presence and the strategic airfield opened at Mount Pleasant

in May 1985. Diplomatic relations were not resumed between the two countries until 1990, when the Falkland Islands Protection Zone (FIPZ) was removed.

The future of the Falkland Islands as a British possession remains a subject for debate, and continues to pose problems for Britain on account of the need to reconcile the islanders' anxiety to 'keep the Falklands British', the British emphasis upon the islanders' rights of self-determination and the Argentine search for sovereignty. The associated defence commitment raises question marks about the realism of a continuing British role in the South Atlantic in the context of more important European and NATO interests.

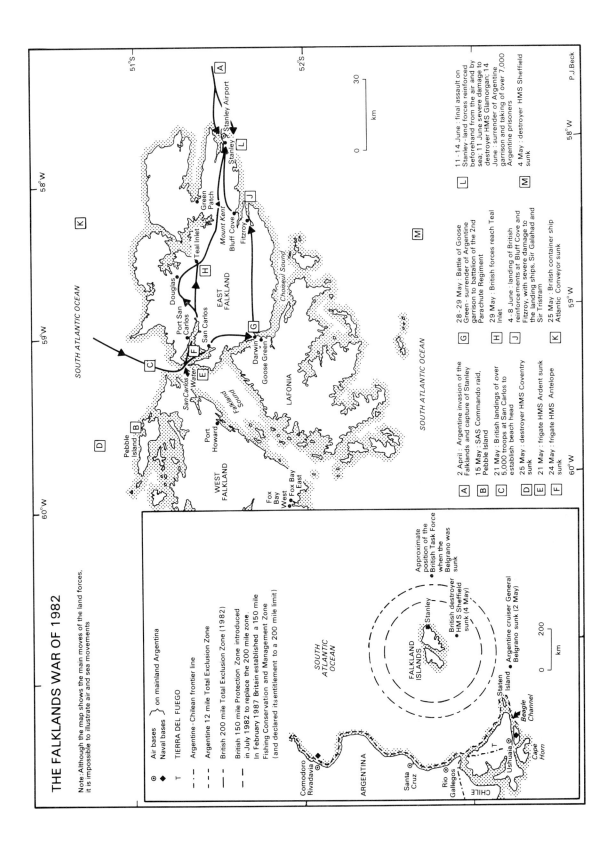

THE FALKLANDS WAR OF 1982

Note: Although the map shows the main moves of the land forces, it is impossible to illustrate air and sea movements

⊙ Air bases ⎱ on mainland Argentina
◆ Naval bases ⎰

T TIERRA DEL FUEGO

–·–·– Argentine-Chilean frontier line

– – – Argentine 12 mile Total Exclusion Zone

– – – British 200 mile Total Exclusion Zone (1982)

––––– British 150 mile Protection Zone introduced in July 1982 to replace the 200 mile zone.
In February 1987 Britain established a 150 mile Fishing Conservation and Management Zone (and declared its entitlement to a 200 mile limit)

A 2 April : Argentine invasion of the Falklands and capture of Stanley

B 15 May : SAS Commando raid, Pebble Island

C 21 May : British landings of over 5,000 troops at San Carlos to establish beach head

D 25 May : destroyer HMS Coventry sunk

E 21 May : frigate HMS Ardent sunk

F 24 May : frigate HMS Antelope sunk

G 28-29 May : Battle of Goose Green - surrender of Argentine garrison to battalion of the 2nd Parachute Regiment

H 29 May : British forces reach Teal Inlet

J 4 - 8 June : landing of British reinforcements at Bluff Cove and Fitzroy, with severe damage to the landing ships, Sir Galahad and Sir Tristram

K 25 May : British container ship Atlantic Conveyor sunk

L 11-14 June : final assault on Stanley - land forces reinforced beforehand from the air and by sea; 11 June severe damage to destroyer HMS Glamorgan; 14 June : surrender of Argentine garrison and taking of over 7,000 Argentine prisoners

M 4 May : destroyer HMS Sheffield sunk

P.J.Beck

Britain's Antarctic and sub-Antarctic possessions

Antarctica, comprising 5.5 million square miles (14 million sq km), occupies about 10 per cent of the world's land surface. Like the nearby Falklands, the region has proved a marginal international interest even for Britain, which possesses a significant Antarctic tradition and controls about 700,000 square miles as British Antarctic Territory.

In 1900 Antarctica remained still largely unknown. During succeeding decades expeditions from several countries, most notably Britain, unveiled the continent and reached the South Pole itself (1911). The 1900s witnessed also the development of sub-Antarctic and Antarctic whaling, and by 1914 about two-thirds of the world's whale oil – utilized for lubricants, soap, margarine and explosives – was derived from the southern oceans. The historical rights acquired through discovery and the taking of possession, in conjunction with economic and other considerations, encouraged the issue of letters patent in 1908 and 1917 to announce British control over the Falkland Islands Dependencies (FID) (see map below).

In 1920 the British government adopted a policy to acquire gradual control over the remainder of the continent, and this attempt 'to paint the whole Antarctic red' resulted in the announcement of British control, albeit under New Zealand and Australian administration, over the Ross Dependency (1923) and Australian Antarctic Territory (1933). By 1933 the British Empire claimed over 60 per cent of Antarctica, even if the initial desire to annex the whole area was being qualified in the light of the emergence of other claimants (i.e. Argentina, Chile, France and Norway) and the USA's non-recognition of claims. The overlapping nature of Argentine, British and Chilean claims caused occasional difficulties, as evidenced in 1952 by the Hope Bay incident.

The Antarctic Treaty of 1959 came into effect in 1961. The resulting establishment of a zone of peace and a 'freeze' on sovereignty

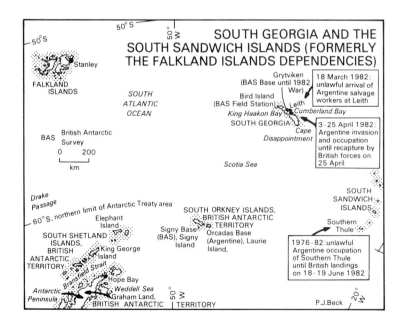

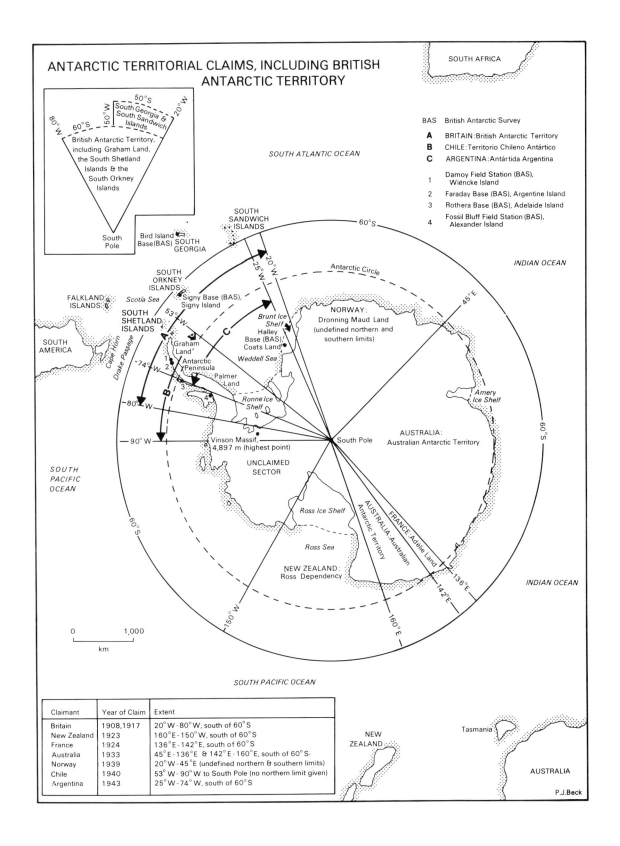

ANTARCTIC TERRITORIAL CLAIMS, INCLUDING BRITISH ANTARCTIC TERRITORY

British Antarctic Territory, including Graham Land, the South Shetland Islands & the South Orkney Islands

South Pole

South Georgia & South Sandwich Islands

SOUTH AFRICA

BAS   British Antarctic Survey

A   BRITAIN: British Antarctic Territory

B   CHILE: Territorio Chileno Antártico

C   ARGENTINA: Antártida Argentina

1   Damoy Field Station (BAS), Wiencke Island

2   Faraday Base (BAS), Argentine Island

3   Rothera Base (BAS), Adelaide Island

4   Fossil Bluff Field Station (BAS), Alexander Island

SOUTH ATLANTIC OCEAN

INDIAN OCEAN

SOUTH SANDWICH ISLANDS

60°S

Antarctic Circle

Bird Island Base (BAS) SOUTH GEORGIA

SOUTH ORKNEY ISLANDS

FALKLAND ISLANDS

Scotia Sea

Signy Base (BAS), Signy Island

NORWAY: Dronning Maud Land (undefined northern and southern limits)

45°E

SOUTH SHETLAND ISLANDS

Brunt Ice Shelf

Halley Base (BAS), Coats Land

SOUTH AMERICA

Cape Horn

Drake Passage

Graham Land

Antarctic Peninsula

Palmer Land

Weddell Sea

Amery Ice Shelf

Ronne Ice Shelf

60°S

SOUTH PACIFIC OCEAN

Vinson Massif, 4,897 m (highest point)

UNCLAIMED SECTOR

South Pole

AUSTRALIA: Australian Antarctic Territory

INDIAN OCEAN

Ross Ice Shelf

FRANCE: Adélie Land

AUSTRALIA: Australian Antarctic Territory

136°E

Ross Sea

142°E

60°S

NEW ZEALAND: Ross Dependency

160°E

150°W

0   1,000
km

SOUTH PACIFIC OCEAN

NEW ZEALAND

Tasmania

AUSTRALIA

Claimant	Year of Claim	Extent
Britain	1908, 1917	20°W-80°W, south of 60°S
New Zealand	1923	160°E-150°W, south of 60°S
France	1924	136°E-142°E, south of 60°S
Australia	1933	45°E-136°E & 142°E-160°E, south of 60°S
Norway	1939	20°W-45°E (undefined northern & southern limits)
Chile	1940	53°W-90°W to South Pole (no northern limit given)
Argentina	1943	25°W-74°W, south of 60°S

P.J.Beck

213

questions has alleviated the impact of the Anglo-Argentine–Chilean territorial problem, while in 1962 British Antarctic Territory was created to cover the Antarctic Treaty segment of the FID (i.e. south of 60°S). Britain performs a major role in the management activities of the Antarctic Treaty System as well as in the conduct of Antarctic science; indeed, British scientists were prominent in identifying and monitoring the depletion of the Earth's ozone layer over Antarctica. The 1982 Falklands War was followed by a significant increase in the funding and work of the British Antarctic Survey (BAS) as part of the post-war enhancement of British visibility in the South Atlantic region.

The island of South Georgia lies 800 miles south-east of the Falklands. Captain James Cook took formal possession for Britain in 1775, and subsequently the island was utilized for fur sealing, whaling (1903–65), BAS scientific research and more recently for fishing. In 1775 Cook also discovered the South Sandwich Islands, a chain of volcanic and relatively inaccessible islands located 460 miles south-east of South Georgia.

In 1908 and 1917 South Georgia and the South Sandwich Islands were placed under British control as part of the FID. They retained this title after the separation and formation of British Antarctic Territory in 1962, but in 1985 the territory was renamed the Dependency of South Georgia and the South Sandwich Islands. Like British Antarctic Territory, this dependency lacks indigenous and permanent inhabitants. Argentina, whose claim to the Malvinas extends to cover this British dependency also, established a meteorological station on Southern Thule in the South Sandwich Islands in 1976, while South Georgia was invaded at the start of the 1982 Falklands War. Britain recaptured South Georgia and Southern Thule in April and June 1982 respectively.

The Commonwealth, 1931–1989

The history of the Commonwealth has often been depicted as a process of constitutional evolution providing for the freedom yet continuing association of former British dependencies. One milestone in this long march was the Balfour Report of 1926 which defined the status of dominions (then Australia, Canada, New Zealand, South Africa, Newfoundland [merged with Canada in 1949] and the Irish Free State) in terms of autonomy and equality while ensuring unity through their common allegiance to the crown. This position was formalized in the Statute of Westminster, 1931. Decolonization in south Asia after the Second World War further altered the Commonwealth structure: Burma's right to secede was recognized and, more important for the future, India's republican status was accommodated by the formula whereby the republic accepted 'the King as the symbol of the free association of the independent Member Nations and as such Head of the Commonwealth'. The title 'Head of the Commonwealth' carried no strict constitutional significance but was to have symbolic potency and practical value; it facilitated the expansion of membership, the accession of an increasing number of republics and the survival of an extremely heterogeneous international association. Britain's expressed intention to convert empire into commonwealth (with a view, so some would argue, to asserting 'informal empire' or 'neo-colonialism' in the post-imperial era) resulted in a wave of fresh applicants for full membership, principally from black Africa and led by Ghana in 1957. At the start of 1988 the Commonwealth consisted of forty-eight members, including the UK but excluding Fiji.

The modern Commonwealth is not bound by a written constitution, nor is it a military alliance. Some members are parties to regional pacts (as are Britain and Canada to NATO), some (like Belize) have defence agreements with Britain, and others (like India) play leading roles in the Non-Aligned Movement. The Commonwealth does, however, pride itself on a tradition of consultation and co-operation, and generally subscribes to an ideology in tune with a multiracial world. The Colonial Conferences, initiated in 1887, became Imperial Conferences for the 1911–37 period, were renamed Commonwealth Prime Ministers' Meetings in 1944 and have been known as Heads of Government Meetings since 1966. In the Singapore Declaration of 1971 members pledged themselves as follows: 'We recognize racial prejudice as a dangerous sickness threatening the healthy development of the human race and racial discrimination as an unmitigated evil of society.' However, the withdrawal of South Africa from the Commonwealth (1961), the Gleneagles Agreement on sporting contacts with South Africa (1977) and the settlement of Britain's Rhodesia/Zimbabwe problem (1980) notwithstanding, the question of race has subjected the association to immense strain over three decades. Since 1985, the issue of sanctions against South Africa has driven a wedge between the United Kingdom and other Commonwealth countries, including her otherwise closest of associates, namely Australia, Canada and New Zealand. The Falklands War (1982), unlike the Suez affair (1956), did not provoke a crisis within the Commonwealth, but the 1983 coup in Grenada followed by US military intervention not only involved the governor-general (the Queen's representative) in controversy but also caused considerable disquiet among members. Most recently, the advent of a racialist (anti-Indian) regime in Fiji as the result of a military coup has led to the lapse of Fiji's membership (1987).

More influential in downgrading the Commonwealth as a national priority than any irritation over Commonwealth criticism of Britain's African or immigration policies has been a fundamental realignment of Britain's defence and economic policies. At the same time Britain has reduced her profile in the association. Indeed, as early as 1951 the term 'British Commonwealth' gave way to 'Commonwealth'; in 1965 the Commonwealth set up its own secretariat (hitherto Whitehall's Commonwealth Relations Office had serviced intra-Commonwealth affairs); in 1971, the year when British forces withdrew from the Singapore base, London ceased to be the automatic venue for Heads of Government Meetings; and on 1 January 1973, ten years after de Gaulle had vetoed Macmillan's application to join the Common Market, Britain became a full member of the European Community. Nevertheless, even though the Thatcher government paid less heed than its predecessors to Commonwealth consensus, in the 1980s Britain still fulfilled a pivotal role in providing the funds and know-how for a wide range of joint ventures in the fields of culture, development, education, health, science and technology.

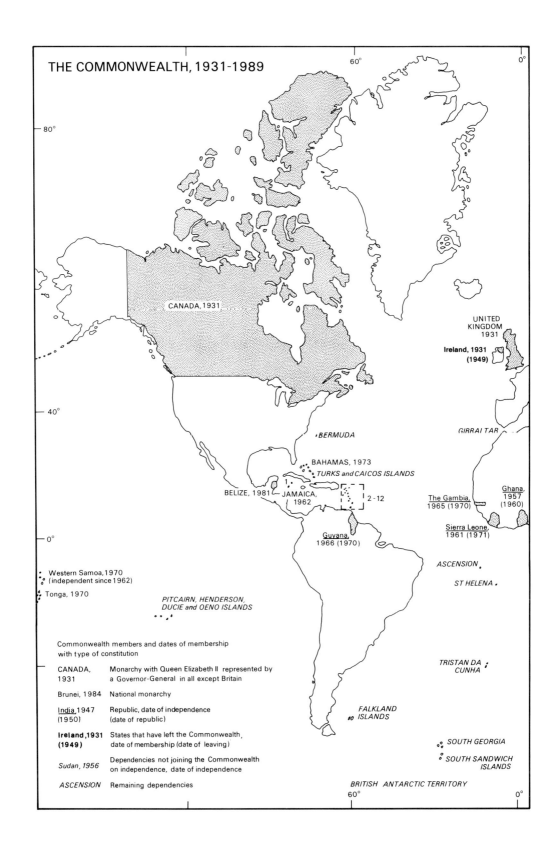

THE COMMONWEALTH, 1931-1989

CANADA, 1931

UNITED KINGDOM 1931

Ireland, 1931 (1949)

GIBRALTAR

•BERMUDA

BAHAMAS, 1973

TURKS and CAICOS ISLANDS

BELIZE, 1981

JAMAICA, 1962

2 - 12

The Gambia, 1965 (1970)

Ghana, 1957 (1960)

Sierra Leone, 1961 (1971)

Guyana, 1966 (1970)

ASCENSION •

ST HELENA •

Western Samoa,1970 (independent since 1962)

Tonga, 1970

PITCAIRN, HENDERSON, DUCIE and OENO ISLANDS

TRISTAN DA CUNHA

FALKLAND ISLANDS

Commonwealth members and dates of membership with type of constitution

CANADA, 1931	Monarchy with Queen Elizabeth II represented by a Governor-General in all except Britain
Brunei, 1984	National monarchy
India,1947 (1950)	Republic, date of independence (date of republic)
Ireland,1931 (1949)	States that have left the Commonwealth, date of membership (date of leaving)
Sudan, 1956	Dependencies not joining the Commonwealth on independence, date of independence
ASCENSION	Remaining dependencies

SOUTH GEORGIA

SOUTH SANDWICH ISLANDS

BRITISH ANTARCTIC TERRITORY

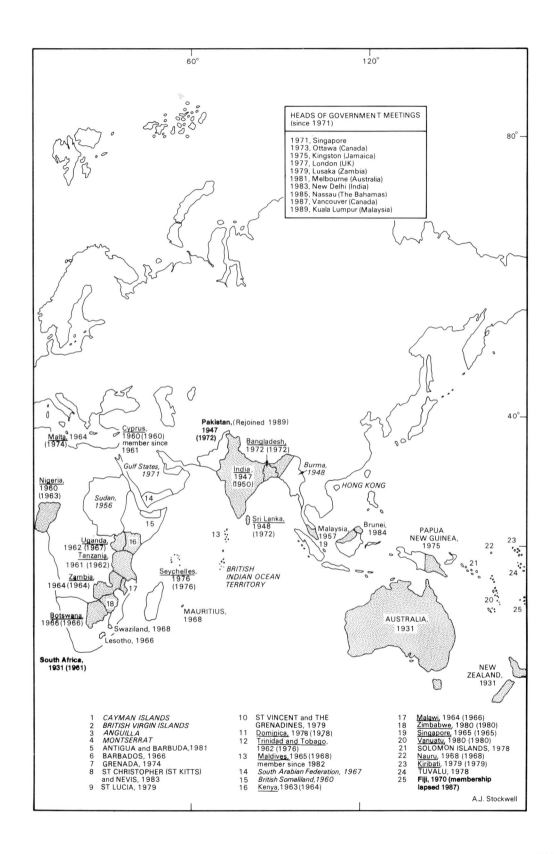

HEADS OF GOVERNMENT MEETINGS
(since 1971)

1971, Singapore
1973, Ottawa (Canada)
1975, Kingston (Jamaica)
1977, London (UK)
1979, Lusaka (Zambia)
1981, Melbourne (Australia)
1983, New Delhi (India)
1985, Nassau (The Bahamas)
1987, Vancouver (Canada)
1989, Kuala Lumpur (Malaysia)

Malta, 1964 (1974)

Cyprus, 1960(1960) member since 1961

Pakistan, (Rejoined 1989) 1947 (1972)

Bangladesh, 1972 (1972)

Burma, 1948

Nigeria, 1960 (1963)

Gulf States, 1971

India, 1947 (1950)

HONG KONG

Sudan, 1956

14

Sri Lanka, 1948 (1972)

Malaysia, 1957

Brunei, 1984

PAPUA NEW GUINEA, 1975

15

13

19

Uganda, 1962 (1967)
Tanzania, 1961 (1962)

16

Seychelles, 1976 (1976)

22

23

Zambia, 1964 (1964)

17

BRITISH INDIAN OCEAN TERRITORY

21

24

Botswana, 1966(1966)

18

Swaziland, 1968

MAURITIUS, 1968

20

25

Lesotho, 1966

AUSTRALIA, 1931

South Africa, 1931 (1961)

NEW ZEALAND, 1931

1	*CAYMAN ISLANDS*	10	ST VINCENT and THE GRENADINES, 1979	17	Malawi, 1964 (1966)
2	*BRITISH VIRGIN ISLANDS*	11	Dominica, 1978 (1978)	18	Zimbabwe, 1980 (1980)
3	*ANGUILLA*	12	Trinidad and Tobago, 1962 (1976)	19	Singapore, 1965 (1965)
4	*MONTSERRAT*	13	Maldives, 1965 (1968) member since 1982	20	Vanuatu, 1980 (1980)
5	ANTIGUA and BARBUDA,1981	14	*South Arabian Federation, 1967*	21	SOLOMON ISLANDS, 1978
6	BARBADOS, 1966	15	*British Somaliland,1960*	22	Nauru, 1968 (1968)
7	GRENADA, 1974	16	Kenya, 1963(1964)	23	Kiribati, 1979 (1979)
8	ST CHRISTOPHER (ST KITTS) and NEVIS, 1983			24	TUVALU, 1978
9	ST LUCIA, 1979			25	**Fiji, 1970 (membership lapsed 1987)**

A.J. Stockwell

217

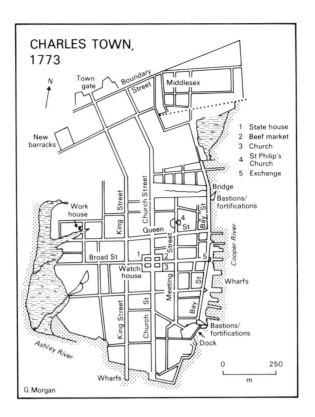

Charles Town

The first permanent settlers in South Carolina located themselves at Albemarle Point on the west bank of the Ashley in 1670. Ten years later they moved to the tip of the peninsula between the Ashley and Cooper rivers. Rapid immigration pushed Charles Town's population to 1,200 by 1690. It was the only metropolis to develop in the colonial south. Charles Town grew because, like Boston and Philadelphia, it attracted family immigrants with modest amounts of capital. Adult sex ratios declined from 380 males to 100 females in 1672 to 153 to 100 in 1703, figures similar to those in New England in the 1630s and Penn-

sylvania in the 1680s. Moreover, since South Carolina lacked the navigable rivers which, penetrating far into the interior, undermined urban development in the Chesapeake, Charles Town was the conduit through which all goods passed. In 1720 around 200 vessels cleared the port. Two years later the assembly passed an Act incorporating the town, but merchants who were excluded from power obtained its disallowance by the Privy Council, and Charles Town remained under the control of the legislature until the end of the colonial period.

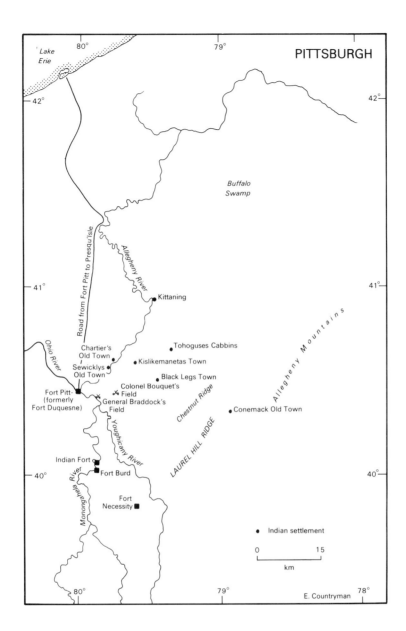

Map labels:
- Lake Erie
- 80°
- 79°
- PITTSBURGH
- 42°
- 42°
- Buffalo Swamp
- Road from Fort Pitt to Presqu'Isle
- Allegheny River
- 41°
- 41°
- Kittaning
- Allegheny Mountains
- Ohio River
- Tohoguses Cabbins
- Chartier's Old Town
- Kislikemanetas Town
- Sewicklys Old Town
- Black Legs Town
- Colonel Bouquet's Field
- Fort Pitt (formerly Fort Duquesne)
- General Braddock's Field
- Chestnut Ridge
- Conemack Old Town
- LAUREL HILL RIDGE
- Youghicany River
- Indian Fort
- Fort Burd
- Monongahela River
- 40°
- 40°
- Fort Necessity
- • Indian settlement
- 0   15
- km
- 80°
- 79°
- E. Countryman
- 78°

Pittsburgh

The point where the Allegheny and Mononga-hela rivers join to form the Ohio was one of the most strategic spots in late colonial America. Whites first occupied it in 1754, when Virginians began building a fort, with the intention of controlling the route west. French troops, already ensconced further north and west, drove them from the site and named it Fort Duquesne, in honour of the governor of Quebec. It remained in their hands until the British recaptured it in 1758 and rechristened it Fort Pitt. Among the notable figures associated with the Anglo-French struggle in its vicinity were Major-General Edward Braddock, whose force of regulars was decimated as it marched to attack the French position in 1756, and the young George Washington, whose attack on French troops in 1754 and surrender at nearby Fort Necessity actually initiated the Seven Years War.

In the last years of the colonial period the region around Fort Pitt became a centre of struggle between the provinces of Pennsylvania and Virginia. Both geopolitical concerns (control of western access) and economic ones (the validation of speculative claims) were at stake. In 1774 Virginia's governor, the Earl of Dunmore, sent officials to take possession and set up local government. The Revolution effectively ended Dunmore's initiative, and in 1776 settlers in the region proposed the establishment of a separate state of 'Westsylvania'. This proposal failed, and commissioners from Virginia and Pennsylvania worked out the latter state's present boundary in 1779. During the War of Independence, Fort Pitt was unimportant militarily, but the Continental Army occupied it until 1792, as a staging point against the Indians to the west. A village was laid out around the fort as early as 1764, but the modern city of Pittsburgh developed afterwards, first as 'the gateway to the west' and later, thanks to rich mineral deposits in its neighbourhood, on the basis of heavy industry.

Bridgetown

Bridgetown increased its share of the Barbados slave population from 4 per cent in 1680 to 12 per cent in 1817, when 9,284 slaves lived in the town. Of these slaves, roughly one-half were

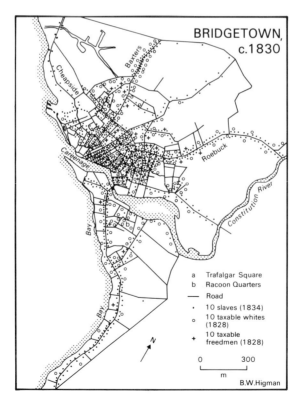

employed as domestics; skilled tradespeople, transport workers and hucksters were also common.

The slaves of Bridgetown were widely dispersed. Their owners, the taxable whites and freedmen, were similarly scattered. Some concentration existed around the wharves and warehouses of the Careenage, and around Trafalgar Square where Nelson's statue was erected in 1813. But settlement was strung out along the major routes connecting town and country, particularly Bay Street, Roebuck Street, Baxters Road and Cheapside. The ratio of taxable whites to slaves was relatively high near the wharves and Racoon Quarters, while freedmen were more obviously concentrated in the area around Marl Hill Street toward Roebuck. But it is certain that the slave and free populations were not segregated into particular zones during slavery. Government buildings were scattered through the town.

Christchurch

Christchurch was the final and most successful colonizing venture launched by Edward Gibbon Wakefield and the New Zealand Company, who wanted to put into practice their distinctive views of planned settlement and draw on the inspiration of religious colonization, last practised in seventeenth-century America. In 1848 Wakefield joined with John Robert Godley and others to form the Canterbury Association with the aim of establishing a model Church of England colony, comprising respectable middle-class emigrants and skilled labourers, complete with churches, schools and other institutions of civilized society. The first migrants, carefully selected and led by their bishop, arrived in 1850–1. The settlement of Canterbury in the eastern South Island was renamed Christchurch after Godley's college at Oxford. Close to the port of Lyttelton, it became one of New Zealand's most populous and prosperous cities, a microcosm of English society transplanted in the antipodes.

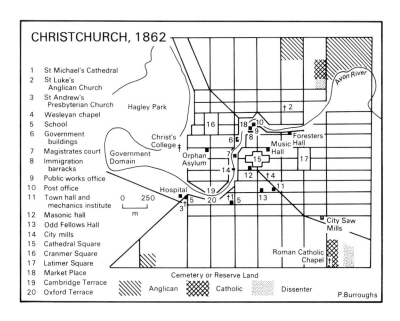

CHRISTCHURCH, 1862

1 St Michael's Cathedral
2 St Luke's Anglican Church
3 St Andrew's Presbyterian Church
4 Wesleyan chapel
5 School
6 Government buildings
7 Magistrates court
8 Immigration barracks
9 Public works office
10 Post office
11 Town hall and mechanics institute
12 Masonic hall
13 Odd Fellows Hall
14 City mills
15 Cathedral Square
16 Cranmer Square
17 Latimer Square
18 Market Place
19 Cambridge Terrace
20 Oxford Terrace

Cemetery or Reserve Land
Anglican   Catholic   Dissenter

P. Burroughs

Grahamstown

Grahamstown was first the military headquarters of Colonel John Graham after the Cape's eastern frontier war of 1812. Following the arrival of the '1820 settlers' it rapidly displaced Bathurst as principal town and administrative centre for Albany district. By 1831 it was second only to Cape Town, the source of intermittently powerful but ultimately ineffective demands for the transfer of government functions from Cape Town or the creation of a separate colony in the eastern Cape. With its newspapers, churches and chapels, Anglican bishopric (1853) and well-known schools, Grahamstown was self-consciously 'civilized'. Beneath this veneer lay less attractive features of colonial small-town life – periodic hysteria about military security, the land speculation and war profiteering which fuelled frontier expansion, the grasping for public office, the habits of segregation. After 1872 when the Cape secured responsible government and under the impact of railways and mineral discoveries, Grahamstown was edged away from the centre of colonial life.

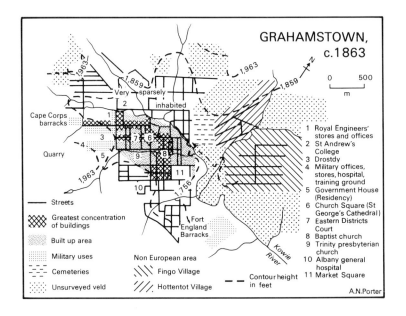

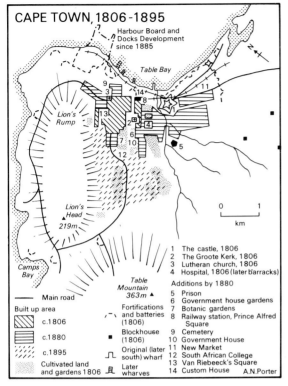

CAPE TOWN, 1806-1895

Harbour Board and
Docks Development
since 1885

Table Bay

Lion's
Rump

Lion's
Head
219m ▲

Camps
Bay

Table
Mountain
363m ▲

─── Main road

Built up area

▨ c.1806

▤ c.1880

░ c.1895

Cultivated land
and gardens 1806

Fortifications
and batteries
(1806)

■ Blockhouse
(1806)

⌐ Original (later
south) wharf

⊥ Later
wharves

1 The castle, 1806
2 The Groote Kerk, 1806
3 Lutheran church, 1806
4 Hospital, 1806 (later barracks)

Additions by 1880

5 Prison
6 Government house gardens
7 Botanic gardens
8 Railway station, Prince Alfred
   Square
9 Cemetery
10 Government House
11 New Market
12 South African College
13 Van Riebeeck's Square
14 Custom House   A.N.Porter

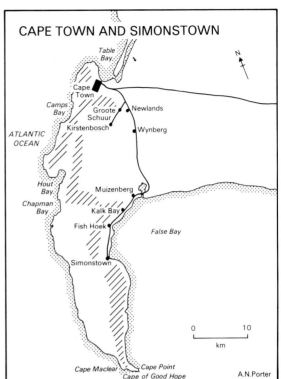

CAPE TOWN AND SIMONSTOWN

Table
Bay

Cape
Town

Camps
Bay

Groote
Schuur

Newlands

Kirstenbosch

Wynberg

ATLANTIC
OCEAN

Hout
Bay

Chapman
Bay

Muizenberg

Kalk Bay

Fish Hoek

False Bay

Simonstown

Cape Maclear

Cape Point
Cape of Good Hope

A.N.Porter

Cape Town

The 'true centre of the Empire' to a Colonial Office official in 1871, Cape Town was probably better known as the 'tavern of the seas', a market for Cape farmers' produce and a provisioning or repair centre for ships passing to and from the east. Always the colony's seat of government, its inconvenience – much as if Britain had been administered from Penzance – emerged as white settlement spread and, after 1880, as its relative economic importance declined. Its elite of administrators, military or professional men and merchants remained somewhat apart from the inhabitants of the interior, at least until railways linked it to Kimberley (1885) and Johannesburg (1892). Its progress was commonplace – a municipality in 1839, chamber of commerce in 1861, local railway by 1864 and consequent suburbs. However, it remained the chief colonial port, and, with its fine harbour and naval station at Simonstown, its immense strategic importance persisted. In 1885 £92 million (14.3 per cent) of Britain's overseas trade followed the Cape route compared with only £66 million via Suez.

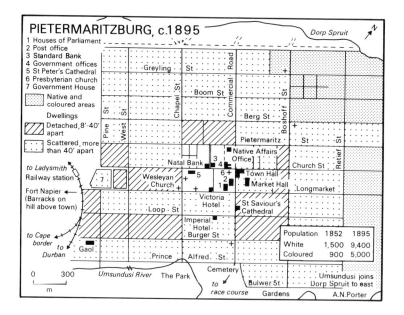

Pietermaritzburg

Commemorating Pieter Retief and Gert Maritz, the Voortrekker leaders, Pietermaritzburg was established following the battle of Blood River. Briefly the seat of the Volksraad of the Afrikaner Republic of Natalia, it remained the centre of government after British annexation in 1842–3 and was rapidly Anglicized. A municipality in 1854, it housed the colony's legislative council set up in 1856. With a hill behind and water on three sides, defence and security crucially determined its site. So too did subsistence. The basic design, eight parallel streets intersected by six at right angles, divided into 300 plots all irrigable from the Dorp Spruit, changed little during the century. Situated 40 miles inland from the larger port of Durban, Pietermaritzburg was reached by railway in 1880 immediately after the Zulu War, and linked with Johannesburg in 1895, following negotiations with the Transvaal by Natal's new responsible government ministry.

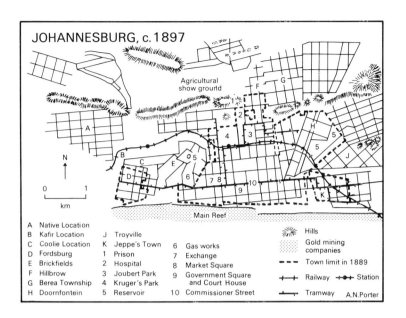

JOHANNESBURG, c. 1897

Agricultural show ground

N

0   1
km

Main Reef

A	Native Location		
B	Kafir Location	J	Troyville
C	Coolie Location	K	Jeppe's Town
D	Fordsburg	1	Prison
E	Brickfields	2	Hospital
F	Hillbrow	3	Joubert Park
G	Berea Township	4	Kruger's Park
H	Doornfontein	5	Reservoir

6	Gas works
7	Exchange
8	Market Square
9	Government Square and Court House
10	Commissioner Street

Hills

Gold mining companies

- - - Town limit in 1889

Railway   Station

Tramway   A.N.Porter

Johannesburg

Johannesburg's hectic transformation from mining camp to major city reflected its central position on the Witwatersrand goldfields, opened in 1886. In 1896 its population was estimated at 102,000, and by 1914 at 250,000. Rand gold production similarly rose to 27 per cent of world output in 1898 and 40 per cent in 1913. Early growth rested on the shallow mining of reef outcrops and, after technical advances and financial reorganization between 1890 and 1893, on expansion southwards of mining at deeper levels. The railways arrived in 1893–5, but living costs remained high. Until after 1900 its inhabitants were predominantly male – American engineers, Cornish miners, Southern Africa's unskilled blacks, European refugees. Drunkenness and crime were common; slums were already being cleared in Brickfields by 1903 as wealthier suburbs rose in the north. Although municipal administration developed only slowly before 1902, residential segregation appeared rapidly, along with pass regulations (1896).

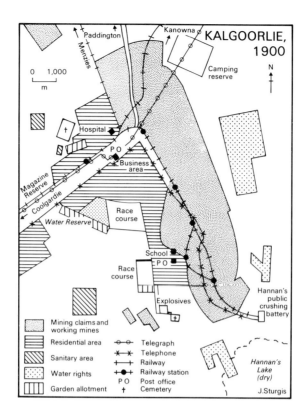

The map shows:

KALGOORLIE,
1900

N

0   1,000
m

Paddington

Kanowna

Menzies

Camping
reserve

Hospital

P O

Business
area

Magazine
Reserve

Coolgardie

Water Reserve

Race
course

School

P O

Race
course

Explosives

Hannan's
public
crushing
battery

Hannan's
Lake
(dry)

J. Sturgis

Mining claims and
working mines

Residential area   ○─○   Telegraph

Sanitary area   ×─×   Telephone

Water rights   ┝━┿   Railway

Garden allotment   ●━●   Railway station
                       P O   Post office
                       †   Cemetery

Kalgoorlie

Dotted throughout the map of Australia are many towns which owed their origins to the discovery of gold. Comparatively, it was late in the day before Western Australia shared in the largesse. Several false starts occurred before the 'Golden Mile' of Kalgoorlie was discovered in 1893. The prospectors endured many hardships, none more trying than the shortage of water. The gold discoveries had the effect at last of providing the colony with an eager supply of immigrants; Kalgoorlie itself within five years numbered 35,000. While some did make quick fortunes, the alluvial deposits were soon superseded in importance by deep-level mining backed by finance capital. As a result the frontier stage of social life soon passed into more settled conditions. The miners, many of them migrants from the east, were to provide the impetus behind the established elite's belated acceptance of federation in 1900. Such influence was not transitory, as gold was to remain economically important for decades to come.

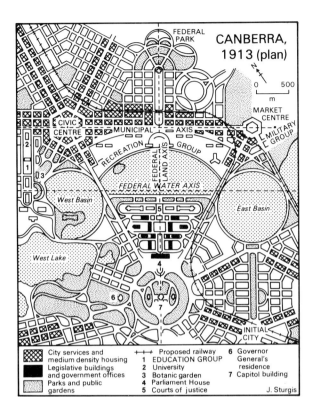

City services and
medium density housing
Legislative buildings
and government offices
Parks and public
gardens

+—+—+ Proposed railway
1 EDUCATION GROUP
2 University
3 Botanic garden
4 Parliament House
5 Courts of justice

6 Governor
   General's
   residence
7 Capitol building

J. Sturgis

FEDERAL PARK

CANBERRA,
1913 (plan)

0   500
         m

MARKET CENTRE

MILITARY GROUP

CIVIC CENTRE   MUNICIPAL   AXIS

RECREATION   GROUP

FEDERAL LAND AXIS

FEDERAL WATER AXIS

West Basin

East Basin

West Lake

INITIAL CITY

Canberra

Typical of the major colonies of white settlement, Australia resorted to a compromise in its choice for a site for its national capital. New South Wales, having rejected an earlier referendum on federation, was only mollified by an amendment which would situate the capital within its borders. Finally in 1911 it was agreed that the Commonwealth would develop a site near Yass. Since this was the height of the 'city beautiful' movement, the plans for the capital were thrown open to international competition. It was won by W. B.

Griffin in 1913 with a bold plan, shown here, which made extensive use of triangular avenues and artificial lakes, and 'grouped' buildings with related functions. Bureaucratic procrastination, personal squabbles, financial cut-backs and world war caused such delay that Parliament was unable to sit at Canberra until 1927. Other parts of the plan were similarly delayed so that realization of vital parts of the original plan came to resemble somewhat the playing out of a national drama.

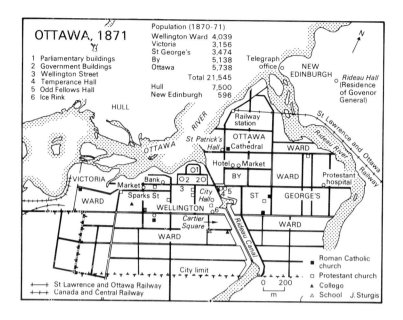

OTTAWA, 1871

1 Parliamentary buildings
2 Government Buildings
3 Wellington Street
4 Temperance Hall
5 Odd Fellows Hall
6 Ice Rink

Population (1870-71)
Wellington Ward 4,039
Victoria 3,156
St George's 3,474
By 5,138
Ottawa 5,738

Total 21,545

Hull 7,500
New Edinburgh 596

Telegraph office
NEW EDINBURGH
Rideau Hall (Residence of Govenor General)

HULL

OTTAWA RIVER

St Patrick's Hall
Railway station
OTTAWA Cathedral
St Lawrence and Ottawa Railway
Rideau River

VICTORIA
Market
Bank
Sparks St
WELLINGTON
WARD

Hotel Market
BY WARD
City Hall
ST GEORGE'S WARD
Protestant hospital

Cartier Square
WARD

Rideau Canal

City limit

0 200
m

St Lawrence and Ottawa Railway
Canada and Central Railway

■ Roman Catholic church
□ Protestant church
▲ College
△ School   J. Sturgis

Ottawa

The Confederation of Canada in 1867 inherited Ottawa as its capital from the period of the United Province of Canada (1841–67). The strife and tensions which had emerged then were too formidable to bear repeating, to say nothing of disregarding the vast expense incurred in constructing the parliament buildings. The choice of a permanent site was so contentious that it had to be referred to Queen Victoria in 1857. Guided very much by the opinion of Sir Edmund Head, the governor-general, her decision was in favour of Ottawa.

The town had emerged in the 1820s as a timber centre as a result of Colonel By of the Royal Engineers locating his construction base there for the building of the Rideau Canal. Despite the impatience often expressed with a capital 'in the backwoods', it was an inspired choice. Located in a most defensible position, its population also reflected the religious and ethnic diversity of Canada with Lower Town (east of the Rideau Canal) being mainly French and Irish Catholic, and Upper Town, British and Protestant.

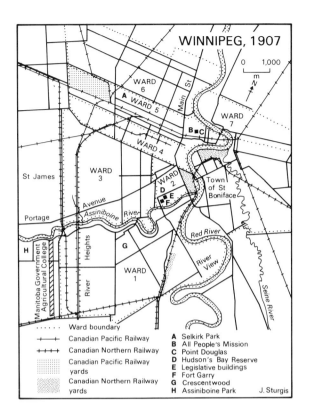

Winnipeg, 1907

·······	Ward boundary
┼──┼──┼	Canadian Pacific Railway
+++++	Canadian Northern Railway
	Canadian Pacific Railway yards
	Canadian Northern Railway yards

A Selkirk Park
B All People's Mission
C Point Douglas
D Hudson's Bay Reserve
E Legislative buildings
F Fort Garry
G Crescentwood
H Assiniboine Park

J. Sturgis

Winnipeg

Winnipeg, a settlement of only a few hundred people in 1871, became the 'shock' city of Canada at the turn of the century. Due very much to intensive immigration from eastern Europe, its population trebled within a decade to 150,000 in 1913. Many of the newcomers settled into ghetto areas in the northern wards of the city, where problems of disease and overcrowding were endemic. Since the city was the main recruiting centre for railway and timber contractors it naturally attracted a high proportion of male and seasonal workers, thus adding to its frontier character. The influx posed a threat to the British and Protestant character of the city which had been stamped upon it by two previous generations of settlers from Ontario. The ethnic tensions spilled over into numerous controversies relative to language rights in schools and the recognition of trade unions in industry. Many agencies took up the task of assimilating the immigrants, especially the Methodist Church and the School Board – a process still under way when multiculturalism became official policy in Canada in 1971.

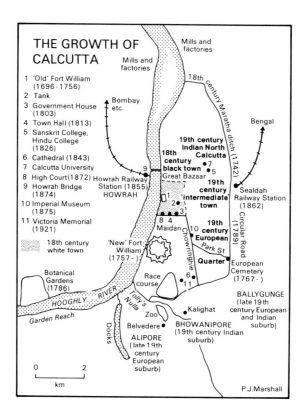

THE GROWTH OF CALCUTTA

1 'Old' Fort William (1696-1756)
2 Tank
3 Government House (1803)
4 Town Hall (1813)
5 Sanskrit College, Hindu College (1826)
6 Cathedral (1843)
7 Calcutta University
8 High Court (1872)
9 Howrah Bridge (1874)
10 Imperial Museum (1875)
11 Victoria Memorial (1921)

18th century white town

Mills and factories

Bombay etc.

18th century black town

19th century Indian North Calcutta

Great Bazaar

19th century 'intermediate' town

Howrah Railway Station (1855)
HOWRAH

19th century European Quarter

Maidan

'New' Fort William (1757-)

Race course

Chowringhie

Park St

Bengal

18th century Maratha ditch (1742)

Sealdah Railway Station (1862)

Circular Road (1789)

European Cemetery (1767-)

BALLYGUNGE (late 19th century European and Indian suburb)

Botanical Gardens (1786)

HOOGHLY RIVER

Garden Reach

Tolly's Nulla

Zoo
Belvedere

Docks

Kalighat

BHOWANIPORE (19th century Indian suburb)

ALIPORE (late 19th century European suburb)

0   2
km

P.J.Marshall

Calcutta

Calcutta, a British foundation that grew into a great port, was virtually created by the East India Company in the late seventeenth century as its headquarters on the Hooghly River, the main commercial artery of Bengal. Even before the establishment of British political dominance after Plassey in 1757, Calcutta had become a very considerable urban centre with at least 100,000 people living in it. It grew as a segregated town, a 'white' town of the company's fort and offices near the river with a much larger sprawling 'black town', of Indian merchants, artisans and labourers to the north. During the nineteenth century Calcutta's growth continued in an entirely unplanned way. The black town grew in area but above all in density of population, while the company's public buildings, such as the new Government House started by Wellesley

in 1799, and large neo-classical private residences spread round the Maidan, the great open space in front of the company's new Fort William.

From 1774 Calcutta was formally the capital of British India and it remained so until it was displaced by Delhi in 1912. Thus the city, which had always been a great centre of trade, became an administrative centre as well, and in time it developed into an industrial complex of jute and cotton mills and engineering works. By 1881 its population was estimated to be about 800,000 and it was continuing to attract waves of migrants from all over eastern India. The massing of people, usually in slums of shanty hutments, had swamped the city's capacity to maintain even the most basic facilities for the majority of its inhabitants.

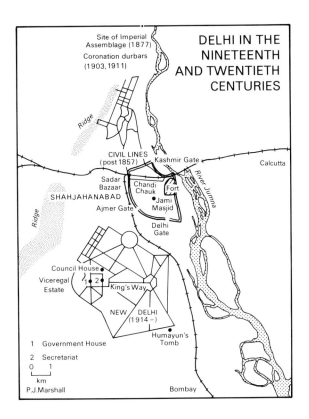

Map caption content within the figure:

DELHI IN THE NINETEENTH AND TWENTIETH CENTURIES

Site of Imperial Assemblage (1877)
Coronation durbars (1903, 1911)

Ridge

CIVIL LINES (post 1857)
Kashmir Gate
Calcutta

River Jumna

Sadar Bazaar
Chandi Chauk
Fort
SHAHJAHANABAD
Jami Masjid
Ajmer Gate
Delhi Gate

Ridge

Council House
Viceregal Estate
1 2
King's Way

NEW DELHI (1914 –)

Humayun's Tomb

1 Government House
2 Secretariat
0   1
km
P.J.Marshall

Bombay

Delhi

When British power was established in northern India at the beginning of the nineteenth century, Shahjahanabad, the seventeenth-century Mughal city of Delhi, was still a considerable place, in spite of the collapse of the Mughal Empire. Mosques, palaces and bazaars (markets) were clustered within its walls. In the first half of the nineteenth century the British presence was not very intrusive, British government offices taking their place within the city walls. In 1857 Delhi was seized by the rebel sepoys, who held it for some months against the British forces encamped on the Ridge above. When the British took the city, they looted it, and much desecration followed, the Mughal imperial palace becoming a British fortress with buildings being cleared to give it a field of fire.

From the 1870s the British began to move out of the walled city and to separate themselves from the mass of the Indian population. At first they went to north of the city, establishing what was called the Civil Station along and under the Ridge. Military cantonments were also built to the north. Meanwhile the city, whose growth had been brutally checked in 1857, underwent a considerable expansion as a commercial and later as a manufacturing centre. By 1881 its population exceeded 200,000.

Delhi's Mughal past gave it a high symbolic importance to the British, who staged the great pageant, called the Imperial Assemblage, outside the city in 1877 to mark Queen Victoria's title of Empress of India. Grand durbars were also held at Delhi in 1903 and

231

1911 for the accessions of Edward VII and George V. By the 1911 durbar Delhi's attractions as an alternative capital to Calcutta were being widely canvassed. In 1912 the change was announced. A new seat of government would be built to constitute 'New' Delhi on a site to the south of the walled city. Edwin Lutyens and Herbert Baker were commissioned as the principal architects to design the new capital. They conceived a spacious city built round a monumental plan of avenues radiating outwards from the massive centrepiece of Lutyens's Viceroy's Palace and Baker's two secretariat blocks. New Delhi was declared to be complete at great ceremonies in 1931. It served as capital of British India for another fifteen years and has been a by no means inappropriate capital for an independent India since 1947.

Simla

Simla, a purely British creation as a 'hill station', was hardly a town at all. By the end of the nineteenth century some 14,000 people lived around a network of ridges 7,000 to 8,000 feet above sea level, covering some six miles between two commanding heights, one called Jakko and the other called Prospect Hill. The main feature of Simla was its bungalows, single-storeyed residences, put up wherever sufficient level ground could be found. Amid the bungalows were more imposing buildings: the Viceregal Lodge, completed in 1888, offices used by the officials of the Government of India and the Government of the Punjab, a military headquarters, a town hall with a theatre, reading room and ballroom, clubs, schools, orphanages and churches. The architecture of these buildings was a pastiche of various European styles, set in an abundance of trees and shrubs. In one of the valleys below the ridges there were playing fields and a race course called Annandale. Travel to Simla was an arduous undertaking until the completion of a railway link in 1903.

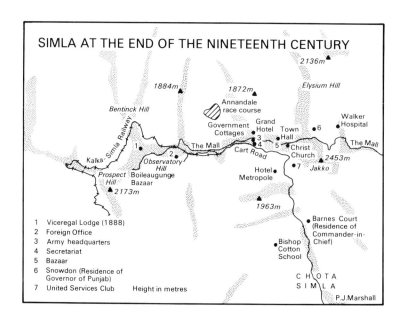

Simla had come into existence as a retreat for Europeans from the heat of the plains during the Indian summer. The land had first been acquired by the British in 1816. A governor-general went to Simla for the first time in 1827. By 1864 Simla had become effectively the summer capital of India. The governor-general left Calcutta between March and May and remained in Simla until October or November. He was followed to Simla by his councillors and many officials. They were joined by the commander-in-chief and the governor of the Punjab. During the summer migrations, the business of ruling the Indian empire was supplemented by a somewhat fevered pursuit of pleasure by some of the migrants and those who accompanied them. In Rudyard Kipling's stories fashionable Simla of the later nineteenth century has found its memorial. Official India, however, insisted that Simla was no holiday resort for them. Only in the cool of the hills could their labours continue uninterrupted.

Hong Kong

Hong Kong has always been primarily a harbour and its inhabitants always predominantly Chinese. The island, when acquired by Britain in 1842, had a rural population of only about 5,000; the great increases in its size have usually been the consequences of political disturbance in China – particularly the Taiping rebellion of the early 1860s, struggles between warlords in the 1920s, Japan's invasion after 1937 and civil war and the

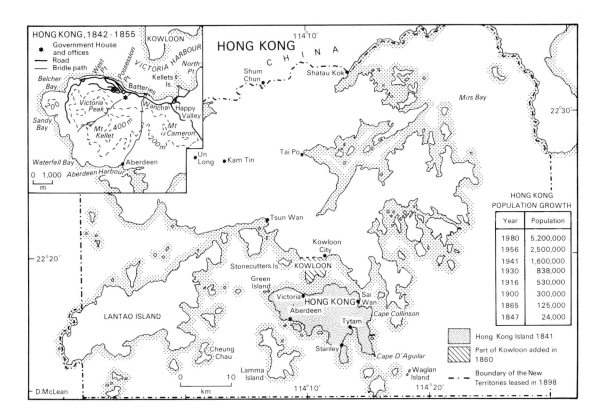

HONG KONG POPULATION GROWTH

Year	Population
1980	5,200,000
1956	2,500,000
1941	1,600,000
1930	838,000
1916	530,000
1900	300,000
1865	125,000
1847	24,000

Communist take-over in the late 1940s. In 1956, for example, about 30 per cent of the population were refugees. Early settlement along the north coast of the island was slower than originally anticipated as Shanghai emerged very quickly in the 1840s and 1850s as a powerful economic competitor.

Hong Kong was originally the centre for opium distribution. Other aspects of its trade and commercial services developed from the 1860s onwards when the colony became more important as an entrepôt for Britain's expanding trade with China and as the centre for the vast Chinese emigration overseas. The lease of the New Territories in 1898 added 355 square miles to Hong Kong and provided the land where much of the population influx since 1945 has lived. Over the years land reclamation also extended the frontage along Victoria Harbour. In the twentieth century Hong Kong has developed manufacturing industries, initially those associated with shipping but more recently textiles, footwear, plastics and electronics – all of which have contributed to the colony's great prosperity and its importance as an international financial centre. Hong Kong reverts to Chinese sovereignty in 1997.

Freetown

Freetown originated on land bought in 1787 by Granville Sharp as a home for 'poor blacks' from Britain. This 'Granville Town' survived two years, a second town being built in 1791 and settled with ex-slaves from North America (the 'Nova Scotians'). It was in 1794 that Freetown itself – soon augmented by Maroon settlers from Jamaica – was laid out, with the characteristic grid pattern that still marks the heart of the city. Following the British abolition of the slave trade, the crown took over Freetown as a colony in 1808, using the town and surrounding villages to settle Africans liberated from captured slave ships. Thereafter Freetown was the centre of the Royal Navy's anti-slaving activities and, for

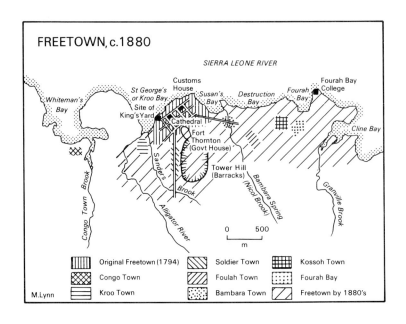

234

short periods in the 1820s and 1840s, the head-quarters of all Britain's West African possessions. By mid-century a cohesive Creole society had emerged within Freetown from its amalgam of ethnic groups, many originally settled in their own subsidiary quarters, and Sierra Leonian traders began pushing down the West African coast and into the interior. British influence followed them, expanding along the coast adjacent to Freetown in the 1860s and culminating in 1896 with the declaration of the Sierra Leone Protectorate.

Lagos

Lagos, whose origins go back to the fifteenth century, emerged as a major trading state around 1800, its importance deriving from its possession of the only natural harbour along many miles of coast. The hub of the town lay around the Oba's palace to the north-west of the island, but from the 1830s freed slaves from Brazil and Sierra Leone began to settle Popo Aguda and Olowogbowo respectively. British intervention in the area, with their attack on the town in 1851 and the creation of a consulate two years later, led to Lagos's annexation in 1861. The handful of European missionaries and traders drawn to Lagos after 1851 settled along the southern side of the island, where the marina and Broad Street were laid out by the 1860s. From here Sierra Leonian and European traders pushed into the interior. Lagos was to become the base for British expansion, first during the 1860s and 1870s into the town's immediate hinterland and then, during the 1890s, in the conquest of what became Nigeria. This was accompanied by the growth of the town beyond its original nucleus; its population reached some 40,000 by the 1890s. A railway to the interior was begun; bridges were completed to the mainland; the island swamps were drained and the harbour's notorious bar dredged. Lagos became the capital first of Southern Nigeria in 1906 and then in 1914 of Nigeria.

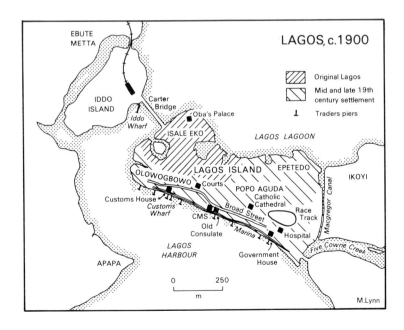

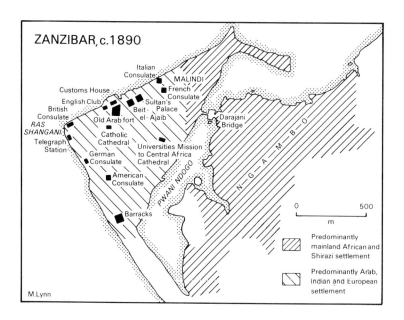

ZANZIBAR, c.1890

Italian Consulate
MALINDI
Customs House
French Consulate
English Club
Sultan's Palace
British Consulate
Beit- el-Ajaib
RAS SHANGANI
Old Arab fort
Darajani Bridge
Telegraph Station
Catholic Cathedral
Universities Mission to Central Africa Cathedral
German Consulate
American Consulate
PWANI NDOGO
N-G-A-M-B-O
Barracks
0   500
m
Predominantly mainland African and Shirazi settlement
Predominantly Arab, Indian and European settlement
M.Lynn

Zanzibar

The nineteenth century saw the remarkable rise of Zanzibar. Under Sultan Seyyid Said (1806–56) it became the effective capital of the Omani Empire and the centre of a fluctuating hegemony over the adjacent African coast. Its role in the development of the slave and ivory trades from the African interior, and the growth of Arab-owned clove plantations on the island, made Zanzibar the pre-eminent entre-pôt on the East African coast. The town's role in the slave trade brought increasing British interest; the signing of Anglo-Zanzibari treaties (1822, 1839, 1845 and 1873), the appointment of a resident British consul in 1841 and the establishment of a British naval presence were all aimed at suppressing the trade. This process culminated in the declaration of a British protectorate over Zanzibar and Pemba in 1890. By this period Zanzibar's maze of crowded streets had an estimated population of 80,000, made up of Arabs, mainland Africans (mainly slaves), Indian traders, the indigenous Shirazi inhabitants and a handful of Europeans. From the 1890s, however, Zanzibar went into decline as the growth of Dar-es-Salaam and the building of the Uganda Railway from Mombasa ended its entrepôt role.

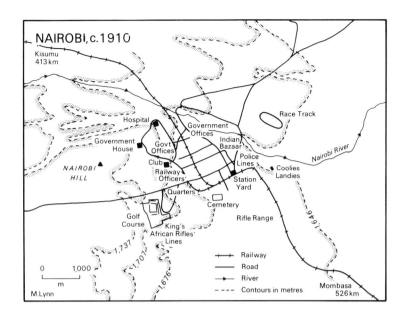

NAIROBI, c.1910

Kisumu 413 km

Hospital

Government House

Government Offices

Govt Offices

NAIROBI HILL

Club

Railway Officers' Quarters

Indian Bazaar

Police Lines

Station Yard

Cemetery

Race Track

Nairobi River

Coolies Landies

Golf Course

King's African Rifles' Lines

Rifle Range

1,646

1,737

1,707

1,676

0 ··· 1,000

m

M.Lynn

Railway
Road
River
Contours in metres

Mombasa 526 km

Nairobi

Nairobi (from the Maasai 'Enkare Nairobi' or 'the place of cold water') had its origins as a railhead established in 1899 during the building of the strategic Uganda Railway from Mombasa to Lake Victoria. The site, chosen because of its space for rail sidings and its convenience for the route through the Highlands, rapidly grew into a major town, with its centre lying in the triangle formed by the railway and the Nairobi River. By the end of 1899 the headquarters of the railway had been moved there, to be followed by the administrative headquarters of Ukamba Province. In 1907, despite calls for the town to be relocated, Nairobi became the capital of British East Africa. Its position made it the gateway into the interior for large numbers of Indian traders and European settlers; an Indian bazaar was established in 1899, and already by 1901 coffee was being grown commercially near by. Large-scale African settlement accompanied the growth of the town; but, while Europeans never numbered more than a tiny fraction of Nairobi's population, it remained the centre of European activity in the colony. With its government offices, golf course and white housing along Nairobi Hill – comfortably above the river and the non-European quarters – Nairobi was in many ways the archetypal colonial settlers' town.

REFERENCES AND FURTHER READING

Atlases

Ajayi, J. F. Ade and Michael Crowder (eds), *Historical Atlas of Africa*, London, 1985.

Barraclough, G. (ed.), *The Times Atlas of World History*, rev. edn, London, 1984.

Bayly, C. A. (ed.), *Atlas of the British Empire*, London, 1989.

Camm, J. C. and J. McQuilton (eds), *Australians: A Historical Atlas*, Broadway, 1987.

Cappon, L., B. Bartz and J. Hamilton, *Atlas of Early American History*, Chicago, 1976.

Cole Harris, R. and Geoffrey J. Matthews (eds), *Historical Atlas of Canada, vol. I: From the Beginning to 1800*, Toronto, 1989.

Davies, C. C., *An Historical Atlas of the Indian Peninsula*, Oxford, 1949.

Kerr, D. G., *Historical Atlas of Canada*, 3rd edn rev., London, 1975.

Natkiel, Richard, *Atlas of Twentieth Century History*, London, 1982.

Schwartzberg, Joseph E. (ed.), *A Historical Atlas of South Asia*, Chicago, 1978.

Walker, E. A., *Historical Atlas of South Africa*, Cape Town, 1922.

Wards, Ian (ed.), *New Zealand Atlas*, Wellington, 1976.

Bristol and the Atlantic, 1480–1509

Andrews, K. R., *Trade, Plunder and Settlement: Maritime Enterprise and the Genesis of the British Empire, 1480–1630*, Cambridge, 1984.

Quinn, D. B., *England and the Discovery of America, 1481–1620*, New York, 1974.

Williamson, J. A. (ed.), *The Cabot Voyages and the Bristol Discovery under Henry VII*, Hakluyt Society, 2nd series, vol. 120, Cambridge, 1962.

Sixteenth-century English oceanic enterprise: the northern hemisphere

Andrews, K. R., *Trade, Plunder and Settlement: Maritime Enterprise and the Genesis of the British Empire, 1480–1630*, Cambridge, 1984.

Morison, S. E., *The European Discovery of America: The Northern Voyages, AD 500–1600*, New York and Oxford, 1971.

Willan, T. S., *The Early History of the Russia Company, 1553–1603*, Manchester, 1956.

Sixteenth-century English oceanic enterprise: the southern hemisphere

Andrews, K. R., *Drake's Voyages: A Reassessment of their Place in Elizabethan Maritime Expansion*, London, 1967.

Foster, Sir William, *England's Quest of Eastern Trade*, London, 1933, reprint 1966.

Wagner, H. R., *Sir Francis Drake's Voyage around the World*, San Francisco, 1926.

Early attempts at settlement in North America

Durant, D. B., *Ralegh's Lost Colony: The Story of the First English Settlements in America*, New York, 1981.

Morison, S. E., *The European Discovery of*

America: The Northern Voyages, AD 500–1600, New York and Oxford, 1971.

Quinn, D.B., *North America: From Earliest Discovery to First Settlements*, New York, 1977.

Virginia: early settlement

Andrews, C.M., *The Colonial Period of American History*, vols I and II, New Haven, Conn., 1934–6.

Craven, W.F., *The Southern Colonies in the Seventeenth Century*, Baton Rouge, La., 1949.

Morgan, E.S., *American Freedom, American Slavery*, New York, 1975.

New England colonies: early settlement

Andrews, C.M., *The Colonial Period of American History*, vols I and II, New Haven, Conn., 1934–6.

Davies, K.G., *The North Atlantic World in the Seventeenth Century*, London, 1974.

Pomfret, J.E. and F.M. Shumway, *Founding the American Colonies, 1583–1660*, New York, 1970.

Chartered companies: the eastern seas

Bassett, D.K., 'Early English trade and settlement in Asia, 1602–1690', in J.S. Bromley and E.H. Kossmann (eds), *Britain and the Netherlands in Europe and Asia*, London, 1968.

Foster, Sir William, *England's Quest of Eastern Trade*, London, 1933, reprint 1966.

Meilink-Roelofsz, M.A.P., *Asian Trade and European Influence in the Indonesian Archipelago between 1500 and about 1630*, The Hague, 1962.

Chartered companies: the Mediterranean

Braudel, F., *The Mediterranean and the Mediterranean World in the Age of Philip II*, trans. from the French by Sian Reynolds, 2 vols., London, 1972.

Ramsay, G.D., *England's Overseas Trade during the Centuries of Emergence*, London, 1957.

Wood, A.C., *A History of the Levant Company*, Oxford, 1935.

Chartered companies: Africa

Andrews, K.R., *Trade, Plunder and Settlement: Maritime Enterprise and the Genesis of the British Empire, 1480–1630*, Cambridge, 1984.

Blake, J.W., *European Beginnings in West Africa, 1454–1578*, London, 1937; reissued as *West Africa: Quest for God and Gold, 1454–1578*, London, 1977.

Willan, T.S., *Studies in Elizabethan Foreign Trade*, Manchester, 1959.

Chartered companies: Russia and the Eastland

Fedorwicz, J.K., *England's Baltic Trade in the Early Seventeenth Century*, Cambridge, 1972.

Hinton, R.W.K., *The Eastland Trade and the Common Weal in the Seventeenth Century*, Cambridge, 1959.

Ramsay, G.D., *England's Overseas Trade during the Centuries of Emergence*, London, 1957.

Ireland: mid-sixteenth to late seventeenth centuries

MacCurtain, Margaret, *Tudor and Stuart Ireland*, Dublin, 1972.

Maxwell, P., *The Scottish Migration to Ulster in the Reign of James I*, London, 1973.

Quinn, D.B., *The Elizabethans and the Irish*, Ithaca, NY, 1966.

The West Indies: plunder and acquisitions in the sixteenth and seventeenth centuries

Andrews, K.R., *The Spanish Caribbean: Trade and Plunder, 1530–1630*, New Haven, Conn., 1978.

Bridenbaugh, C. and R., *No Peace beyond the Line: The English in the Caribbean, 1624–1690*, New York, 1972.

Dunn, R.S., *Sugar and Slaves: The Rise of the Planter Class in the English West Indies, 1624–1713*, Chapel Hill, NC, 1973.

South Carolina, North Carolina and Georgia

Lefler, Hugh T. and William S. Powell, *Colonial North Carolina*, New York, 1973.

Sirmans, M. Eugene, *Colonial South Carolina: A Political History, 1663–1763*, Chapel Hill, NC, 1966.

Weir, Robert M., *Colonial South Carolina*, New York, 1983.

Maryland, Pennsylvania, Delaware and New Jersey

Nash, Gary B., *Red, White and Black: The Peoples of Early America*, 2nd edn, Englewood Cliffs, NJ, 1982.

Pomfret, John E., *Colonial New Jersey*, New York, 1973.

Quinn, David B. (ed.), *Early Maryland in a Wider World*, Detroit, 1982.

Simmons, R.C., *The American Colonies: From Settlement to Independence*, Oxford, 1976.

New York and New Hampshire

Archdeacon, Thomas J., *New York City, 1664–1710: Conquest and Change*, Ithaca, NY, 1976.

Bonomi, Patricia U., *A Factious People: Politics and Society in Colonial New York*, New York, 1971.

Kammen, Michael, *Colonial New York*, New York, 1975.

European rivalries in the New World, 1650–1713

Bridenbaugh, C. and R., *No Peace beyond the Line: The English in the Caribbean, 1624–1690*, New York, 1972.

Davies, K.G., *The North Atlantic World in the Seventeenth Century*, London, 1974.

Scammell, Geoffrey, *European Expansion, 1500–1715*, London, 1987.

Emigration from Britain in the seventeenth century

Bridenbaugh, Carl, *Vexed and Troubled Englishmen, 1590–1642*, New York, 1967.

Galenson, David, *White Servitude in Colonial America*, Cambridge, 1981.

Gemery, Henry A., 'Emigration from the British Isles to the New World 1630–1700', *Research in Economic History*, 5, 1980, 179–231.

—— 'European immigration to North America, 1700–1820: numbers and quasi-numbers', *Perspectives in American History*, new series 1, 1984, 283–342.

Horn, James, 'Servant emigration to the Chesapeake in the seventeenth century', in Thad W. Tate and David Ammerman (eds), *The Chesapeake in the Seventeenth Century*, New York, 1979, 51–95.

McCusker, John J. and Russell R. Menard, *The Economy of British America, 1607–1789*, Chapel Hill, NC, 1985.

Beginnings of empire in India, to 1765

Chaudhuri, K.N., *The Trading World of Asia and the English East India Company 1660–1760*, Cambridge, 1978.

Marshall, P.J., 'British expansion in India in the eighteenth century', *History*, LX, 1975, 28–43.

Marshall, P.J., *Bengal: The British Bridgehead: Eastern India 1740–1828*, Cambridge, 1987.

Spear, P., *Master of Bengal: Clive and his India*, London, 1975.

Canada at the British conquest, 1763

Frégault, Guy, *Canada: The War of the Conquest*, trans. Margaret M. Cameron, Toronto, 1969.

Neatby, Hilda, *Quebec: The Revolutionary Age 1760-1791*, Toronto, 1966.

Rich, E.E., *The Fur Trade and the Northwest to 1857*, Toronto, 1967.

Stanley, George F.G., *New France: The Last Phase 1744-1760*, Toronto, 1968.

The British North American empire in 1776

Bailyn, Bernard, *The Ideological Origins of the American Revolution*, Cambridge, Mass., 1967.

—— *The Peopling of British North America: An Introduction*, New York, 1986.

Christie, I.R. and B.W. Labaree, *Empire or Independence 1760-1776*, Oxford, 1976.

Countryman, Edward, *The American Revolution*, New York, 1985, and London, 1987.

Morris, Richard B., *The Peacemakers: The Great Powers and American Independence*, Boston, 1983.

Steele, Ian K., *The English Atlantic, 1675-1740: An Exploration of Communication and Community*, Oxford, 1986.

Tucker, R.W. and D.C. Hendrickson, *The Fall of the First British Empire*, Baltimore, 1983.

Boston

See under Charles Town, Boston, Pittsburgh, p. 249.

The British North Atlantic trading system of the later eighteenth century

Davis, R., 'English foreign trade 1700-74', *Economic History Review*, 2nd series, XV, 1962-3, 285-303.

—— *The Rise of the Atlantic Economies*, London, 1973.

Farnie, D.A., 'The commercial empire of the Atlantic, 1607-1783', *Economic History Review*, 2nd series, XV, 1962-3, 205-18.

British exports to the Atlantic area

Davis, R., *The Industrial Revolution and British Overseas Trade*, Leicester, 1979.

Minchinton, W.E., *The Growth of British Overseas Trade in the Seventeenth and Eighteenth Centuries*, London, 1969.

Exports from the North American colonies

McCusker, J.J. and R.R. Menard, *The Economy of British America, 1607-1789*, Chapel Hill, NC, 1985.

Perkins, E.J., *The Economy of Colonial America*, New York, 1980.

Walton, G.M. and J.F. Shepherd, *The Economic Rise of Early America*, Cambridge, 1979.

Exports from the West Indies

Pares, R., 'The London sugar market 1740-69', *Economic History Review*, 2nd series, XI, 1956, 254-70.

—— *Merchants and Planters*, supplement to *Economic History Review*, 1960.

Sheridan, R.B., *Sugar and Slavery: An Economic History of the British West Indies*, Baltimore, Md, 1974.

British exports from West Africa

Anstey, R.T., *The Atlantic Slave Trade and British Abolition 1760-1810*, London, 1975.

Gemery, H.A. and J.S. Hogendorn (eds), *The Uncommon Market: Essays in the Economic History of the Atlantic Slave Trade*, New York, 1979.

Lovejoy, P.E., *Transformations in Slavery*, Cambridge, 1983.

The War of the American Revolution

Alden, John Richard, *The American Revolution*, New York, 1954.

Hoffman, Ronald *et al.* (eds), *Arms and Independence: The Military Character of the*

American Revolution, Charlottesville, Va, 1984.

Makesy, Piers, *The War for America, 1775–1783*, London, 1964.

British expansion in India, 1765–1805

Barnett, R.B., *North India between Empires: Awadh, the Mughals and the British 1720–1801*, Berkeley, Calif., 1980.

Forrest, D., *Tiger of Mysore: The Life and Death of Tipu Sultan*, London, 1970.

Ingram, E., *Commitment to Empire: Prophecies of the Great Game in Asia 1797–1800*, Oxford, 1981.

Nightingale, P., *Trade and Empire in Western India 1784–1806*, Cambridge, 1970.

India, south-east Asia and China, 1784–1826

Bassett, D.K., *British Trade and Policy in Indonesia and Malaysia in the Late Eighteenth Century*, Hull, 1971.

Greenberg, M., *British Trade and the Opening of China 1800–42*, Cambridge, 1951, repr. 1969.

Tarling, N., *Anglo-Dutch Rivalry in the Malay World 1780–1824*, Brisbane, 1962.

Wurtzburg, C.E., *Raffles of the Eastern Isles*, London, 1954.

Exploration and exploitation of the Pacific in the late eighteenth century

Beaglehole, J.C. (ed.), *The Journals of Captain James Cook on his Voyages of Discovery*, 3 vols, Cambridge, 1955, 1961, 1967.

Frost, Alan, *Convicts and Empire: A Naval Question 1776–1811*, Melbourne, 1980.

Mackay, David, *In the Wake of Cook: Exploration, Science and Empire 1780–1801*, London, 1985.

Steven, Margaret, *Trade, Tactics and Territory: Britain in the Pacific 1783–1823*, Melbourne, 1983.

The Hudson's Bay Company

See below under British North America, *c.* 1760–1837.

Jamaica, *c.* 1810

Higman, B.W., *Slave Population and Economy in Jamaica, 1807–1834*, Cambridge, 1976.

—— 'The spatial economy of Jamaican sugar plantations: cartographic evidence from the eighteenth and nineteenth centuries', *Journal of Historical Geography*, 13, 1987, 17–39.

Turner, Mary, *Slaves and Missionaries: The Disintegration of Jamaican Slave Society, 1787–1834*, Urbana, Ill., and London, 1982.

Britain's empire in 1815

Bayly, C.A., *Imperial Meridian: The British Empire and the World, 1780–1830*, London, 1989.

Geggus, D., *Slavery, War and Revolution: The British Occupation of St Domingue 1793–8*, Oxford, 1982.

Ingram, E., *Commitment to Empire: Prophecies of the Great Game in Asia 1797–1800*, Oxford, 1981.

Lynch, J., 'British policy and Spanish America 1783–1808', *Journal of Latin American Studies*, I, 1969, 1–30.

British North America, *c.* 1760–1837

Craig, G.M., *Upper Canada: The Formative Years 1784–1841*, Toronto, 1963.

Friesen, Gerald, *The Canadian Prairies: A History*, Toronto and London, 1984.

Harris, R.C. and John Warkentin, *Canada before Confederation: A Study in Historical Geography*, New York and London, 1974.

MacNutt, W.S., *The Atlantic Provinces: The Emergence of Colonial Society 1712–1857*, London and New York, 1965.

Meinig, D.W., *The Shaping of America: A*

Geographical Perspective on 500 Years of History, New Haven, Conn., and London, 1986.

Mitchell, R.D. and Paul A. Groves (eds), *North America: The Historical Geography of a Changing Continent*, London, 1987.

Ouellet, F., *Lower Canada 1791–1840: Social Change and Nationalism*, Toronto, 1980.

The settlement of Australia before 1860

Blainey, G., *The Tyranny of Distance: How Distance Shaped Australia's History*, Melbourne, 1966.

Burroughs, Peter, *Britain and Australia 1831–1855: A Study in Imperial Relations and Crown Lands Administration*, Oxford, 1967.

Clark, C.M.H., *A History of Australia*, vols 1–4, Melbourne, London and New York, 1962, 1968, 1973, 1978.

Madgwick, R.B., *Immigration into Eastern Australia, 1788–1851*, Sydney, 1969.

Ritchie, J., *Punishment and Profit*, Melbourne, 1970.

Roberts, Stephen H., *The Squatting Age in Australia 1835–1847*, Melbourne, 1935, and London and New York, 1964.

Serle, G., *The Golden Age: A History of the Colony of Victoria 1851–1861*, London and New York, 1968.

Sherrington, G., *Australia's Immigrants 1788–1918*, Sydney, 1980.

New Zealand, 1840–1870

Adams, P., *Fatal Necessity: British Intervention in New Zealand 1830–1847*, Auckland, 1977.

Belich, James, *The New Zealand Wars and the Victorian Interpretation of Racial Conflict*, Auckland, 1986.

Oliver, W.H. (ed.), *The Oxford History of New Zealand*, Oxford and Wellington, 1981.

Sinclair, Keith, *A History of New Zealand*, London, 1969.

British exploration in Africa, 1770–1890

Bovill, E.W., *The Niger Explored*, London, 1968.

Cairns, H.A.C., *Prelude to Imperialism: British Reactions to Central African Society 1840–1890*, London, 1965.

Curtin, P.D., *The Image of Africa: British Ideas and Action, 1780–1850*, London, 1965.

Hallett, Robin, *The Penetration of Africa*, London, 1965.

Hibbert, C., *Africa Explored*, London, 1982.

Rotberg, R.I., *Africa and its Explorers*, London, 1970.

Southern Africa, 1795–1854

Duly, L., *British Land Policy at the Cape, 1795–1844: A Study of Administrative Procedures in the Empire*, Durham, NC, 1968.

Elphick, Richard and Hermann Giliomee (eds), *The Shaping of South African Society 1652–1840*, London and Cape Town, 1989.

Galbraith, John S., *Reluctant Empire: British Policy on the South African Frontier, 1834–1854*, Berkeley, Calif., 1963.

Ross, Andrew, *John Philip (1775–1851): Missions, Race and Politics in South Africa*, Aberdeen, 1986.

Wilson, M. and L.M. Thompson (eds), *The Oxford History of South Africa, vol. I to 1870*, Oxford, 1969.

Emigration from Britain, 1815–1914

Carrothers, W.A., *Emigration from the British Isles*, London, 1929.

Coleman, Terry, *Passage to America*, London, 1972.

Cowan, Helen I., *British Emigration to British North America*, Toronto, 1961.

British West Indies, c. 1820–1860

Higman, B.W., *Slave Populations of the British Caribbean, 1807–1834*, Baltimore, Md, 1984.

Wood, Donald, *Trinidad in Transition: The Years after Slavery*, London, 1968.

British expansion in India, 1805–1885

Gillard, D., *The Struggle for Asia 1828–1914*, London, 1977.

Jeffrey, R. (ed.), *People, Princes and Paramount Power: Society and Politics in the Indian Princely States*, Delhi, 1978.

Thompson, E., *The Making of the Indian Princes*, Oxford, 1943.

Yapp, M.E., *Strategies of British India: Britain, Iran and Afghanistan 1798–1850*, Oxford, 1980.

Revolt in India, 1857–1858

Metcalf, T.R., *The Aftermath of Revolt: India 1857–70*, Princeton, NJ, 1964.

Sen, S.N., *Eighteen Fifty-Seven*, New Delhi, 1957.

Stokes, E.T., *The Peasant and the Raj*, Cambridge, 1975.

—— *The Peasant Armed: The Indian Revolt of 1857*, Oxford, 1986.

Britain and China, 1842–1900

Edwards, E.W., *British Diplomacy and Finance in China 1895–1914*, Oxford, 1987.

Fairbank, J.K., *Trade and Diplomacy on the China Coast: The Opening of the Treaty Ports 1842–1854*, Stanford, Calif., 1969.

Lowe, Peter, *Britain in the Far East*, London, 1981.

Young, L.K., *British Diplomacy in China 1895–1902*, Oxford, 1970.

Britain in south-east Asia, 1824–1914

Cowan, C.D., *Nineteenth-Century Malaya: The Origins of British Political Control*, London, 1961.

Hall, D.G.E., *A History of South-East Asia*, 4th edn, London, 1981.

Sardesai, D.R., *British Trade Expansion in Southeast Asia 1830–1914*, New Delhi, 1977.

Britain in the Middle East before 1914

Busch, B.C., *Britain and the Persian Gulf 1894–1914*, Berkeley, Calif., 1967.

Gillard, D., *The Struggle for Asia 1828–1914*, London, 1977.

Greaves, R.L., *Britain and the Defence of India 1884–1892*, London, 1959.

Kent, M., *Oil and Empire: British Policy and Mesopotamian Oil 1900–1920*, London, 1976.

McLean, D., *Britain and her Buffer State: The Collapse of the Persian Empire 1890–1914*, London, 1979.

British expansion in West Africa, 1820–1914

Fage, J.D., *A History of West Africa*, Cambridge, 1969.

Hargreaves, J.D., *Prelude to the Partition of West Africa*, London, 1963.

—— *West Africa Partitioned*, 2 vols, London, 1974, 1985.

Hopkins, A.G., *An Economic History of West Africa*, London, 1973.

British expansion in East Africa, c. 1840–c. 1900

Galbraith, John S., *Mackinnon and East Africa 1878–1895*, Cambridge, 1972.

Oliver, R. and G. Mathew (eds), *History of East Africa, vol. I*, Oxford, 1963.

Robinson, R. and J. Gallagher with A. Denny, *Africa and the Victorians: The Official Mind of Imperialism*, London, 1961.

Britain, Egypt and the Sudan, 1870–1914

Collins, R.O., *Land beyond the Rivers: The Southern Sudan, 1898–1918*, New Haven, Conn., and London, 1971.

Daly, M.W., *Empire on the Nile: The Anglo-*

Egyptian Sudan 1898–1934, Cambridge, 1987.

Hopkins, A.G., 'The Victorians and Africa: a reconsideration of the occupation of Egypt, 1882', *Journal of African History*, 27, 1986, 363–91.

Robinson, R. and J. Gallagher with A. Denny, *Africa and the Victorians: The Official Mind of Imperialism*, London, 1961.

Sanderson, G.N., *England, Europe and the Upper Nile, 1882–1899*, Edinburgh, 1965.

Britain and the partition of South Africa, 1854–1910

Kiewiet, C.W. de, *The Imperial Factor in South Africa*, Cambridge, 1937.

Marks, Shula, 'Southern Africa, 1867–1886' and 'Southern and Central Africa, 1886–1910', in Roland Oliver and G.N. Sanderson (eds), *The Cambridge History of Africa, vol. 6 from 1870 to 1905*, Cambridge, 1985.

Porter, A.N., *The Origins of the South African War: Joseph Chamberlain and the Diplomacy of Imperialism 1895–99*, Manchester, 1980.

Schreuder, D.M., *The Scramble for Southern Africa, 1877–1895: The Politics of Partition Reappraised*, Cambridge, 1980.

Britain and the partition of Central Africa, 1875–1910

Galbraith, John S., *Crown and Charter: The Early Years of the British South Africa Company*, Berkeley, Calif., and London, 1974.

Hanna, A.J., *The Beginnings of Nyasaland and North-Eastern Rhodesia 1859–95*, Oxford, 1956.

Palmer, R.H., *Land and Racial Domination in Rhodesia*, London, 1977.

Phimister, I.M., *An Economic and Social History of Zimbabwe 1890–1948*, London, 1988.

Wills, A.J., *An Introduction to the History of Central Africa*, 4th edn, London, 1985.

The South African War, 1899–1902

Pakenham, Thomas, *The Boer War*, London, 1979.

Spies, S.B., *Methods of Barbarism? Roberts and Kitchener and Civilians in the Boer Republics, January 1900–May 1902*, Cape Town, 1977.

Warwick, Peter (ed.), *The South African War: The Anglo-Boer War 1899–1902*, London, 1980.

―――― *Black People and the South African War 1899–1902*, Cambridge, 1983.

Imperial defence: army garrisons, 1848 and 1881

Senior, Elinor K., *British Regulars in Montreal: An Imperial Garrison, 1832–1854*, Montreal, 1981.

Spiers, Edward M., *The Army and Society 1815–1914*, London, 1980.

Strachan, Hew, *Wellington's Legacy: The Reform of the British Army 1830–1854*, Manchester, 1984.

Imperial defence: naval stations, 1848, 1875 and 1898

Bartlett, C.J., *Great Britain and Sea Power 1815–1853*, Oxford, 1963.

Graham, G.S., *The China Station: War and Diplomacy 1830–1860*, Oxford, 1978.

Kennedy, Paul M., *The Rise and Fall of British Naval Mastery*, London, 1976.

Protestant missionaries and the Anglican Church overseas, 1780–1914

Ajayi, J.F.A., *Christian Missions in Nigeria 1841–1891*, London, 1965.

Cnattingius, H., *Bishops and Societies: A Study of Anglican Colonial and Missionary Expansion 1698–1850*, London, 1952.

Cohen, P.A., 'Christian missions and their impact to 1900', in J.K. Fairbank (ed.), *The Cambridge History of China, vol. 10*, Cambridge, 1978.

Fingard, J., *The Anglican Design in Loyalist Nova Scotia 1783–1816*, London, 1972.

Gunson, Neil, *Messengers of Grace: Evangelical Missionaries in the South Seas 1797–1860*, Melbourne, 1978.

Laird, M.A., *Missionaries and Education in Bengal 1793–1837*, Oxford, 1972.

Latourette, K.S., *Christianity in a Revolutionary Age*, 5 vols, New York, 1957–61.

McCracken, John, *Politics and Christianity in Malawi 1875–1940*, Cambridge, 1977.

Morrell, W.P., *The Anglican Church in New Zealand: A History*, Dunedin, 1973.

Neill, Stephen, *A History of Christianity in India 1707–1858*, Cambridge, 1985.

—— *A History of Christian Missions*, 2nd edn, Harmondsworth, 1986.

Oliver, Roland, *The Missionary Factor in East Africa*, 2nd edn, London, 1965.

Porter, Andrew, 'Cambridge, Keswick and late nineteenth-century attitudes to Africa', *Journal of Imperial and Commonwealth History*, V, 1, 1976, 5–34.

—— '"Commerce and Christianity": the rise and fall of a nineteenth-century missionary slogan', *Historical Journal*, 28, 3, 1985, 597–621.

Yates, T.E., *Venn and Victorian Bishops Abroad: The Missionary Policies of Henry Venn and their Repercussions upon the Anglican Episcopate of the Colonial Period 1841–1872*, Uppsala and London, 1978.

Canada, 1867–1949

Bothwell, Robert, Ian Drummond and John English, *Canada since 1945: Power, Politics and Provincialism*, Toronto, 1981.

—— *Canada 1900–1945*, Toronto, 1987.

Brown, R.C. and Ramsay Cook, *Canada 1896–1921*, Toronto, 1974.

Waite, Peter B., *Canada 1874–1896: Arduous Destiny*, Toronto, 1971.

Australia and federation, 1901

Clark, C.M.H., *A History of Australia, vol. 5 1888–1915*, Melbourne, 1981.

Hodgins, Bruce W., Don Wright and W.H. Heick (eds), *Federalism in Canada and Australia: The Early Years*, Waterloo, Canada, 1978.

Martin, A.W. (ed.), *Essays in Australian Federation*, Melbourne, 1969.

Norris, Ronald, *The Emergent Commonwealth: Australian Federation, Expectations and Fulfilment, 1889–1910*, Carlton, 1975.

Britain and the Pacific

Kennedy, P.M., *The Samoan Tangle: A Study in Anglo-German—American Relations 1878–1900*, Dublin and New York, 1974.

Morrell, W.P., *Britain in the Pacific Islands*, Oxford, 1960.

Ward, J.M., *British Policy in the South Pacific, 1786–1893*, Sydney, 1948.

Communications: principal steamer routes and coaling stations, 1889

Farnie, D.A., *East and West of Suez*, Oxford, 1969.

Greenhill, Robert, 'Shipping 1850–1914', in D.C.M. Platt (ed.), *Business Imperialism 1840–1930*, Oxford, 1977.

Hyde, Francis E., *Far Eastern Trade 1860–1914*, London, 1973.

Porter, Andrew, *Victorian Shipping, Business and Imperial Policy: Donald Currie, the Castle Line and Southern Africa*, Woodbridge and New York, 1986.

Communications: telegraphs, 1865–1914

Bright, Charles, *Submarine Telegraphs: Their History, Construction, and Working*, London, 1898.

Kennedy, P.M., 'Imperial cable communications and strategy, 1870–1914', *English Historical Review*, 86, October 1971, 728–52.

PP (1902) XI, Cd 1056 and Cd 1118, *First and Second Reports of the Inter-Departmental Committee on Cable Communications, with Minutes of Evidence*, London.

The First World War, 1914–1918

Darwin, John, *Britain, Egypt and the Middle East: Imperial Policy in the Aftermath of War, 1918–1922*, London, 1981.

First, Ruth, *South West Africa*, Harmondsworth, 1963.

Green, R.H., M.-L. Kiljunen and K. Kiljunen, *Namibia: The Last Colony*, London, 1981.

Iliffe, John, *A Modern History of Tanganyika*, Cambridge, 1979.

Kent, Marion (ed.), *The Great Powers and the End of the Ottoman Empire*, London, 1984.

Louis, W.R., *Great Britain and Germany's Lost Colonies, 1914–1919*, Oxford, 1967.

Monroe, Elizabeth, *Britain's Moment in the Middle East 1914–56*, London, 1963.

Ogot, B.A. and J.A. Kieran (eds), *Zamani: A Survey of East African History*, Nairobi and London, 2nd edn, 1973.

Britain and the Middle East after the Treaty of Lausanne (1923)

Darwin, John, *Britain, Egypt and the Middle East: Imperial Policy in the Aftermath of War, 1918–1922*, London, 1981.

Monroe, Elizabeth, *Britain's Moment in the Middle East 1914–56*, London, 1963.

Nicolson, Harold, *Curzon: The Last Phase 1919–1925*, London, 1934.

Sachar, H.M., *The Emergence of the Middle East, 1914–1924*, New York, 1969.

The partition of Ireland, 1914–1922

Boyce, D.G., *Englishmen and Irish Troubles: British Public Opinion and the Making of Irish Policy, 1918–1922*, London, 1972.

Lyons, F.S.L., *Ireland since the Famine*, London, 1973.

Mansergh, P.N.S., *The Irish Question 1840–1921*, rev. edn, London, 1965.

Townshend, Charles, *The British Campaign in Ireland, 1919–1921: The Development of Political and Military Policies*, Oxford, 1975.

Communications: imperial airways, 1918–1950

Higham, Robin, *Britain's Imperial Air Routes, 1918–1939*, Hamden, Conn., 1960.

Killingray, David, '"A swift agent of government": air power in British colonial Africa, 1916–1939', *Journal of African History*, 20, 1984, 429–44.

McCormack, R.L., 'Imperialism, air transport and colonial development: Kenya 1920–1946', *Journal of Imperial and Commonwealth History*, XVII, 3, 1989, 374–95.

Britain in India, to 1939

Gallagher, John, *The Decline, Revival and Fall of the British Empire*, Cambridge, 1982.

Moore, R.J., *The Crisis of Indian Unity, 1917–1940*, Oxford, 1974.

Tomlinson, B.R., *The Indian National Congress and the Raj, 1929–1942: The Penultimate Phase*, London, 1976.

Britain and the war in the Mediterranean, 1942–1945

Barnett, Corelli, *The Desert Generals*, London, 1960.

Bryant, Sir Arthur, *The Turn of the Tide, 1939–1943*, London, 1957.

—— *Triumph in the West, 1943–1946*, London, 1959.

Howard, Michael, *The Mediterranean Strategy in the Second World War*, Cambridge, 1966.

The war against Japan, 1941–1946

McIntyre, W. David, *The Rise and Fall of the Singapore Naval Base, 1919–1942*, London, 1979.

Stockwell, A.J., *British Policy and Malay Politics during the Malayan Union Experiment, 1942–1948*, Kuala Lumpur, 1979.

Thorne, Christopher, *Allies of a Kind: The United States, Britain and the War against Japan, 1941–1945*, Oxford, 1978.

The partition of India

Jalal, Ayesha, *The Sole Spokesman: Jinnah, the Muslim League and the Demand for Pakistan*, Cambridge, 1985.

Moore, R.J., *Escape from Empire: The Attlee Government and the Indian Problem*, Oxford, 1983.

Tomlinson, B.R., *The Political Economy of the Raj, 1914–47: The Economics of Decolonization*, London, 1979.

Britain in the Middle East, to 1954

Cohen, Michael J., *Palestine, Retreat from the Mandate: The Making of British Policy 1936–45*, London, 1978.

Louis, Wm Roger, *The British Empire in the Middle East 1945–1951*, Oxford, 1984.

Sachar, H.M., *Europe Leaves the Middle East, 1936–1954*, New York, 1972.

Sykes, Christopher, *Cross Roads to Israel*, London, 1965.

Decolonization in south-east Asia: the Malayan Emergency, 1948–60

Chin, Kin Wah, *The Defence of Malaysia and Singapore: The Transformation of a Security System, 1957–1971*, Cambridge, 1983.

Cloake, John, *Templer, Tiger of Malaya*, London, 1985.

Short, Anthony, *The Communist Insurrection in Malaya 1948–60*, London, 1967.

Decolonization in south-east Asia: the Union of Burma, and Malaysia

Sopiee, Mohd. Noordin, *From Malayan Union to Singapore Separation: Political Unification in the Malaysia Region, 1945–65*, Kuala Lumpur, 1974.

Stockwell, A.J., 'British imperial policy and decolonization in Malaya, 1942–52', *Journal of Imperial and Commonwealth History*, XIII, 1, October 1984, 68–87.

Tinker, Hugh, (ed.), *Burma: The Struggle for Independence, 1944–48*, 2 vols, London, 1983–4.

Singapore

Turnbull, C.M., *The Straits Settlements 1826–67: Indian Presidency to Crown Colony*, London, 1972.

—— *A History of Singapore, 1819–1975*, Kuala Lumpur, 1977.

The resources and products of the Commonwealth, 1952

Bangura, Yusuf, *Britain and Commonwealth Africa: The Politics of Economic Relations 1951–1975*, Manchester, 1983.

Day, A.C.L., *The Future of Sterling*, Oxford, 1954.

Morgan, D.J., *The Official History of Colonial Development*, 5 vols, London, 1980.

Britain and the South-East Asia Treaty Organization, 1954

Lyon, Peter, *War and Peace in South–East Asia*, London, 1969.

Modelski, George (ed.), *SEATO: Six Studies*, Melbourne, 1962.

Royal Institute of International Affairs, *Collective Defence in South East Asia: The Manila Treaty and its Implications*, London, 1956.

The Baghdad Pact, 1955

Carlton, David, *Anthony Eden: A Political Biography*, London, 1981.

Young, John W. (ed.), *The Foreign Policy of Churchill's Peacetime Administration, 1951–55*, Leicester, 1988.

The Cyprus revolt, 1955–1959

Alastos, Doros, *Cyprus Guerrilla: Grivas, Makarios and the British*, London, 1960.

Foley, Charles, *Island in Revolt*, London, 1962.

Grivas, General George, *The Memoirs of General Grivas*, ed. Charles Foley, London, 1964.

Stephens, Robert G., *Cyprus: A Place of Arms*, London, 1966.

The Suez crisis, 1956

Louis, Wm Roger, and Roger Owen (eds), *Suez 1956: The Crisis and its Consequences*, Oxford, 1989.

Nutting, Anthony, *No End of a Lesson: The Story of Suez*, London, 1967.

Thomas, Hugh, *The Suez War*, Harmondsworth, 1970.

Verrier, Anthony, *Through the Looking Glass: British Foreign Policy in an Age of Illusions*, London, 1983.

British decolonization in Africa, 1956–1970

Austin, D., *Politics in Ghana 1946–1960*, London, 1964.

Darwin, John, *Britain and Decolonization: The Retreat from Empire in the Post-war World*, London, 1988.

Hargreaves, J.D., *Decolonization in Africa*, Harlow, 1988.

Holland, R.F., *European Decolonization 1918–1981: An Introductory Survey*, London, 1985.

Low, D.A. and Alison Smith (eds), *History of East Africa, vol. III*, Oxford, 1976.

Pearce, R.D., *The Turning Point in Africa: British Colonial Policy 1938–1948*, London, 1982.

Porter, A.N. and A.J. Stockwell, *British Imperial Policy and Decolonization 1938–1964*, 2 vols, London, 1987, 1989.

Britain's presence east of Suez

Darby, Phillip, *British Defence Policy East of Suez, 1947–1968*, Oxford, 1973.

Mayhew, Christopher, *Britain's Role Tomorrow*, London, 1967.

Paget, Julian, *Last Post: Aden, 1964–1967*, London, 1969.

The Falkland Islands and Antarctica

Beck, Peter J., *The International Politics of Antarctica*, London, 1986.

—— *The Falkland Islands as an International Problem*, London, 1988.

—— 'British relations with Latin America: the Antarctic dimension', in Victor Bulmer-Thomas (ed.), *Britain and Latin America: A Changing Relationship*, Cambridge, 1989, 164–85.

Cawkell, Mary, *The Falklands Story 1592–1982*, Oswestry, 1983.

Freedman, Lawrence, *Britain and the Falklands War*, Oxford, 1988.

Fuchs, Sir Vivian, *Of Ice and Men: The Story of the British Antarctic Survey 1943–73*, Oswestry, 1982.

The Commonwealth, 1931–1989

Mansergh, Nicholas, *The Commonwealth Experience, vol. 2 From British to Multiracial Commonwealth*, 2nd edn, London, 1982.

Miller, J.D.B., *Survey of British Commonwealth Affairs: Problems of Expansion and Attrition, 1953–1969*, London, 1974.

The Round Table, the Commonwealth journal of international affairs.

Charles Town, Boston, Pittsburgh

Bridenbaugh, Carl, *Cities in the Wilderness: The First Century of Urban Life in America, 1625–1742*, New York, 1971.

Earl, Carville, 'The first English towns of North America', *Geographical Review*, 67, 1977, 34–50.

Jennings, Francis, *Empire of Fortune: Crowns, Colonies and Tribes in the Seven Years War in America*, New York, 1988.

Labaree, Benjamin W., *The Boston Tea Party*, Boston, 1964, reprint 1979.

Nash, Gary B., *The Urban Crucible: Social Change, Political Consciousness and the Origin of the American Revolution*, Cambridge, Mass., 1979.

Rutman, Darrett B., *Winthrop's Boston: A Portrait of a Puritan Town, 1630-1649*, New York, 1972.

Sosin, Jack M., *Whitehall and the Wilderness: The Middle West in British Colonial Policy 1760 to 1775*, Westport, Conn., 1961, reprint 1981.

Bridgetown

Higman, B.W., *Slave Populations of the British Caribbean, 1807-1834*, Baltimore, Md., 1984.

Christchurch

Graham, Jeanine, 'Settler society', in W.H. Oliver (ed.), *The Oxford History of New Zealand*, Oxford and Wellington, 1981.

Hamer, D.A., 'Towns in nineteenth-century New Zealand', *New Zealand Journal of History*, XIII, 1, 1979, 5-20.

Hight, James and C.R. Straubel, W.J. Gardner and W.H. Scotter (eds), *A History of Canterbury*, 3 vols, Christchurch, 1957, 1965, 1971.

Grahamstown, Cape Town, Pietermaritzburg, Johannesburg

Cordeur, B.A. le, *The Politics of Eastern Cape Separatism 1820-1854*, Cape Town, 1981.

Hattersley, A.F., *The British Settlement of Natal: A Study in Imperial Migration*, Cambridge, 1950.

Immelman, R.F., *Men of Good Hope, 1804-1954*, Cape Town, 1955.

Onselen, Charles van, *Studies in the Social and Economic History of the Witwatersrand 1886-1914*, 2 vols, Harlow, 1982.

Shorten, J.R., *Cape Town*, Cape Town, 1963.

Thomson, D.H., *A Short History of Grahamstown*, Grahamstown, n.d.

Kalgoorlie, Canberra, Ottawa, Winnipeg

Artibise, A.F.J., *Winnipeg: An Illustrated History*, Toronto, 1977.

Blainey, G., *The Rush That Never Ended: A History of Australian Mining*, Melbourne, 1978.

Knight, David B., *Choosing Canada's Capital: Jealousy and Friction in the Nineteenth Century*, Toronto, 1977.

Statham, P., *The Origins of Australia's Capital Cities*, Cambridge, 1989.

Wigmore, L., *The Long View: A History of Canberra, Australia's National Capital*, Melbourne, 1963.

Calcutta, Delhi, Simla

Gupta, N., *Delhi between Two Empires 1803-1931*, Delhi, 1981.

Irving, R.G., *Indian Summer: Lutyens, Baker and Imperial Delhi*, New Haven, Conn., 1981.

King, A.D., *Colonial Urban Development: Culture, Social Power and Environment*, London, 1976.

Nilsson, S., *European Architecture in India 1750-1850*, London, 1968.

Sinha, P., *Calcutta in Urban History*, Calcutta, 1978.

Hong Kong

Endacott, G.B., *A History of Hong Kong*, London, 1958.

Lethbridge, H.J., *Hong Kong: Stability and Change*, Hong Kong, 1978.

Freetown, Lagos, Zanzibar, Nairobi

Aderibigbe, A.B., *Lagos: The Development of an African City*, London, 1975.

Bennett, N.R., *A History of the Arab State of Zanzibar*, London, 1978.

Fyfe, C. and E. Jones, *Freetown: A Symposium*, Freetown, 1968.

Morgan, W.T.W., *Nairobi, City and Region*, Nairobi, 1967.

INDEX

Entries refer first to the pages in the text, then to the maps by page number, and finally provide the map references by longitude and latitude.

Jos, Map 106: *10/11*
Juba, Maps 110, 164–7: *32/4*
Jubaland, 154, Map 153: *42/2*
Julundur, Map 92: *75/30*

Kaarta, Map 104: *9/13*
Kabul, Map 159: *69/34*
Kachin Hills, Map 100: *98/27*
Kachins, 182, Map 181: *98/26*
Kaduna, Maps 106, 164–7: *8/12*
Kagoshima, Map 134: *130/32*
Kaifeng, Maps 96, 134: *14/33*
Kaipara Harbour, Map 75: *174/36*
Kaitaia, Map 129: *173/35*
Kajang, Map 135: *102/3*
Kalahari Desert, Map 155: *20/25*
Kalgoorlie, 226, Maps 128, 141, 226: *122/30*
Kalimantan (Borneo), Maps 180, 185: *115/0*
Kalkfontein, Map 155: *18/28*
Kamaran, Map 208: *43/15*
Kambia, Map 104: *13/9*
Kamerun, 152
Kampala, Maps 108, 153, 164–7: *33/0*
Kanara, Map 54: *75/13*
Kanazawa, Map 134: *136/37*
Kandy, 172, Maps 15, 127, 174: *80/7*
Kangar, Map 181: *100/6*
Kangaroo Is., Map 73: *137/35*
Kankan, Map 104: *8/11*
Kano, Maps 77, 79, 106, 164–7: *8/13*
Kanpur, Maps 92, 127, 164–7, 169: *81/26*
Kantara, Map 199: *32/31*
Kapenguria, Map 206: *35/1*
Kapunda, Map 141: *139/34*
Kara Sea, 3, Map 4: *70/75*
Karachi, 148, 166, Maps 145–7, 149–51, 164–7, 169: *67/25*
Kareima, Map 164–7: *32/18*
Karenni State, 182, Map 183: *98/20*
Karens, 182
Karikal, Map 37: *80/11*
Karimnagar, Map 127: *79/17*
Karonga, Map 115: *34/10*
Karoo, 82
Karpass Peninsula, Map 196: *34/35.30*
Karpathos, Map 17: *27/35.30*
Kasemy, Map 164–7: *30/0*
Kashmir, 177, Maps 90, 169, 176, 194: *77/32*

Kaskaskia, Map 33: *90/37*
Kassala, Map 110: *37/15*
Kassem, General, 195
Kat River, Map 131
Kat River settlement, 82, Map 83: *26.30/32.30*
Katanga, 116, Map 115: *28/10*
Kathykos, Map 196: *32.30/35*
Katsina, Maps 77, 106: *8/14*
Kaw-Thu-Lay, Map 183: *98/18*
Kayes, Map 104: *12/14*
Kecoughtan, Map 11: *76.20/37*
Kedah, Maps 98, 101, 181, 184: *100/6*
Keetmanshoop, Map 155: *17/27*
Keewatin, Diocese, Map 125: *95/55*
Keiskamma, Map 131
Kelantan, Maps 98, 101, 181, 184: *102/5*
Kelowna, Map 138: *120/50*
Kelung, Maps 145–7, 149–51: *121/25*
Kemal, Ataturk, 160–1
Kenora, Map 138: *95/50*
Kent County, 30, Map 29: *75.30/39*
Kentucky, 41
Kenya, 152, 154, 190, 202, 205–7, 209, Maps 108, 153, 201, 206, 208, 216–17: *40/0*; Kenya African Democratic Union (KADU), 207; Kenya African National Union (KANU), 207; Lancaster House Conference (1960), 205: Mau Mau, 205; Provinces: Ukamba, 237; White Highlands, 152
Keri Keri, Map 129: *174/35*
Kermadec Islds, Map 143: *180/23*
Kerman, Maps 102, 149–51: *58/30*
Kesang, Map 185: *103/2*
Keta, Map 106: *1/6*
Khartoum, 111, Maps 79, 110, 164–7: *32/15*
Khasi Hills, Map 127: *91/24*
Khilafat Movement, 168
Khorassan, Map 159: *58/35*
Khorremabad, Map 102: *48/33*
Kianning, Map 134: *119/26*
Kiaowchow, Map 96: *120/35*
Kienyang, Map 134: *119/26*
Kigoma, Maps 115, 153: *30/4*
Kilkenny, Map 23: *7.30/52.30*
Killarney, Map 23: *9/52*
Kilwa Kivinje, Maps 108, 115, 153, 164–7: *40/9*

Kimberley, 116, 223, Maps 113, 117, 155, 164–7: *25/28*
Kimberley and Kuruman, Diocese, Map 131: *25/25*
King Is., Map 73: *144/37*
King's County, 30, Map 31: *74/40.20*
King George Sound, Map 145–7: *118/35*
Kingston (Jamaica), Maps 62, 126, 164–7: *76.50/18*
Kingston (Ontario), Maps 69, 138: *76.30/44.30*
King William's Town, Maps 83, 113: *27.30/33*
Kingsale, 22, Map 23: *8.30/51.30*
Kionga, 154
Kionga Triangle, Map 153: *41/11*
Kipini, Map 108: *41/3*
Kipling, Rudyard, 233
Kiribati (formerly Gilbert Islds, q.v.), Maps 143, 217: *170/0*
Kirkuk, Maps 157, 159: *44/35*
Kiskiack, Map 11: *76.40/37.15*
Kismayu, Maps 108, 110: *43/0*
Kisumu, Maps 108, 153, 164–7: *35/0*
Kitale, Map 108: *36/1*
Kitchener, Sir Herbert H., 111, 116
Kittaning, Map 219: *79.30/41*
Kitty Hawk, Map 9: *75.40/36.10*
Kitui, Map 77: *38/2*
Kitwanga, Map 125: *129/55*
Kiukiang, Maps 94, 134: *116/29*
Kiungchow, Map 94: *110/20*
Klaarwater, Map 81: *23/29*
Klang, Map 135: *102/3*
Klerksdorp, Maps 117, 145–7: *26/27*
Kobe, Map 134: *135/35*
Koenigsberg, 20
Kofu, Map 134: *138/36*
Kohima, Map 174: *94/25*
Kok, Adam, 84, Map 113
Kokstad, Map 83: *29/31*
Kolhapur, Maps 92, 127: *75/16*
Kolobeng, Map 77: *25/24*
Komaggas, Map 131
Komati Poort, Map 117: *32/26*
Komenda, Map 106: *2/5*
Kong, Map 106: *4/9*
Koningow, Map 135: *117/5*
Kootenay, Diocese, Map 125: *116/50*
Kootenay House, Map 61: *116/50*
Kordofan, 111

London Missionary Society, 60, 114, 124, 133, Maps 126–31, 134–5; Methodist Church of Canada, Map 125; Missionary Society of the Church of England in Canada, Map 125; Netherlands Missionary Society, Map 134–5; North African Mission, Map 130–1; North American missions, Maps 125–31, 134–5; Plymouth Brethren, Map 130–1; Rhenish Missionary Society, Map 134–5; Society for the Propagation of the Gospel, Maps 125–7, 130–1, 134–5; United Brethren (Moravian) Missionary Society, Maps 125–6, 130–1; Universities Mission to Central Africa, 136, Map 130–1; Wesleyan Methodist Missionary Society, 124, 132, 133, Maps 125–31

Mitla Pass, Map 199: *33/30*

Mito, Map 134: *140/36*

Mao, Map 135: *128/9*

Mobile, 34, Maps 33, 145–7: *88/31*

Moeraki, Map 129: *171/45*

Mogadishu, Map 110: *47/3*

Mohammerah, Map 102: *48/30*

Mojanga, Map 149–51: *46/16*

Mokotling, Map 131

Mollendo, Map 149–51: *72/17*

Moluccas, 5, 14, 55, Maps 15, 56, 99: *128/5*

Mombasa, 109, 121, 236, Maps 15, 77, 79, 108, 123, 149–51, 153, 164–7, 206: *40/6*

Mombasa, Diocese, Map 130

Monrovia, Map 104: *11/6*

Monte Cassino, 170, Map 171: *14/41*

Montego Bay, Maps 62, 126: *77.55/18.30*

Montevideo, Maps 145–7, 149–51, 164–7: *56/35*

Montgomery, General Bernard, 170

Montreal, 38, 40, 51, 60, Maps 33, 39, 61, 69, 138, 164–7: *73/45*

Montreal, Diocese, Map 125: *75/47*

Montserrat, 26, Maps 25, 33, 35, 42, 216–17: *63/16*

Moorea, Map 129: *150/17*

Moose Factory, Maps 61, 125: *81/51*

Moosejaw, Map 138: *105/50*

Moosonee, Map 138: *81/51*

Moosonee, Diocese, Map 125: *80/51*

Morant Bay, Maps 62, 126: *76.25/17.55*

Moratuc, Map 9: *76.45/35.50*

Moreton Bay, Map 128: *154/26*

Morley, Map 125: *114/51*

Morocco, 18, Maps 19, 201: *5/30*

Morristown, Map 52(N): *74.30/40.30*

Morija, Map 131

Morogoro, Map 153: *37/6*

Moruga, Map 88: *61.20/10.05*

Moruya, Map 71: *150/35*

Moshi, Maps 153, 164–7: *37/4*

Mosquito Coast, Maps 33, 43: *85/15*

Mossamedes, Map 149–51: *12/15*

Mossel Bay, Maps 81, 83: *22/34*

Mosul, Maps 157, 159: *43/36*

Motito, Map 131

Moulmein, Maps 127, 135: *98/16*

mountains: Mt Cameroon, Map 106: *9/4*; Mt Elgon, Map 108: *34/1*; Mt Kenya 78, Maps 77, 79, 108: *37/0*; Mt Kilimanjaro 78, 152, Maps 77, 79, 108, 153: *37/3*; Mt Olympus, Map 196: *33/35*

Mountbatten, Lord, 172, 175, 182

Mount Charles, Map 126: *77/18*

Mount Gambier, Map 141: *150/23*

Mount Morgan, Map 141: *140/36*

Mount Pleasant, 210, Map 210: *58.30/52*

Mozambique, 114, Maps 15, 115, 117, 201: *38/14*

Mozambique (town), Maps 115, 145–7, 149–51, 164–7: *41/15*

Mozambique Channel, Map 15: *41/22*

Mozambique Company, 114

Mpika, Map 164–7: *31/12*

Mshweshwe, 84

Msiri's, Map 115: *29/12*

Mudros armistice, 160

Mughal Empire, 16, 89, 93, 231, Map 15

Mukden, Map 134: *122/41*

Multan, Maps 127, 169: *71/29*

Mumia's, Map 108: *35/0*

Murshidabad, Maps 37, 127: *89/23*

Murzuk, Map 77: *14/26*

Muscat, Maps 15, 102, 145–7, 159, 208: *58/23*

Muscovy Company, 3, 20

Muslim League, 170, 175, 177

Muslims, 132, 168, 170, 175

Mussadiq, Dr, 179

Mussolini, Benito, 170

Mwanza, Map 164–7: *33/3*

Myconos, Map 17: *25.30/37.30*

Myitkina, Map 127: *100/25*

Mysore (city), Map 127: *77/12*

Mysore (state), 53, Maps 37, 54, 90, 169, 176: *77/13*

Naauwpoort, Map 117: *25/31*

Nablus, Map 178: *35/32.30*

Nachtigal, Gustav, 78

Nafa, *see* Okinawa

Naga Hills, Map 127: *93/25*

Nagano, Map 134: *138/37*

Nagasaki, 172, Maps 134, 145–7, 149–51, 174: *130/33*

Nagoya, Map 134: *137/35*

Nagpur, 91, Maps 54, 90, 127, 169: *80/21*

Nagpur, Diocese, Map 127

Nain, Map 125: *62/57*

Nairobi, 237, Maps 108, 153, 164–7, 206, 237: *37/1*

Namib Desert, Map 155: *14/20*

Namibia, 156

Nana, of the Itsekiri, 107

Nanaimo, Map 125: *124/49*

Nanchang, Map 134: *116/28*

Nanking, Maps 94, 96, 134: *123/32*

Nantucket Is., Map 13: *70/41*

Napier, Maps 129, 145–7: *177/39*

Naples, Maps 17, 149–51, 171: *14/41*

Napoleon, 76

Nara, Map 134: *136/35*

Naragansett Bay, Map 13: *71.30/41.30*

Narva, 20, Map 21: *28/59*

Nasik, Map 127: *74/18*

Nasirabad, Map 92: *75/26*

Nassau, Maps 145–7, 149–51, 164–7: *72/25*

Nassau, Diocese, Map 126: *75/25*

Nasser, President Gamal, 195, 198–200

Natal, 84, 112, 116, 224, Maps 113, 117, 164–7: *31/29*

Natal, Diocese, Map 130

Natalia, Republic of, 224

80/41; Altamaha, Map 27: 82/32; Appamatuck, Map 11: 77.30/37.10; Arkansas, Map 33: 100/37; Ashley, 26, 218, Maps 27, 218: 80/33; Atbara, Map 110: 36/12; Athabasca, Map 39: 112/57; Athi, Map 206: 37/3; Bahr al-Ghazal, Map 110: 28/8; Bashee, Map 113: 28/32; Benuc, 78, Maps 77, 78, 106: 12/9; Berg, Map 81: 19/33; Black, 28, Map 27: 79/35; Black Volta, Maps 106, 203: 4/13; Blue Nile, Maps 77, 110: 34/10; Bushmans, Map 83: 26.30/33.30; Caledon, Maps 83, 113: 26/30; Cape Fear, 28, Map 27: 79/35; Casamance, Map 104: 15/13; Chattahoochie, Map 27: 85/32; Chaudiere, Map 69: 71/46; Chawanoac, see Chowan; Chickahominie, Map 11: 77.10/37.30; Chindwin, Map 100: 96/25; Chowan, Map 9: 76.45/36.10; Churchill, Map 61: 97/57; Cipo, see Pamlico; Cohansey, 28, Map 29: 75/39.30; Congo, 78, 133, Maps 77, 79: 20/0; Connecticut, Maps 13, 31: 72.30/44; Cooper, 26, 218, Map 27: 80/33; Cross, Maps 77, 106: 9/7; Darling, Maps 71, 73: 145/30; Delaware, 28, 30, Maps 29, 31: 75/41; Derwent, Map 71: 147/42; Dvina, 20, Map 21: 25/56; Edisto, 26, Map 27: 81/33; Elbe, Map 21: 11/53; Euphrates, 156, Maps 102, 157, 159: 45/32; Gambia, 20, Maps 19, 77, 104: 14/13; Ganges, 53, 89; Goulburn, Map 71: 146/36; Gouritz, Map 81: 21.30/34; Great Fish, Maps 81, 83: 26/33; Gwai, Map 115: 28/19; Harts, Maps 83, 113: 24/28; Hooghly, 230, Map 230; Housatonic, Map 31: 73.30/41.30; Hudson, 28, 30, 51, 53, Maps 13, 29, 31, 39, 69: 74/42; Hunter, Maps 71, 73: 152/32; Hutt, Map 75: 175/41; Irrawaddy, Maps 100, 183: 95/20; James, 10, 12, 26, Map 11: 77.30/37.30; Juba,

Map 108, 110: 43/2; Jumna, 89; Kafue, 116, Map 115: 27/14; Karun, Map 102: 50/32; Kei, Maps 81, 83: 27/32; Keiskamma, 112, Maps 81, 83, 113: 27/33; Kennebec, 10, Map 13: 70/45; Kowie, Map 83: 26.30/33.30; Kwa Ibo, Map 106: 7/5; Lachlan, Maps 71, 73: 147/33; Limpopo, Maps 83, 115, 117: 32/23; Mackenzie, Maps 39, 61: 124/62; Macleay, Map 71: 153/30: Manawatu, Map 75: 175/40.30; Manning, Map 71: 153/31; Mattaponi, Map 11: 77/37.40; Meherrin, Map 9: 77/36.30; Mekong, Map 100: 100/25; Mellacourie, 103, 105, Map 104: 13/11; Menam, Map 100: 101/15; Merrimac, 32, Maps 13, 31: 71.30/43; Mississippi, 40, 41, 68, Maps 33, 39: 92/47; Missouri, Map 33: 100/40; Moa, Map 104: 11/7; Modder, Maps 83, 117: 26/29; Mohawk, 30, 32, 41, 51, Maps 31, 69: 75/43; Molopo, Map 113: 23/26; Molyneux, Map 75: 170/46; Monongahela, 219, Map 219: 80/40; Moose, Map 61: 82/50; Moratuc, see Roanoke; Murray, Maps 71, 73: 141/33; Murrumbidgee, Map 71: 146/34; Nairobi, 237, Map 237: 37/1; Nelson, Map 61: 96/57; Neuse, 28, Maps 9, 27: 76.40/35; Niemen, Map 21: 24/54; Niger, 76, 78, 80, 105, 107, 133, 136, Maps 19, 77, 79, 104: 6/14; Nile, 76, 78, 109, 158, 198, Maps 77, 110: 32/25; North, see Hudson; North Saskatchewan, Maps 39, 61: 110/54; Nun, Map 106: 6/4; Nunez, 103, Map 104: 15/11; Ob, 3; Oder, Map 21: 21/52; Ogun, Map 106: 3/8; Ohio, 40, 41, 68, 219, Maps 33, 39, 43, 219: 85/38; Oil Rivers, Map 106: 5/5; Olifants, Maps 81, 83: 19/32; Orange, 84, Maps 81, 83, 117: 22/29; Orinoco, 24, Maps 25, 33: 65/8; Ottawa, 68, Maps 61, 228: 76/45; Pamlico, 28, Maps 9, 27: 76.40/35.20; Pamunkey,

Map 11: 77.10/37.40; Pangani, Map 108: 38/5; Peace, Map 61: 113/59; Pee Dee, Map 27: 80/35; Piscataqua, 32, Map 31: 71/43.30; Plate, 5, 65; Pongola, Map 113: 31/27.30; Pongos, 103, Map 104: 14/10; Potomac, Maps 11, 29: 76.30/38; Pungwe, Map 115: 35/19; Rangitikei, Map 75: 175/40; Rappahannock, Map 11: 76.40/38; Red (Manitoba), 61, 139, Map 229; Red (Texas), Map 33: 95/34; Rhine: 198; Rio Grande, Map 33: 102/30; Roanoke, Maps 9, 27: 77/36; Rokel, Map 104: 12/9; Rovuma, 78, Maps 108, 153: 40/11; Rufiji, Maps 108, 153: 38/8; Sabi, Map 115: 34/21; Saco, Maps 13, 31: 71/44; Saguenay, Map 69: 70/48; St John's, Map 27: 81.30/30; St Lawrence, 40, 41, 68, Maps 33, 39, 43, 61, 66, 69: 73/42; St Mary's, Map 27: 81.30/30.30; Salween, Maps 100, 183: 99/24; Santee, 26: Map 27: 81/33.30; Saskatchewan, 38, 139; Savannah, Map 27: 82/33; Scarcies, 103, 105, Map 104: 13/9; Schoharie, 32, Map 31: 74.30/42.30; Schuykill, 30, Map 29: 76/40.30; Senegal, 20, 103, 105, Maps 19, 77, 104: 14/15; Severn, Map 61: 90/55; Shangani, Map 115: 29/18; Shannon, 22, Map 23: 8/53; Sherboro, 20, Map 19: 12/6; Shire, 78, Maps 79, 115: 35/15; Sobat, Map 110: 35/8; South Saskatchewan, Maps 39, 61: 104/51; Stono, 26; Sundays, Maps 81, 83: 25/33; Susquehanna, 30, Map 29: 77/40; Tana, Maps 77, 108: 40/1; Tamar, Map 71: 147/41; Thames, 14; Tigris, 156, Maps 102, 157, 159: 45/33; Tsavo, Map 206: 37/3; Tugela, Maps 83, 113: 31/29; Ubangi, Map 79: 20/4; Umba, 109, Map 108: 39/5; Umkusi, Map 113: 32/28; Umtanvana, Map 113: 30/31; Umtata, Maps 81, 83, 113: 29/32; Umzimkulu, 112,

Maps 81, 83, 113: *30/31*;
Umzimvubu, Maps 81, 113:
29/32; Vaal, 84, Maps 81, 117:
25/28; Vistula, 20, Map 21:
21/52; Volta, Maps 19, 106,
203: *0/8*; Waikato, Map 75:
175/38; Waipa, Map 75:
175/38; Wairau, Map 75:
174/41; Waitaki, Map 75:
171/45; Waitara, Map 75:
175/39; Wallkill, Map 31:
74.30/41.30; Wanganui, Map
75: *175/39*; Warrego, Map 73:
145/25; White Nile, 107, Maps
77, 79, 110: *33/12*; White
Volta, Maps 106, 203: *1/11*;
Wouri, Map 106: *10/4*;
Wyoming, 41; Yangtze, 95,
Map 94: *110/30*; York, Map
11: *76.50/37.25*; Youghicany,
Map 219: *79.30/40*; Zambezi,
78, 80, 114, 115, Maps 77, 79,
115: *32/15*
Roanoke Is., 8, 10, Map 9:
75.40/35.50
Roberts, Lord, 116
Rockhampton, Map 141: *150/23*
Rockhampton, Diocese, Map 128:
145/22
Roebuck Bay, *see* Broome
Roggeveld, Map 81: *20/32*
Rohlfs, Gerhard, 78
Rohtak, Map 92: *76/27*
Rolfe, John, 10
Rolling River, Map 125: *103/51*
Roma (Indonesia), Map 135:
128/8
Roma (Queensland), Map 141:
148/27
Roman Catholics, 28, 32, 41, 74,
161, 163, 228
Rome, 170, Maps 164-7, 171:
12/42
Rommel, Field-Marshall E., 179
Roosevelt, President F.D., 170
Ross, Map 23: *7/52.30*
Ross Dependency, 212, Map 213:
170/70
Roti, Map 135: *124/11*
Rotorua, Map 129: *176/39*
Rotterdam, Map 149-51: *4/52*
Round Lake, Map 125: *105/51*
Royal African Company, 50
Royal Air Force, 163, 210, Maps
164-5, 198, 208, 211
Royal Geographical Society, 80
Royal Navy, 121-4, 132, 144-52,

154, 156, 163, 175, 207-9,
234-5, Maps 122, 123, 199,
208, 211
Royal Niger Company, 107; (*see
also* National African Company)
Ruanda-Urundi, 152, Map 153:
30/3
Rudd, C.D., 114
Rupert, Prince, 60
Rupert's Land, 61, Map 61
Rupert's Land, Province and
Diocese, 133, Map 125: *100/50*
Rururu, Map 129: *151/23*
Russell, *see* Kororareka
Russia, 3, 20, 60, 91, 95, 101-3,
109, 111, 118, 121, 124, 156,
158, 160, 172, 179, 193, Maps
21, 155, 171
Rustenburg, Map 83: *27/25.30*
Rutbah, Map 164-7: *40/33*
Rwanda, Map 201: *30/2*;
(formerly Ruanda-Urundi,
q.v.)
Rye, Map 13: *71/42.50*
Ryuku Islds, Map 143: *125/26*

Sabah, Maps 185, 208: *117/5*; (*see
also* North Borneo)
Saco, Map 13: *70.30/43.25*
Sadiyah, Map 127: *95/27*
Safi, 18, Map 19: *9/33*
Saga, Map 134: *130/33*
Sagar, Map 92: *78/23*
Sahara, 78
Saigon, Maps 145-7, 149-51, 180:
107/11
St Ann's Bay, Map 126: *77/18*
St Augustine, 26, 34, Maps 27,
33, 43: *81.30/30*
St Bartholomew, Map 126: *63/18*
St Christopher, *see* St Kitt's
St Domingue (Haiti), 49, 65,
Maps 33, 64: *73/19*
St Eustatius, Maps 33, 126: *63/17*
St Helena, Maps 7, 64, 119, 120,
122-3, 145-7, 216: *5/13*
St Helena, Diocese, Map 131
St John (New Brunswick), Maps
66, 138, 145-7: *66/45*
St John's Kaffraria, Diocese, Map
131: *30/32*
St John's (Newfoundland), Maps
39, 66, 138, 145-7: *52.30/47.30*
St Joseph, Map 88: *61.25/10.40*
St Kitts, 24, 34, 49, Maps 25, 33,
35, 42, 126, 216-17: *63/17*

St Lawrence, Gulf of, 40, 41, Map
66: *60/48*
St Leger, Colonel Barry, Map
52(N)
St Louis, Maps 104, 145-7,
149-51: *17/16*
St Lucia, 121, Maps 64, 122-3,
145-7, 216-17: *61/14*
St Lucia Bay, Map 113: *33/28.30*
St Martin, Map 126: *63/18*
St Mary (Madagascar), Map
145-7: *50/17*
St Mary's (Gambia), Map 129:
16/15
St Mary's (Maryland), Map 29:
76.30/38.15
St Paul de Loanda, *see* Loanda
St Pierre, 40, Map 39: *56/47*
St Thomas (Canada), Map 69:
81/43
St Thomas (West Indies), Map
149-51: *65/18*
St Vincent, *see* Cape Verde Islds
St Vincent, (West Indies), 49,
Maps 126, 145-7, 216-17:
62/13
Sakhalin, 172
Salaga, Map 106: *1/11*
Salamis, Map 196: *34/35.15*
Saldanha Bay, Map 81: *18/33*
Salerno, Map 171: *15/41*
Salem (Cape Colony), Map 83:
26.30/33.30
Salem (Massachusetts), 14, Map
13: *71/42.30*
Salina Cruz, Map 149-51: *95/16*
Salisbury, 114, 202, Maps 115,
164-7: *31/17*
Salisbury, 3rd Marquess of, 111
Saltpond, Map 106: *1/6*
Samar, Map 180: *125/12*
Sambalpur, Map 127: *86/21*
Samma, Map 19: *3/4*
Samoa, Maps 129, 143: *173/14*
Samori, 105, Map 104: *7/11*
Samothrace, Map 17: *25.30/40.30*
San'a, Map 208: *44/15*
San Augustin, *see* St Augustine
San Buenaventura, Map 145-7:
115/32
San Carlos, 210, Maps 210-11:
59/51.30
Sandakan, Maps 135, 149-51:
117/6
San Diego, Map 145-7: *117/33*
San Fernando, 89, Map 88:
61.30/10.15

273

Vigo, Map 149–51: *9/42*

Virginia, 12, 26, 28, 41, 46, 51, 53, 220, Maps 29, 42, 43, 47: *78/39*; 'North Virginia', 10; 'South Virginia', 10

Virginia Company, 10

Vizagapatam, Map 127: *83/16*

Vladivostok, Map 145–7: *132/43*

Voi, Maps 153, 206: *39/3*

Volksrust, Map 117: *29/27*

Volta River Project, *see* Gold Coast

von Lettow Vorbeck, General, 154

Vryburg, Maps 113, 117: *24.30/27*

Vryheid, Map 113: *31/28*

Wa, Maps 106, 203: *3/12*

Wadelai, Maps 108, 110: *31/3*

Wadi Halfa, Maps 110, 164–7: *31/22*

Wafd, 177

Wagadugu, Map 106: *2/14*

Wagga Wagga, Maps 71, 73: *148/34*

Waiapu, Diocese, Map 129: *176/39*

Waikanae, Map 129: *175/41*

Waikato, 76

Waikato Heads, Map 129: *175/37*

Waikawa, Map 129: *169/16*

Waimate, Map 129: *174/35*

Wairau, Map 129: *173/42*

Wairoa, Map 129: *174/36*

Waitangi, Maps 75, 129: *174/35*

Waitangi, Treaty of, 74, 132

Waitara, 76

Wake Is., Map 143: *155/25*

Wakefield, E.G., 70, 72, 74, 221

Wales, 28, 30, 36

Wallaroo, Map 141: *138/32*

Wallis, Captain Samuel, 57, Maps 58–9

Walloons, 30

Walsingham, Francis, 8

Walvis Bay, 154, 156, Maps 77, 117, 155: *14/23*

Wandiwash, Map 37: *79/11*

Wanganui, 76, Map 129: *175/40*

Wangaratta, Diocese, Map 128: *147/35*

Wankie, Map 115: *26/18*

Warri, Map 106: *6/6*

Warrnambool, Map 141: *143/36*

Wars: American Independence, 41, 49, 51–3, 220, Map 52; Anglo-American (1812), 68, 89; Asante, 105, 107, 116; Burma,

91, 97; Crimean, 121; Falklands, 209–10, 215, Map 211; French Revolutionary, 65, 80, 121; Gurkha, 91; Korean, 189, 191, 193; Maori, 74–6, 118; Matabele, 114, 115; Napoleonic, 57, 65, 76, 121; Northern, 74; Opium, 55, 93; Seven Years, 40, 49, 57, 67, 220; Sikh, 91; South African, 112, 116–18, Map 117; World War I, 124, 142, 152–63, 187, Maps 153, 155, 157; World War II, 166, 170–5, 187, Maps 171, 173–4; Yoruba, 105, 107; Zulu, 114

Warsheik, Map 110: *47/3*

Warwick (Rhode Island), 14, Map 13: *71.30/41.30*

Warwick (Queensland), Map 141: *152/27*

Washington, George, 51, 53, 220, Map 52 (N and S)

Washington Conference, 142

Watauga, Map 43: *83/37*

Waterboer, Andries, 84

Wau, Map 110: *28/8*

Wavell, Lord, 175

Waymouth, George, 3

Weapemeoc, Map 9: *76.30/36.15*

Weddell Sea, Map 212–13: *40/69*

Weihaiwei, Maps 96, 123: *122/37*

Weipa, Map 128: *142/14*

Welland Canal, Map 69: *79/43*

Wellesley, Lord, 53–5, 65, 89

Wellington (Cape Colony), Map 81: *19/33.30*

Wellington (New Zealand), 74, 76, Maps 75, 85, 122–3, 129, 145–7: *175/41*

Wellington (New Zealand), Diocese, Map 129

Wellington Valley, Map 128: *149/32*

Wenchi, Map 203: *2.30/7.30*

Wepener, Map 117: *27/30*

Werewocomoco, Map 11: *76.40/37.20*

Wesley, John, 124

Wesleyans, 74

Wesleyville, Map 131

West Indies, 24, 26, 30, 32, 44–6, 49, 67, 118, 124, 127, 132, Maps 25, 47, 49, 126; French, 40, 49; (*see also* individual islands)

West Irian, Map 185: *133/2*

Westchester County, 32, Map 31: *74/41*

Western Australia, 72, 74, 226, Maps 73, 119, 141: *120/25*

Western China, Diocese, Map 134: *100/30*

Western Equatorial Africa, Diocese, Map 130: *10/15*

Western India States Agency, Map 169: *72/22*

Western Pacific High Commission, Map 143

Western Samoa, Map 143: *175/10*

Western Thrace, 161, Map 159: *27/41*

Westport, Map 145–7: *172/42*

Wethersfield, 14, Map 13: *41.30/73*

Wexford, Map 23: *6.30/52.15*

Whangarei, Map 145–7: *174/36*

Whangaroa, Map 129: *174/35*

White, John, 8

White Fish River, Map 127: *118/55*

White Horse, Map 138: *135/61*

White Sea, 3, Map 4: *38/66*

Whitlock, Sir George, Map 92

Whydah, Map 106, *2/6*

Wicklow, Map 23: *6/53*

Williamsburg, Maps 43, 52(S): *77/37.30*

Willoughby, Hugh, 3

Wilmington (Delaware), 30, Map 29: *75.45/39.45*

Wilmington (N. Carolina), Map 52(S): *78/34*

Wilson, Harold, 207

Wimble Shoals, *see* Cape Kenrick

Windhoek, Map 155: *17/23*

Windsor (Connecticut), 14, Map 13: *73/41.45*

Windsor (Ontario), Maps 69, 138: *83/42*

Windward Coast, 103, Maps 45, 50, 104: *15/10*

Windward Islds, Maps 25, 42, 119: *63/12*

Windward Islds, Diocese, Map 126: *63/12*

Winnebah, Map 203: *1.45/5.30*

Winnipeg, 229, Maps 125, 138, 229: *97/50*

Winnsboro, Map 52(S): *81/40*

Winterberg, Map 81: *26/32*

Winton, Map 164–7: *143/22*

Winyah Bay, 26, Map 27: *79/33*

Witu, Map 108: *41/2*